Intergovernmental Relations in Transition

The field of intergovernmental relations has changed substantially over the past five decades. It maintains a critical and evolving role in the US federal system as well as in public policy and administration. Building upon the legacy of Deil S. Wright's scholarship, this collection of essays by distinguished scholars, emerging thought leaders, and experienced practitioners chronicles and analyzes some of the tensions and pressures that have contributed to the current state of intergovernmental relations and management.

Although rarely commanding media attention by name, intergovernmental relations is being elevated in the public discourse through policy issues dominating the headlines. Many of these intergovernmental issues are addressed in this book, including health insurance exchanges under the now-threatened Affordable Care Act, and the roles of the federal, state, and local governments in food safety, energy, and climate change. Contributors interpret and assess the impacts of these and other issues on the future directions of intergovernmental relations and management. This book will serve as an ideal text for courses on intergovernmental relations and federalism, and will be of interest to government practitioners and civic and nonprofit organization leaders involved in public policy and management.

Carl W. Stenberg is the James E. Holshouser, Jr. Distinguished Professor of Public Administration and Government at the School of Government, University of North Carolina at Chapel Hill, USA.

David K. Hamilton retired as Associate Professor of Public Administration and Director of the Center for Public Service at Texas Tech University, USA.

Intergovernmental Relations in Transition

Reflections and Directions

Edited by Carl W. Stenberg and David K. Hamilton

Routledge
Taylor & Francis Group

NEW YORK AND LONDON

First published 2018
by Routledge
711 Third Avenue, New York, NY 10017

and by Routledge
2 Park Square, Milton Park, Abingdon, Oxon, OX14 4RN

Routledge is an imprint of the Taylor & Francis Group, an informa business

© 2018 Taylor & Francis

The right of Carl W. Stenberg and David K. Hamilton to be identified as the authors of the editorial material, and of the authors for their individual chapters, has been asserted in accordance with sections 77 and 78 of the Copyright, Designs and Patents Act 1988.

Library of Congress Cataloging-in-Publication Data
A catalog record for this book has been requested

ISBN: 978-0-8153-9642-0 (hbk)
ISBN: 978-0-8153-9643-7 (pbk)
ISBN: 978-1-351-18216-4 (ebk)

Typeset in Times New Roman
by Keystroke, Neville Lodge, Tettenhall, Wolverhampton
Printed and bound by CPI Group (UK) Ltd, Croydon, CR0 4YY

In memory of Deil S. Wright for his pioneering scholarship and furthering understanding of intergovernmental relations.

Contents

Contributors

J. Edwin Benton is Professor of Political Science and Public Administration at the University of South Florida. He has written extensively about county government, state–local relations, urban government and politics, intergovernmental fiscal behavior, and American federalism and has a forthcoming book on *Revenue Sources of Local Governments: How They Pay the Bills amid Continuing Challenges and Emerging Opportunities*. He is the Managing Editor of *State and Local Government Review* and the recipient of the Manning J. Dauer Award from the Florida Political Science Association for sustained research contributions to scholarship on Florida government and politics and the SIAM Service Award from the ASPA Section on Intergovernmental Administration and Management.

Donald J. Borut has more than 40 years' experience in municipal government and organizational leadership in the public interest sector. He served as the Executive Director of the National League of Cities from 1990 to 2012. Prior to his NLC appointment, he was Deputy Executive Director of the International City Management Association (ICMA). He received the Neil Staebler Distinguished Service Award from the Ford School of Public Policy, University of Michigan and the National Public Service Award from the American Society for Public Administration and the National Academy of Public Administration.

Ann O'M. Bowman is Professor and Hazel Davis and Robert Kennedy Endowed Chair in the Bush School of Government and Public Service at Texas A&M University. State and local governments are her primary research foci.

Jeffrey L. Brudney is the Betty and Dan Cameron Family Distinguished Professor of Innovation in the Nonprofit Sector at the University of North Carolina Wilmington and Academic Director of Quality Enhancement for Nonprofit Organizations (QENO). His current teaching interests include nonprofit management, volunteer management, and quantitative methods. He has published extensively in public affairs journals, and has served most recently as the editor of *Nonprofit and Voluntary Sector Quarterly*. His books include *Fostering Volunteer Programs in the Public Sector: Planning, Initiating, and Managing Voluntary Activities* (1990); *Advancing Public Management: New Developments in Theory, Method, and Practice* (2005, with Laurence J. O'Toole and Hal G. Rainey); and nine editions of *Applied Statistics for Public and Nonprofit Administration* (with Kenneth J. Meier and John Bohte).

Brendan F. Burke is Associate Professor at Suffolk University. His research and teaching interests include organizational theory, administrative reform, executive leadership, and collaborative public management. He has published in the *American Review of Public Administration*, *Public Administration Review*, *Publius: The Journal of Federalism*, *State and Local Government Review*, and other journals.

Benjamin H. Deitchman drafted this chapter while serving as a Visiting Assistant Professor of Public Policy in the Saunders College of Business at the Rochester Institute of Technology (RIT). Among his other duties at RIT were additional research, teaching, and playing the role of the Institute's tiger mascot at a minor league baseball game. Dr. Deitchman currently works at the Georgia Public Service Commission. His son, Isaac, was born in 2016.

Samuel Gallaher is Data Analytics and Methodology Specialist at the City and County of Denver Auditor's Office. Sam received his Ph.D. in Public Affairs from the University of Colorado Denver where he was part of the Workshop of Policy Process Research. His research interests include water and energy policy, as well as examining how local governments participate and affect large issues, such as climate change, at the local, state, and federal levels.

Brian J. Gerber is Associate Professor and Director of the Emergency Management and Homeland Security program at Arizona State University. His research interests include hazards governance and public policy issues related to emergencies, disasters and security issues. He is a PLuS Alliance Fellow, an Honorary Associate Professor at the University of New South Wales in Australia, and a Senior Sustainability Scholar at ASU's Wrigley School of Sustainability.

Parris N. Glendening has been a participant in intergovernmental relations for 50 years. A three-decade member of the University of Maryland faculty, he has numerous publications on federalism and intergovernmental relations. As an elected official (city and county council, county executive and Governor of Maryland) and leader of several national public interest groups, he was actively involved in intergovernmental struggles ranging from welfare reform to the creation of the Department of Homeland Security and was twice named "outstanding Public Official of the Year" by *Governing* magazine. Glendening serves as President of Smart Growth America's Leadership Institute, a national environmental NGO. He is an elected Fellow in the National Academy of Public Administration, and served as Senior Advisor to the President and National Council of the American Society of Public Administration.

David K. Hamilton recently retired from Texas Tech University where he was director of the MPA program and Director of the Center for Public Service. He has published articles in a number of journals including *Public Administration Review*, *Journal of Urban Affairs and Urban Affairs Review*. His books include *Governing Metropolitan Areas: Growth and Change in a Networked Age* and *Measuring the Effectiveness of Regional Governance: A Comparative Study of City Regions in North America*.

Benoy Jacob is Associate Professor in the University of Nevada Las Vega's School of Public Policy and Leadership and serves as Director for the School's Urban Leadership Program. His research focuses on the growth and governance of cities. Prior to joining UNLV, he was an Assistant Professor at both the University of Colorado, Denver's School of Public Affairs and the School of Politics and Economics at Claremont Graduate University.

Jocelyn M. Johnston is Professor of Public Administration and Policy at American University. She has published in leading public administration journals on government contracting, inter-organizational and inter-sectoral service collaboration, and intergovernmental programs. She earned an MPA and a PhD in Public Administration from the Maxwell School at Syracuse University after serving for ten years in local government administering intergovernmental programs.

Richard C. Kearney recently retired from North Carolina State University's School of Public and International Affairs.

John Kincaid is the Robert B. and Helen S. Meyner Professor of Government and Public Service and Director of the Meyner Center for the Study of State and Local Government at Lafayette College. He is former Executive Director of the U.S. Advisory Commission on Intergovernmental Relations and has written many articles on federalism and intergovernmental relations, edited *Federalism* (4 vols, 2011), and co-edited *Courts in Federal Systems: Federalists or Unitarists?* (2017), *Intergovernmental Relations in Federal Systems: Comparative Structures and Dynamics* (2015), *Political Parties and Civil Society in Federal Countries* (2015), and the *Routledge Handbook of Regionalism and Federalism* (2013).

Dale Krane was the Frederick W. Kayser Chair Professor and is now Professor Emeritus in the School of Public Administration, University of Nebraska, Omaha. His scholarship includes books and journal articles on policy implementation and evaluation, federalism and intergovernmental relations, state and local government administration, performance management and collaborative governance. He was the 1995 recipient of the Donald C. Stone award for Outstanding Research in Intergovernmental Relations presented by ASPA's Section on Intergovernmental Administration and Management. Email: dkrane@unomaha.edu.

Ricardo (Rick) S. Morse is Associate Professor at the University of North Carolina at Chapel Hill's School of Government. His research, teaching, and consulting focuses on public leadership, collaborative governance, and civic engagement. He is the author of numerous articles and book chapters, lead-editor of *Transforming Public Leadership for the 21st Century* (2007), and *Innovations in Public Leadership Development* (2008), and lead author of *The Citizens Academies Handbook* (2017). Dr. Morse holds Bachelor and Master degrees in public policy from Brigham Young University and a PhD in public administration from Virginia Tech. Connect with him on Twitter @MorseSOG

Shihyun Noh is Assistant Professor of Public Administration at the State University of New York College at Brockport. He teaches health policy and administration courses. His research includes health policy and administration, intergovernmental implementation of federal programs, and state and local government administration. His related work has been published in *Publius: The Journal of Federalism* and *State and Local Government Review*. Email: snoh@brockport.edu

Susan C. Paddock, Ph.D., University of Oregon, is a University of Wisconsin-Madison Emeritus Professor. She previously served on the faculty of Arizona State University and currently lives and works in Las Vegas, NV. She established and directed Certified Public Manager programs in Arizona and Wisconsin and conducted research on issues related to program management. She has published in the areas of leadership, ethics, professional and organizational development and human resources, and is an active student and researcher on organizational and individual improvement in state and local government and education.

Bruce J. Perlman, Ph.D. is Director of the University of New Mexico's School of Public Administration and Regents' Professor of Public Administration. Professor Perlman's research interests and publications are in the areas of state and local government and organizational studies and reform both in the U.S. and internationally. He served as Chief Administrative Officer for the City of Albuquerque and Deputy Chief of Staff to the Governor of New Mexico.

Paul L. Posner was Professor and Director of the Masters of Public Administration program at George Mason University's Schar School of Policy and Government at the time of his passing in July 2017. Previously, he was the Managing Director for Strategic Issues at the U.S. Government Accountability Office (GAO). Paul's GAO career spanned more than 30 years, working on federal budget and intergovernmental fiscal policy and management issues. He was a Fellow and served as Chairman of the Board of the National Academy of Public Administration and as past President of the American Society for Public Administration. He was co-author of *Governing Under Stress* and *The Pathways to Power* and author of *The Politics of Unfunded Mandates*. Paul was a valued member of and contributor to the Section on Intergovernmental Administration and Management, and he will be remembered as an accomplished teacher, engaged scholar, and dedicated public service advocate. Our knowledge and appreciation of the dynamics and directions of federalism, intergovernmental relations, and intergovernmental management were enhanced by Paul's work, and we are honored to feature one of his last professional papers in this volume.

Michael J. Scicchitano, Ph.D. is Director of the Florida Survey Research Center at the University of Florida, where he directs the Master's Program in Public Affairs in the Department of Political Science. He is editor of the *State and Local Government Review*. His research interests and publications are in the areas of state and local policy and management.

Carl W. Stenberg is the James E. Holshouser Jr. Distinguished Professor of Public Administration and Government at the School of Government, University of North Carolina at Chapel Hill. Previously he served as Executive Director of the Council of State Governments and Assistant Director of the U.S. Advisory Commission on Intergovernmental Relations. He is a Fellow and former Chair of the Board of Directors of the National Academy of Public Administration and past President of the American Society for Public Administration. Email: stenberg@sog.unc.edu.

Rebecca Yurman is Professorial Lecturer in the Department of Public Administration and Policy in American University's School of Public Affairs, where she also received her PhD in 2016. Her research interests include regulatory policy, contract management, and other issues in public management, federalism, and food safety policy. Prior to entering academia, Rebecca was a Senior Analyst in the Natural Resources and Environment team at the U.S. Government Accountability Office (GAO).

Yahong Zhang, Ph.D. is Associate Professor at the Rutgers University-Newark's School of Public Affairs and Administration where she is Director of International Studies. She serves as Director of the Rutgers Institute of Anti-Corruption Studies. Professor Zhang's research interests and publications are in the areas of relationships in politics and administration, performance analysis, and local government human resource management.

Preface

This book is the result of research papers and commentaries originally delivered at Deil S. Wright symposia at American Society for Public Administration National Conferences. Wright was one of the founding scholars in federalism, intergovernmental relations, and intergovernmental management. Wright's book, *Understanding Intergovernmental Relations*, first published in 1978, and his subsequent scholarship, helped to establish intergovernmental relations (IGR) as a field of research, teaching, and practice in public administration and political science.

The inaugural symposium was held at the American Society for Public Administration National Conference (ASPA) in Washington, D.C. in March 2014, organized by the Section on Intergovernmental Administration and Management, of which Dr. Wright was a charter member. The purposes of the 2014 symposium and its successors were to reflect on the evolution and direction of IGR since the 1960s, assess the significant changes that have taken place over the past five decades, and identify future directions, tensions, and trends.

Deil Wright's scholarship and the writings of others who were inspired by him has made significant contributions to the understanding of IGR. Intergovernmental relations have undergone several transitions since the pioneering work of the founders. Wright's work and that of other early writers serves as a springboard for the contributors to use as a basis for examining the dynamic nature of IGR. This volume chronicles and analyzes some of the tensions and pressures that have contributed to the current state of IGR and will likely reshape the field.

The authors include distinguished scholars, emerging thought leaders, and experienced practitioners. Their research adds new dimensions and fresh perspectives to the understanding of developments, issues, and trends.

IGR is a process, not an end state, and it is an enticing and stimulating field to study and practice. We are encouraged by the growth in the number of undergraduate and graduate courses dealing with aspects of federalism and IGR, another indication of resurgence. We hope that this volume will help to spark interest among scholars in researching this rich and expanding field as well as among students who may be interested in pursuing careers in government. Finally, for those toiling in the intergovernmental trenches, we hope this book will provide helpful information and guidance on some of the issues and initiatives that are reinforcing and reshaping the intergovernmental management environment as well as restore and reenergize the commitments of IGR practitioners to making federalism work.

Carl W. Stenberg and David K. Hamilton

1 Introduction: Intergovernmental Relations in Transition

David K. Hamilton and Carl W. Stenberg

During the 1960s and 1970s, intergovernmental relations (IGR) was an exciting area for research and practice. There was substantial interest in the field with studies from the U.S. Advisory Commission on Intergovernmental Relations (ACIR) and research by noted academics such as Deil Wright, Daniel Elazar, Martha Derthick, and Morton Grodzins contributing scholarship to broaden and deepen understanding of the field. With the advent of the Great Society in the 1960s, the federal government assumed a leadership role in IGR practice through domestic policy initiatives, grants-in-aid, and regulations. The federal government forged direct relations with local governments during this period at an unprecedented scale. States were increasingly left out of the loop as local leaders were building direct relationships with federal funding and regulatory agencies.

Particularly significant was the work of intergovernmental institutions in Washington DC during this time. As a symbol of the growing importance of the field, Congress established and funded the Advisory Commission on Intergovernmental Relations in 1959 to conduct research and make recommendations on intergovernmental issues as well as to identify emerging trends and friction points. Although a miniscule organization by Washington standards, the ACIR, with its professional research staff, dedicated public official members, and access to thought and practice leaders, quickly became the preeminent bipartisan, independent organization for the study and understanding of IGR. By the 1980s about half of the states had established an ACIR-type body. This was a halcyon time, undoubtedly a golden age for IGR research.

Decline of Intergovernmental Relations

A major transition in the field occurred when the Reagan Administration sought to extricate the federal government from its leadership role in IGR by cutting or capping many intergovernmental programs, cancelling others, and devolving still others to the states. Nevertheless, overall the number of grant programs and the amount of aid continued to grow thanks to Congress. Yet, other important transitions were under way as the recipients of federal aid shifted from places to people, regulatory federalism, preemptions, and unfunded mandates exploded, and relationships between the levels of government became more coercive and less cooperative. During this period, the states became more involved in executive and legislative capacity-building, strengthening state-local relationships, and serving as "laboratories of democracy."

Symbolically, the ACIR was defunded in 1996 as part of a cost-cutting move by Congress. Neither the Clinton Administration nor the "Big 7" Public Interest Groups representing state and local governments in Washington, DC (e.g. National Governors Association, National Conference of State Legislatures, Council of State Governments, National Association of Counties, National League of Cities, United States Conference of Mayors, International City/County Management Association) mounted a strong defense of the Commission (McDowell 1997). Some of the federal government's institutional capacity for understanding and monitoring IGR was also dismantled. This deinstitutionalization included eliminating the grant management unit in the Office of Management and Budget, downplaying the policy role of the White House Office of Intergovernmental Affairs, and weakening the influence of the federalism subcommittees of Congress.

Until recently, because of these and other transitions, the IGR field languished from its previous prominence. There was little political interest in IGR and no national organization other than the U.S. Government Accountability Office (GAO) with the bipartisan status of the former ACIR to keep federalism, intergovernmental relations, and intergovernmental management before political leaders and the public. Efforts to recreate the ACIR proved futile (Stenberg 2011: 174–176). The "Big 7" Public Interest Groups lost much of their influence in shaping intergovernmental policy and programs as they were increasingly treated as just one of many special interest groups by members of Congress and federal administrators. Federalism considerations were rarely raised on the political radar screen in debates over issues such as tax reform, program management improvement, and regulatory policy implementation.

Members of Congress gain little or no political credit for being federalism champions, and few have followed in the IGR leadership footsteps of U.S. Senator Edmund S. Muskie (Maine) and Representative L.H. Fountain (North Carolina). Vertical and horizontal relations among governments are complex, difficult to understand, and hard to explain. Not surprisingly, the public and media have little comprehension of, interest in, or appreciation for IGR so the state of the federal system rarely becomes a campaign issue.

One example of the lack of political interest and support for significant intergovernmental change is the fate of proposals to "divide the job" or "sort out" functional responsibilities to reduce duplication and bolster efficiency and effectiveness. United States Senator (and former Tennessee Governor) Lamar Alexander (2013) and Alice Rivlin, founding director of the Congressional Budget Office and former Director of the Office and Management and Budget (1992), have called for a transfer of federal and state government responsibilities, building on recommendations put forward by the ACIR in the 1960s. Basically, the federal government would turn most of its programs in education, housing, highways, social services, economic development, and job training over to the states. States would carry out a "productivity agenda" to help revitalize the American economy through investments in education and infrastructure to increase productivity and raise income. Common shared taxes would give the states adequate revenues to carry out their new functional responsibilities and would reduce interstate competition and intrastate disparities. The federal government would retain responsibility for domestic programs requiring national uniformity like Social Security and health care.

In the early 1980s, President Reagan utilized the first part of the concept of sorting out responsibilities to propose devolving a number of federal programs to the states in what became known as New Federalism. Tax sharing to provide adequate revenues for the states to carry out the programs was not part of the President's grand exchange. However, the federalization of Medicaid in return for the turnback of several domestic programs to states and localities was a bold stroke at rebalancing the federal system. But after receiving tepid or no support from members of Congress, governors and state legislators, and local elected officials, the proposal was abandoned. Politics and pragmatism trumped systematic sorting out of functional responsibilities. The failure of this initiative also signaled the lack of trust between the federal government and the states as well as between and among state and local governments, conditions that persist to this day.

Resurgence of Intergovernmental Relations

Recent developments signal a resurgence of interest in IGR. Through the establishment of the Department of Homeland Security, financial responses to the Great Recession, and enactment of high profile domestic legislation under both the Bush and the Obama Administrations—including the No Child Left Behind Act, the American Recovery and Reinvestment Act (ARRA), and the Affordable Care Act—the federal government has reasserted itself in the intergovernmental arena as a stimulator and standard-setter. This transition took place even though the federal government wallowed in massive debt and faced serious challenges in financing health care, retirement, defense, and other commitments.

Particularly noteworthy were the impacts of fiscal stresses caused by the Great Recession. The federal government's $800 billion economic stimulus package helped reduce layoffs of teachers and police officers and provided increased unemployment benefits. ARRA also funded "shovel ready" public infrastructure projects through fund transfers to states and localities. During the recession, several states reduced their financial support to local governments, substituting federal dollars for their own dollars. This practice created financial problems when ARRA funds ended and local and state governments had to cope with less aid while still wrestling with slowly recovering tax revenues (Rubin 2015). News stories reported municipal bankruptcies and state and local government lay-offs of over 700,000 employees (Huffington Post 2012). The long-term viability of some local governments' capacity to finance and manage services became problematic, and sluggish economic growth continues to be a concern at all levels.

The intergovernmental environment within which this federal expansion has occurred is much different than in the past. IGR has changed dramatically partly in response to the growth of "wicked" problems like health care, education, environmental sustainability, infrastructure, and job creation that do not respect traditional governmental boundaries. The concept of intergovernmental relations as vertical dealings between governments in the federal system no longer accurately defines the field. While the institutional, fiscal, and functional policy issues of the 1960s and 1970s are still relevant, IGR is increasingly recognized as including nongovernmental actors and horizontal as well as vertical relationships in more of a regional, collaborative, and networked governance environment (Rosenbaum, Glendening, Posner, and Conlan 2014). According to scholars and practitioners, evidence of the need for cross-boundary collaboration is everywhere.

The old way of conceptualizing IGR does not cover the range of intergovernmental responses to public policy and programs. Kettl (2015) argues that interweaving of functions, tools, and organizations has become the primary instrument of public action. The Affordable Care Act, for example, is a complex of federal standards and subsidies with insurance offered through private companies coordinated through federal and state exchanges with the actual health care provided through for-profit and nonprofit medical centers. The federal government's response to the Ebola virus in 2014 came through federal standards, transmitted through state public health agencies, and administered through local governments and regional nonprofit health care facilities. Intergovernmental programs now often combine governmental and nongovernmental efforts to implement national policies and priorities and feature mandates and preemptions which may or may not be accompanied by federal funds.

The expansion of federal domestic involvement has also occurred in a highly partisan environment and in areas that were previously regarded as predominantly private and state regulated programs. The most recent example is health care. Expansion of the federal role in health care has been extremely contentious, which has made delivery of the program difficult. Supreme Court decisions, such as invalidating part of the Affordable Care Act dealing with mandated expansion of Medicaid coverage, have made implementation more complex. Political polarization of leaders at the national level and increasingly in state capitals does not allow for a serious bipartisan, pragmatic, and collaborative approach to the federalism issues facing America. The challenges are severe, and the institutional capacity to address them is almost nonexistent.

Implementation Challenges

Despite its resurgence, the federal government no longer unilaterally sets the domestic agenda or operates in a top-down environment where it establishes the regulations and the program parameters. States are pushing back against what some governors and legislators consider federal overreach and intrusions. Contrary to the view of many governors and legislators during the 1980s that the 10th Amendment to the U.S. Constitution was a "hollow shell," as a result of Supreme Court interpretations of the Commerce Clause signaling a "green light" to Congress to expand its domestic program and regulatory activities, state leaders have reasserted the states' key role in program design and implementation. They have sought to shape federal programs to better reflect their needs and priorities, resist federal mandates and preemptions, and even turn down federal funds. To increase flexibility and recognize their capacity and commitment, some states have been granted waivers in many instances from federal rules and regulations that determine how federal dollars are spent. Many IGR programs are initiated by the states or local governments, and federal agencies must negotiate with sub-national program implementers. States have also established programs that are in direct violation of federal policy and law, such as legalizing marijuana. Federal funds are still a major force, but increasingly more decision making and IGR initiatives in areas like gay marriage, minimum wages, environmental quality, education, and immigration are being generated by the states and local governments working with non-profit and for-profit program partners.

Relations between the states and local governments also changed during the Great Recession. Many states passed laws either providing greater flexibility to local governments or restricting their functional and fiscal authority. For example, California enacted legislation enabling cities to bargain with creditors short of bankruptcy, while Michigan and Rhode Island passed laws that gave the state authority to take control of local governments in the event of fiscal exigency and override or replace local officials with a state appointee (Rubin 2015). State-local relations are in flux and are gaining visibility. Municipal and county leaders are seeking to determine whether state officials are partners or adversaries, or both. The cover of the April 2016 issue of *Governing* magazine sent a powerful message: "We Interrupt This Program . . . Some states will step in to cut off local government actions any chance they get." For example, a 2017 survey by the National League of Cities found that 42 states had imposed tax and expenditure limitations on localities. Additionally, 37 states had preempted local authority in ride sharing, 24 had done so with respect to the minimum wage, 17 states had preempted paid leave policy, and another 17 had taken such action on municipal broadband authority (Cigler et al. 2017: 3).

In summary, implementation of intergovernmental programs has always been complicated, involving multiple levels of governments and often nongovernmental actors. The IGR concept was designed to recognize that implementation of intergovernmental policies and programs was dependent on relationships between actors at different levels of government. The term "intergovernmental management" (IGM) has been used to underscore that effective implementation of programs requires skill in managing the various actors involved and navigating through complex intergovernmental and intersectoral relationships. The federal government's response to Hurricanes Katrina and Sandy showed the vulnerability of intergovernmental programs in the face of natural disasters, especially the difficulty of coordinating rapid responses. Coordination and communication breakdowns, together with unrealistic time lines for deliverables, led to the botched roll-out of the Obamacare website by the Department of Health and Human Services and private contractors, and helped fuel the debate over the repeal and replacement of the ACA during the 2016 Presidential campaign and since the inauguration of President Donald Trump. These examples also reveal that politics is always a key factor in the implementation of intergovernmental policy and programs.

Trump Federalism?

The election of Donald Trump as the nation's 45th President opened a new chapter in the evolution of intergovernmental relations and management. The President's policy pronouncements and initiatives during his first 100 days in office sent shock waves across federal, state, and local governments. Some proposals, such as to spend $1 trillion on infrastructure improvements and to reinvent the Veterans Administration, were generally well-received. Particularly distressing to the "Big 7" organizations representing state and local officials in Washington, DC, however, were proposals in the administration's 2018 federal budget to shift $54 billion in federal spending from domestic discretionary accounts to defense. Forecasts that, in view of the growth in the federal debt and record budget deficits, cutbacks in discretionary spending for grant-in-aid programs could be anticipated look very likely to occur. The initial congressional response to the massive proposed budget shift did not indicate a clear direction or prospects for consensus. Just as during the Reagan administration when the Congress had resisted and restored cutbacks, similar political, constituent, and interest group pressures could thwart Trump budget cutters and perpetuate the status quo.

The President's initiatives to deregulate, defund, and devolve federal programs and agencies also have been a wake-up call to subnational units. Governors, legislators, and local elected leaders will likely confront tough choices, such as whether: (1) to agree to the trade-off of more discretion and flexibility in moving federal funds to their priority areas in exchange for less federal funds (i.e. Medicaid block grants); (2) to reduce or increase the level of regulations (i.e. air and water quality, climate control, immigration and Sanctuary Cities for immigrants); and (3) to continue to support former federal programs that are on the chopping block (i.e. Community Development Block Grants, Appalachian Regional Commission, Supplemental Nutrition Assistance, Planned Parenthood).

Tax reform is a third policy area that could have substantial intergovernmental impacts. For example, since many state tax systems are linked to the federal tax code, proposals to eliminate the deductability of interest on state and local bonds on federal tax returns could prove costly. Efforts to simplify and standardize the federal tax system, such as through a flat tax or national sales tax, could also threaten state economies.

As indicated in some of the chapters that follow, it is quite possible that more attention will be devoted to intergovernmental management and budget balancing in the years ahead than at any time since the Reagan administration. Whether there will be a new wave of initiatives to "sort out" responsibilities or "divide the job" along the lines suggested by Reagan, Alexander, and Rivlin remain to be seen. The GAO has prepared several reports to Congress identifying program duplication, agency overlap, and high risk management areas, and the recommendations for remedial action offer a promising point of departure (GAO 2011). GAO has also called attention to the serious and growing impacts of entitlement spending on the federal budget. But whether these proposals will gain traction in the administration and Congress and with the "Big 7" remain to be seen. Alternatively, "turmoil" rather than systematic "transition" may be the defining characteristic of future intergovernmental relations.

From Practice to Theory: Is Intergovernmental Relations Relevant or Obsolete?

The preceding overview of IGR in transition highlights how and why intergovernmental relations has changed significantly since publication of Wright's book, *Understanding Intergovernmental Relations*, in 1978. IGR has gone through many twists, turns, and permutations in reaching its present state, and continues to evolve. The major focus of Wright's book and others that were written during the period between 1970 and 1990 was largely on the impact of federal policies on state and local governments. Federal grants-in-aid, program management, and federal-local relations were the major topics.

In the third edition of his book (1988), Wright identified seven phases of intergovernmental relations during the history of our Republic: the conflict, cooperative, concentrated, creative, competitive, calculative and contractive phases. As will be seen in Part 1 of this book, these phases have been the basis for much debate among scholars. Some suggest that the field is now in a new phase, while others claim that intergovernmental relations has basically remained the same since the 1960s, albeit more coercive and partisan.

The authors also are divided on whether Wright anticipated the directions that IGR would take and the relevance of his three intergovernmental relations models (see Figure 1.1). Under the co-ordinate authority model, the state and federal levels were independent insofar as their spheres of authority were concerned. Their powers did not overlap. The inclusive or the unitary model held that the federal government was supreme and the state governments were subject to its policy direction. In the third model, overlapping authority, power was shared between various levels of governments simultaneously working together or independently within the same sphere on the same issues.

Although Wright's models and the study of IGR in that period were firmly institutional based, some scholars argue that his overlapping model did anticipate the type of networked governance that we have today, and is a good representation of IGR as it has evolved (Agranoff and Radin 2015; Burke 2014). These scholars claim that the overlapping model is a valuable and appropriate approach to use in the study and analysis of the type of networked governance that is evident. According to Agranoff and Radin (2015: 152), "The evolving nature of IGR in the quarter century since Wright's third edition was published has done little to disparage the power of the overlapping model. Indeed, it is even more appropriate as a place to begin to look for developments."

Others claim that the IGR orientation on government institutions of that period missed the dynamic changes that were occurring in intergovernmental relations as it moved to a networked

Figure 1.1 Deil Wright's Intergovernmental Relations Authority Models.

Source: Wright (1978)

system. Barnes (2014) claims that with the focus of IGR scholars on institutional arrangements and relations among governments, the increasing involvement and impact of nongovernmental actors in the public policy arena was overlooked or downplayed. He argues that scholarship in IGR was left behind because of this orientation on the institution rather than on the governance question of how policy is addressed and implemented with the various actors and influences involved. IGR scholarship was stuck in institutional research questions while the practice was in networks and collaboration. Thus the new generation of scholars researching in this area did not identify with the IGR field as it had been developed in the 1960s and 1970s. Toward the end of his life, Wright wondered whether federalism, intergovernmental relations, and intergovernmental management were becoming obsolete, as revealed in a content analysis of titles of articles published in the *Public Administration Review* (Wright, Stenberg, and Cho 2011).

"Big Questions" About IGR and IGM Revisited

In 2011 John Kincaid and Carl Stenberg co-authored a concluding article on "'Big Questions' about Intergovernmental Relations and Management: Who Will Address Them?" (2011) for a symposium in the *Public Administration Review* on the impacts of the 1996 demise of the U.S. Advisory Commission on Intergovernmental Relations and assessment of prospects for restoring intergovernmental institutional capacity. Overall, the contributors' views were pessimistic.

Kincaid and Stenberg posed 15 questions to provoke discussion about the future directions of intergovernmental relations (IGR) and management (IGM). The former was defined as a term "that encompasses all types of interactions between elected and nonelected officials of federal state, and local governments," featuring policy-making through laws and regulations "in which elected officials and agency heads are important actors." IGM was "a less comprehensive term, encompassing the implementation and management of intergovernmental policies . . . in which nonelected agency heads and street level bureaucrats are prime actors" (Kincaid and Stenberg 2011: 196). The intergovernmental landscape at that time featured local and state actions to respond to the national economic crisis together with significant federal domestic leadership initiatives such as the American Recovery and Reinvestment Act and the Affordable Care Act.

The intergovernmental world has changed dramatically since 2011, and its future contours and directions are unclear and uncertain. IGR and IGM have become more fractious and contentious while relationships have become more horizontal and intersectoral. Nevertheless, many of the "Big Questions" remain relevant. We have recast eight of them below, in consultation with Kincaid. Two contributors to this volume—John Kincaid and Parris Glendening—share their insights from academic and practitioner perspectives, respectively. Other authors have expressed their views on questions that are relevant to their chapter.

1 Deinstitutionalization

How important is the absence of institutions that monitor intergovernmental trends and developments, convene meetings, and conduct research to the health of the federal system? Will the need to rebalance the federal government's financial and programmatic roles call for more and sustained attention to intergovernmental management?

No serious effort has been made to rebuild institutional capacity to understand intergovernmental relations and management since the demise of the U.S. Advisory Commission on Intergovernmental Relations in 1996 and of most of the state ACIRs. Proposed federal budget reforms, reorganizations, and program eliminations have potentially significant impacts on states and localities. Yet, the likely consequences of these initiatives are not well appreciated and often not even considered in the policy-making process.

2 Sorting Out

The federal budget has been driven by the "four d's" for decades—debts, deficits, demographics, and defense—and there have been no serious initiatives to reign in federal spending. Given the political and policy shifts that have taken place recently in Washington, DC and several states, what are the prospects for budget reform and what are the implications for states and localities? Has the time come to systematically sort out functions or divide the job intergovernmentally, as advocated by Alice Rivlin and Senator Lamar Alexander, and if so who should take the lead?

No agreement has been reached on ways to close the widening "credibility gap" between federal spending and revenues. Medicare, Medicaid, Social Security, defense, and deficit spending have long been targets of budget reformers, but they remain "sacred cows" in the IGR pasture. The day of reckoning might be on the horizon and one option is to "divide the job" systematically, as was attempted by President Reagan in 1981–1982. Who would champion such an initiative in Congress and the Administration, or would this be just another exercise in futility given the strength of Wright's shared authority model?

3 Block Grants

Are block grants feasible instruments for reforming federal grants-in-aid through consolidation, deregulation, and devolution? What criteria should be used? What does the record show about the trade-off of fewer federal dollars for greater recipient flexibility and discretion?

Block grants have been a used since 1966 to give state and local recipients flexibility in targeting federal funds to their priority needs within a broad functionally related area. Typically, more discretion is provided than in narrower categorical grants. Block grants have been considered instruments for federal aid reform, especially consolidation of categorical programs such as under the 1974 Housing and Community Development block grant. They also have been proposed as a means of reducing federal expenditures by lowering administrative costs through devolution or authority. Yet, only 21 block grants have been enacted since the Partnership for Health program in the mid–1960s and block grants account for only between 10–15 percent of the federal aid total. Will block grant proposals be a part of discretionary program cuts that will be on the federal budget balancer's agenda?

4 State–Local Relations

Why are states increasingly imposing unfunded or underfunded mandates on local governments, and restricting municipal and county authority in economic, social, and environmental policy? What are the prospects for "fend-for-yourself localism?"

Across the 50 states there is wide variation in the extent to which states have accorded local governments home rule authority over their structures, functions, and finances. In some states, local officials have considered governors and legislators partners in meeting citizen needs, while in others there is an adversarial relationship. Recent years have witnessed a growing number of state laws preempting or restricting local authority, shifting functional responsibility without commensurate resources, and cutting local financial aid. While weak state revenue conditions have been cited as a reason for these actions, the rising cost of Medicaid and the shifting partisan and ideological landscapes also have been contributors.

5 Regional Cooperation

If, as Beverly Cigler states, cooperation is "an unnatural act among nonconsenting adults" what strategies and tools can states and localities use to encourage interlocal service sharing and joint action on "wicked" problems (Cigler 2007)?

Contrary to expectations that a "New Normal" would emerge from the Great Recession, in which the local government footprint would be shrunk by outsourcing and permanent cutbacks, most counties and municipalities have rebounded from the economic crisis without making fundamental changes in their services or structures. While there is general recognition that "wicked" problems require intergovernmental, intersectoral, and interdisciplinary approaches, local autonomy and parochialism have inhibited regional cooperation in many places. What "carrots" or "sticks" could be used to encourage local governments to work across boundaries on serious problems?

6 "Coercive" Federalism

What are the prospects for continuation of "coercive" federalism? Is a return to cooperative federalism, as reflected in the work of the U.S. Advisory Commission on Intergovernmental Relations and previous respect accorded the state and local Public Interest Groups, likely in the future?

John Kincaid coined the term "coercive" federalism to describe the steady growth of federal policy-making power in the federal system, often at the expense of subnational units. In recent years, however, state leaders have pushed-back against federal authority in health care, environmental regulation, and other areas. The Trump administration and members of Congress have launched initiatives to "deconstruct the administrative state" by shrinking federal career personnel, reorganizing agencies, reducing regulations, and cutting discretionary expenditures. While the outcomes of these proposals are unclear, another chapter in the "New Federalism" story is unfolding and the "coercive" aspects of IGR and IGM could be challenged or reinforced.

7 Networks and Partnerships

Will the networked and collaborative nature of IGR and IGM continue as efforts are under way to diminish the federal government's intergovernmental role as was attempted during the Reagan administration?

Federal policies and program initiatives in past decades have expanded and added complexity to IGR and IGM. Governance arrangements have also become more common in recent years both horizontally and vertically. Elected officials and administrators from all levels of government, together with private sector actors, are more involved in public policy and implementation than previously. As the federal government retrenches, what effect will that have on networked and collaborative partnerships?

8 Partisanship

To what extent is partisan polarization affecting IGR and IGM? To what extent does the party in power in Washington DC seek to impose its policy preferences nationwide regardless of state and local preferences?

Many observers have highlighted contention in IGR and IGM, though especially IGR; yet, much of this contention is partisan. Republican states bucked President Obama and Democratic states are bucking President Trump. There is a high degree of party congruence in the state-federal system in 2017–2018 as Republicans control the White House and Congress, and conservatives make up the majority on the U.S. Supreme Court. At the state level, Republicans control 33 governorships and both the governorship and the legislature in 25 states (counting Nebraska as *de facto* Republican). The current partisan contention is the six states where Democrats control the governorship and legislature. Will state-federal relations be mostly cooperative for two-thirds or more of the states or, will intraparty differences produce policy and program stalemate as was evidenced in congressional efforts in the spring of 2017 to repeal and replace the Affordable Care Act?

Introduction to the Chapters that Follow

In the chapters that follow, which build on this overview of IGR in transition, the authors cover several aspects of intergovernmental relations and management, adding insights and furthering understanding of the current state and possible future directions of IGR. The authors give their perspectives on how intergovernmental relations have evolved over the past 40–50 years, and the policies and issues that have contributed to those changes. They also offer their prognosis on how IGR will continue to evolve, and there is consensus in some areas and disagreement in others.

The first section of the book deals with the federal government's shifting role and impact in the context of the evolution of the federal government's domestic leadership and the phases of IGR developed by Deil Wright. The authors differ in their assessments of these developments and trends, but they share a number of concerns about the implications for research and practice. The second section considers contemporary and emerging fiscal issues affecting intergovernmental relations and management, together with their institutional impacts. The third section of the book focuses on recent developments in program implementation. Four contemporary—and controversial—areas are showcased: health care, food safety; energy policy; and climate change. The fourth section moves the discussion of IGR from a national focus on phases of IGR and state-local implementation of federal programs. The subnational levels are examined from the viewpoints of state relationships with local units and street level collaboration. The fifth section presents two seasoned practitioner's reflections "from the trenches" and their perspectives on the future directions and challenges confronting the intergovernmental system. In the concluding chapter, the co-editors summarize some of the major themes that emerge from the various authors in the context of the "Big Questions" and identify related areas for further research.

References

Agranoff, Robert and Beryl A. Radin. 2015. "Deil Wright's overlapping model of intergovernmental relations: The basis for contemporary intergovernmental relationships." *Publius* 45(1): 139–159.

Alexander, Lamar. 2013. "Speech given at outset of the Tennessee General Assembly." January 10. Retrieved from www.lamaralexander.com/news?ID (accessed January 12, 2016).

Barnes, Bill. 2014. "Emerging issues: The kind of problem the intergovernmental system is." *PA Times* 37(3): 12.

Burke, Brendan F. 2014. "Understanding intergovernmental relations, twenty-five years hence." *State and Local Government Review* 46(11): 63–76.

Cigler, Beverly. 2007. "Post-Katrina emergency management: Forum overview." *The Public Manager* (Fall).

Cigler, Beverly, Nicole DuPuis, Trevor Langan, Christiana McFarland, Angelina Panettieri, and Brooks Rainwater. 2017. *City Rights in an Era of Preemption: A State-by-State Analysis*. Washington, DC: National League of Cities.

GAO. 2011. *Opportunities to Reduce Potential Duplication in Government Programs, Save Tax Dollars, and Enhance Revenue*. GAO-11-318SP (March). Washington, DC: U.S. Governmental Accountability Office.

Huffington Post. 2012. "Newly-red states account for nearly half of government layoffs: report." *Huffington Post* (March 27). Retrieved from www.huffingtonpost.com/2012/03/27/government-jobs-cuts_n_1382989. html (accessed January 13, 2016).

Kettl, Donald F. 2015. "The job of government: Interweaving public functions and private hands." *Public Administration Review* 75(2): 219–228.

Kincaid, John and Carl W. Stenberg III. 2011. "'Big questions' about intergovernmental relations and management: Who will address them?" *Public Administration Review* 71(March): 196–202.

McDowell, Bruce D. 1997. "Advisory Commission on Intergovernmental Relations in 1996: The end of an era." *Publius: The Journal of Federalism* 27(2): 111–127

Rivlin, Alice M. 1992. *Reviving the American Dream: The Economy, the States and the Federal Government*. Washington, DC: The Brookings Institution.

Rosenbaum, Allan, Parris Glendening, Paul Posner, and Tim Conlan. 2014. "America's invisible governmental crisis: Intergovernmental relations in a time of transition and uncertainty." *PA Times* 26(4): 6, 20–21.

Rubin, Irene. 2015. "Past and future budget classics: A research agenda." *Public Administration Review* 75(1): 25–36.

Stenberg, Carl W. 2011. "An ACIR perspective on intergovernmental institutional development." *Public Administration Review* 71(2): 169–176.

Wright, Deil S. 1978. *Understanding Intergovernmental Relations*. Boston, MA: Duxbury Press.

Wright, Deil S., Carl W. Stenberg, and Chung-Lae Cho. 2011. "Historic relevance confronting contemporary obsolescence? Federalism, intergovernmental relations, and intergovernmental management." In Donald C. Menzel and Harvey L. White, eds. *The State of Public Administration: Issues, Challenges, and Opportunities*. Armonk, NY: M. E. Sharpe: 297–315.

Part I
Phases of Intergovernmental Relations Revisited

2 Intergovernmental Relations in the Early Twenty-First Century

Lingering Images of Earlier Phases and Emergence of a New Phase

J. Edwin Benton

In crafting the U.S. Constitution and setting into motion what Tocqueville (1999) would call the "novel American Experiment," the Founding Fathers probably never envisioned the complex system of intergovernmental relations (IGR) and ubiquitous interactions that would result in the new republic. From the launching of the new democracy in 1789 until the end of the nineteenth century, the scope of government activity and the impact on governmental decisions were in line with the Jefferson proclamation that "government that governs best . . . governs least." This period was marked by Americans embracing the notion of *laissez-faire* and many of the basic tenets of Social Darwinism, while the dominant political culture could be characterized as a mixture of the traditionalistic and individualistic types (Elazar 1984). With the national government, and even state governments, performing only a limited number of functions and providing a relatively short menu of services, there was little opportunity for these governments, and subsequently, their officials, to come into contract or interact with one another. State–local relations could be characterized by a top-down approach, with states exercising oversight authority over their creations (local governments), while national–state relations could be viewed as "two ships passing in the night," and each respecting the sphere of authority of the other. That is, these two planes (levels) of government tended to act independently of each another and generally did not encroach on the other (Zimmerman 2008). The concept of "Dual Federalism" seemed to be an appropriate depiction of the operation of American federalism and subsequent IGR for over 100 years.

IGR was destined to change, however, with the dawning of the twentieth century, as the seeds for change were visible even before 1900 (see O'Toole 2000: 6–7). Deil Wright (1988: 65) explained the coming IGR changes and the reason for them in this way: "It is an accepted fact that since 1900 the U.S. political system has experienced major shifts that represent dramatic, if not evolutionary, upheavals." He was obviously referring to history-changing events and significant political and public policy decisions that are listed here in abbreviated form and in no particular order: sixteenth (individual income tax), seventeenth (direct election of U.S. Senators), eighteenth (prohibition), nineteenth (women's suffrage), twenty-first (repeal of prohibition), twenty-third (right to vote for citizens of the District of Columbia), twenty-fourth (prohibition against poll tax), and twenty-sixth (lowering of voting age to 18 years of age) Amendments to the U.S. Constitution, World War I, Great Depression, World War II, Civil Rights Movement, Congressional enactments and U.S. Supreme Court cases in areas like health care, welfare, housing, labor relations, civil rights and civil liberties, environment, homeland security, immigration, and so forth.

To better understand and explain how these events and policy decisions contributed to the evolution of our political system as well as changes in patterns of relations in IGR in the U.S., Wright identified and described seven phases or periods of IGR (see Table 2.1). The descriptive nature and nuances of each phase crystallized upon Wright's consideration of the following questions:

- What underlying forces precipitated the changes?
- What were the directions and subtle shapes of the shifts?
- Around what policy issues did the changes revolve, and what were the mechanisms by which the changes were implemented?
- What were the short- and long-term effects of the shift?

Table 2.1 Phases of Intergovernmental Relations

Phase Descriptor	Main Problems	Participants' Perceptions	IGR Mechanisms	Federalism Metaphor	Approximate Climax Period
Conflict	Defining boundaries Proper spheres	Antagonistic Adversary Exclusiveness	Statutes Courts Regulation	Layer-cake federalism	19th century–1930s
Cooperative	Economic distress International threat	Collaboration Complementary Mutuality Supportive	National planning Formula grants Tax credits	Marble-cake federalism	1930s–1950s
Concentrated	Service needs Physical development	Professionalism Objectivity Neutrality Functionalism	Categorical grants Service standards	Water taps (focused or channeled)	1940s–1960s
Creative	Urban-metropolitan Disadvantaged clients	National goals Great Society Grantsmanship	Program planning Project grants Participation	Flowering (proliferated and fused)	1950s–1960s
Competitive	Coordination Program effectiveness Citizen access	Disagreement Rivalry	Grant consolidation Reorganization	Picket-fence (fragmentation) federalism	1960s–1970s
Calculative	Accountability Bankruptcy Constraints Dependency Federal role Public confidence	Grantsmanship Fungibility Overload	General aid-entitlements Bypassing Loans Crosscutting regulations	Façade (confrontational) federalism	1970s–1980s
Contractive	Borrowing and balanced budgeting Federal aid cuts and changes Juridicial decision making Managing mandates	Aggressiveness Contentiousness Defensiveness Litigiousness	Congressional statutes/Court decisions Information sources Negotiated dispute settlement Privatization	De facto federalism Telescope(s) federalism Whiplash federalism	1980s–1990s

Phase Descriptor	Main Problems	Participants' Perceptions	IGR Mechanisms	Federalism Metaphor	Approximate Climax Period
Kaleidoscopic	Redefining boundaries Economic decline Fiscal woes Globalization Pension reassessment	Polarization Inaction Indecisiveness Convolution Collaboration	State legislation Court challenges Mandates Interlocal agreements	Fragmented federalism Push-back federalism Nuanced federalism Fend-for-yourself federalism Collaborative federalism	1990s–2010s

Source: Wright (1988: 67); the Kaleidoscopic Phase was added by the author

Over the last 25 years, few scholars (including Wright) have either identified or described a new phase of IGR beyond his seventh "Contractive Phase." Do the principal components associated with the "Contractive Phase" (that is, the main problems or policy issues dominating the public agenda, participants' perceptions, and IGR mechanisms) still accurately describe and explain the workings of IGR or has a new phase emerged? Given changing citizenry and private sector needs and expectations and profound national and global events, have the basic contours of IGR and roles of various governments and subsequently relations among these governments' elected and appointed public officials been reshaped and redefined? While remnants of Wright's seventh phase may still be evident, is it possible that enough has changed in the workings of IGR to suggest the emergence of a new eighth phase of IGR? The purpose of this chapter is to explore the possibility that we have already entered into a new eighth phase of IGR.

Before proceeding to the principal objective of this paper, it is instructive for us to know something about how Wright arrived at identifying his seven phases of IGR. A brief description of the methodology he utilized is provided below.

Wright's Seven Phases of Intergovernmental Relations: From Whence They Came

Deil Wright's identification and characterization of seven distinctive periods or phases in the U.S. that were evident during the twentieth century has served as an invaluable and insightful guidepost for scholars and practitioners in their desire to better understand and appreciate the dynamic relations and interactions among levels of government, especially among their elected and appointed officials. Therefore, it is important that any effort to determine if a new phase has emerged should start with a review of the significant political and economic happenings and defining moments in IGR that preceded the opening of the new century. A condensed overview of the distinctive features (i.e., main problems, participants' perceptions, IGR mechanisms, federalism metaphors, and approximate climax period) of each of Wright's phases is presented in Table 2.1 (for a thorough description of each phase, see Wright 1988: 66–110).

A general familiarity with the distinctive features of each of Wright's phases, however, is not sufficient to be able to fully grasp or appreciate the dynamics of IGR or the transition from one phase to another. As Wright put it, two clarifications are important to "understanding the exposition and interpretation of the phases and their one-word descriptors" (1988: 66). First, the descriptors do not include *all* aspects of intergovernmental interaction during the period indicated for each phase. For instance, while conflict is the predominant characteristic of the period prior to 1930, it does not preclude the possibility or probability of important cooperative IGR activities. Second, since the dates for each period are approximate and not finite, this means that the phases overlap. Therefore, the term "climax period" not only identifies a time of peak prominence but also leaves open the possibility for the continuation of a phase beyond the dates given. For example, even though the conflict phase climaxed before and during the 1930s, the conflict relationship did not end then but often reappears in future periods as a subsidiary theme of the present dominant phase. Wright (1988: 66) describes what happens in this manner:

> Like successive, somewhat porous strata that have been superimposed on each other (by the interactions and perspectives of public officials), no phase ends at an exact point—nor does it in fact disappear. Each phase is continuously present in greater or lesser measure, bearing the weight, so to speak, of the overlying strata (subsequent phases).

Each phase has "carryover effects" much wider than the climax periods indicated in Table 2.1. As a consequence, the state of IGR at any point in time is actually the product of manifold overlays of each of the preceding phases.

Intergovernmental Relations Since the Late 1990s

From Wright's description and analysis of the main problems of each of the seven phases of IGR, it is reasonable to speculate that intergovernmental relations in the American federal system is subject to major change over time.[1] Unanticipated (or even anticipated) national and international events, public opinion and philosophical shifts, technological and scientific advances, volatile and precarious economic forces, climate and ecological changes, and the advent of a globalized world can serve as underlying causes and catalysts for the development of new patterns in IGR. Have these and other harbingers of change resulted in the emergence of a new eighth phase of IGR or does the seventh phase persist albeit in a transitional form?

In the last edition of *Understanding Intergovernmental Relations*, published in 1988, Wright projected that what he labeled the Contractive Phase of intergovernmental relations was likely to continue through at least the end of the twentieth century. A review of "The State of American Federalism" that has appeared in *Publius* on an annual basis during the 1980s and 1990s, as well as many articles devoted to American federalism and IGR, indicates that the conduct of IGR closely resembled what Wright had predicted. IGR participants' perceptions of relations and interactions (aggressiveness, contentiousness, defensiveness, and litigiousness) were clearly visible. In fact, by the first few years of the twenty-first century, there was still visible evidence of what would now appear to be the lingering presence of some aspects of the Contractive Phase.

Even as far back as the last half of the 1990s, there were mounting signs that a new phase was beginning to surface as the "winds of IGR" were shifting direction. This new phase was propelled by several problems and events. A Republican-controlled House of Representatives under the leadership of Speaker Newt Gingrich was at loggerheads with the Clinton White House and sharp ideological differences between Democrats and Republicans in Congress were emerging to the point that relations were nastier than they had ever been on Capitol Hill. Then, the fateful event of 9/11 changed the world forever as we knew it. And, by the second half of President Bush's second term, the nation and the world were rapidly falling into the most devastating downturn in the economy since the Great Depression of the 1930s (the Great Recession), the effects of which will probably be felt for several more decades. These events and others, as applied to the operation of all governments and IGR, have resulted in what many have acknowledged to be a "New Normal."[2]

Returning to the questions posed above, does the 7th (Contractive Phase) persist or have we entered into a new or 8th phase of IGR or are we in the process of transitioning? In an effort to provide answers to these questions, it will be useful to examine three distinctive sets of IGR relationships separately: federal–state, federal–local, and federal–state–local relations; state–local relations; and inter-local relations.

Federal–State, Federal–Local, and Federal–State–Local Relations

In the 2012–2013 Annual Review of Federalism published in *Publius: The Journal of Federalism*, Bowling and Pickerill (2013: 315) reported that "the state of American Federalism was arguably more chaotic, complex, and contentious than ever before" and "fragmentation continues as policy implementation occurs in a piecemeal fashion" (ibid.: 341). Little has changed since then, as noted by the authors of subsequent updates of the Annual Review (Bowling and Pickerill 2014; Rose and Bowling 2015; Bowling and Rose 2016).[3] This appears to be an accurate characterization of the state of federal–state, federal–local, and federal–state–local relations. Earlier descriptions of federalism and IGR and federalism metaphors like "layer cake," "marble cake," and "picket fence" are too one-dimensional and time constrained to accurately describe the relationships between administrators at the national, state, and local levels in the last decade or two. Moreover, federalism and IGR are no longer either "cooperative," "creative," "competitive," "coercive," or "calculative." All of these descriptions and approaches, as well as many others, depict the operation and relations of the federal system, even within the same policy area. As Bowling and Pickerill (2013: 315) observe, the Patent Protection and Affordable Care Act (PPACA) is a good example of this point, as this piece of legislation contains cooperative (grants-in-aid), creative (health exchanges and mandates for individuals), coercive (penalties for citizens and businesses), and calculative (cross-cutting regulations and confrontational politics) elements. In fact, the foregoing description of IGR does bear some resemblance to the depiction of IGR that Wright provided for the "Contractive" phase as he saw it in the 1980s and 1990s, except for the caveat that a new federalism metaphor (fragmentation) should be added to the three suggested by Wright.

In recent years, the President and Congress and both major political parties have been preoccupied with the increasing federal debt, balance of trade deficit, devaluation of the dollar versus other currencies, and slow recovery from the Great Recession. No quick solutions have been forthcoming in any of these and other related daunting economic challenges as sharp ideological and partisan differences have brought the federal budgetary process to a virtual standstill and gridlock has taken Washington hostage in what could be called a war of perpetual attrition. Democrats and Republicans (and liberals and conservatives) seem content and committed "to slugging it out" until the last man/women falls. In the *Publius* Annual Review of Federalism in 2011–2012, Gamkhar and Pickerill (2012: 359) wrote: "The federal executive branch remained embroiled in political standoffs with Congress on debt and budget issues." This statement is still a fairly accurate description of fiscal federalism. Ideological and partisan roadblocks not only threaten vital federal programs but also create uncertainty about intergovernmental transfers for state and localities' budgeting efforts. Currently, Congress (certainly Democrats and enough disgruntled Republicans) and the Trump administration are at loggerheads over efforts to repeal and replace the PPACA. This is significant because budgetary decisions at the federal level will be pivotal as intergovernmental transfers continue to constitute a considerable proportion of state and local government budgets.

More than in previous decades, states and their local governments are still in a precarious and vulnerable position. Although total state revenue collections were exceeding prerecession levels by FY2014 and FY2015, the growth rate in state revenues were beginning to decline noticeably by midway through 2016 and expected to carry over into 2017 (NASBO 2016). There is growing concern that the sluggish and uncertain growth in state revenues coupled with the potential loss of federal funds for Medicaid, infrastructure projects, Community Development Block Grants, and other staple federal aid programs cut from the Trump administration's proposed budget could mean a continuation of uncertain fiscal times for states as they strive to make ends meet (see Parrott, Reich, and Shapiro 2017; Harkness 2017; Benton forthcoming).

Local governments also continue to be challenged financially. It has taken longer for them to recover from the Great Recession than has been the case for states. Local government revenues dropped substantially when the housing bubble burst. A saturated housing market, along with massive foreclosures, combined to significantly reduce the value of real estate and subsequently caused assessed valuation to drop precipitously. This meant that property tax revenues plummeted, unless local governments were willing to raise millage rates in the wake of people already losing their homes to foreclosure and homeowners being in no mood to have their taxes increased. Most local officials did not attempt to raise tax rates and, in essence, gave homeowners a de facto tax break that resulted from lower property assessments coupled with unchanged millage rates. Consequently, local governments had a very difficult time balancing their budgets and were forced to slash spending and/or draw down heavily on their "rainy day funds." The net loss of federal aid (even when accounting for ARRA stimulus funding) served to exacerbate the local government budget situation.

Federal grant-in-aid programs, both competitive and matching, have increased the dependence of states and their local governments on national funding (Bowling and Pickerill 2013: 332). Although the number of federal grants has varied since the 1960s, more state agencies receive federal funding than previously, with 75 percent of them receiving federal monies (U.S. Department of Education 2016). In fact, over half of those receiving federal funds are dependent on intergovernmental transfers for more than one-quarter of their total budgets (ibid.). Because of this dependence, reductions in federal grants-in-aid would have a tremendous impact on state and local governments.

In the same way that fiscal federalism continues to define IGR in the early part of the twenty-first century, constitutional federalism also continues to shape federal–state, federal–local, and federal–state–local relations. In the last several years, the U.S. Supreme Court has decided cases with significant federalism consequences. While some of these decisions have provided further protection for sovereign state immunity, others have reasserted the legal authority of the national government via federal legislation to preempt state laws.

In perhaps the most celebrated case to be handed down in several decades, the Supreme Court in *National Federation of Independent Business v. Sebellius* (*NFIB*) (507 S. Ct. 2566, 2012) ruled on the constitutionality of the controversial PPACA that was proposed by President Obama and enacted by Congress along strict partisan lines. Writing for the 5–4 majority, Chief Justice John

Roberts upheld almost the entire Act, as well as the controversial "individual mandate" that compels individuals to buy health insurance and penalizes those who can afford to purchase insurance but do not do so. Seen by many, including the media, as a victory for President Obama, the majority opinion was "a nuanced one that, while upholding the act under Congress's taxing power, also established some clear and potentially important limitations on federal power with protections for states" (Bowling and Pickerill 2013: 333). In an odd twist and as a surprise to many Court observers, Roberts reasoned that the individual mandate could not be upheld using the commerce clause but could be upheld under Congress' power to tax. In this respect, the Court's decision can be viewed as buttressing and possibly expanding the restrictions placed on the commerce clause in two influential decisions of the Rehnquist Court—*United States v. Lopez* (514 U.S. 549, 1995) and *United States v. Morrison* (529 U.S. 598, 2000).

Upon further consideration, *NFIB* may serve to limit federal authority in another respect and create a conundrum of sorts for members of Congress in the future. Since the Court concluded that the individual mandate could be sustained legally because the penalty for not purchasing health insurance is really a tax, the inference is that for Congress to enact analogous policies in the future, it will have to do so through policy procedures that would make it a tax. Although the Court's decision would make such policies constitutional from a legal perspective, "members of Congress might find themselves in a politically untenable or at least unpopular position since they would have to justify such policies as a tax" (Bowling and Pickerill 2013: 334).

While the NFIB case was the most widely known case pertinent to federalism, the Court decided two other cases that visibly represent a continuing tendency of providing constitutional protections for state sovereignty since the early 1990s. In *Coleman v. Court of Appeals of Maryland* (132 S. Ct. 1327, 2012) and *Nevada Department of Human Resources v. Hibbs* (538 U.S. 721, 2003), the Court provided further protection for states from law suits and reinforced and adhered to the high bar that Rehnquist Court decisions had set for abrogating sovereign immunity.

The Court has taken several opportunities to restrict federal authority and even reaffirm support for state sovereignty and has also remained active in deciding cases involving federal preemption of state laws. The holdings in these more recent cases have been consistent with earlier Rehnquist Court decisions in siding with the federal government. In *Arizona v. United States* (132 S. Ct. 2492, 2012) (cited and discussed in another context later in this chapter), the Court held that three of four provisions of an Arizona law (known as SB 1070) intended to discourage and curb illegal immigration into the state were preempted by federal regulation laws. Also, in 2012, the Court decided in *Kurns v. Railroad Friction Products Corp.* (132 S. Ct. 1261) that a federal law (Locomotive Inspection Act) extensively regulated all design aspects of locomotives and preempted state law on any issues involving design effects.

Shelby County v. Holder (133 S. Ct. 2613, 2013) extended the Rehnquist Courts' constraint on federal power. The Court's ruling effectively restricted the reach of Congress' powers under Section 2 of the Fifteenth Amendment, which authorizes it to enact "appropriate" legislation to carry out the amendment's prohibition on racial discrimination in voting (Somin 2016). The case arose out of a challenge to congressional authority to force state and local governments in the South (and a few other areas) to "preclear" with the U.S. Justice Department changes to their voting laws as required by the Voting Rights Act of 1965.

So what is new in the federal–state, federal–local, and federal–state–local spheres of IGR? According to Bowling and Pickerill (2013: 316), "fragmented federalism" is becoming more and more noticeable from the burgeoning "patchwork of policies that are popping up across the country." Historically, American federalism has both made it possible and encouraged states to devise policies in a myriad of areas (e.g., education, health care, welfare, conservation and environment, public safety, transportation, etc.) that are tailored to the unique preferences, needs, and affordability of their citizens. Obviously, this has created a tremendous amount of variation across states, as states continually serve as laboratories of democracy where creative or innovative ideas or policy experimentation are permitted and advanced. In recent years, however, one sees differentiation occurring not necessarily because of the particularistic needs of the state or its efforts to improve the quality of services or even to enhance service-delivery efficiency or service effectiveness. Instead, and as argued by Bowling and Pickerill (2013), differentiation is driven by several reasons or motivating forces. Five of them are discussed here.

Political Polarization

Increasing political party polarization continues to have an influence on both short- and long-term governance at all levels of government as well as on IGR. For many observers both inside and outside of government, the distance between the two major political parties has never been greater (see Voteview.com 2012). Intense partisanship was a marked feature characterizing the conduct and impact of the 2008, 2012, and 2016 elections and will likely continue to shape federalism and IGR in the years ahead. Evidence of this lasting effect can be seen from legislative and policy decision-making that occurs within the context of the ongoing ideological divide between the Democratic and Republican parties. According to Bowling and Pickerill (2013: 317), "there is a prominent and prolonged level of heightened partisanship that accompanies seemingly every major policy, budget, and implementation decision at the state and federal levels of government as well as the interactions between them." And nothing changed during the remainder of the Obama administration or during the first few months of the Trump administration (Read 2016). If anything, partisan polarization has become more intense and bitter. Tensions at the national level between the two parties have resulted in them being unable to reach compromises on most important policy issues, but especially the federal budget. Simply stated, the increasing party polarization has brought gridlock to an entirely new level in the past few years. With increasing frequency, one sees political parties (along with factions within the parties, interest groups, and unions) engaging in protracted and passionate battles often depicted as zero-sum games, where there is only a winner or loser and no thought being given to a compromise between divergent views.

Unlike the national government which has been embroiled in gridlock, many state governments with conservative Republican governors and Republican-controlled legislatures have been able to make changes to state policy more easily (Bowling and Pickerill (2013: 318). Specifically, Republicans in these states have been able to advance policy agendas on controversial issues like abortion, public sector unionization, gun control, elections, and immigration. Many of these policies have resulted in an exaggerated form of "fragmented federalism" or a patchwork of policies across the country created by factions and implemented in fragments. This is perhaps best illustrated by some states' immigration laws.

Extreme partisanship has also been responsible for intense "pushback" scenarios, most notably in the fields of health care, education, and elections (for example, see Bulman-Pozen and Metzger 2016; Chapter 7, this volume). States and local governments have always objected to federal government intrusion into the first of these arenas and have seen federal actions as treading on state sovereignty. With respect to health care and education, state and local governments question the extent to which the federal government should be involved in the regulation of health care choices and educational goals. Even in the area of elections where the federal government has the authority to insure against discrimination in both voter registration and the operation of elections, state and local governments express a strong dislike for the imposition of a "Big Brother" type oversight.

The PPACA will probably be remembered as one of the most controversial pieces of legislation to be adopted by the Congress in recent memory. Several parts of the law that are aimed at requiring changes in insurance systems, and thereby regulatory in nature, have gone into effect. They include requiring insurance companies to provide coverage for adult children (until the age of twenty-six years), requiring coverage of preventative services, limiting the percentage of funds that insurance companies can spend on administration, and prohibiting insurance policies from creating or enforcing yearly or lifetime benefits limits as well as preexisting conditions exclusions. To follow was a new round of partisan bickering that began over two larger, and more expensive and expansive, provisions of the law—required Medicaid expansion and the creation of state insurance exchanges. The result has been pushbacks in two different directions—state governments pushing back against the federal government and the federal government pushing back against the states.

On one hand, partisan state pushback has resulted where the U.S. Supreme Court in *NFIB* invalidated the excessively coercive requirement that all states expand Medicaid coverage or lose large amounts of federal money. In reality, the decision to expand or not expand is a sovereign state choice and not a federal mandate. On the other hand, pushback by the federal government toward the states has put conservative states in an untenable position with respect to the creation of health exchanges. That is, their choices are either to adopt the minimal undesired standards required by the progressive federal policy or step aside and permit the federal government to operate the health exchanges. By all accounts, states' actions have certainly added complexity to IGR through its diverse and fragmented implementation (see Chapter 7, this volume). In short, there is no doubt that shared implementation will leave oversight fragmented, unless, of course, Republicans in Congress and the Trump administration are able to repeal the PPACA and the issue becomes a moot point.

Federal Inaction, Indecisiveness, and Convoluted Policies

Variance and fragmentation in federalism and subsequently in IGR is also created by the failure (or perception of failure) of the federal government to act or demonstrate indecisiveness in areas traditionally seen in their domain. In many of these areas, federal policies are seen as giving mixed signals and resulting in convoluted policy directives. Subsequently, a number of states have resisted the federal government or adopted their own laws in immigration policy and regulation of "fracking." In the area of education, frustrated state and local government officials operate in an environment of uncertainty due to a myriad mandates and unrealistic expectations relative to the federal share of K–12 public education funding and therefore must proceed as best they can due to the lack of guidance from the federal government. A case in point is No Child Left Behind (NCLB) where the federal government has been granting waivers to states to give them more flexibility and discretion in the face of mounting criticism from state officials (McGuinn 2016; Mann 2015).

Historically, citizenship requirements come under the scope of federally-delegated powers and immigration has traditionally been a national, rather than a state, policy concern. However, numerous failures to enact meaningful immigration reform at the national level have been used as justification for a dramatic increase in states adopting their own legislation in this area. Since 2001, Congress has considered but failed to adopt several pieces of immigration legislation, including the Secure America and Orderly Immigration Act (2005), two Comprehensive Immigration Reform Acts (2006 and 2007), and other pieces of immigration reform legislation under headings like Development, Relief, and Education for Alien Minors (DREAM). One DREAM measure did pass the House of Representatives in 2010 but the measure failed to even get a Senate floor vote. In 2012, President Obama issued an executive order to protect immigrants who would have been eligible for relief under the 2010 Act that granted them work permits and relief from deportation. Also, in 2012 and as mentioned earlier in this chapter, the Supreme Court struck down some provisions of Arizona's controversial immigration law in *Arizona v. United States*. Yet, the Court left intact a provision authorizing state and local police to investigate the immigration status of individuals they encounter in the course of their duties. On some level, these recent federal actions might be interpreted as a reassertion of national government authority in the realm of immigration policy. Nevertheless, there is still no comprehensive action on the part of Congress, even though the Trump administration has touted immigration reform as a top priority.

Since passage of the Elementary and Secondary Education Act (ESEA) in 1962 and creation of the U.S. Department of Education, the federal government has been playing an increasingly important and visible role in education. States and local school districts more than ever look to the federal government for leadership, financial support, and accountability. Yet, in recent years, assistance in these and in other areas has diminished. Not only has the federal government been unable to act quickly, decisively, and boldly in important educational matters, it has also created an environment of uncertainty for state and local governments.

According to Bowling and Pickerill (2013: 326–327), four policies worked together to produce uncertainty. First, the NCLB component of the 2001 reauthorization of the ESEA drove state governments and the federal government toward an inevitable fiscal showdown. States faced a 2014 deadline to meet the goal of having 100 percent of students reach proficiency in reading and math with threat of loss of federal funds. Approximately 80 percent of schools would not have met the goal and would have lost a considerable amount of federal funding, with less affluent school districts projected to have been hit the hardest (Hechinger and Brower 2011). The crisis was averted when President Obama and the Department of Education granted waivers and extensions (Wong 2015). The ESEA was eventually reauthorized (the 2015 Every Student Succeeds Act—ESSA), but not before creating a political backlash from the states and school districts (McGuinn 2016).

The inability or unwillingness of members of Congress to compromise on issues like the creation of charter schools, state flexibility in the use of federal funds, and teacher accountability also contributed to uncertainty for state and local education systems (Hyslop 2013). In the absence of new reauthorizing congressional legislation, President Obama and U.S. Secretary of Education Arne Duncan resorted to executive authority to grant waivers to states that had not met specific requirements (e.g., new state standards, new methods of evaluating and aiding low performing schools, new personnel evaluation systems, and streamlining state reporting systems). Most states applied for and received waivers (U.S. Department of Education 2016). However, these states remained concerned whether the reforms they have implemented would mesh with federal guidelines if ESEA were eventually reauthorized (see McMurrer and Yoshioka 2013).

As Bowling and Pickerill (2013: 326) conclude, "uncertainty is made worse by federalism 'end-runs' around partisan factions."

The third federal policy, which was part of the Obama administration's federal stimulus package, was the Race to the Top (RTTT). RTTT grants were awarded to states that applied and agreed to meet the criteria of the program, which are comparable to the rules required by NCLB waivers. The most difficult element of RTTT was securing agreement on the use of new performance-based teacher and principal evaluations and pay scales that are tied to increases in students' test scores (McGuinn 2016). Other complicating factors included problems in implementing programs due to opposition from teachers' unions and lobbies and states refusing to apply for grants (Bowling and Pickerill 2013: 326–327). Thus, uncertainty loomed large for states and school districts.

A fourth factor that created uncertainty was the anticipation of the end of the American Recovery and Reinvestment Act (ARRA) stimulus funding. Beginning in 2009, over $100 billion of stimulus funding was allocated to education and about a third of this money came as part of budget stabilization funds that permitted states and local school districts to dodge the layoff of some employees and service cutbacks (Alliance for Innovation 2011). Although state revenue collections had been improving in the post-recession period, they were not necessarily increasing as fast as the stimulus funds had been shrinking (NASBO 2013). In some instances, states had to make up the difference by shifting funds previously allocated to other program areas. However, if the threats posed by the implementation of federal sequestration had materialized after 2014, education funding would have been in peril.

Fracking represents an unusual case of the (un)involvement of the federal government in a newly emerging area. Historically, the federal government has played a primary role in regulatory policy in commerce matters by setting broad parameters and state and local governments acting as the principal implementers. But fracking is unusual because, unlike a classic federalism problem in which states act in the absence of federal regulation, the federal government has largely and deliberately cut itself out of the regulatory picture (Warner and Shapiro 2013). The consequence of what amounts to an abdication of federal regulatory authority has been the development of a fractured and fragmented regulatory policy nationwide, increased court action, and interstate conflict over the transport of fracking waste across state lines (ibid.).

From the perspective of the authors of the last two Annual Reviews in *Publius*, two things are clear. First, while "there are some signs of policy convergence. . .partisan gridlock continues to stall the passage of federal legislation [and] policy activity has shifted outward to other venues [like] state legislatures, voters, federal and state executive branches, and the court system" (Rose and Bowling 2015). In short, "inertia and centrifugal force" continue to characterize—even plague—the federal system (ibid.). Second, and as a consequence, "in many ways, gridlock and state pushback necessitate alternative decision-making and implementation arrangements" (Bowling and Rose 2016: 279).

Federal Mandates

Differentiation and fragmentation in federalism and subsequently IGR are the product of state efforts to cope with federal mandates or satisfy conditions of aid in areas like education, elections, and health care. Federal–state hybrids emerge as states seek to retain elements of their own programs even as mandates, preemptions, and conditions of aid create new processes and dependencies. In health care, states have been permitted to reinvent themselves as far back as the Clinton administration. In education, however, state and local government are hit with a "double whammy." Federal mandates and conditions of aid not only create uncertainty but also present daunting challenges to state and local governments in their efforts to achieve compliance in the implementation of federal policy. As seen above, states and their local school districts have had to continually request waivers when compliance with mandates such as those in NCLB and RTTT has not been possible. This places not only undue burdens on these governments but also creates a fragmented and disjointed array of different compliance standards and exceptions for different states and areas of the country. For example, this fragmentation in the elections and health care policy areas creates complex networks of dependencies and interdependencies between the national and sub-national governments (Shelly 2013; Nussbaumer 2013; Hale and Brown 2013).

Navigating mandates or even conditions for federal aid, as two scholars (Nugent 2009; Shelly 2013) have suggested, has meant that state and local governments increasingly feel the need to engage the federal government over the terms of programs for which they traditionally have had implementation responsibility (e.g., education, elections, and health care). More and more, state and local officials think that they can no longer depend on constitutional protections of their power and federal deference to state supremacy on certain policy issues of vital interest to them and their citizens. Since 1990, waivers have become an important "informal and extra-constitutional safeguard" of state power and one of the most common methods by which federal and state governments have reached accommodation on mandates and conditions for aid that cause dispute (Nugent 2009). Both the federal government and the state governments have numerous reasons to seek flexibility in the implementation of conditions attached to federal grants-in-aid and compliance with federal mandates. For their part, state and local officials want to continue to receive federal funding and gain input into the content of the program they will implement, as well as benefit from a reduction in federal oversight and even be permitted to modify policies to fit specific state needs (Weissert and Weissert 2008). Federal policy makers often perceive that state and local governments have considerable experience in certain issues or knowledge of relevant conditions, and thus can provide an opportunity to "borrow strength" from the states or create a sense of *raison d'être* or legitimacy for federal involvement (see Manna 2006). As was the case during the Obama administration, Congress and the President likely viewed waivers as an occasion to force decisions on polarizing topics that could derail legislation onto administrators and to avoid difficult decisions about the nuts and bolts of policy implementation and assign blame went wrong (Shelly 2013: 454–455).

Waivers permit states with less developed capacity to still participate in a program. States with more developed capacity may be able to experiment with alternative approaches and may become models for future nationwide reform. However, the increasing incidence of state and local governments "cutting deals" with federal authorities via waivers ultimately results in a patchwork of implementation policies scattered across the country rather than a uniform set of standards for everyone to follow. Waivers have produced both the illusion and reality of "factious federalism" (Thompson and Gusmano 2014). Others have also referred to the increasing use of waivers as "variable speed federalism" because it "reflects the growing challenge of accommodating a more polarized process across all levels of the U.S. federal system" (Conlan and Posner 2016).

Growing use of waivers has been a direct by-product of the noticeable shift in discretion permitted to the federal executive branch (see Thompson 2013; Thompson and Gusmano 2014). This has resulted in what some have labeled the administrative presidency, in which there is the commitment and ability of the White House and top political executives (rather than career executives) to shape who gets what from federal programs without changes in law (Shapiro and Wright 2011).

Recent presidents, as a means to further their policy objectives, increasingly have resorted to taking unilateral action through executive orders, proclamations, directives, signing statements, and other written guidance. This pattern was especially evident in the administrations of Bill Clinton and George W. Bush, as they sought to shape—or reshape—Medicaid to fit their political philosophy (Aberbach 2007). Then, Barack Obama employed the same strategy with respect to both Medicaid, generally, and to the PPACA, specifically (see Thompson 2013). Most recently, Donald Trump has taken advantage of this strategy with regard to immigration reform. Partisan polarization that has engulfed Washington for part of the last three decades, along with the accompanying congressional gridlock, serves to encourage the administrative presidency (ibid.).

State–Local Relations

The state of state–local relations, whether it is a snapshot of the present or an assessment over time, must always be considered within the context or knowledge of local governments being creatures of their state. From the outset, state–local relationships were cast in the form of an inferior entity (local governments) doing the bidding of a superior entity (state governments). These early notions about state–local relations were reinforced when Dillon's rule was promulgated in what seemed to be an obscure ruling of an Iowa judge in 1868 in the case of *City of Clinton v. Cedar Rapids and Missouri Railroad Company* (24 Iowa 455). Over time, however, the grant of various degrees of home rule to counties and municipalities has resulted in a moderation in this rather hierarchical, top-down legal arrangement. Nonetheless, the present-day legal relationship between states and their local governments was the case, as over 100 years ago, still sets the tone for state–local relations.

When functioning as administrative arms of their state government or as semi-autonomous local governments, counties and municipalities (as well as townships and school and special districts) are still legally creatures of the state. This arrangement therefore can lead to relations ranging from cooperation to conflict and from harmony to friction. Interactions fitting these descriptions are found in a number of policy areas, but especially with issues relating to revenue-raising limits, state mandates, and home rule.

In sizing up state–local relations since the approximate beginning of Wright's contractive phase, it is reasonable to conclude that not much changed. Local officials complain about overbearing state regulatory oversight, top-down management approach, lack of revenue flexibility and shared governance, burdensome and costly state mandates, and insensitivity to or lack of respect for a local government perspective. State officials counter by saying that, given the unitary nature of the legal status of local governments and expectations of citizens, they are obligated to maintain a vigilant watch for overzealous, incompetent, or even corrupt local officials. Some of the heightened tension found in state–local relations has been exacerbated because Congress has become more polarized, the president and Congress are constantly at loggerheads (i.e., divided government), intense partisanship has become a fixture at the national and state level, and the slow Great Recession recovery is still causing lingering economic pains. From a macro-level perspective, it is easy to see that local officials are not reticent about pushing back at state officials[4] and engage in negotiation over divisive issues. A pattern of "fend-for-yourself" federalism seems like an accurate portrayal of state–local relations since the 1990s. This descriptor of state–local relations is most evident with respect to the related issues of state programmatic cut-backs, dwindling state aid, and inflexibility in local revenue options. In the last two to three decades, state revenues have been erratic and revenue stability has eluded many states because of significant downturns in the economy and changing taxpayer moods.

The service hit the hardest by state cuts has been public education, since it is the largest discretionary budget item in state control; states have also cut higher education funding radically. K–12 education cuts led to the loss of thousands of jobs among teachers and support staff and produced a huge outcry from the public and, of course, from local school districts and employee unions. In response to these cuts, numerous lawsuits were filed. Additional fallout from these funding cuts occurred when local school districts and city and county-operated schools fell out of compliance with state education budgeting rules and legislation as well as mandated requirements associated with NCLB and RTTT.

Although welfare is not a big budget item for states, welfare programs also were hit hard during the Great Recession, undermining the national social safety net when it was most needed. Nationwide, the welfare cuts affected roughly 700,000 families and 1.3 million children who were dropped from various assistance programs at the height of the crisis (Schott and Pavetti 2011). This situation heightened state–local tensions when local officials in major urban centers and large central cities with large dependent populations had to find ways (possibly through reallocation of funds from other programmatic areas) to assist the truly needy.

State budget woes in recent years did not bode well for local governments for other reasons. The Great Recession resulted in significant reductions in state aid to local governments. Using data from the U.S. Census Bureau, *Governing* magazine compared the most recent 2014 figures on state aid to local government with 2007, 2008, and 2009 and found that local governments and school districts in 16 states incurred inflation-adjusted cuts that exceeded 10 percent. These data indicate that, while state aid grew by nearly 10 percent in 2014, it has slowed down considerably from the 17–18 percent growth rate from 2007–2010. Looking back further, real state financial assistance grew nearly three times slower than localities' own-source general revenue since 2000 (Maciag and Wogan 2017). While local officials have held out hope that cuts in state aid would be temporary, the sluggish state revenue growth does not bode well for a return to pre-recession aid levels.

One of the most contentious state–local issues has to do with state restrictions on revenue-raising abilities. State governments have long imposed controls on nearly all aspects of local financial management—assessment, taxation, indebtedness, budgeting, accounting, auditing, financing, and revenue sources. In the 1970s, local governments stepped up the pace of lobbying state legislatures for greater authority to set reasonable property tax rates (subject to citizenry approval) and to tap a larger variety of revenue sources. Yet, state governments have for the most part been reluctant to acquiesce to pleas to grant greater latitude and flexibility in revenue schemes. Another state-imposed limitation on local finances is local borrowing, and this can sometimes encourage localities to bypass limits by creating special districts and authorities. While this may solve one problem, it can also create two other problems—the negative side-effects of producing fragmentation in service delivery and less accountability.

A sore spot in state–local relations is the issue of costly and burdensome mandates, many of which are unfunded. Mandates serve to worsen state–local relations when revenues are in short supply and state aid is shrinking. This situation has prompted Zimmerman to refer to mandates as "the principal irritants of state-relations" (1987: 78). While some mandates cost relatively little money, their collective effects can have a dramatic impact on local government budgets. In fact, the cumulative effect of big-ticket service expenditures in areas like health care, education, land use, judicial and court systems, and environmental protection can overwhelm county and munici-pal budgets (Berman 2008: 47). Without mandate reimbursement or mandate rollbacks, local governments facing their own financial constraints and fiscal stress are hard put to provide simul-taneously mandated services and services identified by constituents as high priorities. Over the years, municipal and county officials who believe that they should not have to both "obey and pay" have lobbied state legislatures basically to no avail in efforts to prevent the enactment or repeal of costly mandates (Benton 2012).

An area of long-standing contentiousness in state–local relations is home rule. Owing to the fact that local units of governments are creatures of their state, local governments have no right to home rule authority. States have advanced slowly and cautiously toward authorizing some types of local home rule, but this progress has done little to change or even challenge fundamental assumptions about the legal status of counties and municipalities. In fact, home rule jurisdictions have few of the protections against capricious state action that private corporations, also chartered by the states, commonly enjoy (Berman 2005). And, although local governments with home rule are usually better off than those that do not have this protection, "local governments, with or without home rule, have limited power to initiate action and spend much time and energy trying to ward off mandates, preemptions, and prohibitions that further limit their authority" (ibid.: 46).

More recent assessments of state–local relations (see Chapter 11, this volume; Bowman and Kearney 2012; Ehrenhalt 2017) reveal that state legislatures continue to enact statutes that are "restrictive in nature, meaning that 'they require local governments to adopt new rules and pro-cedures or they prohibit certain practices' in three primary areas (finance, government structure, and human resources)." Along these lines, some states in the last few years in extreme cases have had to assert themselves as overseers or managers of the finances of several cities or to help them formulate a recovery and redemptive plan after they had to file for bankruptcy.[5] On a more positive note, Bowman and Kearney (Chapter 11, this volume) also report that some recent state legislation has actually empowered local government in areas such as land use, infrastructure, economic development, and business licensing.

Inter-Local Relations

For many years, inter-local relations was marred by turf wars, jurisdictional jealousies, and petty rivalries. Common descriptions of local officials by media and state officials was that they were too laid back, lazy, incompetent, intellectually challenged, corrupt, inept, and operate with a backwater mentality. Consequently, state and local textbook and commission report treatments of local governments and their officials often have characterized them in unflattering ways. Moreover, anecdotal stories of urban politics, service delivery, and governance-styles seemed to confirm these characterizations. Most importantly, local governments seemed to follow a "go it alone" approach in the provision of myriad services (many of which had metropolitan or area-wide implications) and only infrequently communicated with one another about common areas of inter-est and a broad spectrum of issues where collaboration made a lot of sense intuitively as well as from a practical perspective. Perhaps most unforgiving was the unwillingness to think beyond their borders and explore opportunities for realizing cost savings and efficiencies which collabora-tion likely could have provided. Not surprisingly, referenda on city-county consolidations (with a handful of some notable exceptions) were rejected by voters after heavy opposition was usually expressed by county and municipal officials.

Beginning in the 1980s, local governments and their officials seemed to be warming up to the idea of pursuing collaborative ventures with other governments. Unlike the relatively few large cities of the mid-1970s that experienced near-fiscal collapse, insolvency, and default of debt, fiscal problems and uncertainly have begun to engulf cities and counties of all sizes in recent years. With encouragement from the federal government and requirements built into the A-95 review process,[6] local governments also began to think regionally in areas like planning and zoning, land use, conservation and environmental protection, water supply, sewage disposal, and solid waste management. But more than anything else, it was the eroding tax base, taxpayer disgruntlement, a faltering economy, and sharp cut-backs in federal grant-in-aid monies (and, in some instances, state aid) that convinced local government officials to put the option of collaborative service provision on the table for serious consideration. Yet, there was still a hesitancy to engage in collaboration when divisive and sticky issues like loss of autonomy and shared governance were collaboration tradeoffs. Local officials, while intrigued with the prospects for inter-local collaboration and the benefits of it, proceeded with extreme caution and doubt. In the end, there was only a modest spike in inter-local collaborative ventures.

The real push to seriously consider inter-local collaboration, however, did not occur until the onset of the Great Recession. It took a major jolt to the economy to persuade local officials to abandon their parochial mentality and get past dislikes for and distrust of jurisdictional neighbors and seriously consider and pursue inter-local collaborative opportunities. As one local government official in Florida in 2009 candidly admitted when asked why his city had begun to actively study and enter into serious negotiations with neighboring cities and the county to jointly fund and provide services like sewage disposal, solid waste management, vehicle purchasing and maintenance, IT training, roadside mowing, and parks and recreation, "it was like a gun had been put to our head and the option of in-house production and provision was no longer a viable one" (Benton, Aikins, and Miller 2009). Carr and Hawkins perhaps sum up the reason why local governments feel compelled more than ever to engage in collaborative efforts. They write that "the fiscal realities many local governments face a 'new normal' in which accountability to the public is a public agenda priority" (Carr and Hawkins 2013: 224). This assessment is congruent with the conclusions drawn by others who have also studied inter-local collaboration (Martin, Levey, and Cawley 2012; Elling, Krawczyk, and Carr 2014; Homsy and Warner 2014). For many local governments, delivering high-quality services within the constraints they now encounter is a serious concern. Therefore, these pressures have prompted greater interest than ever before in creating more shared service delivery arrangements and focused attention on the difficulties involved in managing complex relationships among participants in cooperative efforts (Zeemering 2007, 2008; Hawkins 2009; LeRoux, Brandenburger, and Pandey 2010; LeRoux and Carr 2010; Scholz and Feiock 2010).

A recent survey of local government officials found that collaboration with other local governments "top[ped] the list of trends taking center stage in 2013" (Reach the Public 2013), while another survey reported an uptick in collaborative efforts among local governments (Perlman and Benton 2012). Organizations like the International City/County Management Association, National League of Cities, and National Association of Counties, as well as "good government" groups and study commissions have endorsed the utilization of collaboration in service. Some state governments are actively pushing local governments to become more proactive in both the consideration of and participation in collaborative service delivery efforts (Franzel, Newfarmer, and Stenberg 2013), and there is some evidence that these efforts have achieved some modest success (see Chapter 12, this volume).

Where Are We Presently—Transition or New Eighth Phase?

From the foregoing assessment of the state of American federalism and IGR over the last two to three decades, it appears that many of the signature features of Wright's Contractive Phase, while still recognizable to some extent, are not as prominent or relevant as they once were. Therefore, at a minimum, we are transitioning from the Contractive Phase to a new eighth phase of IGR. However, one could argue persuasively that we have already made the transition and are in the midst of a new phase that is labeled the "Kaleidoscopic Phase" (see the bottom row of Table 2.1, in italics).

Change has occurred, and some of it has been significant and even dramatic in the last two decades. Furthermore, this change has had an obvious and profound impact on the content and tenor of federalism and relations between officials at the federal, state, and local levels of government. These changes, like changes in the past, have been prompted by the necessity to respond to extraordinary political, economic, and social problems and to the realities associated with public opinion, ideology, and partisan shifts. What was happening in the 1990s and early years of the twenty-first century in the federal system and to IGR can be best described as a continuous process of further refining or flushing out of the basic contours and boundaries of the Contractive Phase. At the same time, there was an unremitting layering or superimposing of some of the earlier phases of IGR on top of the Contractive Phase. Nevertheless, there is increasing corroboration that a new phase of IGR has emerged, as evidenced by the following:

- Increased fragmentation in federal–state, federal–local, and federal–state–local relations, resulting in a patchwork of policies across the country.
- More incidences within the federal–state and state–local arenas where state—but especially local—governments must "go it alone" in efforts to finance their operations and continue to provide staple services for their citizens.
- Greater occurrences in the inter-local arena of collaboration and cooperation among local governments or between local governments and non-profit or for-profit entities.

The significance of these new developing patterns leads to the suggestion of the following six federalism metaphorical descriptors for the new Kaleidoscopic Phase: "fragmented federalism" (or "bottom-up federalism"), "push-back federalism," "fend-for-yourself federalism,"[7] and "collaborative federalism" (see Table 2.1). This table also lists the main problems, participants' perception, and IGR mechanisms of the Kaleidoscopic Phase.

The first person to use the term "kaleidoscope" to describe or explain how the American federal system works and subsequent IGR play out was Joseph Zimmerman (2008: 201–202). However, his usage of the term was limited to national-state relations. In short, the scope of the term is greatly expanded in this chapter to also include national–state–local, interstate, state–local, and inter-local relations.

Concluding Thoughts

In addition to these observations about American federalism and IGR and the conclusion that a new Kaleidoscopic Phase has evolved and is currently being flushed out, it is important to consider the need for some qualifications as to how various phases of IGR are depicted and subsequently viewed. First, in examining the scholarly literature and the ongoing intellectual dialogue about

IGR, it seems that less consideration is given to inter-local relations than federal–state, federal–local, and federal–state–local despite the fact there are more inter-local IGR actors and more governments involved than at the national and state levels. Moreover, it is reasonable to speculate that local governments—having now to "go-it-alone" in a "New Normal" of less financial support from both the federal and state governments—are more likely to seek out and forge cooperative arrangements with their neighboring local governments as a means to provide more efficiently staple services to a citizenry that is adverse to higher taxes and fees. Given these new developments, additional scholarly attention to inter-local relations could assist in providing a more balanced and accurate depiction of the substance and nature of evolving IGR.

Greater scholarly attention should also be directed toward state–local relations. The importance of what has been happening in state–local relations in recent years—but especially in the aftermath of the Great Recession—is becoming more critical for state and local officials and the citizens they serve. State and local governments continue to have difficulty "making ends meet." The rapidly growing costs associated with complying with the PPACA mandates are certain to stretch the financial capacity of many states that also will feel the pressure from citizens who expect that greater attention and resources be directed to welfare, education, and environmental concerns as well as pressure from local officials to provide fiscal assistance to their localities. This scenario is likely to lead to greater episodes of "third-order devolution," with more unfunded state mandates, transfer of functional responsibility to local governments, and shrinking state aid or shared state revenue. This situation could become more contentious if states are reluctant to grant greater home rule and revenue flexibility. Yet, there is also the possibility and already some evidence that state legislatures will be more receptive to local pleas for greater governance and revenue authority.

Likewise, it appears that inadequate attention is paid to another IGR arena—interstate relations.[8] Over the years, states have been entering into interstate compacts in myriad areas from operation of port authorities to rendition of criminal suspects to sharing of natural resources like water to cooperation in criminal investigations. In recent years, states (through the National Governor's Association) have been a major force in urging the adoption of common curriculum and standards in education called Common Core. In addition, attorney generals in 29 states led the unsuccessful legal challenge to the PPACA, arguing that states' rights have been abridged. Presently, a potential storm may be brewing in interstate relations with respect to the "Full Faith and Credit" Clause, since states are enacting vastly different statutes with respect to same-sex marriages. Similar discord in interstate relations could also be looming because of sharply differing state statutes pertaining to abortion and legalization of marijuana for medical treatment.

A second qualification would be to view, study, and describe IGR, in general, and IGR phases from a "multi-angled" perspective. While efforts to generalize about a subject matter as broad and heterogeneous as IGR have their usefulness, much is lost for the sake of brevity and identifying overall common characteristics. Simply stated, the diversity of relations, richness of context, uniqueness of mission and goals, and countless nuances implicit in the various IGR arenas are often lost in attempts to summarize and generalize. This perspective takes on added credence in light of the following assessment offered about the evolving state of federalism and IGR by Bowling and Pickerill (2013: 341): "These myriad trajectories point to no single direction for federalism." Therefore, it may be useful for a better understanding of the federal system and resulting IGR if one were to view them through a kaleidoscope. The utility of this approach is that it may lead to varied and yet more all-encompassing assessments and portrayals of American federalism and IGR because it allows for the possibility that IGR participant perceptions and IGR mechanisms may differ noticeably from one arena to another.

Finally, it is argued that any definition of IGR and any subsequent characterizations of IGR (that is, the state of American federalism and IGR) include all possible interaction scenarios. Put differently, it is argued that all relevant and notable interactions in the federal–state, federal–local, federal–state–local, state–local, interstate, and inter-local areas should be reflected in past, current, and future descriptions of the state of IGR. The degree to which this is accomplished is of the utmost importance, since whether we have a new phase ultimately depends on how one defines or conceptualizes IGR.

Notes

1   See also Elazar (1962) and Grodzins (1966).
2   Perhaps, the best description of the "New Normal" has been given by Martin, Levey, and Cawley (2012). It was precipitated by the Great Recession of 2008–2009 and represented a critical breakpoint for local governments with implications that were likely to last long after any economy recovery. The aftermath for local governments was projected to consist of fewer resources, smaller workforces, and new ways of delivering services.
3   At this writing, it is too early to make any safe prediction about any affect that the Trump administration will have on the state of American federalism.
4   For excellent discussions of local governments pushing back against state policies, see Riverstone-Newell (2012, 2014, 2017).
5   See Ammons, Smith, and Stenberg (2012) for an excellent examination of how state (and localities) have responded to the recent increase in local government bankruptcies.
6   Established by the Intergovernmental Cooperation Act of 1968, it established the state clearinghouse grant review process, which required that all state and local federal grant applications be reviewed for regional consistency and coordination.
7   For a more recent discussion and assessment of "fend-for-yourself" federalism, see Pagano and Hoene (2003).
8   See Zimmerman (2012, 2015) for more elaboration on this point.

References

Aberbach, Joel. D. 2007. "The executive branch in red and blue." In *A Republic Divided* (Annenberg Democracy Project), 157–193. New York: Oxford University Press.

Alliance for Innovation. 2011. *What's the Future of Local Government? An Alliance White Paper Intended To Provoke a Needed Conversation*. Phoenix, AZ: Alliance for Innovation.

Ammons, David N., Karl W. Smith, and Carl W. Stenberg. 2012. "The future of local governments: Will current stresses bring major, permanent changes?" *State and Local Government Review* 44 (Supplement 1) (August): 54S–75S.

Benton, J. Edwin. 2012. "State–city and state–county fiscal relations: A look at the past and present and a glimpse at the future." In *Networked Governance: The Future of Intergovernmental Management*, edited by Jack W. Meek and Kurt Thurmaier, 39–63. Washington, DC: CQ Press.

Benton, J. Edwin. Forthcoming. "Local government service roles in the U.S.: Constancy and change." In *Handbook of International Local Government*, edited by Richard Kerley, Joyce Liddle, and Pamela Dunning. New York: Routledge.

Benton, J. Edwin, Stephen Aikins, and Michael J. Miller. 2009. *Coping with Dwindling Property Tax Revenues: The Tale of Municipalities and Counties in Florida*. Report prepared for the Florida City/

County Management Association, Florida League of Cities, Florida Association of Counties, and the Florida Government Finance Officers' Association, August 24.

Berman, David R. 2005. "State–local relations: Partnerships, conflict, and autonomy." *2005 Municipal Yearbook*. Washington, DC: International City/County Management Association.

Berman, David R. 2008. "State–local relations: Authority and finances." *2008 Municipal Yearbook*. Washington, DC: International City/County Management Association.

Bowling, Cynthia J., and Mitchell Pickerill. 2013. "Fragmented federalism: The state of American federalism 2012–13." *Publius: The Journal of Federalism* 43 (Summer): 315–342.

Bowling, Cynthia J., and Mitchell Pickerill. 2014. "Polarized parties, politics, and policies: Fragmented federalism in 2013–14." *Publius: The Journal of Federalism* 44 (Summer): 369–398.

Bowling, Cynthia J., and Shanna Rose. 2016. "The Obama administration and American federalism: Introduction to the special issue." *Publius: The Journal of Federalism* 46 (Summer): 275–280.

Bowman, Ann O'M., and Richard C. Kearney. 2012. "Are U.S. cities losing power and authority? Perceptions of local government actors." *Urban Affairs Review* 48: 528–546.

Bulman-Pozen, Jessica, and Gillian E. Metzger. 2016. "The President of the United States: Patterns of contestation and collaboration under Obama." *Publius: The Journal of Federalism* 46 (Summer): 308–336.

Carr, Jered B., and Christopher V. Hawkins. 2013. "The costs of cooperation: What the research tells us about managing the risks of service collaboration in the U.S.." *State and Local Government Review* 45 (December): 224–239.

Conlan, Timothy J., and Paul L. Posner. 2016. "American federalism in an era of political polarization: The intergovernmental paradox of Obama's 'new nationalism'." *Publius: The Journal of Federalism* 46 (Summer): 281–307.

Ehrenhalt, Alan. 2013. "Devolution and arrogance: States can't resist the temptation to boss their localities around." *Governing* (September): 26: 14–15.

Elazar, Daniel J. 1962. *The American Partnership*. Chicago, IL: University of Chicago Press.

Elazar, Daniel J. 1984. *American Federalism: A View from the States*. New York: Harper & Row.

Elling, Richard C., Kelly Krawczyk, and Jared B. Carr. 2014. "What should we do? Public attitudes about how local government officials should confront fiscal stress." *Local Government Studies* 40: 380–402. Doi:10.1080/03003930.823408.

Franzel, Joshua, Jerry Newfarmer, and Carl Stenberg. 2013. "Collaborative service delivery: How states are pushing change." Presentation at the International City/County Management Association Annual Conference, Boston, MA, September 22–25.

Gamkhar, Shama, and J. Mitchell Pickerill. 2012. "The state of American federalism 2011–2012: A fend for yourself and activist form of bottom-up federalism." *Publius: The Journal of Federalism* 42 (Summer): 357–386.

Grodzins, Morton. 1966. *The American System: A New View of Governments in the United States*. Chicago, IL: Rand McNally.

Hale, Kathleen, and Mitchell Brown. 2013. "Adopting, adapting, and opting out: State response to federal voting system guidelines." *Publius: The Journal of Federalism* 43 (Summer): 428–451.

Harkness, Peter A. 2017. "Trump-watching from City Hall." *Governing* 30 (May): 16–17.

Hawkins, Christopher V. 2009. "Prospects for and barriers to local government joint ventures." *State and Local Government Review* 41 (2): 108–119.

Hechinger, John, and Kate Anderson Brower. 2011. "No Education Agenda Left Behind Becomes Obama Legal Hurdle." Bloomberg News. Retrieved from http://bloomberg.com/news/2011-06-20/no-education-agenda-left-behind-becomes-obama-hurdle-as-congress-deadlocks.html (accessed June 14, 2014).

Homsy, George C., and Mildred E. Warner. 2014. "Intermunicipal cooperation: The growing reform." *The Municipal Yearbook* 80: 53–66.

Hyslop, Anne. 2013. Waiver watch: The real lessons learned from the Senate Waiver Hearing. February 14. Retrieved from www.newamerica.net/taxonomy/term/1753 (accessed May19, 2014).

LeRoux, Kelly, and Jered B. Carr. 2007. "Explaining local government cooperation in public works: Evidence from Michigan." *Public Works Management and Policy* 12: 344–358.

LeRoux, Kelly, P. W Brandenburger, and S.K. Pandey. 2010. "Interlocal service cooperation in U.S. cities: A social network explanation." *Public Administration Review* 70 (March/April): 268–278.

Maciag, Mike and J. B. Wogan. 2017. "With less state aid, localities, look for ways to cope." *Governing*, 30 (February): 32–37.

Mann, Elizabeth. 2015. "The long term impact of NCLB waiver on ESEA renewal." *Brookings Brown Center Chalkboard*, December 20.

Manna, Paul. 2006. *Schools In: Federalism and the National Education Agenda*. Washington, DC: Georgetown University Press.

Martin, Lawrence L., Richard Levey, and Jenna Cawley. 2012. "The 'new normal' for local government." *State and Local Government Review* 44 (December): 17S–28S.

McGuinn, Patrick. 2016. "From no child left behind to every student succeeds act: Federalism and the education legacy of the Obama administration." *Publius: The Journal of Federalism* 46 (Summer): 392–415.

McMurrer, Jennifer, and Nanami Yoshioka. 2013. "States' perspectives on waivers: Relief form NCLB, concern about long-term solutions." Center on Education Policy. Retrieved from www.cep-dc.org/displayDocument.cfm?DocumentID=418 (accessed May 25, 2014).

NASBO. 2013. "Fiscal survey of the states." Fall 2013. Retrieved from www.nasbo.org/sites/default/files.Fall%20201320 Fiscal520Survey.pdf (accessed March 3, 2014).

NASBO. 2016. *State Expenditure Report: Examining Fiscal 2014–2016 State Spending*. Retrieved from www.nasbo.org/sites/ default/files/State%20Expenditure%20Report%20%28Fiscal%202014–2016%20Data %29.pdf (accessed March 3, 2014).

Nugent, John Douglas. 2009. *Safeguarding Federalism: How States Assert Their Interests in National Policymaking*. Norman, OK: University of Oklahoma Press.

Nussbaumer, Kirsten. 2013. "The election law connection and U.S. federalism." *Publius: The Journal of Federalism* 43 (Summer): 392–427.

O'Toole, Jr., Lawrence J. 2000. *American Intergovernmental Relations*, 3rd edition. Washington, DC: CQ Press.

Pagano, Michael A., and Christopher W. Hoene. 2003. "'Fend-for-yourself' federalism: The impact of federal and state deficits and American cities" *Government Finance Review*, 19 (October): 36–42.

Parrott, Sharon, David Reich, and Isaac Shapiro. 2017. *Trump's Skinny Budget Will Be Short on Details, But Troubling Fiscal Agenda Is Emerging*. Washington, DC: Center on Budget and Policy Priorities. March 15.

Perlman, Bruce, and J. Edwin Benton. 2012. "Going it alone: New survey data on economic recovery strategies in local government." *State and Local Government Review* 44 (December): 5S–16S.

Reach the Public. 2013. "Collaboration is a hot trend for state and local government" Retrieved from www.govdelivery.com/blog/2013/collaboration-is-a-hot-trend-for-state-and-local-governments (accessed March 8, 2014).

Read, James H. 2016. "Constitutionalizing the dispute: Federalism in hyper-partisan times." *Publius: The Journal of Federalism* 46 (Summer): 337–365.

Riverstone-Newell, Lori. 2012. "Bottom-up activism: A local political strategy for higher policy change." *Publius: The Journal of Federalism* 42 (Summer): 401–421.

Riverstone-Newell, Lori. 2014. *Renegade Cities, Public Policy, and the Dilemmas of Federalism*. Boulder, CO: Lynn Rienner Publishers.

Riverstone-Newell, Lori. 2017. "The rise of state preemption laws in response to local policy innovation." *Publius: The Journal of Federalism* 47 (Summer): 403–425.

Rose, Shanna, and Cynthia J. Bowling. 2015. "The state of American federalism 2014–15: Pathways to policy in an era of party polarization." *Publius: The Journal of Federalism* 45 (Summer): 351–379.

Scholz, John, and Richard C. Feiock, eds. 2010. *Self-Organizing Federalism: Collaborative Mechanisms to Mitigate Institutional Collective Action Dilemmas*. New York: Cambridge University Press.

Schott, Liz, and LaDona Pavetti. 2011. "Many states cutting TANF benefits harshly despite high unemployment and unprecedented need." *Center on Budget and Policy Priorities*. Retrieved from www.cbpp.org/cms/?fa=3498 (accessed March 9, 2014).

Shapiro, Sidney A., and Ronald F. Wright. 2011. "The future of the administrative Presidency: Turning administrative law inside-out." *University of Miami Law Review* 65 (2): 577–620.

Shelly, Bryan. 2013. "The bigger the better: Cross-variation in federal education and Medicaid waivers, 1991–2008." *Publius: The Journal of Federalism* 43 (Summer): 452–473.

Somin, Ilya. 2016. "Federalism and the Roberts Court." *Publius: The Journal of Federalism* 46 (Summer): 441–462.

Thompson, Frank J. 2013. "Health Reform, Polarization, and Public Administration." *Public Administration Review* 73 (Special Issue) (September/October): S3–S12.

Thompson, Frank J., and Michael K. Gusmano. 2014. "The Administrative Presidency and Fractious Federalism: The Case of Obamacare." *Publius: The Journal of Federalism* 44 (Summer): 426–450.

Tocqueville, Alexis de. 1999. *Democracy in America*. New York: Westvaco.

U.S. Department of Education. 2016. ESEA Flexibility. Retrieved from http://ed.gov/esea/flexibility (accessed June 29, 2016).

Voteview.com. 2012. "The polarization of congressional parties." Retrieved from www.voteview.com/political_polarization.asp (accessed March 2, 2014).

Warner, Barbara, and Jennifer Shapiro. 2013. "Fractured, fragmented federalism: A study in franking regulatory policy." *Publius: The Journal of Federalism*, 43 (Summer): 474–496.

Weissert, Carol S., and William G. Weissert. 2008. "Medicaid waivers: License to shape the future of federalism." In *Intergovernmental Management for the Twentieth-First Century*, edited by Timothy J. Conlan, Paul L. Posner, and National Academy of Public Administration, 157–175. Washington, DC: Brookings Institute.

Wong, Kenneth K. 2015. "Federal ESEA waivers as reform leverage: Politics and variation in state implementation." *Publius: The Journal of Federalism* 45 (Summer): 405–426.

Wright, Deil S. 1988. *Understanding Intergovernmental Relations*, 3rd edition. Belmont, CA: Brooks/Cole Publishing Company.

Zeemering, Eric S. 2007. "Who collaborates? Local decisions about intergovernmental relations." Dissertation, Indiana University, IN.

Zeemering, Eric S. 2008. "Governing Interlocal Cooperation: City Council Interests and the Implications for Public Management." *Public Administration Review* 68 (July/August): 731–741.

Zimmerman, Joseph F. 1987. "The State Mandate Problem." *State and Local Government Review* 19 (Spring): 78–79.

Zimmerman, Joseph F. 2008. *Contemporary American Federalism: The Growth of National Power*, 2nd edition. Albany, NY: State University Press of New York.

Zimmerman, Joseph F. 2012. *Interstate Cooperation: Compacts and Administrative Agreements*, 2nd edition. Albany, NY: State University of New York Press.

Zimmerman, Joseph F. 2015. *Unifying the Nation: Article IV of the United States Constitution*. Albany, NY: State University of New York Press.

3 Why Coercion and Cooperation Coexist in American Federalism

John Kincaid

Deil Wright pioneered important contributions to our knowledge of intergovernmental relations in the United States. His *Understanding Intergovernmental Relations* (1988) was the most commonly assigned text in public administration courses on intergovernmental relations and management (Box 1995). His passing in 2009 was a loss that deprived us of continuing mutual engagement. Yet, a scholar's work endures to invite critical engagement. This essay questions some aspects of Wright's work and seeks to reconcile Wright's findings on the generally cooperative character of intergovernmental administration with my findings on coercive federalism (Kincaid 1990, 2011).

Metaphoric Phases versus Federal-Aid Trends

The study of American federalism and intergovernmental relations has been dominated by metaphors that owe their origin to Corwin's coining of "dual federalism" (1934: 48) and Grodzins's (1966: 8) "marble-cake" federalism. Stewart (1984) identified 497 metaphors. Wright criticized metaphors as an "invent-your-own federalism game" that often politicized federalism studies (Wright 1978: 19); yet 18 such metaphors are listed in the index of his 1988 text, and he coined metaphors for what he called "phases" of intergovernmental relations. These phases, some of which overlap, oddly correspond exactly with decades: conflict (19th century–1930s), cooperative (1930s–1950s), concentrated (1940s–1960s), creative (1950s–1960s), competitive (1960s–1970s), calculative (1970s–1980s), and contractive (1980s–1990s). Inexplicably, the 1950s and 1960s are each included in three phases, the 1930s, 1970s, and 1980s in two phases, and the 1990s in only the last phase. The phases also speed up. The conflict phase was of indeterminate length (141 years?); the cooperative and concentrated phases each lasted 30 years; and the last four phases lasted 20 years each. But history does not unfold in such lock steps; institutional inertia and path dependencies defy imposition of a decennial motif. The names of all the phases, moreover, begin with "c." The rationale for this convention was apparently Wright's "penchant for alliteration and metaphors" (Burke 2014: 63).

The pitfalls in this metaphoric method can be illustrated by Wright's last textbook phase, the "contractive" phase (1980s–1990s). Wright attributed four characteristics to this phase, but only the first—captured in his statement "[f]ederal aid is shrinking" (Wright 1988: 99)—is amenable to empirical testing. Did federal aid shrink from 1980 to 1999? Wright's contractive phase was apparently based on current-dollar declines in aid that occurred in 1982 and 1986. Otherwise, aid increased every year during the contractive period for a total 1980-1999 increase of 193 percent.

The better historical measure is constant dollars. In those terms, aid declined in 1980, 1981, 1982, 1983, and 1987, but otherwise increased every year for a total 34 percent increase from 1980 to 1999. Constant-dollar aid had increased by 49 percent during the previous calculative phase. Hence, the growth rate slowed during the contractive period, but aid continued growing, not shrinking. Furthermore, constant-dollar aid soared by 140 percent from 1990 to 2009, but aid is expected to increase by only 14 percent from 2009 to 2022—a rate 19 percentage points lower than the growth rate during Wright's contractive phase.

Figure 3.1 shows the brief constant-dollar decline in federal aid after 1978 followed by resumed increases. The decline of federal aid after 1978 is almost universally attributed to President Ronald Reagan (e.g., Shannon 1987; Wright 1988). This is incorrect. In constant dollars, federal aid to state and local governments increased by 7 percent in President Jimmy Carter's (1977–1981) first full budget year (1978)—the historic high point at the time—but then declined by 12 percent over his next three budget years. Aid declined by 15 percent in Reagan's first full budget year (1982) but increased by 4 percent by his fourth budget year and declined again by 5 percent by his last budget year. Overall, aid increased by 2 percent from Reagan's first to last budget year. Aid growth bounced back by 36 percent under President George H. W. Bush (1989–1993) and 38 percent under Bill Clinton (1993–2001). Notable in Figure 3.1 is a federal aid roller coaster under President Barack Obama: a sharp one-year increase in federal aid in his first full budget year because of the American Reinvestment and Recovery Act stimulus, a decline of 15.6 percent for 2011–2013, and then a 19 percent increase to 2017. Overall, aid increased by 4 percent under Obama. In 2017, OMB projected a 5.7 percent aid increase during Donald Trump's four years.

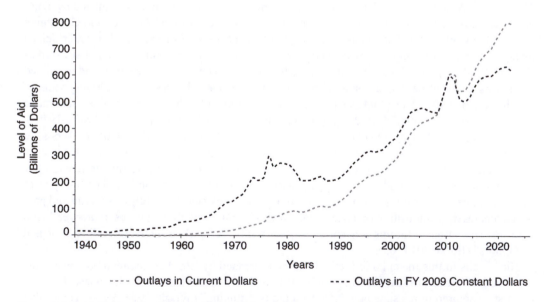

Figure 3.1 Total Outlays for Grants to State and Local Governments, 1940–2022.

Source: Executive Office of the President (2017: 268–269)

Note: 2017–2022 are estimated.

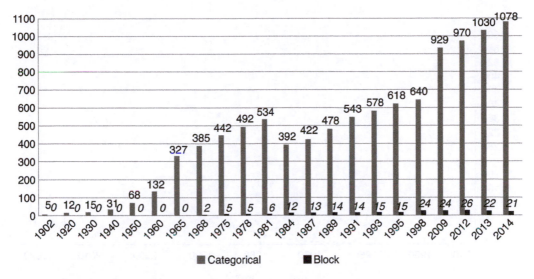

Figure 3.2 Funded Federal Grants to State and Local Governments, 1902–2014.

Source: Dilger (2014)

Another measure of aid trends is the number of grants-in-aid. The trend since 1902 is consistently upward (see Figure 3.2), except for 1984 when the number of categorical grants dropped from 534 to 392. Growth resumed thereafter, and did not abate from 1987 to 2014. Furthermore, 77 categorical grants and two block grants had been consolidated into nine new block grants in 1982 (Walker, Richter, and Colella 1982). The grants count is a poor trend measure, though, because even when the growth of federal dollars slows, grants can proliferate as interest groups compete for slices of the aid pie. The Figure 3.2 data indicate considerable slicing and dicing of the federal-aid system since 1998.

The fact that federal aid did not shrink during the contractive phase illustrates the danger of using short-term phenomena to project long-term trends. In addition, common criteria were not used to define Wright's seven phases. For instance, supposedly shrinking aid is the leading characteristic of the contractive phase, but aid trends are not criteria for any other phase. Furthermore, Wright's descriptions of the phases do not, for the most part, lend themselves to empirical tests.

Efforts to identify periods in American federalism need to be consistent, cognizant of path dependencies, and amenable to empirical verification. Periods should reflect trends that depart markedly from previous trends and persist over a long time with little or no interruption. For instance, a trend not identified by Wright but evident when he termed the 1980s–1990s "contractive" was the shift of federal aid from places to persons displayed in Figure 3.3. "It is difficult to discern any dramatic or distinctive shifts in the composition of federal aid programs since 1975," he wrote in his text's third edition (Wright 1988: 207). Yet aid to places was already declining. The year 1978, when 67 percent of all aid went for place functions, marked the last hurrah of aid to places, while 1988 marked the crossover of aid to persons beginning its steady march to dominance of the federal-aid system.

By aid to places, I mean grants to state and local governments for public investments and enhancements of public places such as infrastructure, economic development, education, and criminal justice. Aid to persons refers to grants for what the U.S. Office of Management and Budget

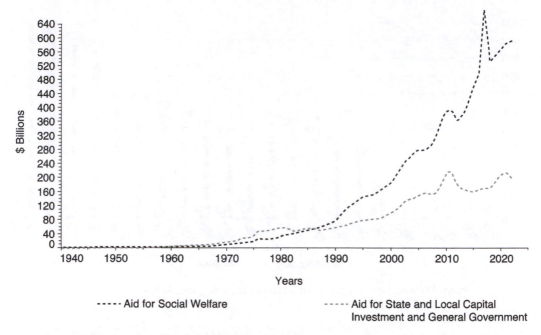

Figure 3.3 Federal Grants-in-Aid to State and Local Governments for Social Welfare and Other Purposes in Billions of Constant (FY 2009) dollars, 1940–2022.

Source: Executive Office of the President (2017: 268–269)

Note: 2017–2022 are estimated.

(OMB) terms payments for individuals such as social welfare and Medicaid. Medicaid now accounts for about 60 percent of all federal aid to state and local governments.

Figure 3.3 shows a dramatic, long-lasting change in the composition of federal aid that differs markedly from the previous era commonly called "cooperative federalism" when aid to places was abundant. This radical shift has had major consequences for state and local governments.

- It has reduced aid for such purposes as infrastructure, criminal justice, economic development, and environmental protection. Place-focused "federal grants—including those for education, highways, weatherization, housing, and other programs—are" also declining as a percentage of GDP (U.S. Government Accountability Office 2010: 6; 2014). A long-term economic impact will be reduced state–local spending on infrastructure, higher education, and other core 'place' functions that have traditionally defined the states' *raison d'être*.
- It has encouraged state and local governments to compensate for this 37-year relative decline of place-focused aid by drawing more nongovernmental actors into the system through public–private partnerships and privatization.
- It has heightened the role of states as administrative agents for the federal government whereby they deliver federally determined social services to individuals under federal rules. Services to individuals, except postal services, were a classic state function.

- It has tied state budgets to social programs susceptible to escalating federal regulation, cost-shifting, and matching state costs and sometimes local costs. Because of population aging, Medicaid will become especially burdensome fiscally. These programs entail substantial federal regulation, even if they permit administrative discretion.
- It has committed substantial portions of state and local budgets to redistributive policies, which some theorists argue should be a federal-government function (Peterson 1995).
- It has increased and intensified the roles of non-profit and for-profit entities in federal program implementation, a trend recently labeled "networked" or "collaborative" governance (Agranoff 2007; O'Leary and Vij 2012; Kincaid and Cole 2016).
- It has been the major factor in the decline of federal aid for local governments since the mid-1970s. States are the primary recipients of federal social-welfare aid. Municipal governments have been affected most acutely because they perform the fewest social-welfare functions. In turn, states have less revenue to send to local governments.
- It also partly explains why, despite increased aid since 1987, federal aid has not significantly alleviated long-term state–local fiscal stress.
- It has increased competition among networked program advocates, between nongovernmental program advocates and state and local governments, among state agencies and among local agencies, between states, between local governments, and between state and local governments. This competition militates against consolidations of the federal government's 1,078 categorical grants (Dilger 2014) into block grants because members of Congress, bureaucrats, and interest groups defend programs that benefit them.

Coercive Federalism

This shift in federal aid from places to persons is one reason why American federalism today can be described as coercive, compared to previous eras when it was often termed dual or cooperative. The current era is coercive because the period's predominant political, fiscal, statutory, regulatory, and judicial trends entail impositions of federal policies and rules on state and local governments. This overt face of American federalism marks an era that began in the late 1960s and succeeded a roughly 35-year era of cooperative federalism. Coercive federalism

> describes an era in which (a) the federal government is the dominant policymaker, (b) the federal government is able to assert its policy will unilaterally over the state and local governments, (c) elected state and local officials are more often lobbyists than partners in intergovernmental policy-making, (d) interactions between federal officials and elected state and local officials are more often consultations than negotiations, (e) there are few constitutional limits on the exercise of federal power, (f) cooperative policy-making, when it occurs, is most often due to the influence of interest groups operating outside the intergovernmental system than to state and local officials operating inside the intergovernmental system, and (g) all important arenas of state and local decision-making are infused with federal rules.
>
> (Kincaid 2011: 13)

Coercive federalism has been characterized by a shift of federal policy-making from the interests of places (i.e., state and local governments) to the interests of persons (i.e., voters, social welfare beneficiaries, and interest groups); increased substantive conditions attached to federal grants requiring states to comply with policies that often fall outside of Congress's constitutional ambit; increased preemptions of state and local powers; increased mandates on state and local governments; restrictions on state and local tax and borrowing powers; nationalization of criminal law; the demise of intergovernmental institutions; the decline of intergovernmental policy-making cooperation; and federal judicial interventions into state and local affairs (Kincaid 1990, 2011).

Empirical evidence of this era is abundant. For instance, from 1970 to 2014, a period of 45 years, Congress enacted 522 explicit preemptions compared to 206 preemptions enacted from 1789 to 1969, a period of 181 years (U.S. Advisory Commission on Intergovernmental Relations 1992; Joseph F. Zimmerman, personal communication, April 23, 2015). Put differently, 72 percent of all explicit preemptions in U.S. history have been enacted during the last 20 percent of years of U.S. history. Not all preemptions can be termed coercive (Zimmerman 2010) but all preemptions displace state authority and nationalize a regulatory field.

As for another example, Congress enacted only two major intergovernmental mandates before 1964, nine during 1964–1969, 25 during the 1970s, and 27 in the 1980s. Although the 1995 Unfunded Mandates Reform Act (UMRA)—one of the few restraints on coercive federalism— reduced to 15 the number of intergovernmental mandates enacted since 1996 having costs above UMRA's threshold, from 2010 to 2016, Congress enacted 370 intergovernmental mandates, each of which fell below UMRA's threshold (U.S. Congressional Budget Office 2015). UMRA's threshold is adjusted annually for inflation; in 2017, it was $78 million for intergovernmental mandates.

Although grants are commonly associated with cooperative federalism, most are very directive. During the nineteenth and early twentieth centuries, federal assistance to states and localities played mostly enabling roles (Elazar 1962; Balogh 2009), but by the mid-twentieth century, most grants became tools for achieving national objectives. Hence, they were increasingly loaded with crossover sanctions and crosscutting regulations. A crossover sanction reduces or terminates federal funding in one program for failure to comply with a rule in another federal program. An example is the 1984 requirement that any state failing to increase its alcoholic-beverage purchase age to 21 would lose 10 percent of its federal highway aid. A crosscutting regulation is a law, such as the National Environmental Policy Act of 1969, that applies to all or most recipients of federal aid. Wright (1988: 369) cited a 1980 OMB study showing that two-thirds of the then extant crosscutting regulations had been adopted during the 1970s—a finding consistent with the temporal pace of coercive federalism as starting around 1968.

Congress's preference for categorical grants also prioritizes federal direction over state and local discretion. Even federally stipulated procedures for state acceptance of federal aid can be so highly directive as to "shape how states internally discuss, deliberate, and decide to join federal programs" (Fahey 2015: 1566) and also constitute coercive rather than voluntary state consent. Federally stipulated procedures can have important policy effects. In 2012, for example, Mississippi's insurance commissioner, a statewide elected official, sent a letter and blueprint to the U.S. Department of Health and Human Services (HHS) declaring Mississippi's intent to establish a health-insurance exchange under the Affordable Care Act (ACA). HHS rejected the application because the ACA requires gubernatorial consent (Fahey 2015). Hence, the federal government established Mississippi's exchange in the absence of gubernatorial consent.

State and local officials still lobby federal officials, but they are rarely partners in federal policy-making. State and local officials usually gain no federal policy concessions or only minor concessions on their own. They ordinarily garner major federal policy concessions only when powerful nongovernmental interests align with state and local goals. Elected federal officials are highly responsive to electoral coalitions, interest groups, and campaign contributors and correspondingly less responsive to elected state and local officials. These officials have no privileged voice in Congress or the White House even though they are the elected representatives of the peoples of the 50 states, 38,910 general-purpose local governments, and 12,880 independent school districts. Instead, they must behave like interest-group lobbyists and compete with all other interest groups in the federal policy-making arena where, frequently, they cannot prevail against powerful interests that bring crucial financial, ideological, and voter rewards and punishments to bear on the electoral fortunes of federal officials. Representatives of the Big 7 state and local associations at the 2014 Deil Wright Symposium described the intergovernmental system as "broken" and termed their influence as limited to occasionally blocking objectionable congressional or executive policy proposals. Grodzins's observation, which was perhaps accurate in 1960, that there is a "comprehensive, day-to-day, even hour-by-hour, impact of local views on national programs" (1960: 274) now reads like ancient mythology.

Party polarization has also weakened state and local influence by producing divisions within the Big 7. Polarization is itself due partly to coercive federalism because the nationalization of so many previously state and local issues, especially white-hot cultural issues, has vastly increased the stakes of controlling the federal government. Ironically, therefore, the State and Local Legal Center, established by the Big 7 in 1983 to defend state and local interests before the U.S. Supreme Court, rarely files *amicus* briefs in major federalism cases, such as *New York v. United States* (1992), *United States v. Lopez* (1995), and *National Federation of Independent Business v. Sebelius* (2012), because members of the Big 7 divide over the policy issues at stake in such cases.

Consequently, state and local officials try to bend the administration of federal policies in cooperative directions through various forms and forums of bargaining and negotiation (Ryan 2011), such as negotiated rulemaking. This process, encouraged by the Negotiated Rulemaking Act (1990), is an administrative law procedure whereby a federal agency negotiates with interest groups, including state and local governments, that will be affected by a proposed rule and seeks agreement on the terms of the final rule promulgated by the agency.

Intergovernmental Administrative Cooperation

Wright was at home in this arena, and he used various metaphors to describe it. He was fond of "picket-fence federalism" (Wright 1988: 83), which conveys a truth that intergovernmental bargaining and cooperation occur mainly within separate policy fields. He and others have criticized this silo reality because it can inhibit coordination, but it does breed familiarity and expertise that facilitate cooperation, and it has not prevented cross-fertilization as in, for example, the infusion of metropolitan, historic preservation, and environmental sustainability objectives in transportation planning.

One can ask, though, why picket-fence federalism—a hierarchical model with the national government on top, states in the middle, and local governments on the bottom—should be preferred over rail-fence federalism—a nonhierarchical model denoting more co-equal cooperation. The picket fence is incompatible with Wright's overlapping-authority model (Wright 1988: 49; Agranoff and Radin 2015), which is presumably nonhierarchical. The rail-fence model can accommodate the overlapping-authority model within each policy rail, thereby capturing much of the reality of intergovernmental cooperation within policy fields, each characterized by more or less overlapping authority.

Wright's overlapping-authority model, while pertinent, is not easily distinguished from Grodzins' marble-cake model. It also is difficult to verify empirically and lacks cognizance of the U.S. Supreme Court's position that comity, which is a norm of intergovernmental courtesy, is a duty that states owe to each other as co-equal sovereigns and the federal government owes to states as sovereigns, but not a duty that states owe to the federal government because the latter is the superior sovereign. In all matters of federal law, the states owe the federal government compliance, not comity (Seinfeld 2015). Thus, while the overlapping-authority model's notion that each government's authority is limited often accurately describes the common practice of federal-policy implementation, legally, the federal government can ultimately command compliance. This renders the model's implicit assumption of co-equality questionable because the federal government can sit at the bargaining table with a big hammer on its lap. For example, after losing on Medicaid expansion in *National Federation of Independent Business v. Sebelius* (2012), the Obama administration began in 2015 to warn officials in states that had not expanded Medicaid that if they refused to do so, the federal government might withhold federal funds to pay health-care providers for uncompensated care for the poor. Florida's governor threatened to sue the administration for linking the state's $1.3 billion uncompensated-care aid to Medicaid expansion (Galewitz 2015).

The model also does not explain why cooperation persists. Even while federal, state, and local elected officials are engaged in mortal political combat, federal, state, and local bureaucrats are generally engaged in cooperation and coordination in policy implementation. From mail surveys, Arneson (1922) found that state highway officials and school superintendents were overwhelmingly satisfied with the federal-aid programs for highways and vocational education. When Macdonald (1928) surveyed 264 state directors of federal-aid programs, 93 percent said federal aid had not "encouraged federal interference with state affairs." The American State Administrators Project (ASAP)—a survey research project founded by Wright in the 1960s that examined the changing intergovernmental world of state administrators over five decades—found a general, though roller-coaster, trend of state administrators reporting increased administrative cooperation and regulatory devolution from 1974 to 2004 (Brudney and Wright 2010). With the exception of the federal courts, federal officials rarely order state and local administrators about like lackeys, and state and local bureaucrats rarely obstruct federal objectives even when adapting them to local circumstances.

Elected state and local officials usually cooperate on implementation, too, though not necessarily when given an entirely voluntary choice, as with the ACA's health-insurance marketplaces. As of April 2017, twelve Democratic states had established a state-based marketplace, compared to only one Republican state (Idaho). Consistent with coercive federalism, though, the federal government established marketplaces in the 28 states that did not do so themselves. Likewise, 15 of the 19 states that have not expanded Medicaid are Republican. However, such uncooperative behavior is ordinarily carried out by elected officials, usually governors (Barrilleaux and Rainey 2014), not administrators. There are, of course, conflicts in intergovernmental administrative relations, but bargaining and negotiation are key conflict-resolution tools.

Administrative cooperation has deep roots. In *Federalist* no. 36, Alexander Hamilton foresaw federal–state cooperation in taxation (Kincaid 2014), and Albert Gallatin, the fourth secretary of the U.S. treasury, articulated ideas for intergovernmental cooperation (Rothman 1972). Intergovernmental cooperation was, as both Grodzins (1960) and Elazar (1962) contended, prevalent from the start of the federal republic and throughout the era of so-called dual federalism. Cooperation intensified during the twentieth-century era of cooperative federalism.

Grodzins especially attributed this cooperation to the country's mildly chaotic non-centralized party system. Reacting against the American Political Science Association's 1950 call for more nationalized and disciplined parties, Grodzins (1960) warned that such parties would destroy cooperative federalism. Grodzins was correct insofar as nationalization of the party system has been a major factor in the rise of coercive federalism, but because of deep institutionalized roots and path dependence, coercive federalism in the policy-making realm has not choked off cooperation in the administrative realm. Implementation of many of the policies imposed on state and local governments requires intergovernmental cooperation for success. This state–local cooperation with federal coercion may seem paradoxical, but it endures because various forces sustain it.

Federal Efficiency and Risk Reduction

Hamilton appears to have regarded federal-state cooperation as efficient. Rather than build a large administrative state, the federal government could contract functions out to the states whose personnel are, moreover, better attuned to local conditions. A grant-in-aid is "in the nature of a contract" (*Pennhurst State School and Hospital v. Holderman*, 1981, 17). In addition, Americans had then, and still have, antipathy toward a 'big' federal government. Furthermore, state and local governments originally occupied virtually all of the policy fields now co-occupied by the federal government. Contracting out also reduces political risks for federal officials because if state performance is negligent, federal officials can deflect blame for policy failures onto the states.

Dual Federalism

Additionally, the U.S. system is not one of executive federalism (as is Germany, for example) whereby states are constitutionally obligated to execute federal framework legislation. The federal government is expected, for the most part, to carry out its own policies or pay the states to do so. Given its very limited administrative capabilities, the federal government must seek the assistance of state and local officials. Federal administrators, therefore, usually have incentives to work cooperatively with their state and local counterparts. Furthermore, cooperative enforcement is sometimes more effective than coercive enforcement (Earnhart and Glicksman 2015).

Also, the federal government does not, *per se*, share revenue with the states or engage in fiscal equalization; thus, it does not need the administrative control and co-decision mechanisms usually required for such policies. Instead, the federal government operates a sprawling grant-in-aid system consisting of more than 1,099 programs, only 21 of which are block grants (Dilger 2014). Given that most federal-aid money flows through categorical grants, the federal government exercises control through the purposes for which the grants are established, but otherwise works cooperatively on the administration of those grants and usually allows state and local officials discretion in implementing those grants as long as each grant's purposes are realized, at least approximately. Block grants afford state and local officials even more discretion, although block grants account for little more than 10–15 percent of all federal aid (U.S. Advisory Commission on Intergovernmental Relations 1995).

Federal-Aid Carrots and Sticks

The carrots and sticks of federal aid play important roles in ensuring cooperation. Federal revenue has accounted for sizable portions of state–local budgets since 1969—ranging in 2013 from 43 percent of state general revenues in Mississippi to 19 percent in North Dakota (Pew Charitable Trusts 2015). Despite numerous conditions, state and local governments embrace most grants-in-aid. All 50 states, for example, complied with the federal drinking age condition attached to surface transportation aid in 1984 because no state could afford to lose the funds and because there is no mechanism for the states to withhold the then 9-cent (now 18.4-cent) federal gas tax collected within their borders.

In addition, the salaries of many state and local government employees and resources for the programs they administer rest in part on direct or indirect federal monies. From 1978 to 2004, the proportion of state agencies receiving and managing federal aid ranged from 69 percent in 1988 to 79 percent in 2004 (Brudney and Wright 2010). Even if only a small percentage of an employee's salary or program resources comes from federal aid, loss of that portion can result in a job or program cutback.

Nongovernmental Organizations

Many intergovernmental programs are administered wholly or partly by nongovernmental organizations and their employees who depend on federal funds often delivered to them via state and local treasuries. Some nongovernmental organizations also have nongovernmental sources of income, but many rely substantially on government funds. Either way, they have strong incentives to welcome federal monies and the regulations that accompany them. This pattern of collaborative administration was initially developed in the early nineteenth century and increased after the Civil War. For example, the first National Asylum for Disabled Volunteer Soldiers established in Milwaukee in 1867 was co-funded by the federal government and the Lady Managers of the Home Society, which also managed the asylum.

Partial Preemption of State Powers

Another federal tool for cooperation is partial preemption, which did not exist during the era of cooperative federalism. Partial preemption allows states to enact their own regulations in a federally preempted field so long as those regulations are equal to or higher than the federal standards. This tool, however, is a one-way federalism. States are free to rise above the federal regulatory floor but are hammered to the floor if they enact policies deemed by the federal government to fall below the floor.

Waivers of Federal Law

Waivers are a more recent tool of cooperation arising from program complexity, public pressure to allow more state discretion to improve outcomes, skyrocketing costs in some programs, such as Medicaid, and polarization that makes it difficult for state and local officials to obtain more discretion, such as block grants, through the legislative process (Kincaid 2001a: 22). Waivers, however, permit only federally sanctioned discretion. Arguably, they also violate the rule of law (Frohnen 2016).

Federal Statutory and Regulatory Penalties

Many federal statutes associated with coercive federalism contain penalties, including, in some cases, civil or criminal penalties, aimed at uncooperative state and local officials. Many federal statutes also enable citizens to sue state and local officials for insufficient or biased compliance with federal laws. Nevertheless, federal officials sometimes accommodate state and local officials by extending compliance deadlines. Because many states have resisted compliance with the REAL ID Act of 2005, the U.S. Department of Homeland Security (DHS) extended compliance deadlines several times, with full enforcement now set for 2018. The extensions, though, did not stem solely from federal cooperation; they also reflected President Obama's dislike of REAL ID and resistance by both conservative and liberal interest groups concerned about government surveillance. By contrast, in 2014–2015, with more than 100 institutions under federal investigation, many public and private higher-education administrators were in a panic to comply with a letter of guidance issued by the U.S. Department of Education setting forth Title IX rules on sexual assaults.

Federal Court Orders

The courts also play roles in intergovernmental relations. Following the massive resistance by southern state and local governments to the federal courts in the 1950s and 1960s, state and local officials became generally cooperative with judicial decisions, which are seen as central to the rule of law. The federal courts stand as potential hammers to compel compliance; hence, state and local officials have incentives to cooperate with federal officials. Numerous federal court consent decrees of long standing, many of which emanated from citizen lawsuits, now govern numerous aspects of administration in all states and perhaps most local governments. Federal officials, in seeking to foster compliance, ordinarily negotiate and bargain with state and local officials before seeking judicial intervention, but the prospect of judicial intervention has a sobering effect on state and local cooperation with federal officials (Goode 2013).

Territorially Dispersed Diversity

Since the fall of massive resistance to desegregation in the South, no cultural, ethnic, religious, or linguistic region in the United States (akin to a Quebec or Catalonia) has had strong incentives to thwart or distort intergovernmental administrative relations. Similarly, partisanship does not play a major role in intergovernmental administration. In the political arena, there may be vigorous partisan conflict over huge intergovernmental programs, such as Medicaid and surface transportation, and over costly mandates, such as environmental regulations, but once federal policies on these matters are enacted into law, bureaucrats have incentives to cooperate across party lines so as to administer the programs as effectively and efficiently as possible. Furthermore, virtually all of the nongovernmental collaborators in policy implementation purport to be nonpartisan, and most of the non-profit participants are legally required to be nonpartisan.

Professional Norms

Due to similar civil service rules and shared professional norms, most federal, state, and local administrators dull the sharp edges of partisanship so as to focus on cooperative task execution under existing rules and budgets. In addition, federal, state, and local administrators within policy fields often share the same education and training pedigrees and interact with each other in the same national and regional professional associations, which are usually more important to them than party affiliations. Federal, state, and local law-enforcement officials, for example, share common training and professional backgrounds, as well as a professional camaraderie, that facilitate intergovernmental cooperation.

Public Sector Unions

The intergovernmental policy sector also is much more unionized than it was in 1960. Federal, state, and local public employee unions and associations have similar goals; they support federal program implementation; and they serve as additional forums for intergovernmental communication and cooperation. State and local public employee organizations usually welcome federal money and rules, and thereby support expansions of federal power. Unions, moreover, have been the originators of some of the landmark U.S. Supreme Court rulings on federalism in litigation over the Fair Labor Standards Act of 1938, which was extended to state and local government employees during the 1960s (Kincaid 1993).

Administrator Lobbying

Additionally, state and local administrators frequently advocate expansive actions and higher spending in their policy field and, thus, often welcome federal intervention. State and local environmental officials, for example, are likely to welcome federal rules that set stricter environmental standards and require more state and local spending on environmental protection. It is not uncommon for state and local bureaucrats to lobby for federal policies that are opposed by state and local elected officials who can be punished at the ballot box for implementing unpopular federal policies or raising taxes in order to pay for state or local implementation of those policies. Deutsch (1948) noted that state mental-hospital administrators often welcomed him to photograph and expose deplorable conditions so as to induce increased state and federal funding and regulation. The American State Administrators Project found over the decades that federal aid and regulations promoted "constant, consequential, and pervasive" state agency autonomy from gubernatorial and legislative oversight (Brudney and Wright 2010: 33).

Interest Group Pressure

Interest groups play a role, too. After achieving a federal policy objective, they pressure state and local governments to cooperate in implementing that objective. There has been tremendous growth in interest-group activity within the states since the late 1960s. One cause of growth has been the need for interest groups to induce cooperative state and local compliance with national policy objectives supported by the interest groups. Advocates for policy causes and rights protections do not hesitate to lobby, protest, and sue state and local governments for noncompliance. In 2014–2016, for example, protests in numerous cities of fatal police shootings of young black men triggered federal interventions to secure local police compliance with federal civil-rights rules, often through consent decrees.

Socialization

Socialization has occurred, as well. The dominance of the federal government in so many policy fields for the past 50 years of coercive federalism became an unquestioned fact of administrative life. Furthermore, many of today's senior federal, state, and local administrators entered public service in the late 1960s and early 1970s with a common passion for reform. For rank-and-file administrators, the origins of their work dictates are less important to them than their preoccupation with how to implement those dictates and satisfy the citizens who will ultimately vote for or against the elected officials who preside in a general and usually distant way over policy implementation.

Congressional Oversight

Grodzins credited congressional interference with federal bureaucrats as another important stimulus for cooperative federalism. "Administrative contacts [are] voluminous, and the whole process of interaction [is] lubricated . . . by constituent-conscious members of Congress" (Grodzins 1960: 270). Congressional casework continues to influence the intergovernmental attitudes and actions of federal administrators, although it is doubtful, for three reasons, that it has the same effects as observed by Grodzins. First, interest groups play much bigger roles in federal programs and intergovernmental administration than they did in the early 1960s. Consequently, the proportion of congressional casework conducted on behalf of the interests of state and local governments as opposed to interest groups is smaller today. Second, although pork-barrel spending dates back to the nation's founding, the rise of contemporary earmarking by members of Congress produces outcomes that often ignore or conflict with the preferences of state and local officials. As a Colorado transportation official remarked: "Why do we spend 18 months at public hearings, meetings and planning sessions to put together our statewide plan if Congress is going to earmark projects that displace our priorities?" (Mullins 2006: A10). Third, Grodzins's evidence dealt overwhelmingly with place-focused programs, such as highways and other infrastructure (e.g., airport development), agriculture, and education. Since then, the federal government has enacted massive social-welfare programs, such that intergovernmental spending on those programs has skyrocketed. As a proportion of all federal aid to state and local governments, social welfare increased from 35 percent in 1960 to 75 percent in 2017. In constant dollars, intergovernmental social-welfare aid increased by 2,934 percent from 1960 to 2017, while aid for programs that preoccupied Grodzins increased by only 302 percent. Hence, the policy content of the intergovernmental fiscal landscape is vastly different from 1960.

For these and perhaps other reasons, cooperative federalism endures in the administrative interstices of coercive federalism. Intergovernmental administrative cooperation is likely to continue unless a new generation of administrators infects it with the same partisan and ideological polarization found in the national and state political arenas.

Big-Question Issues

Most of the trends suggested in the big questions posed in Chapter 1 of the volume are likely to continue but few, if any, of the reforms are likely to materialize.

ACIR Redux?

Cooperative intergovernmental administration is fairly well institutionalized and continues despite the dismantling during the 1990s of nonpartisan or bipartisan institutions devoted to monitoring intergovernmental developments. Significant barriers impede revival of such institutions. For one, the intergovernmental grants system is both complex and segmented by diverse regimes. There were 643 federal grant programs when Congress defunded the U.S. Advisory Commission on Intergovernmental Relations (ACIR) in 1996. Now there are 1,099 grants (see Figure 3.2), each with its own intergovernmental management regime consisting of federal, state, and often local government agencies and nongovernmental organizations. The ACIR had long advocated rationalization and consolidation of the grants system; yet grants proliferated from 132 at the ACIR's founding in 1959 to 643 at its demise. The ACIR also advocated block grants, but as Figure 3.2 shows, block grants never achieved prominence. The ACIR also recommended turning back to the states the federal highway program and its federal revenue sources (U.S. Advisory Commission on Intergovernmental Relations 1987).

The intergovernmental system's picket-fence character would make it difficult for a new monitoring institution to obtain a commanding-heights view of intergovernmental management and even harder to effectuate change against resistance from the more than 1,000 intergovernmental regimes. These regimes are often characterized as networked or collaborative governance (Agranoff 2007), but they also have characteristics of cartels that strongly defend the federal programs and budget allocations that benefit them.

Another barrier is the extent to which regulatory issues arising from a service economy involve extensive intergovernmental relations. The ACIR was established just as the U.S. economy was shifting from an urban-industrial era to a service era. The intergovernmental management literature is dominated by such issues as infrastructure, transportation, economic development, housing, urban renewal, public safety, education, environmental protection, and health care. Less attention has been devoted to intergovernmental relations in such service sectors as banking, financial securities, insurance, consumer protection, telecommunications, information and computing, franchising, entertainment, and occupational licensing (Mitchell and Nunn 2017). Any new monitoring institution would need expertise in the service sector. Moreover, the ACIR avoided addressing the most important and contentious intergovernmental issues of its first two decades, such as civil rights, racial desegregation, and abortion. A new entity would likely do the same.

The main barrier to reviving nonpartisan monitoring institutions is partisan politics. The ACIR was established at a unique moment in U.S. history when polarization was very low and bipartisanship was high (Kincaid 2011). Conceived as an independent bipartisan entity, the ACIR operated for its first two decades under a generally liberal consensus, but as partisan polarization emerged during the 1970s, the commission was increasingly buffeted by partisan forces that made it difficult for it to function effectively. Furthermore, the national associations (e.g., National Governors Association) from which presidents appointed state and local members of the ACIR are themselves now rent by partisan conflict. Consequently, they are unable to support a genuinely bipartisan ACIR-like entity. Additionally, the ACIR was created when there were few think tanks, but as partisan think tanks proliferated, they challenged the ACIR's work, offered alternate analyses of intergovernmental issues, and in at least one case, Heritage, lobbied for the ACIR's abolition.

Any nonpartisan entity established to monitor and evaluate intergovernmental relations (assuming such an entity could be created) would be pushed aside and ignored by the political process, in part because many of the leading intergovernmental issues are political. Medicaid, for example, is the single largest federal grant program, accounting for about 60 percent of all federal aid to state and local governments and serving more people than any other single health-insurance system in the world. The leading intergovernmental debate has been whether to end Medicaid as an open-ended matching grant by capping the federal reimbursement or converting Medicaid into a block grant. The latter options are preferred by most congressional Republicans but opposed by most Democrats in Congress. Hence, this major intergovernmental issue is not amenable to resolution by an independent entity. Nevertheless, consistent with the analysis above, the federal government has responded to states' concerns through waivers. Waivers accounted for 14 percent of total federal Medicaid spending in 2005, 17 percent in 2010, and 33 percent in 2015. The federal government spent $29 billion on waiver demonstrations in 31 states in 2005 and $109 billion in 40 states in 2015 (U.S. Government Accountability Office 2017).

In summary, Congress and the White House are unlikely to create or endorse any ACIR-like body to monitor intergovernmental relations (Kincaid 2001b).

Sorting Out?

Continual deficit spending has occurred since the rise of coercive federalism in the mid-1960s. Since 1960, the federal budget has run annual deficits every year except for 1969 and 1998–2001. The deficit drivers are (a) domestic programs, especially entitlement programs, that began proliferating during the Great Society and (b) the unwillingness of members of Congress to levy taxes commensurate with their policy appetites. The prospects for federal budget reforms that would reduce deficits and debt are slim because reforms would require politically suicidal tax hikes and program cuts, as well as federal withdrawal from fields that benefit members of Congress and presidents. Nongovernmental interests would resist any sorting out that would reduce or end federal funding in their policy areas. Deficit spending makes Congress a more reliable funding source for these interests than state and local governments, which face balanced budget rules.

Thus, sorting out of functional responsibilities is unlikely. The governors foolishly rejected President Reagan's swap proposal in 1982, which would have transferred Medicaid to the federal government, and Congress never acted on the ACIR's proposals to turn back the highway program and many welfare programs to the states. Advocates of sorting out also overlook the extent to which the federal government would retain regulatory roles in devolved functions that impinge on federal powers, such as interstate commerce, and judicial roles pertaining to civil rights and other matters. Clean breaks would be impossible.

Block Grants?

Block grants are less attractive than appeared to be the case in the past for two reasons. First, block grants would be instituted mainly as budget-saving devices for the federal government, allowing it to cap its expenditures and require state and local governments to make hard choices about cutting services or raising taxes. Second, block grants experience some re-categorization over time as Congress and the executive branch add regulations and conditions of aid.

Ordinarily, Congress prefers categorical grants that give federal officials more say over program expenditures. Also, many nongovernmental interests that benefit from categorical grants would resist having their categorical benefits folded into block grants that would require them to compete for funds in the state and local arenas.

It is possible that Medicaid will be converted to a block grant. This would be a revolutionary change in the grant-in-aid system and possibly major devolutionary change as well. This development, however, would not be motivated by a desire to reform the grants system but to restrain federal spending and require states to fund future Medicaid expansions.

State–Local Depredations?

The principal state–local cleavage today divides Democratic cities and Republican states. Notably, in the 2016 election, every one of the country's 493 wealthiest counties, almost all being urban, voted for Hillary Clinton. The remaining 2,623 counties, most of them suburban, small-town, or rural, supported Donald Trump (Luce 2017). Republican legislatures and governors often seek to block anti-Republican policies, such as minimum-wage hikes and sanctuary-city actions, enacted by Democratic cities and counties.

Nevertheless, state–local relations vary considerably across the states, and states are not uniformly constricting local authority. To the extent states could improve their revenue position, they could help alleviate fiscal pressures on local governments. However, there are barriers to accessing new revenues. Voters resist sales taxes on services. The federal Internet Tax Freedom Act of 2015 prohibits federal, state, and local taxes on Internet access and discriminatory Internet-only taxes such as bit, bandwidth, and email taxes. Congress also has failed to pass a statute authorizing state sales taxation of out-of-state mail-order purchases, although states are becoming more successful in taxing such purchases. A looming revenue constraint is that most states and many local governments face huge pension liabilities.

Regional Cooperation?

Despite more than a century of agitation by reformers, metropolitan consolidation is off the table (Kincaid 1993), although many forms of interlocal cooperation occur in metropolitan areas (Miller and Cox 2014). Interlocal cooperation is not likely to increase markedly without coercive state action, in part because the transaction costs for local officials are high. Most elected local officials are part-time, many localities have a small number of employees, most local government employees are fully occupied by local duties, and there are so many local governments that coordination, communication, and negotiation are onerous. However, neither political party has strong incentives to force this issue lest they alienate suburban voters.

Coercive or Cooperative Federalism?

Coercive federalism is here to stay, and so is cooperative federalism. As already noted above, coercive federalism characterizes policymaking in the federal system. Since the mid-1960s, the role of state and local officials in formulating federal intergovernmental policies has been diminished greatly, freeing the federal government to impose historically unprecedented numbers of mandates, preemptions, conditions of aid, and court orders on states and localities. At the same time, intergovernmental administration and management have remained largely cooperative.

More Networked Governance?

Nongovernmental organizations have played important roles in public functions since the republic's early days. Daniel J. Elazar (1970) mapped these organizations in medium-sized metropolitan areas in the late 1960s. Such public–private collaboration shows no signs of abating.

Polarization

Although each party supports states' rights that correspond to their policy preferences, both parties seek to impose their policy preferences nationwide. Polarization is largely a consequence of coercive federalism, which nationalized a huge array of policy issues previously reserved to the states and also overrode states' policy preferences by increasingly imposing national policies on the states. Policy conflicts that were previously diffused across the states, such as abortion, education, and marriage, achieved white-heat intensity in Washington, DC. One function of a federal system is to diffuse conflict in an arrangement where political actors agree to disagree, but nationalization motivates actors only to disagree and battle each other to the death.

Conclusion

Deil Wright helped make intergovernmental relations a field of study in public administration; he also tried to make sense of the intergovernmental system. As such, he provided food for critical engagement.

This chapter has highlighted some problems with his phases of intergovernmental relations in light of long-term federal-aid trends and sought to explain the seemingly paradoxical persistence of intergovernmental administrative cooperation in the face of coercive federalism. It illustrates the complex multidimensionality of the federal system, which, while comprehensible, defies simplistic explanation and metaphoric description.

It might be argued that the concepts of networked and collaborative governance have outdated Wright's conceptions of intergovernmental relations (Burke 2014) as reflected in the rise of these new terms in the literature (Wright, Stenberg, and Cho 2009). But Wright is still right about the centrality of intergovernmental relations, and many in public administration still concur on that centrality (Kincaid and Cole 2016). Those relations lie at the heart of today's administrative networks, in part because those networks are permeated by federal, state, and local dollars and rules. Nongovernmental organizations seek to join networks in order to leverage public dollars and influence government rulemaking. Consequently, the new concepts contain certain normative assumptions that can produce confirmation biases in determining, for example, whether a network is a collaboration or a cartel. 'Intergovernmental relations' is a neutral term carrying no normative assumptions. Such benign terms as 'nongovernmental' and 'nonprofit' can obscure the extent to which these entities are also interest groups.

Furthermore, contemporary public–private intergovernmental networks are more autonomous and free from oversight by elected state and local officials compared to the heyday of cooperative federalism when elected state and local officials had more voice in all aspects of intergovernmental relations. Indeed, the formation of these networks was accelerated by the proliferation of grants under President Lyndon B. Johnson's 'creative federalism,' one purpose of which was to circumvent state and local governments so as to deliver power to the people (Greenstone and Peterson

1973). However, the extent to which intergovernmental relations have been taken over by non-governmental organizations whose leaders face no electoral retribution raises critical questions about the viability of public accountability and democratic self-government.

A further challenge is rising partisan polarization that could weaken intergovernmental co-operation over the long term, especially if polarization seeps into the ranks of bureaucrats. In the short term, apparent conflict will be more bluster than reality. For example, former Republican Texas Attorney General Greg Abbott was famous for saying, "I go into the office, I sue the federal government and I go home." But this statement belies the huge range of intergovernmental co-operative and regulatory activity, such as Medicaid, transportation, agriculture, law enforcement, and most of environmental protection, that functioned routinely in Texas during his tenure. Furthermore, Abbott filed only 31 lawsuits against the federal government during his twelve years as attorney general. Texas won seven, lost eleven, withdrew eight, and still has five pending (Satija, Carbonell, and McCrimmin 2017). Ironically, as governor of Texas in 2017, Abbott withheld $1.5 million in criminal justice grants from Travis County because of the sheriff's refusal to cooperate with federal immigration authorities.

President Donald Trump's proposals for deep cuts in discretionary spending, program terminations, such as the Community Development Block Grant, sanctions on sanctuary cities, environmental cutbacks, and federal marijuana law enforcement would seem to presage considerable intergovernmental conflict. However, Congress is unlikely to approve such deep cuts. Trump's presidency will likely disrupt some intergovernmental programs but not alter the fundamentals outlined above because cooperative intergovernmental administrative relations are highly institutionalized and defended by numerous interests. The media and some scholars will emphasize federal-state conflict over such issues as education, environmental protection, illegal immigrants, and marijuana, but conflicts will occur mostly with Democratic states just as many conflicts occurred with Republican states under President Obama. Furthermore, despite conflicts that occur over certain issues in education, environmental protection, and so on, the vast majority of intergovernmental programs in these fields will function as usual.

Overlooked, moreover, is the high degree of party congruence in the state–federal system in 2017–2018. Republicans control the White House and Congress, and conservatives make up the majority on the U.S. Supreme Court. Republicans control 33 governorships and both the governorship and the legislature in 25 states (counting Nebraska as *de facto* Republican). The loci of combat, therefore, will be the six states where Democrats control the governorship and legislature; otherwise, state–federal relations will likely be mostly cooperative for two-thirds or more of the states. This congruence could, of course, be wiped out if Democrats capture the U.S. House and/ or U.S. Senate, along with more governorships and state legislative seats, in 2018, but even this outcome will little alter cooperative intergovernmental administrative relations across the federal government's 1,099 grant programs and thousands more regulatory regimes.

References

Agranoff, Robert. 2007. *Managing Within Networks: Adding Value to Public Organizations*. Washington, DC: Georgetown University Press.

Agranoff, Robert and Beryl A. Radin. 2015. "Deil Wright's Overlapping Model of Intergovernmental Relations: The Basis for Contemporary Intergovernmental Relationships." *Publius: The Journal of Federalism* 45 (1): 139–159.

American Political Science Association. 1950. "Toward a More Responsible Two-Party System." *American Political Science Review* 44 (Supplement, September).

Arneson, Ben A. 1922. "Federal Aid to the States." *American Political Science Review* 16(3): 443–454.

Balogh, Brian 2009. *A Government Out of Sight: The Mystery of National Authority in Nineteenth-Century America*. Cambridge: Cambridge University Press.

Barrilleaux, Charles and Carlisle Rainey. 2014. "The Politics of Need: Examining Governors' Decisions to Oppose the 'Obamacare' Medicaid Expansion." *State Politics and Policy Quarterly* 14 (4): 437–460.

Box, Richard C. 1995. "Teaching Intergovernmental Relations and Management." *Journal of Public Administration Education* 1(1): 23–38.

Brudney, Jeffrey L. and Deil S. Wright. 2010. "The 'Revolt in Dullsville' Revisited: Lessons for Theory, Practice, and Research from the American State Administrators Project, 1964–2008." *Public Administration Review* 70 (1): 26–37.

Burke, Brendan F. 2014. "Understanding Intergovernmental Relations, Twenty-Five Years Hence." *State and Local Government Review* 46 (1): 63–76.

Corwin, Edward S. 1934. *The Twilight of the Supreme Court: A History of Our Constitutional Theory*. New Haven, CT: Yale University Press.

Deutsch, Albert. 1948. *The Shame of the States*. New York: Harcourt, Brace.

Dilger, Robert Jay. 2014. *Federal Grants to State and Local Governments: An Historical Perspective on Contemporary Issues*. Washington, DC: Congressional Research Service.

Earnhart, Dietrich H. and Robert L. Glicksman. 2015. *International Review of Law and Economics* 42(1): 135–146.

Elazar, Daniel J. 1962. *The American Partnership: Intergovernmental Co-operation in the Nineteenth-Century United States*. Chicago, IL: University of Chicago Press.

Elazar, Daniel J. 1970. *Cities of the Prairie: The Metropolitan Frontier and American Politics*. New York: Basic Books.

Executive Office of the President. 2017. *The Budget for Fiscal Year 2018*. Washington, DC: U.S. Government Printing Office.

Fahey, Bridget A. 2015. "Consent Procedures and American Federalism." *Harvard Law Review* 128(6): 1561–1629.

Frohnen, Bruce P. 2016. "Waivers, Federalism, and the Rule of Law." *Perspectives on Political Science* 45(1): 59–67.

Galewitz, Phil. 2015. "Tennessee, Kansas Also Get Warning: Expand Medicaid Or Risk Hospital Funds." Retrieved from http://kaiserhealthnews.org/news/tennessee-and-kansas-also-get-warning-expand-medicaid-or-risk-losing-hospital-funds (accessed April 24, 2017).

Goode, Edward. 2013. "Some Chiefs Chafing as Justice Dept. Keeps Closer Eye on Policing." *New York Times* (28 July): 14–15.

Greenstone, David and Paul E. Peterson 1973. *Race and Authority in Urban Politics: Community Relations and the War on Poverty*. Chicago, IL: University of Chicago Press.

Grodzins, Morton. 1960. "The Federal System." In *Goals for Americans: The Report of the President's Commission on National Goals*, edited by the American Assembly, 265–282. Englewood Cliffs, NJ: Prentice-Hall.

Grodzins, Morton. 1966. *The American System: A New View of Government in the United States*. Edited by Daniel J. Elazar. Chicago, IL: Rand McNally.

Kincaid, John. 1990. "From Cooperative to Coercive Federalism." *Annals of the American Academy of Political and Social Science* 509 (May): 139–152.

Kincaid, John. 1993. "Constitutional Federalism: Labor's Role in Displacing Places to Benefit Persons." *PS: Political Science & Politics* 26(2): 172–177.

Kincaid, John. "Regulatory Regionalism in Metropolitan Areas: Voter Resistance and Reform Persistence." *Pace Law Review* 13 (Fall): 449–480.

Kincaid, John. 2001a. "The State of U.S. Federalism, 2000-2001: Continuity in Crisis." *Publius: The Journal of Federalism* 31(3): 1–69.

Kincaid, John. 2001b. "Reviving the ACIR Would Be Wonderful–But It's Unlikely." *State Tax Notes* 20(5) (January 29): 369.

Kincaid, John. 2011. "The Rise of Social Welfare and Onward March of Coercive Federalism." In *Networked Governance: The Future of Intergovernmental Management*, edited by Jack W. Meek and Kurt Thurmaier, 8–38. Los Angeles: Sage/CQ Press.

Kincaid, John. 2014. "*The Federalist* and V. Ostrom on Concurrent Taxation and Federalism." *Publius: The Journal of Federalism* 44(2): 275–297.

Kincaid, John and Richard L. Cole. 2016. "Is the Teaching of Federalism and Intergovernmental Relations Dead or Alive in American Public Administration?" *Journal of Public Affairs Education* 22(4): 515–530.

Luce, Edward. 2017. *The Retreat of Western Liberalism*. New York: Atlantic Monthly Press.

Macdonald, Austin F. 1928. *Federal Aid: A Study of the American Subsidy System*. New York: Thomas Y. Crowell.

Miller, David Y. and Raymond W. Cox III. 2014. *Governing the Metropolitan Region: America's New Frontier*. London: Routledge.

Mitchell, Matthew and Ryan Nunn. 2017. "Rule Reversal: How the Feds Can Challenge State Regulation." *Wall Street Journal* (July 7): A15.

Mullins, Brody. 2006. "As Earmarked Funding Swells, Some Recipients Don't Want It." *Wall Street Journal* (December 26): A1, A10.

National Federation of Independent Business v. *Sebelius*. 2012. 132 S.Ct. 2566.

O'Leary, Rosemary and Nidhi Vij. 2012. "Collaborative Public Management: Where Have We Been and Where Are We Going?" *American Review of Public Administration* 42(5): 507–522.

Pennhurst State School and Hospital v. *Holderman*. 1981. 451 U.S. 1.

Peterson, Paul E. 1995. *The Price of Federalism*. Washington, DC: The Brookings Institution.

Pew Charitable Trusts. 2015. "Federal Funds Provide 30 Cents of Each Dollar of State Revenue." Retrieved from www.pewtrusts.org/en/research-and-analysis/analysis/2015/02/25/federal-funds-provide-30-cents-of-each-dollar-of-state-revenue (accessed April 17, 2015).

Printz v. *United States*. 1997. 521 U.S. 898.

Rothman, Rozann. 1972. "Political Method in the Federal System: Albert Gallatin's Contribution." *Publius: The Journal of Federalism* 1(2): 123–141.

Ryan, Erin. 2011. "Negotiating Federalism." *Boston College Law Review* 52(1): 1–136.

Satija, Neena, Lindsay Carbonell, and Ryan McCrimmin. 2017. "Texas vs. the Feds—A Look at the Lawsuits." *Texas Tribune* (January 17). Retrieved from www.texastribune.org/2017/01/17/texas-federal-government-lawsuits (accessed April 19, 2017).

Seinfeld, Gil. 2015. "Reflections on Comity in the Law of American Federalism." *Notre Dame Law Review* 90(3): 1309–1343.

Shannon, John. 1987. "The Return to Fend-for-Yourself Federalism: The Reagan Mark." *Intergovernmental Perspective* 13 (Summer/Fall): 34–37.

U.S. Advisory Commission on Intergovernmental Relations. 1987. *Devolving Selected Federal-Aid Highway Programs and Revenue Bases: A Critical Appraisal*. Washington, DC: ACIR.

U.S. Advisory Commission on Intergovernmental Relations. 1992. *Federal Statutory Preemption of State and Local Authority: History, Inventory, and Issues*. Washington, DC: ACIR.

U.S. Advisory Commission on Intergovernmental Relations. 1995. *Characteristics of Federal Grant-in-Aid Programs to State and Local Governments*. Washington, DC: ACIR.

U.S. Congressional Budget Office. 2015. *Review of CBO's Activities in 2014 Under the Unfunded Mandates Reform Act*. March. Washington, DC: CBO.

U.S. Government Accountability Office. 2010. *State and Local Governments' Fiscal Outlook: March 2010 Update*. GAO-10-358. Washington, DC: GAO.

U.S. Government Accountability Office. 2014. *State and Local Governments' Fiscal Outlook: 2014 Update*. GAO-15-224SP. Washington, DC: GAO.

U.S. Government Accountability Office. 2017. *Medicaid Demonstrations: Federal Action Needed to Improve Oversight of Spending*, GAO-17-3132, April. Washington, DC: GAO.

Walker, David B., Albert J. Richter, and Cynthia Cates Colella. 1982. "The First Ten Months: Grant-in-Aid, Regulatory, and Other Changes." *Intergovernmental Perspective* 8(1): 5–22.

Wright, Deil S. 1978. *Understanding Intergovernmental Relations Public Policy and Participants' Perspectives in Local, State, and National Governments*. North Scituate, MA: Duxbury Press.

Wright, Deil S. 1988. *Understanding Intergovernmental Relations*, 3rd edition. Pacific Grove, CA: Brooks/Cole Publishing.

Wright, Deil S., Carl W. Stenberg, Cho, Chung-Lae. 2009. "American Federalism, Intergovernmental Relations, and Intergovernmental Management." Foundations of Public Administration. Retrieved from www.aspanet.org/PUBLIC/ASPADocs/PAR/FPA/FPA-FEDIGR-Article.pdf (accessed April 23, 2015).

Zimmerman, Joseph F. 2010. *Congress: Facilitator of State Action*. Albany, NY: SUNY Press.

4 Why We Fight

Conflict and "Coping" in Twenty-First-Century Intergovernmental Relations

Brendan F. Burke and Jeffrey L. Brudney

In the 2010s we find ourselves in some of the most contentious political conditions that the United States has faced since the Civil War, combined with some of the largest government interventions since the ramp-up to World War II. War analogies are appropriate, as the conservative strategy of policy constraint, preferred in spirit if not tactic by about half of the American population, is pushed aggressively in Congress and in Republican state houses, while activist efforts favored by nearly half of the population are approved and implemented in a strategic, calculated fashion. Each succeeding generation of public policy participants hears that "the political situation is worse than ever."

Deil Wright pointed out that politics and power are not always as they would seem, or as conventional theories would indicate. Power and influence were a frequent theoretical study for Wright, especially through the American State Administrators Project (ASAP) (Dometrius et al. 2008). He devised three contrasting authority models to characterize intergovernmental relations. The first, Coordinate Authority, is institution-based, with a representation of the separate powers between nation and states, as reflected in the Tenth Amendment. Further, local governments are "creatures of the state" in keeping with Dillon's Rule (1868). A second version is offered in the Inclusive Authority model, wherein the nation is preeminent; it controls politics and policy at the state level, and local government is again subservient to the state. Third, and likely the most practically valid depiction, is the Overlapping Authority model; each of the national, state, and local levels of government have their own domains of authority, and in most cases, the authority is shared with other levels. This version is commonly at the center of current observation and analysis (Agranoff and Radin 2015), but in this chapter, we highlight an alternative perspective on "Inclusive" Authority. Although the nation has long-running periods of hegemony over the system, as seen within the ebb and flow of the "phases" of federalism (Wright 1988), the subnational levels can gain prominence depending on conditions. At this writing, because of internal disagreement and an increasing desire at the state level to adjudicate differences with the nation, "inclusion" within the higher level is inaccurate on several major policy issues. Wright used phrases like "tectonic shift" and "tsunami" in describing some systems changes during the late twentieth century. Commensurate with the force of those statements, it is as if gravity is nearly reversed, with active efforts to keep the nation's largest policy initiatives from falling to ground level.

This chapter analyzes the roots and impacts of the peculiar revision of the inclusive authority model. Contemporary characterizations are of a "fragmented" federalism (Pickerill and Bowling 2014); the forces here do indeed pull in opposing directions. During the Obama presidency, a conservative national legislature was unified in its opposition to almost any activist policy that the president proposed; the opposition took the form of vetoes and inaction, with especially low levels of legislative activity. A Congress that has been even less active than the 1940's "do-nothing" version was allied with a passionate adjudication-oriented opposition among Republican governors and their attorneys general. At the beginning of the Trump presidency, we see the potential for GOP-based dismantling of activist government policies and activities. Democratic governors and mayors are the font of resistance to national government retrenchment and reductions. So the approach to federalism that currently holds sway is akin to a "monkey wrench" in the "machinery" of the national engine.

Will this antagonistic approach to federalism last? History shows occasional equilibrium shifts and policy punctuations (Baumgartner and Jones 1993). The 2016 election serves as a punctuation of sorts, one with the potential to either solidify the antagonism or highlight the need for more collaboration in coming years. Current conditions arise from unclear and contradictory federalism philosophies, characterized as "Kaleidoscopic" elsewhere in this volume (see Chapter 2). Presidents George W. Bush and Barack Obama both pressed for several of the largest budgetary appropriations and reorganizations of American government in the nation's history. "Line in the Sand" Federalism, with only judicial resolution was in some ways a rational response to Presidential leadership that spawned the Department of Homeland Security; two simultaneous foreign wars; the Troubled Assets Relief Program; the American Reinvestment and Recovery Act; and the Patient Protection and Affordable Care Act, all within a single decade.

With the push and pull between a constricting conservative philosophy and a stream of activist political moves to "grow" complex government activity, local program managers and other participants have limited guidance from nation and state. At this level community-based public participants meet their greatest challenge, to work through literal and figurative government shutdowns while keeping an eye out for "shovel ready" opportunities. The variety of mechanisms to create change in public efforts has grown dramatically since the 1990s, leading to an increasingly unfamiliar but expanding and "interweaving" public administration (Kettl 2016).

This chapter considers the three levels of intergovernmental relations (rather than the levels of government), the contrasts among philosophy, pragmatic politics, and managerial engagement as related levels to understand the new complex functioning of our intergovernmental system. All three areas display upheavals in method and strategy. It is more than ever a crucial challenge for academics and practitioners to understand the new patterns.

In Wright's later life, he perceived a "tidal shift" in American public administration, building from the reforms of the 1990s (Brudney, Hebert, and Wright 1999; Brudney and Wright 2002; Burke, Cho and Wright 2008). Although intergovernmental relations in itself was not a reform wave, its interaction with reforms in budgeting, performance management, contracting, and organizational design do illuminate the field (Radin 2012). For that reason, our starting point for assessing the future of intergovernmental relations is the "reform decade," orienting the developments of the early twenty-first century. The chapter proceeds through five steps:

1   It briefly characterizes the contrasts between federalism, intergovernmental relations, and intergovernmental management highlighted by Wright and coauthors beginning in 1990.
2   It assesses the relatively coherent theme of federalism up to the 1990s, and then a turn away from any ordered pattern into the twenty-first century.
3   It builds off of the beginnings of the global reform focus and the outsourcing strategies that solidified in the 1990s, to characterize their current and possibly future political development in several policy areas.

4   With the growth in administrative complexity and possibility that emerged in the 1990s, we provide an assessment of administrative capacity for the middle twenty-first century.

5   With these interactive themes, we predict the health of the intergovernmental system moving into its future during a Trump presidency and beyond.

The Separate Lenses of Federalism, Intergovernmental Relations, and Intergovernmental Management

To understand the variegated dynamics of the intergovernmental system, Wright presented a three-tiered approach, not linked to the levels of government but grounded instead in dialogue and action among participants in different parts or ranks of the system. Although Wright did not introduce the terminology, he was instrumental in synthesizing the concepts into a platform for analysis and research (Wright, Stenberg, and Cho 2009, 2011).

At the highest level, federalism (FED) determines the rationale behind our decentralized system. Starting with the Framers and building through Wilson's (1887) expression of a responsive and high-performing structure, FED focuses on the nexus between political philosophy and highest political action. Presidents and Congress have been the initiators of a progressive movement over time to mesh new capacities and constraining challenges as they arise; the Supreme Court has a frequent mediating role, rendering a constitutional assessment on the growth or contraction of American national power. The states may have an opinion on the direction of FED, but this opinion is usually limited. Local governments, as "creatures of the state," are not represented specifically in the FED dialogue.

Within the broad FED philosophy lies the political interaction to create the intergovernmental system. Presidents propose legislation and budgets to carry out their Federalist vision; Congress, through committee engagement, designs more specific guidance parameters. This level of action, the intergovernmental relations (IGR) within the system, brings state politicians and administrators as well as local jurisdictions to the forefront, developing ideas that balance a national philosophy, the expressed intent of executives and legislatures, and localized need. Morton Grodzins characterized a layered and then fused intergovernmental system through the "layer-cake" and "marble-cake" metaphors, respectively; Wright (1988) envisioned a "picket-fence" nature to the system. Each picket ran through the national, state, and local levels via policy communities, where officials at all three levels worked through the particulars of issue debates. While Wright codified much of the IGR content within this field (ibid.), he consistently credited William Anderson with its initial specification (Wright et al. 2011).

Borrowing from Lipsky (1980), "Street-Level" action carries through on the statutory design adopted within the IGR system. Legislation turns into programmatic content, and as the complexity of localized problems, boundary-related and boundaryless interactions, potential service delivery agents, and ongoing fiscal constraint to respond to local conditions converge, intergovernmental administration becomes key. The local engagement and implementation of IGR system particulars occurs through intergovernmental management (IGM). Not only are the national, state, and local levels represented, but the private and non-profit sectors are active delivery agents. As jurisdiction boundaries are crossed, so too are the legal authorizations of single governments, giving rise to multiple-party contractual and bylaw arrangements. The IGM term was molded in a symposium within *Public Administration Review* in 1975, but early development of the term arose from Agranoff and Lindsay (1983), Derthick (1987), Wise (1990), and others.

Wright developed the three-fold discussion of FED, IGR, and IGM with his peers during the 1980s, leading to three definitional articles in the 1990s (Wright 1990; Krane and Wright 1997; Wright and Krane 1998). The three dimensions provide order to the field, as well as a base for important contrasts in IGR writ large. We treat the FED, IGR, and IGM dimensions or dynamics in turn. FED has become extremely contentious in the past few years (Bowling and Pickerill 2014). We posit that antagonism within the FED dialogue, both before and since the 2016 election, is a reaction to expansionist and unconventional trends in IGR. With less order in the systems "above" administrators, IGM has become a font of creativity and innovative responsiveness. The 1990s are an appropriate period in which to assess the development of the current tug-of-war between a FED fraught with energetic attempts at limitation of national power, offset with multi-faceted and multi-responsive IGR.

Federalism's Current Phase: Contingent and Contentious

Over his career, Wright developed a summative history of FED with representation through important phases. Starting in the 1930s with the New Deal, the phases built out of the "dual federalism" characterization to match broad historical trends and events, matched with the political philosophies of Presidents and potentially Congresses of a given era. While unequal in length and overlapping in foci, the phases provide a reasonably intuitive vision of the American nation-state dynamic over time.[1] Until the 1990s. Phases that summarized the general expansion of national power until the 1960s (cooperative, concentrated, and creative) tended to give way over the next decades to a lessening of national authority and resource deployment (competitive, calculative, and contractive). At the time of the 1994 mid-term elections, FED involved a solid philosophical discourse around the expansion of state powers, combined with sophisticated political engagement between a pragmatic Democratic president and, for a period, a quite disciplined Republican Congress.

"Devolution" is among the global reforms that swept many Western nations by the 1990s (Kettl 2005). Different countries pursued a decentralization of power or a refocus of local powers in myriad ways. President Bill Clinton was elected as a Washington outsider and intended to join the decentralization movement through the National Performance Review, even as he simultaneously pushed for a national health care reform. The 104th Congress solidified the dialogue to press powers back to the states, most successfully through its welfare reform legislation and to a lesser degree, the Unfunded Mandate Reform Act. National power, not necessarily on the wane, was at least checked in and around 1995. Both the Democratic President and the Republican Congress could claim victory as they worked toward shared interests to streamline a large and convoluted welfare system and facilitate innovative responses among the states to tailor responses to their localized circumstances (Cammisa 1998). Devolution occurred over a short period in a decade otherwise fraught with contradictions; witness President Clinton's successful promise to provide national funding for 100,000 local police officers, contrasted with the insertion of enhanced citizen participation in the spending plans for the Intermodal Surface Transportation Efficiency Act (ISTEA). Such programmatic moves earned a musing from Wright that this period was the ever-changing "Kaleidoscopic" phase (Shafritz 1997; Chapter 2, this volume). But an even more contradictory period was to come.

The second President Bush provided widely divergent policy initiatives, running the spectrum from an emphasis on state powers to dramatic expansion of national capacity and control. The

Department of Homeland Security and the Patriot Act centralized national authority on a relative newcomer to the policy agenda (the "War on Terrorism"); deregulation within economic (for example, banking and home loans) and environmental (for example, "Negotiated Regulation") policy were overriding themes during the middle years of his presidency; but as the economy turned at the end of his tenure, a huge national stimulus swung the pendulum back toward national influence with the $700 billion authorization to the Troubled Assets Relief Program. Wright (2003) described this FED phase as "Contingent Collaboration," while Conlan (2006) used the term "Opportunistic."

The 2010s revived a conflict between a President's view of federalism and the direction that Congress sought to pursue. But the dynamics have been more polarized, and thus far we have no indication of reconciliation of party differences that occurred at the peak of the 1990s devolution movement. The current inconsistent and potentially self-interested nature of the politics of federalism also describe the new trend in intergovernmental jurisprudence wherein a large number of states bring suit against the national government. In *Utility Air Group v. EPA* (2014), 14 states failed in a suit against the national regulatory agency for treating carbon dioxide as a pollutant. The Court found that the Environmental Protection Agency could treat greenhouse gases under the scope of regulation of other pollutants from large utility-based sources. Twenty-eight states sued against the national government's efforts to create a national health care policy shortly after the passage of the Patient Protection and Affordable Care Act of 2010 (ACA). In *National Federation of Independent Business v. Sebelius* (2012), the plaintiff states lost on their central Commerce Clause challenge, wherein they contended that the national government cannot force individuals to purchase insurance, but they won a split decision regarding revisions to Medicaid policy (Rosenbaum 2013). The legislation was built on significant decentralizing features, including the intention for states to form their own health care exchanges. This intent became a subsequent focus for a constitutional challenge in *King v. Burwell* (2015), whereby four Virginia residents highlighted the omission of specific authority for the national government to support the ACA through tax breaks. This challenge was overturned, as the Court protected the broad incentive for all Americans to purchase health insurance. This pattern continued in the lawsuit initiated by 17 states against President Obama's Deferred Action for Parents of Americans and Lawful Permanent Residents (DAPA), his administrative actions to revise immigration policy, passed by executive order.

The battleground shifted with the 2016 election, as President Trump removed the need for conservative states to challenge executive authority on health care, climate change, and immigration issues. But current political alignments fare no better at providing consensus-based solutions to these and other policy problems. Currently, it is the more liberal cities and states that sue national policy to defend "sanctuary" protections for immigrants, the rollback of the recently enacted Clean Power Plan, and other Presidential actions that potentially specify President Trump's federalism philosophy.

State challenges against national initiatives are not new. Witness the opposition toward various civil rights actions in the U.S. Senate and in state houses during the 1960s. But in previous instances, the Supreme Court was not so frequently involved, nor were the challenges brought across such a wide range of policy issues. The depth of the state-national conflict is evident in the widespread rejection of national funding incentives for health care. Thirty-six states opted out of creating their own health insurance exchanges under the ACA despite significant grant resources to do so. The reasons for opting out, thus placing the burden back on the national government, vary. Current state avoidance of implementation parallels state antagonism toward the Affordable

Care Act at the time of its passage. A number of Republican governors earlier denied receipt of the stimulus money that Congress would have provided them through the American Recovery and Reinvestment Act. Fiscal federalism conflicts play out in a more conventional way at the time of writing, possibly even with the formation of a bipartisan alliance among governors to protect against major national funding cuts.

Wright's "inclusive authority" model may not be permanently invalidated, but with the strong assertion of power among the states against the President's major initiatives, it continues to reside in "contemporary obsolescence" (Wright et al. 2011). That phrasing arose with regard to the historical or traditional study of intergovernmental relations, but the practice of IGR has become more vibrant as a result of initiatives that arose out of the "reform decade." Excitement for those who appreciate innovation and activist government is the offset to the conflict-based approach toward government activism described above. In the next section, we elaborate the innovations that likely prompted the broad backlash toward a wide range of national activist policy.

Intergovernmental Expansion: Crossing Sectoral and Jurisdictional Boundaries

The "global public management revolution" (Kettl 2005) may not have rendered the term Intergovernmental Relations obsolete, but it is currently far less adequate to capture contemporary systems of public administrative interaction. The 1990s reform wave came about as a response to increased citizen or "customer" demands of government; advancements in technological solutions to governmental problems; increased capacity of knowledge workers to meet service needs; emulation of "best practices" from comparable jurisdictions; and the advancement world wide of acceptability of business models and strategies in governmental service delivery (Borins 1995). The reforms planted the seeds for transformation of national–state–local interaction in many ways. Two major revisions to American IGR are singled out here as their strategies are just approaching their full potential. First, many jurisdictional borders, including national ones, have been rendered far less significant in policy and administrative contexts. Second, the private, non-profit, and government sectors are far more intricately intertwined. When "boundarylessness" (Kettl 2006) and "governance" across sectors is combined with the potential for fast-paced programmatic effort, political tensions mount. As we explore below, these reform themes create both opportunities and challenges.

New public management highlighted the boundaryless nature of public administration, in that new models could come from unexpected foreign jurisdictions (like New Zealand) and policy problems increasingly ignored territorial boundaries (Kettl 2005, 2006). Prior to the "reform decade," Wright described limited examples of boundarylessness, such as the common practice of US states to engage in diplomacy abroad on behalf of their own economic development. This state- or city-to-nation diplomacy is comparatively commonplace now. For example, American subnational governments signed on to the Convention on the Elimination of All Forms of Violence Against Women and the Kyoto Protocol when the national government balked at endorsement (Cigler 2012). Administrative approaches for interaction among Mexican, American, and Canadian governments at all levels address a number of large-scale policy problems. Immigration and drug trafficking concerns along the US-Mexico border have led to a variety of inter-state, inter-local, and nation-to-state cooperative agreements that mesh American and Mexican governmental programs (Covarrubias 2012).

Privatization arose as a government strategy abroad, and came into American policy debates during the Reagan administration (Savas 1982). Contracting in American government dates as far back as the American Revolution (Radin 2012), but would grow steadily through the 1990s and into the 2000s through public-private partnerships; government contracts with non-profit human service, arts, education, and other service-providing agencies; and collaborative service delivery agreements across governmental units. By 2004, over 75 percent of state government agencies entered into some form of cross-sectoral contracting (Choi et al. 2005).

Cross-national and contracting themes unite in the case of the North American greenhouse gas (GHG) reduction initiatives, and illuminate the potential and challenges of contemporary IGR. Around the time of the national failure to endorse the Kyoto Protocol to establish worldwide limits to GHG production, a number of American states moved into an activist stance to respond (Rabe 2004). Upon the platform of single-unit responses, ten northeastern states devised a cross-border compact to pool their capacity to reduce emissions. Building on previous American state and Canadian provincial collaboration to address acid rain, the Regional Greenhouse Gas Initiative (RGGI, or "Reggie") established cap-and-trade policy, whereby participating jurisdictions would auction credits to reduce power plant emissions. This action has created strong incentives for emissions reductions that led to a host of conservation solutions. Proceeds from the auctions have been pooled so that the participating governments can offer tax breaks and incentive grants for energy efficiency. Private and non-profit contractors are networked to implement renewable energy options across communities through the RGGI compact.

Two other climate compacts have met with less success. The Western Climate Initiative brought together seven Western states and four Canadian provinces to prepare a cap-and-trade model, but ultimately it would shrink down to two participating governments, California and Quebec.[2] A Midwestern compact among states and provinces held initial planning meetings but disbanded following electoral losses among the governors who were its strongest advocates in 2010 (Rabe 2015). These state and cross-national networks had fluid participation between 2007 and 2017, but their participants did gain some of the impetus for change within their individual jurisdictions. Ontario, an observer of the Western Climate Initiative, has eliminated coal fired power generation from its energy portfolio. Massachusetts, one of the founding RGGI partners, will achieve this status in 2017. Cities around the World show potential to devise and share climate change solutions through networks such as the C40 Cities and the International Council for Local Environmental Initiatives (ICLEI) (Barber 2013). These networks of cities have simpler formal structure, serving only to share ideas rather than collaborate on resource management like RGGI. In the current IGR environment, national borders may be no more constraining than borders within a federation. For example, a leading energy executive claims that it is no more difficult to negotiate transfer of electric power between Quebec and Massachusetts than between Quebec and Ontario (Vandal 2015).

The new public management techniques, such as public-private arrangements, did not arise through an intentional design, but have spread as a tidal shift across American governments. This phenomenon may be part of what led to the state-level resistance to sweeping national initiatives with major contracted elements. The scope of public-private involvement and interaction has grown in the past ten years through legislation that alters the American economy, such as the American Recovery and Reinvestment Act (ARRA) and the Affordable Care Act (ACA). Both of these have complex cross-sectoral components. While the system of FED is seen as "fractious" and "fragmented" (Bowling and Pickerill 2014), the conservative response should be fully expected in the face of such unconventional and innovative growth in the IGR system. Among the important current characteristics of these major legislative acts has been the speed of their execution. One of the most important criteria for new stimulus projects was their potential for quick economic impact. A "shovel-ready" project, funded through ARRA, could create jobs quickly, but potentially at the cost of more important, well-developed projects that languished earlier in the design process.

The stimulus money produced many quiet successes, as well as highly publicized failures. North of Boston, an innovative bridge replacement project was carried out in record time. The "Fast 14" plan was executed over ten weekends, to replace 14 aging bridges along Interstate 93. Normally, this project would have taken four years, but with new modular technology and experimentation with traffic patterns, the project is an enduring example of a highly-needed transportation project, executed on time and under budget—but with limited publicity. By contrast, a similar phrase, "fast and furious," is associated with a failed use of $40 million of stimulus money to create a "sting" operation against gun runners along the Mexican border. The latter project received much more national press, and underlies some of the turn against far-reaching and complex IGR undertakings. Ironically, perhaps the only way that "Fast 14" would have made major news and endured in our memory is if it had led to disruptions and traffic delays.

Wright has catalogued the history of IGR, both through case studies of political-administrative interaction and by collating the academic analysis underlying the field (Wright, Stenberg, and Cho 2009). He observed that, starting in the 1940s, this field demonstrated the difficulty or even futility of separating politics from administration. When considering the recent history of FED and IGR, it is natural that localized community needs may diverge from the intentions of political masters at the state or national level. But responsiveness to a broader public good is the first principle for local civil servants (Wilson 1887). With less concrete guidance for policy response from conservative political forces, but more innovative methods to pursue policy ideas, how might public administration adjust to remain accountable to political communities and effective in addressing the needs of local stakeholders?

How We Collaborate: "Coping" in the Twenty-First Century

When Wright published the last edition of his classic text, *Understanding Intergovernmental Relations* (1988), the term *intergovernmental management* (IGM) was only introduced in the concluding remarks. But the project to highlight its distinction from FED and IGR was well under way. His own coverage of IGM would remain as an overview, with other scholars to develop the details (McGuire 2006; O'Leary 2009; Koliba 2012; Agranoff 2012). This assessment does not differentiate IGM from the more common and contemporary terms of network models and collaborative public management (CPM) (Agranoff and McGuire 2003; O'Leary and Vij 2012; Emerson and Nabatchi 2015).

Wright's IGR coverage laid the foundation for IGM's practical and pragmatic focus. The "picket fence" metaphor describes policy networks across levels of government, on specialized issues. For example, transportation officials at the national, state, and local levels collaborate within their "picket," exchanging ideas, plans, resources, and assessments through a variety of associations like the American Association of State Highway and Transportation Officials (AASHTO) and the Transportation Research Board (TRB). Many contract agents are included in the transportation picket's activities. The overlapping authority model is amenable to current IGM/CPM systems, aligning ad hoc pairings, triumvirates, or even larger numbers of participants. The diagram is sufficiently complicated with just national, state, and local actors, but the complexity of cross-sectoral networks is commonplace (Agranoff and Radin 2015).

This chapter has suggested that the current antagonistic nature of FED is an outgrowth of fast-paced, expansive developments in IGR. No causal link is assumed between the dynamics at the "top" of the FED/IGR system and the current rich field of IGM/CPM. Innovative approaches to day-to-day management would likely have arisen regardless of the political environment in the national and state capitals. In fact, many of the components of CPM emerged during the "reform decade," a period that at least began with more amenable political alignments between Congress and the White House than we witness in the 2010s. While networks have existed in American government or governance for decades, rich cases in local environmental and economic develop-ment policy (Agranoff and McGuire 2003), emergency management (Moynihan 2005; Brudney and Gazley 2009), community health programming (Burke 2014), and other areas have illumi-nated the possibilities of non-hierarchical, shared authority on boundaryless problems. Removed from Washington politics, many of these local solutions arise with facilitation from a national grant program or constraint from a regulatory instrument.

At the time of writing, one of the most salient examples of network management is seen in the response to opioid addiction and abuse. The dimensions of the fight to regulate and respond to opiates are intergovernmental, but also networked and collaborative. For starters, the opioid crisis is affecting regions and the American states differently. This is still a small problem in some states, but has reached tragic proportions in Ohio, West Virginia, Massachusetts, and New Hampshire (Kaiser Family Foundation 2017). It may in time affect the entire nation uniformly, but it began within regions. It is an eminently cross-sectoral dilemma, as it started with overprescription of opioid-based pharmaceuticals in some areas. So the problem arose in conjunction between the drug industry and doctors, who in some cases received incentives to prescribe certain opioids. A high level of addiction led to adverse economic impacts, crime, and increased deaths from overdoses.

But this proves to be a problem that falls outside of traditional intergovernmental relations in its response. Is this a business ethics problem? Public health? Public safety, or something else? It is another example of a "wicked problem." No one government agency, or level for that matter, con-trols the response; police departments, hospital emergency rooms, Medicaid administration, public and private addiction treatment agencies, pharmaceutical companies, and many others have a hand in the treatment of this epidemic. Innovations arise, such as from police chiefs who move the issue from crime and prosecution to social work and rehabilitation. Naloxone, or "Narcan," the treatment for overdose, moves from hospitals to common access, if it is made affordable (by both the producers and insurance companies). The dimensionality of responding to this problem is still unfolding. But with the rise in addicts and overdose deaths, the response is urgent for affected communities.

What does all of this mean for the future direction of IGR and IGM? In the massive overhaul to health care proposed by the Republicans in early 2017, there are daunting statistics, such as, 20 million or more Americans will lose their health insurance under the proposals, putting six percent of our population at a much higher risk of bankruptcy in addition to poorer treatment of health care issues. But focusing more tightly—national government support for the opioid crisis is endangered under most Republican proposals for health reform, just as the issue is spreading across the country.

To coin Tip O'Neill's phrase that "all politics are local," most collaborative networks are as well. The opioid crisis is especially a community problem; proactive communities will respond, or "cope," regardless of the shortsightedness of Republican-led health care reform. Democrats and Republicans will band together, find shared ground, and innovate their way through the opioid crisis in coming years. Networks overcome professional, political, and other surmountable differences.

Among the current projects in the IGM/CPM realm is the expansion of the short list of coping and negotiation-related skills that Wright initiated in 1990. Koliba (2012: 76–84) has developed a list of "coordinating strategies," including oversight; resource provision; negotiation and bargaining; facilitation; boundary spanning/brokering; and systems thinking. Agranoff (2012: 66–67) identifies activities underlying a network process: Activation; framing; synthesizing; and mobilization. Koliba and Agranoff agree that ties to bureaucratic activity exist within networks, but that the methods of bureaucratic functioning are inadequate in this new environment. Gulick's POSDCORB is dismissed or converted briefly in the description of network strategy, but little is made of the transition from orthodox public administration to the dynamics of twenty-first-century administrative effort. They are worth elaboration here, as we offer a sense of the contemporary topics that might enrich training on IGM/CPM functions.

Planning

Public administration effort strives for a rational ideal plan, but "satisficing," working within resource, knowledge, and feasibility constraints, is necessary for authentic program implementation. IGR has consistently featured a range between high-minded and sophisticated national planning effort and local pragmatism (Wright 1988). Large policy efforts are hamstrung in their planning process if they involve "wicked problems." Here, rational discourse is limited by the difficulty of narrowly defining a problem, overcoming ethical debates, treating the newness of this type of problem, and avoiding unintended consequences that result from policy intervention (Rittel and Webber 1973; Horiuchi 2008). "Wicked" problems have complicated boundaries that point them toward two possible solutions—either the given executive or agency will attempt to tame a small portion of the problem within their jurisdiction and formal authority, or a wider, cross-disciplinary and cross-jurisdictional coalition can form, deliberate, and move toward broader solutions (Burns 2000). Agranoff's (2012) description of the learning process within networks is appropriate to gain leverage on wicked problems.

Organizing

Top-down bureaucracies appear irrelevant to the multiple-actor and cross-sectoral nature of networks; but "many hands" has been a complication of intergovernmental project implementation as well (Pressman and Wildavsky 1973). When mapping out networks and their interactions, the appearance is quite distinct from a traditional organization chart, but within the network reside many bureaucratic processes and techniques. Both intergovernmental settings and networks use contracts, grants, loans and guarantees, bylaws, insurance provisions, tax expenditures, vouchers, regulations, and other interactive instruments (Agranoff 2012). The more formal the network, the more complex will be the crafting and negotiation among participants for these varied tools.

Avoidance of excessive complexity in the design stages may be possible through an assessment of the needs and goals of the network. Networks may operate with limited goals; they may form simply to share a dialogue to educate members of various groups. They may have an advocacy agenda, such as the pooling of participants to increase lobbying effectiveness. Their combined talents may provide the spark to seek outside resources or to recruit further expertise. Or, the collaboration may be the basis for a new service. Different levels of organizational energy, commitment, and formality may be needed for contrasting types of collaborative network (Agranoff and McGuire 2003). While IGR relied on solid understanding of different governmental processes, procedures, and alignments, IGM/CPM also necessitates a clear understanding of non-profit organizations, and in coming years, of hybrid private corporations that contain both a for-profit arm and a non-profit component devoted to corporate social responsibility (CSR). How does a town government collaborate with Nike's desire to provide community recreation resources through its CSR efforts, or with the Wal-Mart Foundation? Through diversification of the traditional intergovernmental tools mentioned above.

Staffing

The history of IGR ties closely to the growth of the civil service at all levels, with much of the state and local growth funded through a variety of grants. This pattern changed during Wright's Contractive phase in the 1980s, as "fend-for-yourself federalism" required state and local governments to calculate their abilities to support staff with reduced intergovernmental revenues. The era of IGM/CPM has no such luxury; the basic assumption and even a prompt for networks is the lack of staff growth to handle new and revised public obligations. Koliba (2012) lays a framework for the allocation of resources to networks, with human resources being just one of many of these resources (for example, political, financial, etc.).

A paradigm shift in human resource approaches is important to function in IGM/CPM settings. Network participation begins with either volunteering time, or possibly having some labor "bought out" through a private or intergovernmental funding source. Network participants move in and out of their employing organizations, as their will and availability changes. In contrast to position design, classification, and compensation issues central in civil service systems, network "staffing" may involve the development aspects of the human resource field to a greater degree. Training and competency in team participation, with focuses on interpersonal skills, negotiation, and stable relationships can enhance network productivity. Comfort with diversity, competing views, and the perspectives of different sectors is a growing focus of public service education related to workforce development (Robinson 2011).

Directing/Leadership

Traditional leadership is outmoded in IGM/CPM. Expertise on the subject matter of the day is helpful, as are rewards to dispense, but command-and-control of the process is likely to fail within IGM settings. Whitaker et al. (2004) described the need to develop mutual benefits in IGM relationships, as each party can learn from the other about bridging gaps in ability among participants. Interdependence rather than contingent leadership approaches keeps interests focused on shared outcomes, rather than "zero-sum" exchanges (Kickert, Klijn, and Koopenjan 1997). Heifetz (1994) describes contemporary leadership challenges as "adaptive," where leaders are not only experts but also facilitators of a participatory process. Followers will need to contribute to the solution of their shared problem; they may be a part of defining the shared problem. This flexible, empathetic approach to participation in network leadership is far removed from the competitive "games" played among participants in IGR (Wright 1988). Negotiation and bargaining were among the core skills identified by Wright (1990); techniques that focus on shared interests facilitate the voluntary participation and development of mutual solutions to network problems (Fisher and Ury 1991).

Coordination

Alignment of varied participants has been an historic focus of public administration and IGR, but frequently with an emphasis on the reconciliation of competing interests. Networks arise out of shared interests and cooperative effort. Network participants contribute value to shared projects based on their "conductivity" (Agranoff 2012), their ability to perceive their own contribution to other organizations as well as their fellow participants' added value to new goals and objectives. Conductivity tends to be a self-sustaining quality; the more practice an organization gains at aligning with partner agencies, the easier and more natural the desired relationships become. Organizational learning is a shared characteristic of all networks. Participants expand problem definitions and learn interdisciplinary approaches to develop responses. The search for innovative linkages between agencies is enhanced through practice across multiple networks. Agranoff (2012) and Koliba (2012) both describe the "boundary-spanner" as the individual public or non-profit manager who see the possibilities across disparate agencies and initiates collaborative agreements to unite partners.

Reporting

In networks a higher mutual commitment to IGM/CPM relationships obtains, involving collaboration toward a public interest rather than cooperation between jurisdictional representatives to gain a divided program-based advantage (McGuire 2006). Collaborative management relationships will be formalized over time, but at first participants sit at the table to work out cross-functional problems. Bylaws and contractual arrangements may specify performance expectations, but accountability across groups to shared measures is a daunting challenge. The development of shared performance measures may emanate from a single professional association or coordinating agency; for example, in emergency management, guides like the National Response Framework orient performance expectations (McGuire, Brudney, and Gazley 2011).

Budgeting

In IGM/CPM settings, the federal budget process may be losing its prominence, especially as funding sources decline. However, major new national initiatives like ARRA and ACA revive the need to understand the national appropriations process. Nongovernmental network participants add new layers of financial complexity; nonprofits increasingly function on fee revenues, and the world of foundations and philanthropy provide new revenue possibilities. The non-profit sector grew throughout the first decade of the twenty-first century, then contracted into a smaller group with more effective business sense (Salamon 2007). Financial management training in public administration needs to grow to cover governmental, private, and non-profit approaches since the public network involves all of these cross-sectoral participants. Robinson (2011) suggests a reinvigoration of business training skills within public affairs programs, since the careers of many future graduates will likely cross sectoral boundaries.

Public administration and its subfields are adjusting to a changing operating environment and to the creation of a range of new innovative tools and approaches. The transition from hierarchical bureaucracy to a new order is irregular across the United States, as befitting a federal system with varied local capacity and responsiveness to policy and programmatic needs. The regions of the country with the least responsive public bureaucracies are the ones where the non-profit sector has developed the most—out of need to respond to public problems and demands. And as the dissonance in politics at the national level and in many states impedes governmental action to some degree, the need for networks to respond through their willing collaborators arises, with varied degrees of urgency depending on local politics and political culture. The lesson plan to bring about a highly effective IGM/CPM system will evolve into new practices and philosophies across America's communities at an uneven rate. The implication of an irregular engagement of network management is discussed below.

Conclusion: Relevance of IGR?

This chapter has described a contrast or contradiction between the broad political theme of FED and the engagement of American IGR to create policy and programming for the citizens of its states and localities. If there is a prevailing political philosophy of governance in our federal system, a near-majority would prefer that it center on constraint of an overgrown system; but even within our system of checks and balances numerous examples of large-scale and high-impact policy activism emerge in recent years to respond to major economic, social, and international challenges. Congress's approach, to dramatically reduce its output and endorsement of intergovernmental initiatives, might be seen as a natural offset to the first two presidents of the twenty-first century, who dramatically increased the scope of their system interventions. Now, with alignment between conservative executive and legislative leadership, there may be intent to shrink the size of government, but the goal will be difficult to achieve (Kettl 2016). Through the confusing fragmentation of guidance from Washington DC, community needs still arise, and local administrators still respond.

In the face of networks approaches, Wright et al. (2011) speculated that IGR had become obsolete. But the theories, lessons, and metaphors collected in *Understanding Intergovernmental Relations* do maintain their relevance, with some adjustment (Burke 2014). And, as we contend in this chapter, the contemporary workings of the intergovernmental system are made clearer through consideration of the FED and IGR dimensions. Although our system reveals tensions, change occurs in the long run, and new patterns emerge. The FED conversation has been active in the past decade (Wright et al. 2009), as practical scholars discussed the appropriateness of the direction of national legislation, rulemaking, and other policy guidance to subnational participants. The dialog became very shallow up to and following the 2016 election, but the issues are too impactful to dismiss through pithy and underdeveloped policy solutions for long. We may be well served to revisit the classic criteria that were considered by the Framers of our federal system. We admire the American federal system for its balance of national and state powers, as a significant subnational level promoted responsiveness to local need, allowed for local political differences, enhanced local accountability, enabled experimentation in the "laboratories of democracy," and created a division of labor across different levels of government. A strong national component could reduce conflict between states, establish stability of some programs and policies, and create equity for all citizens. As our system allows myriad state challenges to national policies, and the national response is weak, the last two advantages are in serious jeopardy.

When a majority of states refused grant incentives to establish their own health care exchanges, and most of these states supported the court challenges to invalidate the ACA, a double standard for American citizens resulted. Those states that supported the legislation and acted to implement it provided a clearer path for their residents to health insurance. National legislation to stabilize the opportunity to purchase health care, subsidized if necessary, may prove to be more desirable than conservative critics expected, but prospects for equal protection of Americans with regard to this support are limited following the 2016 election. Health care is only the most prominent example of disparity in social services across American states.

While advancements in collaborative capacity are encouraging, inconsistent local implementation of progressive, adaptive solutions will likely create even greater inequality. Bishop (2007) demonstrates that not only are there "red" conservative and "blue" activist states, but that the breakdown is at the community level, so that the prevailing value set can create stable and enduring differences between communities and their priorities. Networks arise not based on mandates or state orders, but on the creativity of local participants. In a case of "success to the successful," some national and state agencies now incorporate incentives within grant programs to reward those governments that develop applications across jurisdictional boundaries. These incentives are advantageous for the citizens of the winners but create an increasing void in local capacity for those that either are unable or unwilling to fill needs because of boundedness in their resources and collaborative attitudes and abilities.

Wright was optimistic about the potential contributions of intergovernmental actors, especially the cross-sectoral participants at the street level. And among those, the most potential for success lies in the actors who keep an open mind with regard to advancements in IGM/CPM. While network participants juggle the complexity of cross-sectoral involvement in response to difficult, even "wicked" problems, they may keep watch out of the corner of their eye for changes from Washington. Eventually, the warring sides may reduce their will to fight.

Notes

1   While the phases illuminate general trends and highlight possible shifts over time, Kincaid determines in Chapter 3 of this volume that the phases are limited in their utility because of their lack of specification. They do provide a starting point for clarifying the overall historical direction of the intergovernmental system.
2   This is a quirky geographic configuration, considering Quebec's decidedly Eastern location. On the other hand, the California-Quebec partnership highlights the pragmatic nature of boundaryless networks in the 2010s.

References

Agranoff, Robert. 2012. *Collaborating to Manage: A Primer for the Public Sector*. Washington, DC: Georgetown University Press.

Agranoff, Robert, and Valerie A. Lindsay. 1983. "Intergovernmental management: Perspectives from human services problem solving at the local level." *Public Administration Review* 43(May/June): 227–237.

Agranoff, Robert, and Michael McGuire. 2003. *Collaborative Public Management: New Strategies for Local Governments*. Washington, DC: Georgetown University Press.

Agranoff, Robert, and Beryl A. Radin. 2015. "Deil Wright's overlapping model of intergovernmental relations: The basis for contemporary intergovernmental relationships." *Publius: The Journal of Federalism* 45(Winter): 139–159.

Barber, Benjamin R. 2013. *If Mayors Rule the World: Dysfunctional Nations, Rising Cities*. New Haven, CT: Yale University Press.

Baumgartner, Frank, and Bryan D. Jones. 1993. *Agendas and Instability in American Politics*. Chicago, IL: University of Chicago Press.

Bishop, Bill. 2007. *The Big Sort: Why the Clustering of Like-Minded America is Tearing Us Apart*. New York: Houghton Mifflin.

Borins, Sandford. 1995. "The New Public Management is here to stay." *Canadian Public Administration* 38(Spring): 122–133.

Bowling, Cynthia J., and J. Mitchell Pickerill. 2014. "Polarized parties, politics, and policies: Fragmented federalism in 2013-2014." *Publius: The Journal of Federalism* 44(Spring): 369–398.

Brudney, Jeffrey L., and Beth Gazley. 2009. "Planning to be prepared: An empirical examination of the role of voluntary organizations in county government emergency planning." *Public Performance and Management Review* 32(Fall): 372–399.

Brudney, Jeffrey L., and Deil S. Wright. 2002. "Revisiting administrative reform in the American states: The status of reinventing government during the 1990s." *Public Administration Review* 62(May/June): 353–361.

Brudney, Jeffrey L., F. Ted Hebert, and Deil S. Wright. 1999. "Reinventing government in the American states: Measuring and explaining administrative reform." *Public Administration Review* 59(January/February): 19–30.

Burke, Brendan F. 2014. "Understanding intergovernmental relations, twenty-five years hence." *State and Local Government Review* 46(Spring): 63–76.

Burke, Brendan F., Chung-lae Cho, and Deil S. Wright. 2008. "Continuity and change in executive leadership: Insights from the perspectives of state agency administrators." Special Issue *Public Administration Review* 68: 29–37.

Cammisa, Anne Marie. 1998. *From Rhetoric to Reform? Welfare Policy in American Politics*. Boulder, CO: Westview Press.

Choi, Yoo-sung, Chung-lae Cho, Deil S. Wright, and Jeffrey L. Brudney. 2005. "Dimensions of contracting for service delivery by American state administrative agencies: Exploring linkages between intergovernmental relations and intersectoral administration." *Public Performance and Management Review* 29(September): 46–66.

Cigler, Beverly A. 2012. "International intergovernmental relations and impacts on American federalism." In *Networked Governance: The Future of Intergovernmental Management*, Jack W. Meek and Kurt Thurmaier, eds. Thousand Oaks, CA: CQ Press.

Conlan, Tim. 2006. "From cooperative to opportunistic federalism: Reflections on the half-century anniversary of the Commission on Intergovernmental Relations." *Public Administration Review* 66 (September/October): 663–676.

Covarrubias, Mauricio. 2012. "The challenges of interdependence and coordination in the bilateral agenda: Mexico and the United States." In *Networked Governance: The Future of Intergovernmental Management*, Jack W. Meek and Kurt Thurmaier, eds. Thousand Oaks, CA: CQ Press.

Derthick, Martha. 1987. "American federalism: Madison's middle ground in the 1980s." *Public Administration Review* 47(January/February): 66–74.

Dometrius, Nelson, Deil S. Wright, and Brendan Burke. 2008. "Strategies for measuring influence over state agencies." *State Politics and Policy Quarterly* 8(Spring): 88–100.

Emerson, Kirk, and Tina Nabatchi. 2015. *Collaborative Governance Regimes*. Washington DC: Georgetown University Press.

Fisher, Roger, and William Ury. 1991. *Getting to Yes: Negotiating Agreement without Giving In*. New York: Penguin Books.

Heifetz, Ronald A. 1994. *Leadership without Easy Answers*. Cambridge, MA: Harvard University Press.

Horiuchi, Catherine. 2007. "One policy makes no difference?" *Administrative Theory and Praxis*. 29 (September): 432–449.

Kaiser Family Foundation. 2017. "State health facts." Retrieved from http://www.kff.org/statedata (accessed August 19, 2017).

Kettl, Donald F. 2005. *The Global Public Management Revolution*, 2nd edition. Washington, DC: Brookings Institution.

Kettl, Donald F. 2006. "Managing boundaries in American administration: The collaboration imperative." Special Issue. *Public Administration Review* 66(December): 10–19.

Kettl, Donald F. 2016. *Escaping Jurassic Government: How to Recover America's Lost Commitment to Competence*. Washington, DC: Brookings Institution Press.

Kickert, Walter J.M., Erik-Hans Klijn, and Joop F. M. Koppenjan. 1997. *Managing Complex Networks*. London: Sage Publications.

Koliba, Christopher. 2012. "Administrative strategies for a networked world: Intergovernmental relations in 2020." In *Networked Governance: The Future of Intergovernmental Management*, Jack W. Meek and Kurt Thurmaier, eds. Thousand Oaks, CA: CQ Press.

Krane, Dale, and Deil S. Wright. 1997. "Intergovernmental management." In *The International Encyclopedia of Policy and Administration*, Jay M. Shafritz, ed. Boulder, CO: Westview Press.

Lipsky, Michael. 1980. *Street-Level Bureaucracy: Dilemmas of the Individual in Public Services*. New York: Russell Sage Foundation.

McGuire, Michael. 2006. "Collaborative public management: Assessing what we know and how we know it." *Public Administration Review* 66(December): 33–43.

McGuire, Michael, Jeffrey L. Brudney, and Beth Gazley. "The 'new emergency management': Applying lessons of collaborative governance to twenty-first century emergency planning." In *The Future of Public Administration around the World: The Minnowbrook Perspective*. Rosemary O'Leary, David Slyke, and Soonhee Kim, eds. Washington, DC: Georgetown University Press.

Moynihan, Donald P. 2005. *Leveraging Collaborative Networks in Infrequent Emergency Situations*. Washington, DC: IBM Center for the Business of Government.

O'Leary, Rosemary. 2009. *The Collaborative Public Manager*. Washington, DC: Georgetown University Press.

O'Leary, Rosemary, and Nidhi Vij. 2012. "Collaborative public management: Where have we been and where are we going?" *American Review of Public Administration* 42(September): 507–522.

Pickerill, J. Mitchell, and Cynthia J. Bowling. 2014. Fragmented federalism: The state of American federalism 2012-2013. *Publius: The Journal of Federalism* 43(Summer): 315–346.

Pressman, Jeffrey L., and Aaron B. Wildavsky. 1973. *Implementation: How Great Expectations in Washington are Dashed in Oakland*. Berkeley, CA: University of California Press.

Rabe, Barry G. 2004. *Statehouse and Greenhouse: The Emerging Politics of American Climate Change Policy*. Washington, DC: The Brookings Institution.

Rabe, Barry G. 2015. "The durability of carbon cap-and-trade policy." *Governance* 29(January): 103–119.

Radin, Beryl A. 2012. *Federal Management Reform in a World of Contradictions*. Washington, DC: Georgetown University Press.

Rittel, Horst, and M. Webber. 1973. "Dilemmas in a general theory of planning." *Policy Sciences* 4: 155–169.

Robinson, Scott E. 2011. "Rebranding public administration for a postsector age." In *The Future of Public Administration around the World: The Minnowbrook Perspective*. Rosemary O'Leary, David Slyke, and Soonhee Kim, eds. Washington, DC: Georgetown University Press.

Rosenbaum, Sara. 2013. *National Foundation of Independent Business v Sebelius* and the Medicaid aftermath. *Public Administration Review* 73(Special Issue): S21–S23.

Salamon, Lester M. 2003. *The Resilient Sector: The State of Nonprofit America*. Washington DC: The Brookings Institution.

Savas, E. S. 1982. *Privatizing the Public Sector*. Chatham, NJ: Chatham House Publishers.

Shafritz, Jay M., ed. 1997 *Classics in Public Administration* (4th ed.). New York: Harcourt Brace.

Vandal, Thierry. 2015. "Energy matters: Challenges and prospects for Canada-U.S. relations." Speech at Bridgewater State University, Bridgewater Massachusetts, April 16.

Whitaker, Gordon, Lydian Altman-Sauer, and Margaret Henderson. 2004. "Mutual accountability between governments and non-profits: Moving beyond 'surveillance' to "service." *American Review of Public Administration* 34(June): 115–133.

Wilson, Woodrow. 1887. "The study of administration." *Political Science Quarterly* 2(June): 197–222.

Wise, Charles R. 1990. "Public service configurations and public organizations: Public organization design in the post-privatization era." *Public Administration Review* 50(March/April): 141–155.

Wright, Deil S. 1988. *Understanding Intergovernmental Relations*, 3rd Edition. Pacific Grove, CA: Brooks Cole Publishing.

Wright, Deil S. 1990. "Federalism, intergovernmental relations, and intergovernmental management: Historical reflections and conceptual comparisons." *Public Administration Review* 50(October/November): 168–178.

Wright, Deil S. 2003. "Federalism and intergovernmental relations: Traumas, tensions, and trends." *Spectrum: The Journal of State Government* 2003: 10–13.

Wright, Deil S., and Dale Krane. 1998. "Intergovernmental Management." In *International Encyclopedia of Public Policy and Administration*, Jay M. Shafritz, ed. New York: Holt Rinehart.

Wright, Deil S, Carl W. Stenberg, and Chung-lae Cho. 2009. *Foundations of Public Administration*. Washington DC: ASPA.

Wright, Deil S., Carl W. Stenberg, and Chung-lae Cho. 2011. "Historic relevance confronting contemporary obsolescence? Federalism, intergovernmental relations, and intergovernmental management." In *The State of Public Administration: Issues, Challenges, and Opportunities*, Donald C. Menzel and Harvey L. White, eds. Armonk, NY: M. E. Sharpe.

Part II

Fiscal and Institutional Issues

5   Scarcity and the Federal System

Paul L. Posner

Deil Wright (1982) said that dollars are a commodity in intergovernmental exchanges over which considerable competition and conflict occurs. Shifts in taxes and spending across the intergovernmental system have wide-ranging effects on who does what, when, where, and how in domestic policymaking.

The system of cooperative federalism, marked by shared involvement by all types of general purpose government across most domestic functions, became the norm in American governance in the 1950s. Some of the largest and most important federal aid programs in existence today, such as education grants for disadvantaged children and Medicaid, were established during this period. State and local governments retained vital bargaining power with national leaders since they could at least threaten to withhold their cooperation that was so vital for national programs to succeed (Ingram 1977).

Major shifts are underway in public finances which will limit the resources available to all levels of government. The financial challenges threaten to erode the fiscal foundations that have underwritten cooperative federalism in the past and enabled partners to join together in expanding public services to meet rising public expectations. As fiscal austerity has become a defining public policy regime, cooperative federalism has been replaced with heightened intergovernmental conflict as all levels of government vie to preempt revenues and shift costs and blame for the difficult choices necessary to resolve fiscal deficits. Going forward, it is unlikely that the federal government could afford to play the role of the fiscal knight in bailing out financially stressed states and localities like it did in the depths of the Great Recession with the $800 billion economic stimulus ushered in by the Obama Administration. Indeed, it is more likely that federal officials will serve to exacerbate state and local fiscal stress as they compete for tax bases and scarce resources.

The shifting and volatile fiscal fortunes of the American intergovernmental system will be exacerbated by the weak institutionalization of intergovernmental fiscal collaboration at the national level. A near record federal stimulus that modeled the best thinking in public finance was quickly followed by federal indifference and passivity in the face of major fiscal pressures experienced by many subnational governments.

The institutions of collaboration that had emerged during the era of cooperative federalism in the 1960s had largely disappeared by the 1990s. Fundamental political incentives that formerly provided incentives for bargaining and collaboration across levels of government collapsed in the wake of the nationalization and centralization of political parties, media, and interest groups. In its wake, federal intergovernmental policymaking became less systematic and more opportunistic–collaborative when, and only when, national officials perceived it to be in their interest to engage state and local capabilities.

This chapter examines these long-term fiscal challenges and explores the question of whether our weak collaborative institutions and incentives can be stepped-up to fashion truly intergovernmental solutions.

Structural Fiscal Challenges

The past several years have been the most difficult times for federal, state, and local governments. Following the Great Recession and the federal stimulus program under the American Recovery and Reinvestment Act of 2009 (ARRA), the federal deficit exploded into the largest peacetime deficit in our history. Federal deficits reached a high of 10 percent of the economy, thanks to collapsing revenues and expanding costs from stimulus spending and the automatic stabilizers built into federal programs.

State tax collections dropped by record levels. Compared to other postwar recessions, it took nearly four times longer for state and local revenues to rebound. The federal stimulus program provided some significant relief to the state and local sectors thanks to reductions in state matching required for Medicaid and major infusions of federal aid for education through the state stabilization fund. Indeed, for the first time in American history, federal assistance became the single greatest source of revenue for state governments in 2009 and 2010. However, federal stimulus funds ended well before state and local governments experienced full economic recovery.

By the 2016 election season, the economy was in recovery mode and state and local finances were improving, as were federal revenues. Federal deficits dropped below four percent of Gross Domestic Product (GDP) and many states were again building up surpluses in reserve accounts. While the sector as a whole is recovering, the recession proved to have far more lasting effects for those governments with the weakest economies and finances. Detroit, San Bernadino, and Central Falls, Rhode Island were among a group of cities that entered bankruptcy to reconcile burgeoning costs with declining revenues (George Mason University Center on Public Service undated).

Even though the short-term economy has recovered, all levels of government face a more daunting set of structural deficits brought about by economic, demographic, and global trends that will affect intergovernmental finances for decades to come. An aging society will transform the spending priorities and revenues of all levels of government. Absent fundamental reforms of expenditure and tax policies, the spending commitments for an aging society will rapidly overwhelm the revenues available to finance them. Escalating pensions, health care, and Social Security costs will together cause deficits to escalate in federal, state, and local budgets.

This long-term fiscal scenario is compounded by slower economic growth expected in the future, thanks to a decline in workforce growth. Simply put, we have not had enough children to provide the workforce necessary to support the growth levels to which we have become accustomed. The baby boom has been followed by a baby bust. A labor force that expanded at an average of 1.6 percent per year during the previous 40 years will grow by only 0.4 percent of GDP over the next 20 years. Since labor force growth accounts for most of the annual potential of the economy to grow, it is no surprise that an economy that had a potential growth rate of over four percent annually from 1952–1973 is now projected by the Congressional Budget Office (CBO) to grow at around two percent a year for the next ten years (2014). Most analysts project that economic growth at full employment will slow from over three percent to two percent in the next several decades.

This means less tax revenue from which to finance the escalating health care, pension, and Social Security costs of the baby boom retirement bulge. The CBO expects that the retirement of the baby boom generation as well as their lower birth rates will cause the number of workers to increase more slowly, leading to sharply lower growth potential for the economy as a whole.

A major component of fiscal pressure now and in the future is health care costs. The growth rate of health care far exceeds the rate of inflation, as the United States now spends far more than any nation in the world in this area.

These trends contribute to unsustainable budgets over the long term. Assuming no further policy changes, the priorities in the federal budget would be overtaken by Social Security and health care program spending. As shown in Figure 5.1, CBO projects that federal spending on health care alone would double as a share of the economy by 2038, while Social Security would increase by 50 percent.

While entitlements grow, domestic discretionary spending appropriated annually by the Congress shrinks as a share of the economy and the federal budget. Most recent projections show that domestic discretionary spending—financing many grants to states and localities—would decline to the lowest level in postwar history.

The "bottom line" is that the federal budget is on an unsustainable course. This is shown in Figure 5.2 with CBO simulations indicating debt exceeding 100 percent of GDP over the next 20 years, approaching the record levels amassed by the nation in World War II. As a low-saving nation, federal debt would crowd out private investment, resulting in declining living standards for the nation as a whole. Foreign investors could provide financing for the burgeoning debt, but the profits would go overseas. Most importantly, the ability of the nation to fund domestic investments, national defense, as well as grants to state and local governments, would erode in the face of rising entitlements. It should be emphasized that these trends are not inevitable, but rather simulations illustrating the implicit policy path that the nation's budget is following based on current law and projected economic and demographic assumptions.

Just like the federal budget, state and local budgets are also on an unsustainable course. Even with the on-going recovery from the recession, the U.S. Government Accountability Office (GAO) estimates that states and localities will face a long-term structural deficit that will exceed three percent of the economy by 2050, as shown in Figure 5.3. As with the federal budget, the primary culprit in long-term state and local imbalances is demography: an aging America is driving up health care and pension costs and liabilities. The states are chained to the health care crisis by their financing role in Medicaid as well as insuring their own employees. States and localities also face

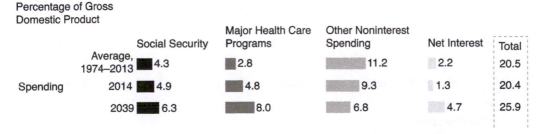

Percentage of Gross Domestic Product		Social Security	Major Health Care Programs	Other Noninterest Spending	Net Interest	Total
	Average, 1974–2013	4.3	2.8	11.2	2.2	20.5
Spending	2014	4.9	4.8	9.3	1.3	20.4
	2039	6.3	8.0	6.8	4.7	25.9

Figure 5.1 Spending and Revenues under CBO's Extended Baseline, Compared with Past Averages.

Source: Congressional Budget Office (2014)

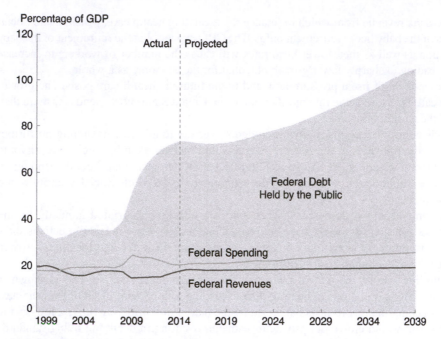

Figure 5.2 Debt Held by the Public, Total Spending, and Total Revenues.

Source: Congressional Budget Office (2014)

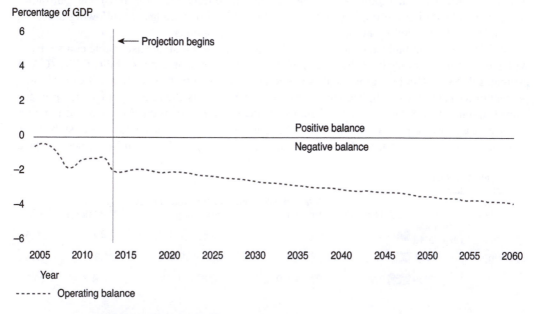

Figure 5.3 State and Local Operating Balance as Share of Gross Domestic Product.

Source: U.S. Government Accountability Office (2014)

unfunded employee pension costs and a revenue system that fails to keep pace with the sources of growth in the economy. In general, states and localities cannot run deficits in their general funds. So the chronic fiscal deficits projected over the longer term indicate the size of the spending cuts and tax increases that state and local officials will have to impose over many decades. In its 2013 report, GAO estimates that the state and local sector would have to reduce spending by over 14 percent annually to bring about an operating balance each year through 2060.

As with the federal government, aging and health care costs will crowd out other priorities in their budgets, assuming no major policy changes in those long-term commitments. The GAO report shows that health care costs nearly double as a share of GDP for states and localities over the next 50 years, while other spending areas decline commensurately. Similarly, pension costs take over more fiscal room in state and local budgets during this period as well. Calculations by Alicia Munnell at the Boston University Center for Retirement Research indicate that state and local pension contributions have already increased from 6.7 percent in 2001 to 17 percent in 2012 (Munnell, Aubrey, and Caferelli 2014).

Other pressures are also at work destabilizing state and local finance as we know it. The sales tax has been eroding for years, thanks to shifts in economic transactions toward services and remote sales–items that conventional sales taxes do not reach. As a result, the productivity of the sales tax has been declining. Moreover, the increasing globalization of economic activity increases opportunities for income shifting and tax planning to avoid taxes in particular states or even at the national level (Scheppach and Shafroth 2008).

Unlike a recession, state and local governments, as well as their federal counterparts, cannot simply grow their way out of this structural fiscal gap through economic expansion or full employment. Rather, the answers lie in complex and difficult choices on the tax and spending sides of the budgets of all levels of government.

Intergovernmental Implications of Long-Term Scarcity

Going forward, federal, state, and local governments will be struggling with the fiscal implications of an aging society and rising health care costs. Whether it be increasing Medicare costs at the national level or employee pensions in state and local governments, all governments will be faced with paying for the elderly and their doctors from a slower growing economy featuring fewer workers. In the past several years alone, pension and health entitlements and revenue slippage are crowding out other priorities, such as education and infrastructure. All governments will be eyeing a shrinking tax base through which to finance expanding commitments. Unlike the past, the federal government will be increasingly less able to serve as the fiscal angel sprinkling debt-financed funds to hard-pressed states and localities in the recessions to come. On its face, it appears we face a grim intergovernmental future of conflict and tension, featuring the passing of the lack of bucks across the numerous actors in our federal system.

Toward Fiscal Centralization

Of course, we have seen such scarcity overtake and reshape other federal systems, most notably in Europe where national and subnational governments struggle to resolve historically high deficits and debt. These systems are undergoing fiscal centralization, as nations yield to central fiscal controllers in the European Union and the International Monetary Fund. In the search for solvency, answers are often forthcoming from central governments with access to the broadest tax base and financing.

Such a process is not without costs, as higher level governments and multilateral institutions impose conditions on public spending, taxation, and debt. Indeed, one observer notes that the European Union is leapfrogging beyond federalism to something approaching a unitary state where the center dictates taxation and spending in ways that would have been unthinkable before the crisis (Zibbitt 2014). Within our states, a comparable process of fiscal and policy centralization is underway as well for cities undergoing bailouts and other extraordinary financial emergencies.

When compared with other federal systems, some suggest that the United States might escape the fiscal centralization scenario befalling other nations. The American federal system is one of the most devolved in the world. Only Switzerland and Canada approach the high levels of fiscal autonomy realized by states and provinces, as most spending is financed by taxes imposed and collected by those units of government. Those traditions have remained strong over time, thwarting national responses to widespread state bankruptcies in the 1840s. Most recently, the notion of federal bailouts or even major grants for hard-pressed bankrupt cities like Detroit has remained off the table. Implicitly, Jonathan Rodden (2006) argues our system of competitive federalism places credit markets rather than governments as the fiscal monitor for state and local governments. Indeed, like Canada, states and localities in the United States must largely fashion their own resolutions to a fiscal crisis (Simeon, Pearce, and Nugent 2014). Thus, in the memorable phrase coined by John Shannon, our federal system can truly be characterized as "fend-for-yourself federalism." From this standpoint, federal, state, and local governments will be like fiscal ships passing in the long night, free to make difficult choices with little or no mutual influence or interference.

But wait just a minute. The fiscal independence of budgetary policy-making among governments in the United States belies their growing fiscal interdependence. In fact, the spending and revenues of different levels of government have become increasingly intertwined. State and local governments, employing nine times as many employees as the federal government, have become the real workhorses of public governance. They are vital partners in implementing many major federal programs, including those involving welfare, health care, and environmental protection. Federal reliance on state and local capacities has accelerated in the past five years, bringing new tensions. Federally devised efforts have extended into policy areas once controlled primarily by lower levels of government–elections administration, fire departments, educational quality, and motor vehicle licensing, among others.

State and local governments have become more dependent on federal aid to fund key services. Federal grants have grown from 15.1 percent in 1992 to 16.6 percent in 2014 of total state and local revenues according to Census data. The percentages remained fairly flat at about 15 percent until the Great Recession. In 2009, intergovernmental transfers increased to 25.6 percent and have since retreated to the current level (U.S. Census Bureau undated). However, in contrast to general revenue sharing programs found in nearly all federal systems, nearly all of the more than 1000 federal grants are conditional and restricted to narrow purposes.

Federal leaders have come to be at the epicenter of a maelstrom of public demands for governmental actions to respond to an increasing range of problems, from climate change to health care to education. In each of these areas, and many others, strong pressures from interest groups and national political leaders themselves call for national action in areas with long-standing and significant state and local involvement. Rather than expand the federal workforce, a nation that retains significant ambivalence about government and national power has implicitly chosen to use state and local and private entities as the shadow workforce implementing new federal initiatives. This is nowhere more clear than the Affordable Care Act, which places states at the center of the expansion of health insurance coverage through an enriched Medicaid program and new health exchanges, to say nothing of augmented powers states can exercise to control insurance rates.

Continuation of Trends Toward Coercive Federalism

Over the past 40 years, federal officials have gone beyond cooperative grants to resort to a wide range of preemptions and mandates to carry out their policies. Frustrated with the carrot, federal officials who are focused on national goals and constituencies have frequently turned to these more coercive methods, notwithstanding their potential to cause greater intergovernmental conflict (Posner 1998; see Chapter 3, this volume). State officials are all too prone to engage in the same kind of unilateral mandates and preemptions in dealing with local governments.

Federal preemptions of their tax bases have also limited states' capacities to handle expanded responsibilities from federal mandates and policies. State and local sales and use tax revenues have been eroded by the rapid growth of remote internet sales—an area which the Supreme Court has ruled off-limits to states unless Congress passes new legislation. This federal regime has not only had an impact on state and local governments, but also has established an uneven playing field where businesses offering products through remote sales gain tax-free advantages over traditional brick-and-mortar retailers.

As the foregoing suggests, unilateral actions can create imbalances in any interdependent system. These actions risk overgrazing the "fiscal commons"—the fixed resources available to each level of government as well as business entities and other taxpayers. In the case of federal or state governments, this unilateral behavior often takes shape by way of spending mandates (more resource demands on the commons) and revenue limitations (more fences). These actions have the effect of both limiting total state and local revenues as well as encumbering the use of those revenues for federally defined purposes. Imbalances can also result when governments separately impose tax burdens on the private economy without carefully considering their aggregate impact on economic efficiency and equity.

National Responses to Fiscal Challenges

As all levels of government face common fiscal challenges in the future, how will governments respond? While this is difficult to predict, we can suggest three potential approaches:

Go it Alone

Comparable to the old dual federalism model, each level of government develops approaches to deficits on their own. While easier to achieve politically, such approaches will fall short in their impact on the economy and on policy effectiveness. For instance, solving the fiscal costs associated with health care is most efficiently accomplished through concerted action. Each government can strike their own deal but be at a disadvantage when negotiating with a complex national industry. Similarly, extending the sales tax to the internet can only be addressed through concerted national action by states working collectively. Each state attempting to tax remote sales risks violating Supreme Court rulings as well as suffering from opportunistic actions of other states

courting national businesses through lower taxes. In fact, states have banded together in a cooperative Streamlined State Sales Tax movement to harmonize conflicting sales tax bases, easing
compliance by remote sellers across the nation, although significant holdouts by key states have
frustrated this initiative.

Fiscal Buck-passing and Off-loading

Federal or state or local governments can off-load their fiscal problems by passing them off to other
governments in our system. The unfunded mandate requiring states to spend nearly $11 billion to
change driver's licenses under the Real ID Act of 2005 is one example of how the federal government
can abuse its constitutional supremacy to pass costs to other governments in our federal system.
Similarly, state or local governments can abuse federal grant funds intended for specific purposes
by using them to replace their own funds, resulting in the undermining of federal program goals.

Fiscal Collaboration

Governments can join together in developing common solutions to common problems. Health
care has great potential to yield to collaborative solutions across governments. The passage of
legislation that yields real cost savings in the delivery of health care would constitute such an
approach, with savings for all governments involved in financing health care.

The fiscal implications of the Great Recession for all levels of government can serve as a bell-
wether for how the nation might respond to the longer term fiscal issues hanging over governments
in our system. The early response to the Great Recession was highly intergovernmental and collaborative, epitomized by the $800 billion economic stimulus program under ARRA authored by
the Obama Administration. One has to go back to the Nixon Administration's General Revenue
Sharing program to find a federal fiscal response that was as helpful to struggling state and local
officials as this initiative. Fueled by stimulus spending, federal aid exploded from $461 billion in
FY 2008 to over $647 billion in FY 2011.

Facing extraordinary expectations for conflicting goals, ARRA inspired remarkable levels of
collaboration among elected officials and their representatives from all three levels of government.
OMB and state and local association representatives instituted weekly conference calls to resolve
administration questions to expedite program implementation. Representing the President's
uniquely personal stakes in Recovery outcomes, the Vice President's office became the chief point
officer (or "sheriff" as the Vice President Joe Biden called himself) to resolve intergovernmental
conflicts and federal programmatic problems before they reached a public boiling point. This
notable level of collaboration among what Samuel Beer called "topocrats"–the highest elected
officials and their staff from all levels of government including the White House, OMB, the nation's
governors, and state budget officers—reflected the degree to which both states and the federal
government needed to collaborate in order to promote their own interests. The President and OMB
relied upon states and local governments as the primary agents to save and create new jobs, and it
was in their interest to make sure that grants and contracts were spent expeditiously on activities
that were beyond reproach (Conlan and Posner 2011).

Other federal systems have followed the fiscal collaboration model when crafting tax and fiscal
policy. For instance, nearly all Organisation for Economic Co-operation and Development (OECD)
nations have a national consumption tax, or a value-added tax (VAT); the United States is the only

major advanced nation without a national consumption tax. When compared with state sales taxes, a VAT has several advantages, including a national and international reach into the service economy and revenue potential that could go a long way toward filling fiscal gaps at all levels of government.

Absent an intergovernmental partnership, the danger to the states from a national consumption tax is very real. A federal government desperate to solve its own billowing deficits could enact a consumption tax unilaterally that would threaten to undermine state sales taxes.

Many federal systems have collaborated with subnational governments to ensure that these units could either piggyback on the expanded consumption tax base or realize proceeds allocated from the collections from this tax. In Australia, the states supported national adoption of a new consumption tax to replace a series of inefficient wholesale taxes. States were able to replace these outmoded taxes by working with national officials to gain the proceeds of the revenues of a new national consumption tax administered by the national government, but reallocated across the states through a complex fiscal equalization formula. Whether states piggyback or gain revenues through such a formula, collaboration between national and state officials is absolutely essential to realize these fiscal reforms (Duncan and Sedon 2011).

While collaboration may very well be essential to protect the fiscal capabilities of all levels of government in our federal system, actions taken to resolve deficits often have a centralizing effect on intergovernmental finance. In the United States, within two years of the 2009 economic stimulus package, national fiscal officials mobilized to deal with the burgeoning deficits that were sparked by the recession and the stimulus, among other initiatives. In comparison to the stimulus, deficit reduction plans hatched in Washington carried a centralizing bias. The proposals authored by the Simpson-Bowles Commission in 2010 had a unilateral centralizing thrust. Plugging a $4 trillion federal fiscal gap, the commission reached into state and local revenue systems for savings, proposing the elimination of state and local tax deductibility as well as the tax exempt bonds (National Commission on Fiscal Responsibility and Reform 2010). Tax-exempt debt had helped state and local governments reduce their borrowing costs by 20 to 50 percent and played a critical role in financing much-needed infrastructure improvements throughout the nation (Hume 2010).

The 2011 Budget Control Act imposing new caps and sequesters on defense and domestic discretionary spending also have potentially negative fiscal consequences for state and local government grants funded by discretionary appropriations. As discussed earlier, the caps on discretionary spending and the budget sequesters together will cause domestic discretionary spending to fall below its current low in the next several years, absent actions by the Congress.

The Deinstitutionalization of Intergovernmental Relations

As the United States sails into these uncharted fiscal waters, it does so without the thick array of intergovernmental collaborative institutions that characterized national policymaking some three or four decades before. By comparison, many other OECD nations have strong intergovernmental traditions of fiscal collaboration and joint stewardship, reflected in fiscal targets for deficits and debt and expenditure limits shared by national and subnational governments. These targets can be established and enforced through a series of well-developed intergovernmental collaborative forums, such as the Premier's Conference in Canada and the Council of Australian Governments. In Germany, new fiscal targets were passed along with a new Stability Council consisting of the ministers of finance of national and state governments working together.

A recent OECD study concluded that the fiscal consolidations of most OECD nations did not involve buck-passing to subordinate governments, but in fact constituted highly proportionate efforts to allocate sacrifices between national and subnational governments (Rudifer, Curto-grau, and Vammalle 2013).

In the United States, those institutions and traditions of fiscal collaboration are weak, if nonexistent. With no institutional focal points, federal and state governments are on their own to craft deficit reduction strategies, often working at cross-purposes as federal officials pass underfunded mandates and budget cuts to states while subnational officials work assiduously to shift their costs to federal programs (Posner and Shafroth 2011). Federal tax policy is an arena where most states adopt federal tax base definitions in their own income taxes, but where federal officials make tax policy decisions with no real involvement by state and local officials.

As noted above, this fiscal interdependence is recognized in the context of individual programs such as President Obama's health care reform where states were given significantly higher Medicaid funds to cover the uninsured. However, the de facto administrative partnerships that increasingly bind together the policy outcomes and fiscal stakes of all levels of government are not explicitly recognized in the development of the budget either within the Administration or by the Congress. While fiscally good periods can lead to greater federal largess to states, there is a real risk that vertical inequities and horizontal equities will both be exacerbated as deficit pressures accelerate at the national level.

The dissolution of cooperative federalism is reflected in a deinstitutionalization of intergovernmental relations. Starting in the 1950s, as federal grants grew with the interstate highway and housing programs, federal institutions grew to better understand the emerging intergovernmental system that was taking shape. Top federal political and senior civil servants recognized the need to develop systematic information on the condition of states and localities as well as to more deeply understand the implications of thickening relationships between the levels of government for national programs and interests.

The most important and preeminent institution was the Advisory Commission on Intergovernmental Relations (ACIR), created in the late 1950s during the Administration of President Eisenhower, a moderate Republican who viewed the growth of the federal role with concern but nonetheless embraced pragmatic solutions that satisfied federal and state interests. The ACIR was appointed by the President and Congress and consisted of top elected officials at all levels of government as well as private citizens. The Commission had a staff of up to 40 at one time, considered to be the best minds in the country on federalism and intergovernmental relations. This body played several vital roles in bringing together governments across our system to address common problems:

- data collection and transparency on finances, personnel, and other features of the intergovernmental system;
- forums bridging differences to test for areas of agreement across parties and levels of government; and
- articulation of agendas for reform in intergovernmental relations at all levels of government.

Over its 37-year lifespan, the ACIR "grew from a nondescript agency that avoided making headlines into a respected voice on intergovernmental issues" (Howell-Maroney and Handley 2009: 8).

Its research and policy recommendations found their way into path-breaking federal grants legislation including the Intergovernmental Cooperation Act of 1968, the Intergovernmental Personnel Act of 1970, the General Revenue Sharing program enacted in 1972, and the unfunded mandates reform legislation passed in 1995. The ACIR was also instrumental in Presidential federalism initiatives, with major involvement in Nixon Administration's block grant proposals and in the Reagan Administration's New Federalism program turn-back and sorting out proposals. The Commission also directed some of its work to the states, establishing a state legislative program including 112 bills for state consideration in 1975 (McDowell 2011).

The ACIR was joined by other institutions that enabled the emergence of an intergovernmental issue network in Washington. These included a separate grants division in the President's budget office, the Office of Management and Budget (OMB), as well as specific subcommittees on federalism and intergovernmental relations on both House and Senate sides of the Congress, chaired by powerful senior members of Congress such as Senator Edmund Muskie. It also included a significant investment in intergovernmental management by the U.S. Government Accountability Office, which did major studies on the grant system, federal funding formulas, and intergovernmental impacts of federal policies (the author led that unit for a number of years from the mid-1980s through 2005).

The rise of these institutions in Washington also reflected efforts by state and local interest groups to frame their concerns in fact-based and neutral ways that would become credible to other national actors in Washington, DC. The ACIR served to increase awareness and lend legitimacy to long-standing state and local complaints about the impacts of federal laws and programs on their own fiscal and legal autonomy. During the 1980s, state and local groups invested in the creation of an Academy for State and Local Government which was intended to perform neutral studies on the intergovernmental system that each group could not perform on its own.

This entire edifice crumbled during the 1980s and 1990s. The ACIR was abolished by a Congress seeking short-term budget savings by eliminating smaller agencies and commissions. The OMB eliminated its grants office in the early 1980s, ironically at the time when federalism received high level attention from President Ronald Reagan as part of his broad scale reform intended to reallocate and devolve powers from the federal government to the states. The Congress abolished its federalism subcommittees. The state and local groups abandoned their Academy, as internal disagreements on priorities and interests among them caused an independent neutral group to lose support. The Treasury Department, which had an Office of State and Local Finance originating from its administration of the General Revenue Sharing program, abolished this office in the late 1980s, shortly after producing a major report on the federal intergovernmental fiscal system (U.S. Treasury Department 1985).

What are the common denominators behind the collapse of the intergovernmental institutional edifice in Washington? Certainly, the shifting landscape of the policy process played a role. The rise of polarized parties, confrontational politics, and interest group advocacy served to erode support for institutions that sought out the vital center and promoted improvements in relationships among governments. The advent of the Reagan Administration marked a new era of more ideological public administration. Newland writes that this era featured a closed group of political advisers acting based on strong ideologies rather than consultation and collaboration with experts and other professional administrators across our intergovernmental system. When they came into office, the new Reagan political officials disavowed the previous agenda of intergovernmental management, which had featured middle-range reform of existing grant programs and management procedures, favoring instead a more fundamental reexamination of the need for many of these programs in the first place. The elimination of the grants management division in OMB was one response to this new vision. Newland (1983: 13) characterizes the Reagan Administration as supporting "the hasty and ideologically uncompromising formulation of intergovernmental and urban policy proposals, without regard for realistic state and local political considerations."

In some respects, the new politicization of intergovernmental relations signaled its growing importance to policymakers and interests throughout Washington, DC. Yet, this same realization prompted the deinstitutionalization of intergovernmental actors and agencies. Most importantly, it signaled the death knell for the ACIR itself in 1996. However the demise of this body was signaled in 1982 in the early Reagan years when the chairman of ACIR was replaced with new leadership who used conservative public choice principles to fundamentally challenge the history of the Commission's work in federalism, grants, and intergovernmental organization. The departure of key staff signaled to some the unraveling of the reputation for independence and neutrality that was the only source of real influence that the Commission enjoyed.

The state and local interest groups also became increasingly less collaborative and capable of forging agreements (see Chapter 14, this volume). Rampant partisan polarization began to affect these groups in the 1980s. The National Governors Association is too divided to take positions and lobby on the major intergovernmental policy initiatives of our era such as the Affordable Care Act of 2010 and Welfare Reform of 1996. The Democratic and Republican Governors Associations now have become the vehicles through which highly partisan alliances of governors express their views to increasingly polarized national officials. On health reform, Republican governors disavowed a consensus on changes in legislation to advance state fiscal interests that was formed at the staff level within the National Governors Association when national Congressional Republican leaders decided to oppose the Obama Administration reform proposal, a position that Republican governors felt obliged to support (Thompson 2012). This development was a stunning reversal from the days when party positions in Washington reflected state and local party interests to a time when such positions are now articulated by national party leaders.

Beyond the shifting nature of policymaking itself, the demise of the ACIR and other institutional foundations for intergovernmental cooperation and collaboration reflected the eclipse of federalism as a fundamental rule of the game in Washington, DC. National elected officials have converted from being ambassadors of state and local party leaders to independent political entrepreneurs anxious to establish their own visible policy profiles to appeal to a diverse coalition of interest groups, media, and an increasingly independent base of voters. Far from allies, the relationship between congressional officials and state and local elected colleagues from their districts resembles more of a competition among independent political entrepreneurs for money, visibility, and votes. It is no surprise, then, that leaders of both parties engaged in what Timothy Conlan (2006) calls "opportunistic federalism" where national leaders anxiously embrace different problems for national attention and legislation, irrespective of their consequences for states and localities or the balance of power between and among governments.

Conclusions: The Contingent Nature of States' Influence

The foregoing suggests that the American federal system is not as robustly inclusive or deferential to the states as it used to be. While still nominally a federal system, the system was aptly characterized by Reagan and Sanzone (1981) as being governed by "permissive federalism." In their view, most national initiatives continue to feature power sharing with states and communities, but the nature and extent of delegation rests upon the permission and permissiveness of the federal government. The nation has become more uniform socially, economically, and culturally, providing a firmer foundation for national goals and homogeneous programs. And the political system has been shorn from its former state and local moorings, becoming more responsive to increasingly well-organized national constituencies and values.

Federal officials retain strong incentives to work through, not around, states due to profound administrative, financial, and political advantages. With all of their conflicts and tensions, intergovernmental systems remain well-suited for many of the "wicked" problems we face today–problems with contestable definitions, wide distribution of the resources and capacities necessary to solve them, and uncertainties about how to best implement these solutions. Complex public policy problems like climate change, health care costs and coverage, and educating the future workforce will call on the compound republic to find ways to work in effective partnerships across boundaries. The growing polarization among states and within the Congress has made it difficult to enact new national initiatives, thereby fortifying the long noted power of states to serve as laboratories for policy reform. However, it has also arguably increased the leverage states have over national policy implementation, if for no other reason than states are more willing than ever before to opt out of national programs for ideological reasons.

The coming environment of fiscal scarcity will make the task of reconciling expansive national policy ideas with intergovernmental management and political realities increasingly more difficult and conflictual. The system of cooperative federalism was once viewed as a win-win, as the federal government gained state participation in building political support for national policy while states gained significant new federal dollars to help expand programs. Increasingly driven with conflicting ideological agendas and fiscal constraints, the federal system now radiates increasing conflicts and tensions between activist policy makers in Washington DC and wary officials in states and communities.

There is no way to underestimate the political difficulties involved with rising to these intergovernmental policy challenges. Federal officials looking after their increasingly shrinking bottom line, may at times have incentives to take the interests of their intergovernmental partners into account when designing and implementing new national programs. The Obama Administration illustrated the delicate balancing act that national leaders must play in this more tension filled environment. While its initial promises and actions created widespread concerns and occasionally loud complaints about policy centralization and standardization, the Administration actually followed a path that was far more nuanced and cooperative than that suggested by early expectations or contemporary rhetoric. While coercive federalism strategies were deployed in health care and sought in climate change, the Administration relied upon older regimes of cooperative grants and regulatory flexibility to engage the states in collective initiatives to achieve economic recovery and regulate the financial sector. Even in the case of health care, the strategy adopted by Congress and the Administration enabled conservative states to opt out of administering new national programs, thereby accommodating the heightened ideological polarization among the states (Conlan and Posner 2011; see also Chapter 7, this volume).

When formulating federal initiatives, states remain on the critical path for national leaders who must rely on their laws, people, and finances to satisfy program goals. In these cases, federalism may not have informed the decisions about *whether* to undertake the growing agenda of national policies, but it most certainly was instrumental in shaping *how* those initiatives would be designed.

The intergovernmental collaboration that was noted by giants in our field like Deil Wright and Martha Derthick is a natural byproduct of a system where all actors share common interests.

It is not so clear that win-win solutions are available on fiscal issues. As federal purse strings tighten, states and localities will compete with compelling and highly organized constituencies of medical providers, elderly organizations, and thousands of other interests for a share of the shrinking federal pie. The ARRA experience shows that, on occasion, federal officials share incentives to finance states and localities when necessary to achieve vital national political interests in jumpstarting a moribund economy. This seemingly new-found federal intergovernmental fiscal role was destined to be short-lived indeed. The budget reductions and fiscal gridlock that followed undercut the recovery of states and localities throughout the nation.

The tightening of the fiscal vise places a new premium on institutions that can help our federal system rise to this endemic and wrenching set of fiscal challenges. In public budgeting, bond markets and other constraints on deficits and debt provide a built-in thermostat to regulate, after a fashion, the fiscal expansion of governments. We have no such natural bulwark protecting the fiscal vitality of our federal system to perform its much needed functions of providing important sources of variability, innovation, and efficiency in providing public services. It is time for leaders in our federal, state, and local government community to design new institutions to fortify the nation's governing capacity to respond to the policy challenges of the next decades.

References

Congressional Budget Office. 2014. *The 2014 Long Term Budget Outlook*. Washington, DC: CBO.

Conlan, Timothy J. 2006. "From cooperative to opportunistic federalism: Reflections on the half-century anniversary of the Commission on Intergovernmental Relations." *Public Administration Review* 66(5): 663–676.

Conlan, Timothy J., and Paul L. Posner. 2011. "Inflection point? Federalism and the Obama administration." *Publius: The Journal of Federalism* 41(3): 421–446.

Duncan, Harley, and Jon Sedon. 2011. "Coordinating a federal VAT with state and local sales taxes." *Tax Notes* 127(9): 1029.

George Mason University Center on Public Service. Undated. "The GMU Municipal Sustainability Project." Retrieved from http://fiscalbankruptcy.wordpress.com/the-reports (accessed July 13, 2014).

Howell-Maroney, Michael, and Donna Handley. 2009. *Restoring the Intergovernmental Partnership: What Needs to Change*. White paper. Washington, DC: International City/County Management Association.

Hume, Lynn. 2010. "Vote for deficit-cutting report falls short." *Bond Buyer* 374(33427): 1.

Ingram, Helen. 1977. "Policy implementation through bargaining: The case of grants-in-aid." *Public Policy* 25(4): 499–526.

McDowell, Bruce. 2011. "Reflections on the spirit and work of the U.S. Advisory Commission on Intergovernmental Relations." *Public Administration Review* 71(2): 161–168.

Munnell, Alicia, Jeanne-Pierre Aubrey, and Mark Caferelli. 2014. *The Funding of State and Local Pensions: 2013–2017*. Boston, MA: Center for Retirement Research at Boston College.

National Commission on Fiscal Responsibility and Reform. 2010. *Moment of Truth*. Washington, DC: National Commission on Fiscal Responsibility and Reform.

Newland, Chester A. 1983. "A midterm appraisal—The Reagan administration: Limited government and political administration." *Public Administration Review* 43(1): 1–21.

Posner, Paul L. 1998. *The Politics of Unfunded Mandates: Whither Federalism?* Washington, DC: Georgetown University Press.

Posner, Paul L., and Frank Shafroth. 2011. *Deficits All Around: The Need for Fiscal Collaboration*. Arlington, VA: George Mason University Center on Public Service.

Reagan, Michael, and John G. Sanzone. 1981. *The New Federalism*, 2nd edition. New York: Oxford University Press.

Rodden, Jonathan. 2006. *Hamilton's Paradox: The Promise and Perils of Fiscal Federalism*. New York: Cambridge University Press.

Rudifer, Ahrend, Marta Curto-grau, and Camila Vammalle. 2013. *Passing the Buck? Central and Subnational Governments In Times of Fiscal Stress*. Paris: Organisation for Economic Co-operation and Development.

Scheppach, Raymond, and Frank Shafroth. 2008. "Intergovernmental finance in the new global economy." In *Intergovernmental Management for the 21st Century*, edited by Timothy J. Conlan and Paul L. Posner, 42–74. Washington, DC: Brookings Institution.

Simeon, Richard, James Pearce, and Amy Nugent. 2014. "The resilience of Canadian federalism." In *The Global Debt Crisis: Haunting U.S. and European Federalism,* edited by Paul E. Peterson and Daniel Nadler, 201–222. Washington, DC: Brookings Institution.

Thompson, Frank. 2012. *Medicaid Politics: Federalism, Policy Durability and Health Reform*. Washington, DC: Georgetown University Press.

U.S. Census Bureau. Undated. "State and Local Government Finance." Retrieved from www.census.gov//govs/local/historical_data_ (accessed July 23, 2017).

U.S. Government Accountability Office. 2013. "State and local governments' fiscal outlook." Retrieved from www.gao.gov/products/GAO-13-546SP (accessed July 23, 2017).

U.S. Government Accountability Office. 2014. "State and local governments' fiscal outlook." Retrieved from www.gao.gov/products/GAO-15-224SP (accessed July 23, 2017).

U.S. Treasury Department. 1985. *Federal-State-Local Fiscal Relations: A Report to the President and Congress*. Washington, DC: U.S. Treasury Department.

Wright, Deil S. 1982. *Understanding Intergovernmental Relations,* 2nd edition. Monterey, CA: Brooks/Cole Publishing.

Zibbitt, Daniel. 2014. "Between centralization and federalism in the European Union." In *The Global Debt Crisis: Haunting U.S. and European Federalism,* edited by Paul E. Peterson and Daniel Nadler, 113–133. Washington, DC: Brookings Institution.

6 Putting the "R" Back in IGR

The Great Recession and Intergovernmental "Relationships"

Bruce J. Perlman, Michael J. Scicchitano, and Yahong Zhang

Since its inception, the study of intergovernmental relations (IGR) in the United States has used a series of models and metaphors (paradigms) to help one understand the relations implicit in U.S. Federalism (Wright 1982). Conceptual models of federalism have attempted to reflect the changes in emphasis in the system. The initial metaphor for IGR was that of the "layer" cake in which the federal, state, and local governments operated, for the most part, independently of the other branches of government. Additional images of IGR, however, the "marble" cake and the "picket fence," suggested more collaboration in which federal and state governments provide funding, local government provide services, and all three provide expertise.

Consequently, as the nature of IGR has changed over time, the paradigms have had to change to catch up to and to replicate reality. For example, the original "layer cake" image was clearly not adequate to describe IGR throughout the entire twentieth century and was replaced first by the "marble cake" notion highlighting the greater interaction among the levels of government and the blurring of hierarchy in the funding and delivery of services. Later, that idea gave way to the "picket fence" image to indicate the change to the cross-cutting nature of service delivery through professional bureaucracies. These changes mirror, in turn, the roughly coequal state and federal sovereignty encapsulated in "dual federalism," the multi-level cooperation of "collaborative federalism" when all governments address problems together, and finally "regulatory federalism," the idea of a directive, but supportive federal government in a leadership role.

While the paradigms of IGR have changed, they have done so only slowly. Mostly, change is reactive and gradual in manner. Frameworks are modified to extend their lives and when finally outmoded are succeeded by new ones in a sort of gradual evolution. As the federal system changes ever more rapidly because of unconstrained domestic or international factors, are these paradigms sufficiently flexible, dynamic, and responsive to provide an accurate, up-to-date characterization of IGR under precipitous change or upheaval? Can they accurately and agilely characterize IGR, for example, under the severe fiscal stress of the past several years in which the federal and state governments did not have the revenues to pass to local governments but still mandated that existing services be provided – and even issued mandates for additional services (Perlman 2010)?

Most likely the answer is no. As history shows so far, IGR paradigms have not evolved into a solid theory that explains, captures, and predicts changes in the federal system. Rather, they are responses to changes that have invalidated prior explanations and attempts to conserve them. Such circumscribed thinking can lead to a sort of cognitive inertia: as much is invested in preserving and extending current models and relating them to old ones as is invested in understanding phenomena. That risk is run when attempts to make sense out of contemporary IGR are constrained by previous theory and seen mostly through prior lenses.

Consequently, this essay takes the point of view that a more flexible and dynamic approach is needed to accurately characterize both big and small changes in IGR. In addition, it presents the idea that this new approach should be based on the bottom-up perceptions of local governments. Although local governments play the crucial operational role in service delivery in the federal system, the governing paradigm maintains that the federal government plays the central role in understanding IGR.

Therefore, the focus of this research is to suggest a more flexible, dynamic, and time sensitive approach to understand the relationship between federal and local governments and state and local governments under severe fiscal stress. This approach is developed from a national survey of city ($N = 306$) and county ($N = 438$) managers and other chief officials of local government. The survey asked a series of questions regarding city and county leaders' perceptions of the relationship between their local government and the federal and state governments. This chapter first provides a review of some of the fundamental descriptive characterizations of American federalism and IGR. Second, it suggests consideration of some limitations of these traditional ways of understanding American federalism and IGR. Third, it recommends an alternative to this sort of understanding by distinguishing between "relationship" and "relations" as the important concept in association with the federal system. Fourth, it presents empirical perceptions of local government managers on the relationship between their local governments and the state and federal governments to illustrate this in practice. It concludes by suggesting that the framework of relationship is a more useful one for understanding the data presented and perhaps for comprehending federalism and IGR in general.

The Old Outworn Paradigms

For most of the U.S. national experience, constitutional law defined federalism–the set of transactions later called *intergovernmental relations* (IGR). Dual federalism, a concept that continues to mark the relations between the federal government and state governments, was originally a descriptor for the balance of power between the two achieved under the doctrine of States' Rights. The idea of dual federalism implied a sort of constitutional hierarchy as well as a dichotomy.

Two ideas are implicit in the view of a "dual" federal system. First, that the federal and state governments have twin or double roles in governance and are more equal than not; they remain supreme in their own areas. Second, both governments have important responsibilities in representing and serving the public in their spheres, much more so than local governments. Local governments were relatively ignored entities in this formal framework as the notion "dual" implies "stepchildren" of the two parent governments.

Beginning with the Great Depression, pressure was put on the division of powers implicit in the idea of a dual federalist system. Increasing citizen demand for governmental support and innovations like the Works Progress Administration and the National Recovery Administration gave a new role to all levels of government. The federal government's and the states' role changed; even localities and the private sector had to become involved in serving public needs. Settled patterns of provision gave way to new arrangements and collaboration across levels of government. In short, the concept of dual federalism became outmoded.

Marble and Layer Cakes and Cooperative Federalism

To characterize the then outmoded view of IGR in dual federalism Mortin Grodzins called it famously, "layer cake" federalism (Grodzins 1960). This was a useful metaphor that illustrated the clear notions of separateness, hierarchy, and rough equality implicit in dual federalism. Moreover, the third layer of the cake suggested a larger role for local jurisdictions than under dual federalism. This was a more accurate model of how people interacted with government and how governments interacted than dual federalism; it was a better model for reflecting IGR in practice.

In tandem with the layer cake metaphor, and really grounded by it, Grodzins also introduced the contrasting simile of the marble cake. This type of federalism, also known as "cooperative" federalism, as the name implies, typifies an IGR system in which the costs, administration, decisions, powers, and responsibilities of the various types of governments are mixed together. As Grodzins says in *The Federal System*:

> The American form of government is often, but erroneously, symbolized by a three-layer cake. A far more accurate image is the rainbow or marble, characterized by an inseparable mingling of differently colored ingredients, the colors appearing in vertical and diagonal strands and unexpected whirls. As colors are mixed in the marble case, so functions are mixed in the American federal system.
>
> (Grodzins 1960: 74)

The federal, state, and even local governments mix together to pay for, set standards for, execute, and evaluate policy activity. One of many examples is the cooperation inherent in constructing, maintaining, and policing highway and road systems. Cooperative federalism is more a description of the informal cooperation that has evolved over time rather than a legalistic encapsulation of formal relations.

Regulatory Federalism

Regulatory federalism marked an important shift in the way federal policy was carried out through states and, to a lesser degree, localities. For the first time, during the 1960s and the 1970s the federal government attempted to bring the states and local governments under far-reaching federal regulation, initially by providing funding through a new system of grants. Expansive interpretation of federal constitutional powers under the U.S. Constitution by the courts coupled with a more restrictive view of the 10th Amendment when applied to the states led to a more centrally guided intergovernmental system administered through the federal grant system (Dilger and Boyd 2014).

This new system was supported by the development of new enforcement mechanisms that conditioned federal financial support on compliance with federal mandates. These included cross-over sanctions, wherein the termination or reduction of aid provided by one grant program was threatened unless the requirements of another program were satisfied, for example tying together highway safety funding with highway beautification requirements. They also included now commonplace enforcement mechanisms like cross-cutting sanctions that apply across the board to all federally funded programs such as requirements of non-discrimination or environmental protection. Once less money became available from the federal government to implement regulations in areas ranging from the natural environment to housing, these sanctions supported the rise of an important concept in the study of U.S. federalism: the unfunded mandate. It reflected the continued requirement for compliance with, but also the new burden of paying for these policies.

A noteworthy change—and mechanism of control—in the way intergovernmental business was conducted during this period was the development of a direct relationship between the federal government and local governments or what has been called "direct federalism" (Advisory Commission on Intergovernmental Relations 1983). One feature of the Johnson Administration's Great Society programs was the creation of new programs with grants made not only to states but also directly to cities, counties, school districts, and not-for-profits and bypassing states entirely in their implementation. Although most of the Great Society programs were implemented through grants for specific purposes–categorical grants–the distribution of funding was done in a way that emphasized a new federal and local partnership.

The Picket Fence Metaphor and Regulatory Federalism

One limitation of metaphors is that they may not be responsive to new developments. This was true of regulatory federalism and the cake metaphor. The federal grant programs that grew in the 1960s designed to address urban problems and to meet the needs of disadvantaged citizens were not well exemplified by the cake metaphor. The bureaucratic actors overseeing categorical grant programs in specific policy areas played a much larger role than before as both federal funding and grant requirements increased: successful grant applications required clear strategies, well developed budgets, public participation, and a sound management plan.

The importance of administrative professionals grew because they understood the technical requirements and legal norms of policy areas addressed in the categorical grants. This allowed them to communicate with similar professionals at other levels of government and successfully obtain funding for and implement programs. So, attention shifted from the programmatic decisions of political actors at each level of government, to the implementation of federal grant programs by like-minded and trained specialists in policy areas. The professional specialty and policy area in which administrative actors were trained and their understanding of the activities and relations in this area were more important than the level of their government employer. It has been pointed out, variously, that these arrangements reduce the power of political officials (Sanford 1967).

Consequently, American federalism was best represented by the metaphor of a picket fence. In this metaphor, the horizontal boards or slats in the fence depict the levels of government, national, state, and local, which are depicted by layers in the cake metaphor. What the picket fence metaphor adds are the vertical, pointed pickets in a picket fence that run from top to bottom and represent specific federal policy or program areas: elementary and secondary education, welfare, and public housing are the sort of cross-cutting program areas represented by the vertical pickets of the fence. The key innovation in this metaphor is the focus on the way programs are carried out by specialized administrative actors at different levels of government: the pickets encapsulate the relations that develop among professional specialists in the various cooperating bureaucracies at all levels of government to enable the implementation of federal policies. Support, communication, and reinforcement are provided by the federal, state, and local governments portrayed by the horizontal slats, but the important activities occur in program areas funded by the federal government and implemented by specialized professionals across the levels of government.

Executive Federalism and Modern Innovations

Thompson (2013) has pointed out that the picket fence metaphor over-emphasizes the role of professionals at the expense of political actors and thus does not characterize well some of the dynamics of modern federalism and IGR. He suggests that the picket fence metaphor does not capture the discretionary decisions of political executives to accept programs, in what form to accept them, and their guidance of implementation through their appointed agents in what has been called "executive federalism." This model places more emphasis on the relationship of political executives and their appointees rather than bureaucratic actors.

There have been other attempts to replace the more conventional metaphors with new ones. An interesting effort has been the work of Schapiro (2009), who has developed a theory of polyphonic federalism. He attempts to address the dualism of contemporary Federalist theories and replace them with one that preserves the differences in points of view and manages to give a small nod to the role of local governments. The chief notion in this schema is that the most effective way to portray U.S. federalism is not visually, but aurally and that rather than using a visual metaphor, a more adequate one would be a musical fugue or canon. This representation purports to have the advantage of assuring that individual voices are not lost in combination, but rather create a new whole while preserving their individual nature.

Likewise, Bidjerano (2004) uses the metaphor of the Internet as a representation of U.S. federalism to suggest a networked federalism and IGR. This is a somewhat unique perspective because rather than trading on the modern preoccupation in public administration with network analysis and networked government, his contribution is more squarely in the tradition of federalism metaphors. Using a case of multi-agency response to the West Nile Virus, he suggests that actors' attempts to get around the pre-existing formal and informal intergovernmental networks resembled more the way nodes on the internet seek to reroute packets of information when desired connections are not available. In addition, he suggests an additional metaphor of "web-weaving" (ibid.: 24) that is the activity to give permanence to the new connections and create new formal networks for IGR.

Limitations of the Paradigms of Federalism

The usefulness of these frameworks has been criticized roundly. Weissert (2011) suggests they do not highlight what is important or useful to an understanding of U.S. federalism. Nathan has suggested that they are repetitive if not redundant (Nathan 2006a). Others submit that the effort to encapsulate American federalism is a "seemingly endless quest for a rational and functional division of governmental responsibilities [that] has produced little of lasting significance" (Bowman and Kearney 2011: 563). For Derthick (2000: 27), an understanding of U.S. federalism defies description and remains "murky."

Attempts to summarize American federalism are largely futile because the scope and placement of activities across governments and organizations is transitory: government reforms, elections, and novel policies all change the nature and functioning of federalism. According to Stever (2005), the efforts to develop meaningful categories for the U.S. federal system remain difficult to pin down in a functional and lasting way and are largely fruitless due to this distribution of activities across governments. As Robert Dilger (2000) has pointed out, much of what we think we know about U.S. government, American federalism, and IGR is not so. Accordingly, it is in the interests of everyone to challenge background assumptions about their workings that are presented in the basic paradigms. When both public officials as well as interest groups operate on received wisdom it affects the policy making process itself.

One widely embraced attempt to supplant these paradigms in public administration has been the study of IGR as a theoretical and empirical effort to understand how the various constituent parts of the U.S. federal system work together at given moments. As the name implies, it focuses on "relations" or transactions among governments operating in the same sectors, such as health or social welfare, or operating mutually to achieve programmatic ends such as building highway systems or providing family assistance. Nevertheless, it is not easy to say what IGR is in practice. As the father of IGR, Deil Wright (1990) points out that it is most appropriately viewed as a set of complementary conceptual frameworks. According to McGuire (2006: 677) an understanding of IGR varies with "the policy area, the policy instruments employed, and even the skills of the administrator." An offshoot, intergovernmental management (IGM), has been questioned as vague in concept and suffering from being of "recent vintage, specialized usage, limited visibility, and uncertain maturity" (Krane and Wright 1998: 1162).

The Federalism Paradigms Over Time

The paradigms in this essay suggest a gradual evolution of U.S. federalism. For example, the allegory of a cake representing separate sovereign and dependent jurisdictions with individual missions serving different jurisdictions, was extended to show how these governments had become involved with each other to ensure the wellbeing of a nation. This metaphor represented the change from dual federalism to collaborative federalism. Likewise, the metaphor of a picket fence preserved the notions of levels of government and collaboration across levels, but highlighted the way the collaboration was implemented in narrow fiscal and technical channels bounded by specific policies. The picket fence parable exemplified the change from collaborative to regulatory federalism in which the federal government drove the system from the top-down using a new arrangement of federal grants to tackle social problems. From that point on much of the discussion about U.S. federalism is about marginal, technical modifications in grant and funding arrangements—categorical, block, or revenue sharing—rather than depiction of change in the echelons or preeminence of different governments or bureaucracies. The description of change is slow and steady and reflects a regular progression.

The paradigms portray a federal system that adapts to change and evolves gradually. Yet, sometimes evolution occurs due to an inability to adapt to exogenous system changes. In such cases evolution is said to be punctual rather than gradual and the paradigms are unable to tell the story of such unsettling events. Large-scale exogenous changes to the federal system might include the Great Depression and World War II, which eradicated dual federalism, or the Vietnam War, which destroyed faith in the federal government and constrained federal funding. The paradigms do not capture these either as models or labels. For example, collaborative federalism could be called "great depression federalism." In the same vein, regulatory federalism could have been styled "Vietnam" (or "civil rights"?) federalism.

One of the main limitations of the frameworks is that they are largely time-bound; they seem incapable of capturing the dynamic and cyclical nature of U.S. federalism. How well do they account for changes in the system that have occurred? Richard Nathan points out about the states that:

> States reshaped programs to their priorities, increased the funding of programs in areas in which the federal government had become less active, and assumed more control over the

activities of local governments and nonprofit organizations. In these ways and others, states expanded their influence vis-à-vis the federal government and in their relationships with local governments and nonprofit organizations.

(Nathan 2006b)

Clearly, the paradigms did not reflect this and such changes in federalism are occurring with greater frequency and intensity. Moreover, the old paradigms of U.S. federalism simply no longer capture or explain what is really going on. Focused on gradual change, the paradigms cannot account well for systemic changes after considerable upheavals in the system itself (Agranoff and McGuire 2001). The most recent example of systemic change due to disruption is the impact of the Great Recession (Perlman and Benton 2012). This near depression-like event from which the nation is still recovering has been felt most at the local level of the economy.

The economic downturn stressed the federal system almost to the breaking point. A federal government trillions of dollars in debt was not financially or politically capable of helping other governments much (see Chapter 5, this volume). Without the possibility of deficit budgeting, state governments devote every available dollar to their own operations and dedicate the lion's share of federal grants-in-aid to the largest and fastest increasing portion of their budgets–Medicare and Medicaid. Local governments have shed jobs and reduced expenditures and waited for help from above that has not come. Meanwhile, shrinking tax bases, growing benefit burdens, increasing service demands, and deteriorating infrastructure put local governments against the fiscal wall. Where and how is any of this reflected in the conventional paradigms and how could it be?

At the time of this writing, local governments are recovering from the Great Recession, but they have done so unevenly. For cities, overall fiscal stability is improving for day-to-day operations. Yet, local budgets continue to confront challenges in the areas of infrastructure, pay and benefits, and retiree support (McFarland and Pagano 2016). Moreover, local governmental recovery is widely disparate in the areas of employment and housing. Their ability to sustain current levels of fiscal stability is uncertain. For example, in 2013, thirteen cities (Baltimore, Boston, Denver, Houston, Los Angeles, Miami, New York, Philadelphia, Portland OR, San Antonio, San Francisco, St. Louis, and Washington) saw increases in property tax revenue collections. Fifteen cities (Atlanta, Chicago, Cleveland, Dallas, Detroit, Kansas City MO, Las Vegas, Minneapolis, Orlando FL, Phoenix, Pittsburgh, Riverside CA, San Diego, Seattle, and Tampa FL) saw declines (Pew Charitable Trust 2017b).

The real threat to sustained recovery of local governments is the irregular recovery of the state governments on which local governments directly depend. This relationship is reflected in the results reported in this work. Even after seven years not all states have recovered all the ground lost to the Great Recession (Pew Charitable Trust 2017a). Slow tax revenue growth leaves many states with little slack in their budgets to help local governments; they continue to feel the pinch from shortfalls in pension and health plans, and not all have picked up in employment. In short, while improving, the fiscal condition of states and localities after the Great Recession continues to be precarious.

The Federalism Paradigms and Local Governments

Another limitation of the conventional ways to understand U.S. federalism is their failure to maintain an equitable focus on national, state, and local activities. This has been particularly problematic

(Zimmerman 1996). Yet the practical evolution of U.S. federalism during more than 200 years has seen the importance of local governments shift from the top to the bottom of the governmental hierarchy (Berman 2003). This emphasis is repeated in the key metaphors and models of American federalism and is extended into IGR and IGM. In fact, according to Agranoff (2001) what would make IGR and IGM useful would be a continuing focus on both state and local relations as well as federal ones. Nevertheless, the emphasis on the federal and state levels ignores the fact that many local governments are quite powerful even though the extent of local discretion, autonomy, and authority varies with state constitution, statute, and precedent. Too, it disregards the current circumstances in which local governments carry the heaviest loads and have become the work-horses of the federal system.

There is another factor in the downplaying of local governments in U.S. federalism. According to Kincaid (1999: 135), in what he calls a shift from "places to persons" in U.S. intergovernmental relations, federal policy and aid is mostly directed to individuals, rather than to local governments and this has led to an effective defunding of cities in the federal system. Once a significant feature of the U.S. system and prominent in Great Society programs, the federal and local government partnership ended in the 1970s. Kincaid points out that even though there has been interest in and demand for moving functions from the federal government to the states and localities since the New Deal—devolution—this tendency has been resisted and slowed in fact because there is less political benefit for federal elected officials to aid jurisdictions rather than individual voters. Thus, there is a tension between local government responsibilities and federal policymaking that leaves the former as less than full partners in the system. While they have clear importance, they are hamstrung in fact.

The significance of local government actors in U.S. federalism has been long noted by authors. For example, in a 1981 study, Gargan advanced the notion that attitudes of local officials coupled with community expectations of adequate service delivery mattered as much as the capacity of local governments to provide services, particularly in financial management. Local fiscal problems result not only from poor processes but as much from local perceptions of those problems which are in turn based on local practices, tradition, and culture.

Nevertheless, when local administrators are studied it is less the role they play in U.S. federalism or even in IGR, but instead their limited, job-related behaviors, views, attitudes, and perceptions. For example, Kearney, Feldman, and Scavo (2002) looked at not only the actions but the sentiments of city managers as patrons of reinvention efforts at the local level, calling them the "prime movers of local government reinvention efforts." Similarly, DeSantis, Glass, and Newell (1992) looked at the influence of city managers' perceptions of community problems and their job satisfaction, finding that the relationship between managers and councilors in confronting these problems was a key determinant. In a like vein, Hoyman and McCall (2010) examined the attitudes of local officials about the suitability of the use of eminent domain in county governments. Too, Lewis (1993) has looked at local administrators' views as a predictor of their productivity improvement efforts.

In sum, most attempts to characterize or capture the U.S. federal system have three limitations in common. First, they employ a label-based metaphorical approach to capture the essential qualities of a large and complex system instead of an approach that captures both sentiments and behavior. Second, they have limited ability to capture changes in the intergovernmental system that are occurring with greater frequency and intensity. Third, they give preeminence, prominence, or emphasis to the federal and state ambits of the American federal system and less, if any, importance to the realm of local governments.

A Relationship Approach

The problems outlined above suggest that the study of American federalism will benefit from a shift in focus. One way of correcting the limitations of the metaphorical approach relates to a conceptual distinction that has been left unnoticed in the discussion of federalism and IGR: that is the difference between the concept of *relations* and the concept of *relationships*. Employing the latter provides a different point of view than the former that may go some ways to address the challenges outlined above.

According to the *Oxford English Dictionary* (OED), the former term, *relations*, is an "attribute" of something that denotes a "connection, correspondence, or contrast" between different things (OED 2014). Also, it is used most often in the context of government entities to connote operational connections or how jurisdictions maintain "political or economic contact with one another" (ibid.). Interestingly, the OED highlights that this usage is most often employed with a "modifying word"; so, this example highlights uses like international relations or intergovernmental relations. In addition, the OED indicates that the word also is used to point out "social interactions and feelings" that exist between individuals or groups. Clearly, the relevant use of this word is the second one: the maintenance of contact among jurisdictions.

On the other hand, the term *relationships*, has a different focus according to the OED. It more clearly highlights the "connections formed between two or more people . . . based on social inter-actions and mutual goals" (OED 2014). This more clearly corresponds to the third usage of the term *relations*, but is much more obviously pointed at human affiliation as the key concept. Although the term *relationship* is related to the term *relation*, it is a specific and isolated case that highlights something different: the human connection, affiliation, and association based on inter-personal interaction, rather than the jurisdictional maintenance of contact among jurisdictions on operational areas like the economy or politics.

Dunn and Legge (2002) point out both that the notion of relationships among officials is an enduring issue and that their perceptions of these is what is genuinely important in understanding their behavior. This is because, like the background conditions, the perceptions of the practitioners themselves change about how things are working. Not metaphor, nor theory, nor framework are useful in understanding them. They depend on the circumstances confronted and do not reach a permanent consensus view about how things mesh.

This notion of relationships becomes increasingly significant when individuals must collaborate to solve problems that are not easily solved by single individuals in one organization or jurisdiction (Agranoff and McGuire 2003). These are precisely the sort of problems that have been faced by local governments after the Great Recession. Since 2008, the environment of U.S. federalism has changed drastically. The programs of jobs, grants, and aid that powered the old system since the Great Depression and through the Clinton Administration, no longer exists. Moreover, the concept of relationships is not hierarchical but lateral and so it does not presuppose the hierarchical arrangement of government importance implicit in the use of the term "relations." In whatever manner U.S. federalism is portrayed, local governments' views have been given less attention than that of the other levels.

The research presented below is an attempt to employ the concept of relationships. It does so by looking at the perceived state of the relationship between local government actors and the states and federal government. It presents the views of managers at the local level concerning their relationships with the other levels of government.

What is suggested here is to shift the study of federalism from the top to the bottom and from formal norms to informal behaviors; especially those driven by attitudes. The former focus is on the relations of federalism. In studying relations, the focus is on describing the activities of the parts of the system and has a structural orientation—behavior is ascribed to jurisdictions and entities. A shift to studying relationships would focus on the actors in the system, their attitudes and the way these attitudes enable or condition their behavior in the carrying out of program activity. It is tempting to see relationships as the infrastructure of federalism on which the formal procedures and processes (relations) are constructed: this complements the descriptions of behavior in implementing formal rules and policies with the descriptions of the bonds forged among the actors that provide the basis for them. The infrastructure provides a basis for the structure. This is a notion based on social capital: encouraging interaction builds trust and positive attitudes, which are lasting, helpful relationships. These provide a foundation for the construction of successful programs. Success depends on the relationships of the actors and their views of each other: attitudes, perceptions, and thoughts about other actors limit the effectiveness of programmatic relations and program outcomes.

The Research

This research uses data collected from a 2012 survey ($N = 744$) of local government administrators—both city and county level—on the actions they have taken to cope with fiscal pressures during and after the Great Recession and their perceptions about the support they receive from the other two levels of government. The questions examine the views of these local managers on the relationship of their governments with the other two levels of governments: the states, on whom they most directly depend, and the federal government from whom they have gotten most of their resources in the recent past.

The research reported here looks at the three important constructs that conform part of the relationship of local governments to their states and the federal government: authority, support, and burdens for local governments from the states and federal government. It examines the way that changes in these constructs by the state and federal governments impact the perceptions of local officials of their relationships with these other two levels after the economic downturn. In short, it looks at the perceived relationship between local governments and the federal and state governments after the Great Recession.

The purpose of the research is to improve our understanding of the current views of the local governments and their relationships with the state and federal governments. That is, to tell the story from the local point of view. The survey asked about four key topics that affect the relationship of local governments to the state and federal governments:

* revenues;
* authority;
* mandated activities; and
* responsibilities.

Data for this analysis was collected from an online survey that was directed to the chief operating officer for a random selection of cities of all sizes and each county in the U.S. The chief operating officer was the city/county manager or mayor in those cities with a strong mayor/mayor only form of government. Multiple reminders were sent to maximize the participation rate. A response rate of approximately 28 percent was obtained. The survey asked a number of questions regarding the actions taken by city or county governments in response to the financial downturn. The survey results permitted this research to examine any changes between local governments and state and federal governments related to resources and authority as well as the perceived relationship between the local governments and the state and federal governments.

Local government managers were asked about an increase or a decrease in revenues, authority, mandates, or responsibilities for a total of eight questions (see appendix to this chapter). The questions were asked first about the local government manager's view of the relationship with the state government and then repeated for the relationship with the federal government. This created 16 data points, eight for the state government and eight for the federal. The responses were scored on an additive scale that ranged from 0 to 4 for increases or decreases in the set of topics. For example, a city or county received a score of "0" if it did not mark any of the questions. If the respondent indicated that the government being considered had decreased revenues and reduced authority they received a score of "2."

A second analysis specifically asked the city or county respondent to assess its relationship with the state and federal governments. This question asked managers to assess changes in the relationship between their government and the state and federal government on a three-point scale that ranged from "worse" to "the same" to "improved." Also, respondents could indicate that they did not know or refuse to answer.

Findings

The following tables present the results of the questions regarding the changes in the resources and authority provided by the state or federal governments for the local governments. The second analyses present the results of the question regarding perceived changes in the relationship between the local government and the state and federal governments.

Increases and Decreases in State and Federal Resources and Support

Table 6.1 presents the results for the responses regarding reduction of state support in the categories of funding, reduction of authority, increase of unfunded mandates, or increase of unfunded responsibilities.

As Table 6.1 indicates, 663 respondents answered the questions that make up the variable. Of those responding, 622, or over 90 percent, indicated one or more reductions in support by their state government, while 442, or over about 65 percent, responded affirmatively to experiencing three to four reductions.

Table 6.2 presents the results for the responses regarding reduction of federal support in the categories of funding, reduction of authority, increase of unfunded mandates, or increase of unfunded responsibilities.

Conversely from Table 6.1, as can be seen on Table 6.2, 204 or about 30 percent of the respondents indicate no reduction at all in federal support, and 331 respondents or just barely half report undergoing zero to two reductions from the federal government. Unlike the states, only 128 or less than one fifth (19 percent) of the respondents reported experiencing three to four federal support reductions.

Table 6.1 State Support Reduction

Number of State Resource Reductions	Freq.	Percent	Cum.
0	41	6.18	6.18
1	85	12.82	19.00
2	123	18.55	37.56
3	182	27.45	65.01
4	232	34.99	100.00
Total	663	100.00	

Table 6.2 Federal Support Reduction

Number of Federal Resource Reductions	Freq.	Percent	Cum.
0	204	30.77	30.77
1	218	32.88	63.65
2	113	17.04	80.69
3	81	12.22	92.91
4	47	7.09	100.00
Total	663	100.00	

Table 6.3 State Support Increase

Number of State Supports	Freq.	Percent	Cum.
0	559	84.31	84.31
1	81	12.22	96.53
2	18	2.71	99.25
3	4	0.60	99.85
4	1	0.15	100.00
Total	663	100.00	

Like the foregoing tables, Table 6.3 presents the results for the responses regarding state increase of funding, increase of authority, decrease of unfunded mandates, or decrease of unfunded responsibilities.

When it comes to increases in support, things are somewhat different than in reductions in support and somewhat more similar between the states and the federal governments. As Table 6.3 makes clear, nearly all the local governments, 559 or 84 percent, did not experience any increase in state support or attendant reduction of unfunded mandates.

Table 6.4 presents the results for the responses regarding federal increase of funding, increase of authority, decrease of unfunded mandates, or decrease of unfunded responsibilities. In these respects, the federal government is almost identical to the states when it comes to support. Nearly all the respondents, 553 or 83 percent, reported no increase in support. The federal and state governments are close to identical in all other categories.

As the results clearly indicate, state governments added significantly more burdens to local governments than did the federal government in the three years before respondents were surveyed.

Table 6.4 Federal Support Increase

Number of Federal Supports	Freq.	Percent	Cum.
0	553	83.40	84.31
1	98	14.78	96.53
2	11	1.65	99.25
3	4	0.60	99.85
4	1	0.15	100.00
Total	663	100.00	

Nevertheless, when it comes adding support for local governments, there is no substantial difference in the change of support between state and federal governments. In other words, although the federal government largely held local governments harmless during this time and kept resources at prior levels and did not add burdens, neither level of government increased support to local governments in most cases during the same time.

What does this mean in practice and what sort of changes are being reflected in these attitudes? On the state level, examples of increased burdens range from state impositions of training requirements for local firefighters or communication capabilities for public safety entities in general to election roll reporting or purging as well as strictures for local hospital access. Reduced aid in the state purview can take the form of decreases in capital or hospital support from state legislatures, to reductions in economic development support at the local or regional level, to withdrawal of financial support for public defenders, medical examiners, or even activities such as participation in issuing or underwriting local revenue bonds. Increased federal burdens are more likely to consist of regulatory impositions such as enhanced environmental safeguards or clean-up strictures, additional requirements for obtaining federal grants such as collaboration, or reduction in local autonomy through preemption in such policy areas as criminal justice processes and local election equipment. Federal aid reductions are most likely to be felt through the reduction of grants in housing and community development, for example in the Home Investment Partnership Program and Community Development Block Grant programs. In addition, through the American Recovery and Reinvestment Act (ARRA) local governments were given more to do, but most of the funding stayed at the state level.

Changes in Local Governments' Relationship with State and Federal Governments

The impact of these findings can be clearly seen in the answers to two other questions asking directly about perceptions of federal and state relations. The tables below summarize the frequencies for two questions on whether relationships have improved, gotten worse, or stayed the same for local government and state and federal governments. These results are reported on the other frequency tables below.

As shown on Table 6.5, perceptions of the respondents are that the relationship between the state and their local jurisdiction has worsened. Almost two thirds, 401 or 61 percent, of the 654 respondents answering report this view. Only 36, a little under 6 percent, think things have improved and only about a third, 217 or 33 percent, even think things are the same. Almost 95 percent in total believe relationships between the localities and states are the same or worse and it is almost two to one that see things worse rather than the same.

Table 6.5 Relationship with the State

Relations	Freq.	Percent	Cum.
Worse	401	61.31	61.31
Same	217	33.18	94.50
Improved	36	5.50	100.00
Total	654	100.00	

Table 6.6 Relationship with the Federal Government

Relations	Freq.	Percent	Cum.
Worse	176	26.55	26.55
Same	449	67.72	94.27
Improved	38	5.73	100.00
Total	654	100.00	

As might be expected, perceived relationships with the federal government are nearly the inverse. Only 176 of the 654 respondents, barely over one quarter or about 27 percent, think the relationship has worsened. The bulk of them believe that interactions with the federal government are primarily the same as before, with a solid two thirds, almost 68 percent, reporting this perspective. Interestingly, just about as many of the local government administrators thought that relationships were improving with the federal government as they did with the states (38 compared with 36 for the states). In sum, 61 percent of local governments think their relationship with state became worse, while 27 percent of them think their relationship with federal government became worse.

Discussion

How should these data be interpreted? Perhaps, taken together, they indicate that from the point of view of local government managers, the prevalent metaphors and theories of U.S. federalism and the IGR system do not capture their intergovernmental reality. Maybe, even more clearly, they do not seem to lend much credence to notions like collaborative or picket fence federalism. If the implicit notion of cooperative or supportive relationships, whether political or professional, that are found in those ideas were dominant in empirical fact, then the data would not so clearly portray a dependence of favorable respondent attitudes on support from other governments. Moreover, there is nothing in the data suggesting that local governments are looking for ways to adjust the system with joint and collaborative formal innovations, such as new regional governance structures, local buying cooperatives, or consolidated services or jurisdictions.

An important point about the data in this study that needs to be emphasized is that the respondents do not report factual claims about reduced or status quo support for local governments from the other levels, but rather involve local perceptions of the behavior of federal and state governments. This is important because, as Dilger (2000) suggests, the views of participants about facts are what conditions their attitudes about policy in the federal system. Accordingly, and important for this research, perceptions of local government managers themselves about the relationship with the states and the federal government are likely to endure beyond any factual changes. That is, behavior of these actors in federalism may be best interpreted for some time to come by their attitudes conditioned in the Great Recession and their views of their relationships and the stories they tell themselves.

There are other examples of this disjunction between perception and reality and the long-lasting effects of these perceptions. In their findings about state and local relations, Bowman and Kearney (Chapter 11, this volume) show that although, as indicated here, the general perception is that states have restricted local authority across the board, this is not completely true. As they point out, many states have passed laws that empower localities rather than restricting their authority. Likewise, practicing local managers indicate in recent interviews that, unlike the perceived wisdom, unfunded mandates are not important drivers for their activities especially in inter-local collaboration. In fact, to the managers interviewed these seem to be nuisances and required objects of complaint, but not important spurs to or constraints on action (Perlman 2015).

The data suggest that, from the standpoint of local governments, the relationship with the other two governments is not ideal, but varies depending on the circumstances of that relationship. Clearly, most local actors have a jaundiced view of their relationship with the states, but a more favorable one of the federal government. As one local government manager responded in an open-ended section of the survey, "Our State eliminated redevelopment funding to balance their own deficits. They took local revenues to meet state obligations to education. They steal from economic development projects and wind up hindering local recovery." Another commented in speaking of the federal government that, "There has been more federal funding available for economic relief and grants through things like ARRA which was successful as far as it went, but stopped too soon. This has led to three years of continuous engagement of federal officials and relationship building."

The data in this study could be portrayed as showing local government officials to be somewhat resentful that states have increased tasks and have withdrawn prior funding. As one local manager commented, "We are seeing more state actions to sweep funds at the state level, to take funds away from the cities, and to reduce state contributions to cities." In short, local governments find themselves continuing to work for the states, but not being supported in that work. Resentment is not directed at the federal government, but at the states and it is the relationship with the states that has suffered. Perhaps, it is going beyond the data to cast the respondents as hopeful about their rescue by the federal government in the future, but clearly, they have a more positive attitude about federal support and a somewhat better relationship. Whether, this is a lingering halo effect or there is hope for the future would take additional research to confirm, but as another respondent commented, "The state keeps taking shared revenues and funding set aside by voters that was supposed to go to Cities. They have an anti-City-County agenda and have been fiscally irresponsible and are now trying to solve their financial problems by taking municipal revenue."

Conclusion: A Relationship Approach and the Future of the Local–Federal Relationship

This research presents a view of the limitations of conventional understanding of U.S. federalism and IGR, attempts to address those limitations with a new notion of relationship rather than relations, and applies it to survey data from local government managers. Indeed, this work supports the belief that IGR should stand for intergovernmental *relationships*. It argues that the attitudes of local government actors about relationships with other levels of government matter and endure and thus are most important for an understanding of change in the American federal and IGR system than are functional or conceptual models. Also, it maintains that this understanding of how to study U.S. federalism and IGR is even more important today in a period of reconfiguration and challenge, just as it was after the Great Depression.

An argument for a concentration on governmental actors in the study of federalism is not without precedent. Both the picket fence metaphor and the notion of executive federalism focus on people and the roles they play in federalism. Nevertheless, that focus is more on formal relations in either legislative and party politics leading to policy outputs or policy implementation than it is a focus on relationships based on attitudes. Neither point of view aims to understand the attitudes of the actors and how, once converted to sentiments, they may last and condition, limit, or facilitate what is possible with respect to the carrying out of government programs. As some research indicates, this is true horizontally in inter-local collaboration in the U.S. system; there is good reason to believe it is true in vertical association as well.

Part of what is necessary to make an effective study of IGR is the focus not so much on formal relations (norms and policies) and program implementation (behavior in the carrying out of norms and policies) but on relationships – the attitudes and ability to cooperate and get along of the actors in the system. For the study of IGR to prosper in the future attention needs to shift from the structure of federalism (relations) to the infrastructure of federalism (relationships). That is, the focus needs to change from the descriptions of behavior found in implementing formal rules and policies to the descriptions of the bonds forged among the actors that provide the basis for the construction of new programs. The infrastructure provides a basis for the structure. This most resembles the notion of social capital: interaction and trust built through relationships affords a foundation for the construction of successful programs. The degree to which programs are successful or even serviceable depends on the relationships of the actors implementing them and their views of each other. Attitudes, perceptions, and thoughts about actors become important because they limit what is possible in the future. Views of the actors are not only the basis for what is possible, but condition what is probable and likely as outcomes. What occurs in jurisdictions is not dictated by planning or incentive, but rather is a product of preexisting trust and the identification of opportunity. The former is likely to be a product of social capital and the latter a product of similar professional background.

This research suggests several benefits for viewing U.S. federalism and IGR using relationships rather than relations. While illustratively useful, traditional metaphors and models of U.S. federalism and IGR are reactive, inflexible, and under-study the local point of view. It is not clear that this can be fixed in any way by changing or using a different "flavor of the month" metaphor or framework. Those attitudes about relationships with other governments matter and endure in local government officials who far outnumber both federal and state officials and who bear the greatest responsibility for the implementation of programs and thus impact the American federal and IGR system in lasting ways. Even though their behavior is paramount, explaining it requires a deeper understanding of what they see when they are acting and to what they are reacting—in this case, their relationships with the other governmental actors.

In addition to the specific results of this research, the relationship approach has several significant implications for the study of federalism and intergovernmental relations. First, relationships are an empirical construct and this research is based on empirical results. The construct of relationship consists of reported perceptions on provided and reduced resources as well as imposed burdens from actual activities to responsibilities. Thus, it is tied to the actual perceptions of local government officials and not what they think the intergovernmental system is at any point in time or what it should be in an ideal sense or the future.

Second, the construct of relationship indicates that there is not just one paradigm or view that accurately characterizes the U.S. federal or intergovernmental system. For example, some states may impose stringent unfunded mandates on local governments while others do not do so. Similarly, local governments vary in their capacity to absorb or generate revenue to cover the costs of such mandates. The intergovernmental system should be thought of not in terms of a single framework, model, or metaphor but as a range of experiences and perceptions of the relationships of the actors.

Third, the relationship approach is not time-bound and does not suffer from having to either depict disruptive change or account for theoretical anomaly. Changes in a relationship based on financial, legislative, or other forces that affect the federal system can be quickly identified and monitored over time. It is not the distribution of functional elements in the system that is the important focus–something that changes over time and circumstance–but rather the level and degree of sentiment among the key officials that is tracked and monitored. This is the empirical basis of the relationship which is the effect of system change.

Fourth, the focus of the relationship approach is the views of local government officials as they perceive the actions of the federal and state governments. Given the undeniable fact that most service delivery, much funding, and most political activity takes place at the local level, the key actors in the intergovernmental system are local, even if they are not the preeminent actors in the constitutional system. Failing to focus on them gives too much credence to regulatory over service delivery regimes and continues to encourage study of the federal system from a top-down rather than bottom-up approach; this distorts the reality of the system for most participants. Moreover, it emphasizes a deductive rather than inductive understanding of U.S. federalism and, ultimately, leads to a better understanding of the intergovernmental system.

Fifth, the relationship approach, as developed through empirical research, provides the basis for formulating and testing theories that can better explain the perception of local government officials. As suggested above, the relationship approach should help to understand the entire system; however, a more profound understanding of the perceptions of local officials themselves is an important step. Other frameworks more closely examine and highlight federal and state actors, but there is comparatively little in this vein about local government players. A focus on them will enhance a theoretical understanding of their activities as well as their system role.

In sum, the results of this research support a focus on the relationship between local government officials and their state and federal counterparts as a fruitful research direction for the future of IGR. Particularly, what is stressed here is a focus on the views of local officials—the view from the bottom of the U.S. federal system. In addition, this research suggests an approach, the focus on relationships, which it is hoped can lead to an improved and deeper understanding of the federal system and local government at the same time. This improvement is sought by moving away from what might be characterized as a functional and transactional view to a sentimental one.

The Future of Local–Federal Relationships

The empirical results reported in this work indicate that the local managers' perceptions of the state and federal government are less than positive, but that the relationship of local managers with their states suffers most. This was primarily due to the greater reduction in state support and the increase in burdens being passed down from them to localities. Conversely, the federal government was perceived as passing fewer burdens, but maintaining a greater, if reduced, level of support. A question for the future of the study of IGR is: what will happen to this relationship, if the level of federal support for local governments is perceived as reduced and imposition of burdens increased? Put another way, what happens to the local–federal relationship if political change in Washington leads to a change for the worse in national budgetary and policy priorities for localities?

Recent Changes at the Federal Level

At this writing, there has been such change in Washington. The advent of the Trump administration and the control of both houses of Congress by the Republican Party is a fact that was not accomplished or even anticipated when data was collected for this work. Although it is too early to know for sure what proposals will be adopted and carried out, their effects on local governments, and the views of local managers of them, the proposed $54 billion reduction in domestic spending in the Trump administration's proposed budget signals its posture toward local governments. The budget proposal of the administration (Office of Management and Budget 2017a), including its budget blueprint (Office of Management and Budget 2017b) and detailed major savings and reforms (Office of Management and Budget 2017c) documents lays out these cuts:

- A $16.2 billion (13 percent) cut to the Department of Transportation results in the freezing of local government transportation grants from the New Starts (projects over $300 million) and Small Starts (projects under $300 million) programs; both are critical for local mass transit.
- The $3 billion, 42-year-old Community Development Block Grant (CDBG) program administered by the Department of Housing and Urban Development (HUD) which supports infrastructure, community building, and anti-poverty projects in 1,185 state and local governments will be eliminated; this includes both Meals-on-Wheels and downtown revitalization.
- HUD will lose $1.9 billion for public housing maintenance, hitting both capital and operations, which will affect the public housing stock in most big cities across the U.S. and lead to its deterioration and increased future maintenance costs.
- Elimination of up to 62 agencies, some of which provide direct aid to localities, including the Department of Commerce's Economic Development Agency ($221 million), the Department of Energy's Weatherization Assistance Program ($121 million) which helps homeowners with energy efficiency grants up to $6,500, and the Department of the Treasury's Community Development Financial Institution grants ($210 million) supporting community banks and credit unions, among others.

The potential cuts in support for local government in the proposed budget outlined above are considerable and they do not include additional increased costs for local governments that are likely to accompany other policy changes proposed both by the administration and in Congress, if adopted. For example, proposed cuts in federal health care insurance subsidies and Medicaid may increase the costs for local governments to run hospitals, emergency rooms, and ambulance services. Likewise, the imposition of mandatory sentencing proposed by the Department of Justice may increase the costs of local police, courts, and corrections. In addition, the plans of the Trump administration and Congress to penalize local governments that do not assist in immigration enforcement may reduce grants for those local governments. For example, H.R. 3003, the No Sanctuary for Criminals Act, broadens the pool of money that cities could lose for not cooperating with federal immigration officials. Moreover, those that do capitulate may be forced to absorb new costs.

Impact of the Proposals on the Local–Federal Relationship

The spending plan put forward by the Trump administration aims to cut domestic outlays, mostly by axing aid to state and local governments. If enacted, this plan will certainly affect the current benign or at least neutral attitudes of local officials concerning the federal government reported in this work and will worsen that relationship. Nonetheless, even if not passed, the announcement of these priorities and the demonstrated willingness by the administration to withdraw support from local governments is likely to negatively affect that relationship. When coupled with additional proposals from the administration, in Congress, and from agencies which pass costs to local governments, the posture looks much the same as the one adopted by the states, about which respondents complained in the research reported here. The most likely outcome of this change over time is decreasing esteem by the locals for the feds.

Only time will determine the actual impact of these proposals. Nevertheless, it is interesting to speculate on what a renewed focus on the relationship of local government managers with the federal government might reveal over time. A more straightforward way to understand future changes is to ask those managers their opinions of that relationship. That was the method used to develop the findings reported in this work. It is suggested that updating this type of survey on a periodic basis is a way to carry out the program of putting the "R" back into IGR. This may be especially efficacious when political change in Washington results in a new policy posture toward local government.

Appendix: Questions Asked of Local Government Managers

In the past three years, has your city/county experienced any of the following in relation to the state/federal government? [Please mark all that apply.]

1   *Decreased* state/federal funding/transfers (i.e. grants, transfers for services, shared/collected revenues, etc.)
2   *Increased* state/federal funding/transfers (i.e. grants, transfers for services, shared/collected revenues, etc.)
3   State/federal actions that *reduced* local authority
4   State/federal actions that *increased* local authority
5   An *increase* in state/federal actions that mandate additional local activities without additional funding
6   A *decrease* in state/federal actions that mandate additional local activities without additional funding
7   An *increase* in state/federal actions that increased local responsibilities without sufficient revenue
8   A *decrease* in state/federal actions that increased local responsibilities without sufficient revenue

- None of the above
- Don't know
- Refuse

References

Advisory Commission on Intergovernmental Relations. 1983. *In Brief: Regulatory Federalism, Policy, Process, Impact and Reform*. Washington, DC: Advisory Commission on Intergovernmental Relations.

Agranoff, Robert. 2001. "Managing within the matrix: Do collaborative intergovernmental relations exist?" *Publius: The Journal of Federalism* 31(2): 31–56.

Agranoff, Robert and Michael McGuire. 2001. "American federalism and the search for models of management." *Public Administration Review* 61(6): 671–681.

Agranoff, Robert and Michael McGuire. 2003. *Collaborative Public Management: New Strategies for Local Government*. Washington, DC: Georgetown University Press.

Berman, David R. 2003. *Local Government and the States*. Armonk, NY: M. E. Sharpe.

Bidjerano, Morris. 2004. "The metaphors of federalism revisited: The web and intergovernmental relations." Annual Meeting of the Northeastern Political Science Association and the International Studies Association, Boston, MA.

Bowman, Ann O'M., and Richard C. Kearney. 2011. "Second-order devolution: Data and doubt." *Publius: The Journal of Federalism* 41(4): 563–585.

Bowman, Ann O'M., and Richard C. Kearney. 2014. "Transforming state–local relations." Annual Conference of the American Society for Public Administration, Washington, DC.

Derthick, Martha. 2000. "American federalism: Half-full or half-empty?" *Brookings Review* 18(1): 24–27.

DeSantis, Victor S., James J. Glass, and Charldean Newell. 1992. "City managers, job satisfaction, and community problem perception." *Public Administration Review* 52(5): 447–453.

Dilger, Robert Jay. 2000. "The study of American federalism at the turn of the century." *State and Local Government Review* 32(2): 98–107.

Dilger, Robert Jay and Eugene Boyd (2014). Block grants: Perspectives and controversies. CRS Report 7-5700 24. Washington, DC: Congressional Research Service.

Dunn, Delmer D., and Jerome S. Legge Jr,. 2002. "Politics and administration in U.S. local governments." *Journal of Public Administration Research and Theory* 12(3): 401–422.

Gargan, John J. 1981. "Consideration of local government capacity." *Public Administration Review* 41(6): 649–658.

Grodzins, Morton. 1960. "The Federal System." In *Goals for Americans: The Report of the President's Commission on National Goals and Chapters Submitted for Consideration of the Commission*. Englewood Cliffs, NJ: Prentice Hall.

Hoyman, Michele M., and Jamie R. McCall. 2010. "'Not imminent in my domain!' County leaders' attitudes toward eminent domain decisions." *Public Administration Review* 70(6): 885–893.

Kearney, Richard C., Barry M. Feldman, and Carmine P. F. Scavo. 2000. "Reinventing government: City manager attitudes and actions." *Public Administration Review* 60(6): 535–548.

Kincaid, John, 1999. De facto devolution and urban defunding: The priority of persons over places." *Journal of Urban Affairs* 21(2): 135–168.

Krane, Dale, and Deil S. Wright. 1998. "Intergovernmental management (IGM)." In *International Encyclopedia of Public Policy and Administration*, edited by Jay M. Shafritz. Boulder, CO: Westview.

Lewis, Edward B. 1993. "Precursors of productivity efforts by appointed county managers." *Public Productivity and Management Review* 16(3): 227–239.

McFarland, Christiana, and Michael A. Pagano. 2016. *City Fiscal Conditions*. Washington, DC: National League of Cities, Center for City Conditions and Applied Research.

McGuire, Michael. 2006. "Intergovernmental management: A view from the bottom." *Public Administration Review* 66(5): 677–679.

Nathan, Richard P. 2006a. "There will always be a new federalism." *Journal of Public Administration Research and Theory*: 16(4): 499–510.

Nathan, Richard P. 2006b. "Updating Theories of American Federalism." Annual Meeting of the American Political Science Association, Philadelphia, PA.

OED. 2014. *Oxford English Dictionary*. Oxford: Oxford University Press.

Office of Management and Budget. 2017a. *A New Foundation for American Greatness*. Budget of the U.S. Government, Fiscal Year 2018. Washington, DC: U.S. Government Publishing Office.

Office of Management and Budget. 2017b. *America First: A Budget Blueprint to Make America Great Again*. Budget of the U.S. Government, Fiscal Year 2018. Washington, DC: U.S. Government Publishing Office.

Office of Management and Budget. 2017c. *Major Savings and Reforms*. Budget of the U.S. Government, Fiscal Year 2018. Washington, DC: U.S. Government Publishing Office.

Perlman, Bruce J. 2010. "Fiscal distress and governance challenges: The perfect storm of the fiscal crisis." *State and Local Government Review* 41(3): 201–207.

Perlman, Bruce J. 2015. "Trust and timing: The importance of relationship and opportunity for interlocal collaboration and agreements." *State and Local Government Review* 47(2): 116–126.

Perlman, Bruce J., and J. Edwin Benton. 2012. "Going it alone: New survey data on economic recovery strategies in local government." *State and Local Government Review* 44(S): 5S–16S.

The Pew Charitable Trust. 2017a. "Fiscal 50: State trends and analysis." Retrieved from www.pewtrusts.org/en/multimedia/data-visualizations/2014/fiscal-50#ind0 (accessed May 17, 2017).

The Pew Charitable Trust. 2017b. "Fiscal health of large U.S. cities varied long after Great Recession's end: Impact of economic downturn persisted for many local governments." Retrieved from www.pewtrusts.org/en/research-and-analysis/issue-briefs/2016/04/fiscal-health-of-large-us-cities-varied-long-after-great-recessions-end (accessed June 17, 2017).

Sanford, Terry A. 1967. *Storm Over the States*. New York: McGraw Hill.

Schapiro, Robert A. 2009. *Polyphonic Federalism: Toward the Protection of Fundamental Rights*. Chicago, IL: University of Chicago Press.

Stever, James A. 2005. "Adapting intergovernmental management to the new age of terrorism." *Administration and Society* 37(4): 379–403.

Thompson, Frank J. 2013. "The rise of executive federalism: Implications for the picket fence and IGM." *The American Review of Public Administration* 43(1): 3–25.

Weissert, Carol S. 2011. "Beyond marble cakes and picket fences: What U.S. federalism scholars can learn from comparative work." *The Journal of Politics* 73(4): 965–979.

Wright, Deil S. 1982. *Understanding Intergovernmental Relations*, 2nd edition. Monterey, CA: Brooks/Cole Publishing Co.

Wright, Deil S. 1990. "Federalism, intergovernmental relations, and intergovernmental management: Historical reflections and conceptual comparisons." *Public Administration Review* 50(2): 168–178.

Zimmerman, Joseph S. 1996. *Interstate Relations: the Neglected Dimension of Federalism*. Westport, CT: Praeger.

Part III

Intergovernmental Management Cases

7   Partisan Polarization, Administrative Capacity, and State Discretion in the Affordable Care Act

Dale Krane and Shihyun Noh

The Patient Protection and Affordable Care Act (ACA) of 2010 (P.L. 111–148) granted state governments substantial discretionary authority over the implementation of the Act's several elements, most notably health insurance exchanges and Medicaid expansion. Given the degree of discretion available to states, it is no surprise considerable variation emerged among the fifty states as to whether a state decided to establish its own state-based health exchange (SBE), rely on the federally-facilitated exchange (FFE), or participate in a state–federal partnership exchange (SPE). Initial research on ACA implementation that focused on the exchange choice treated it as a simple binary issue: state-based exchange versus federally facilitated exchange. By May 2014, sixteen states and the District of Columbia established an SBE, 20 states opted for the FFE, 14 states entered into an SPE. Within these three seemingly distinct choices, there exists considerable variation in the degree of federal versus state control over key programmatic components. If one takes into account this variation in administrative responsibility, then ACA implementation is even more nuanced than these three basic forms. This chapter presents a more detailed approach to classifying the variation in state exchange choices in terms of the federal–state distribution of responsibility for specific program elements.

ACA Health Insurance Exchanges—Politics Leads to Diversity

The Affordable Care Act restructured the nation's health insurance market by altering the way individuals and small businesses gain access to insurance plans. The Act did so by requiring the states and the District of Columbia to establish health insurance marketplaces (hereafter referred to as exchanges) in which eligible persons could compare and purchase insurance plans from private issuers of health coverage (U.S. Government Accountability Office 2013b; Starr 2013). The exchanges are new entities for purchasing coverage in "a more organized and competitive market for health insurance by offering a choice of plans, establishing common rules regarding the offering and pricing of insurance, and providing information to help consumers better understand the options available to them" (Kaiser Family Foundation 2010). The ACA also required states to establish Small Business Health Options Program (SHOP) exchanges so that small employers could shop for and purchase health insurance for their workers (U.S. Government Accountability Office 2013c). Both types of exchanges create new incentives in the health coverage market through new regulations and subsidies so as to reduce the number of individuals without health insurance, while at the same time controlling or even reducing costs.

The ACA's goals include better access to and improved quality of health care, lower cost of health services, and expanded consumer protections against discrimination by health insurance companies (Barr 2011). The Act addressed better access by establishing the new mechanisms of health insurance exchanges and by encouraging states to expand Medicaid. Also, cost containment was expected to occur through changes to the Medicare program and new sources of tax revenues. Better quality was anticipated to be attained by an expansion and restructuring of primary care services, and by a major expansion of comparative effectiveness research (ibid.). Through the ACA's two pillars for better access, insurance exchange and Medicaid expansion, it was estimated to cover 32 million non-elderly Americans by 2016 (Congressional Budget Office 2011). Simply put, the Act's goal was to end the previous "system that guaranteed millions of people would be left without any [health] protection" by making coverage affordable (Starr 2013: 240).

To negate the "socialized medicine" attack that doomed the Clinton era effort, the Obama plan leading to the ACA adopted the private health care marketplace concept, long advocated by Republicans and the conservative Heritage Foundation think tank (Doonan 2013: 117; Haeder and Weimer 2013: 2). The pre-passage political maneuvering over various elements to be included in the ACA focused not just on access, cost, and quality concerns, the legislative debates also revolved around the Act's implementation (Starr 2013: 21–23). The question of who would administer the exchanges was resolved through the application of a well-established regulatory strategy—the partial preemption (Wright 1988: 371–373; Conlan and Posner 2011). The states were required to establish separate exchanges for individuals and small business employees, and if a state chose not to operate these exchanges by January 1, 2014, or its application to run these exchanges was denied by the Centers for Medicare and Medicaid Services (CMS), then the ACA directed the DHHS Secretary to establish and operate an exchange in the state, either directly or through a nonprofit entity, which is referred to as a Federally-facilitated exchange (FFE). States deciding to implement their own exchange had to submit an application "blueprint" to DHHS by December 14, 2012 which described how the state-based exchange would implement the essential functions required by the ACA (U.S. Government Accountability Office 2013a). The deadline for states to choose to operate their own exchange was subsequently moved to June 2015 (Carey 2014).

State-based exchanges (SBEs) and the federally facilitated exchange (FFE) administer the core functions required by DHHS: eligibility, enrollment, plan management, consumer assistance, and financial management. SBEs must administer the required core functions and may use federal services for premium tax credit and cost sharing reduction determination, exemptions, risk adjustment program, and reinsurance. The FFE operated by DHHS performs the core functions, but states may elect to use federal services for reinsurance and for Medicaid and CHIP eligibility assessment or determination (Dash, Monahan, and Lucia 2013). This initial either-or choice was soon augmented with a third option: State Partnership Exchanges (SPEs). As described by Dinan (2014), DHHS had to devise an alternative that could induce states that were reluctant to operate all core exchange functions or were undecided between the two choices. In SPEs a state has responsibility for plan management, consumer assistance, or both, and could elect to perform or use federal services for reinsurance and for Medicaid and CHIP assessment or determination (Center for Consumer Information and Insurance Oversight 2012).

While few state officials opposed the concept of an insurance exchange (Vestal 2011), they differed widely in their preferences for the type of exchange their state would select. "The response to the federal reforms by state political leaders," as Starr (2013: 271) noted, "depended largely on their party ideology." Progressive Democratic governors embraced SBEs, while Republican governors typically opposed SBEs, and ironically given their resistance to dictation by federal agencies, nevertheless preferred the FFE. It should be noted there were some exceptions to the partisan pattern, for example, California's Republican governor signed the first state law establishing an SBE. Some state officials waited to make a decision until the U.S. Supreme Court ruled on the Act's constitutionality in the summer of 2012, and others waited for the results of the 2012 presidential election (Bowling and Pickerill 2013). Even after the Court upheld the Act and President Obama was re-elected, many state governments did not move to embrace SBEs. By September 2013, only 16 states and the District of Columbia had established a SBE, 7 states chose an SPE, and 26 states preferred the FFE option (Burke and Kamarck 2013: 4–5). The 2012 election results complicated state decisions on exchanges as the number of one-party Republican states increased from 20 to 24. Furthermore, another 14 states had divided government which put Republicans in a position to block SBEs in 38 states (Starr 2013: 293).

But the creation of new options did not stop with three types of exchanges. Desire by DHHS to induce uncommitted states as well as its own interest in reducing the Department's workload led to a willingness to negotiate with reluctant states. At the same time, some state officials pursued negotiations to wrest concessions from federal officials (Dinan 2014), while others simply waited to see if the Act would survive not just court challenges (Vestal 2012), but also the normal snafus typically associated with the initiation of a new public program (Mitchell 2014). A second variant of the FFE appeared—the marketplace plan management (MPM)—which allowed a state to conduct plan management but leave the other core functions to DHHS (Dash, Monahan, and Lucia 2013). By November 2014, fourteen states adopted an SBE, seven states decided on an SPE, seven states chose an MPM, and twenty states preferred an FFE (Kaiser Family Foundation 2015). The interaction of DHHS objectives and the preferences of state officials has resulted in considerable variation in the assignment of responsibility between the federal government and the states over different elements of the ACA. Initial studies of state choice of exchange type focused on the original binary choice: state-based versus federally facilitated exchange, but given the diversity among the state exchanges a more nuanced approach is required.

State Government Implementation of ACA Health Insurance Exchanges

That the ACA gave state officials discretion over several important policy choices continued the long-standing practice of shared governance in U.S. domestic public policy (Grodzins 1966; Elazar 1966). Interactions between the national and state governments are characterized by interdependence, which necessitates the development of cooperative, mutually beneficial arrangements between "working partners" to make federalism "work" (Sundquist and Davis 1969). But American shared governance is not always a smooth relationship, rather it is "an uneasy partnership" in which negative power to veto each other's actions has to be taken into account in policy implementation (Williams 1980: 44). It is common to argue the national government determines the share of state authority and participation in the joint administration of programs (Reagan 1972), but "control within the federal arrangement is reciprocal" despite the power asymmetry between the national and state governments (Krane 1992: 251; Pressman 1975). This is so because state governments possess the ability to take (or not take) actions which affect the design of federal policy as well as how nationally enacted programs operate at the state and local level (Krane 1993; Nugent 2009).

This "uneasy partnership" is grounded in the U.S. Constitution's language, and has led historically to "an appropriately endless argument over the proper balance between federal and state authority—an argument whose intensity ebbs and flows and whose content evolves, but which is never really settled" (Donahue 1997: 17). Recent experience exhibits numerous instances of sharp intergovernmental disagreements, but few have been as rancorous as the conflict over Obamacare. The philosophical, political, fiscal, economic, and administrative reasons for the struggle over the passage of the ACA and its implementation have been discussed at length elsewhere (Thompson 2012; Gray, Lowery, and Benz 2013; Doonan 2013). For our purpose, what is important to note is the diversity in the choices made by state government officials in response to the ACA's partial preemption provision, as displayed on Table 7.1.

Initial Findings

Early research (excluding GAO reports) on the implementation of the health exchanges focused on factors affecting state officials' decisions to establish a state-based exchange or to leave the operation of the exchange to the national government. These studies reported that partisanship was a powerful influence on state decisions (Haeder and Weimer 2013; Rigby and Haselwerdt 2013; Burke and Kamarck 2013). In 2013, thirty states had Republican governors, and twenty-six states had Republican dominated state legislatures (National Conference of State Legislatures 2013), so it is no surprise that twenty-four Republican governors opted for an FFE (Burke and Kamarck 2013: 6). Haeder and Weimer's analysis of exchange choices prior to the November 2012 presidential election found that an electoral change to a Republican governor had a strong negative effect on the timely establishment of an SBE, while a unified Democratic legislature had a strong positive effect. Their analysis indicated that if the state insurance commissioner was elected, this also negatively impacted exchange establishment, while more resources in the state insurance agency were a positive factor. Rigby and Haselwerdt discovered that the insurance commissioner's party affiliation affected progress with Republican commissioners acting to slow progress. Additionally, Rigby and Haselwerdt, using pre-May 2012 data, charted the states' progress through the administrative steps necessary to establish an exchange. Their results affirmed both other studies but added an important factor—public opinion. Politically liberal states where 50 percent or more of the public favored the ACA made the most progress, while those states where 45 percent

Table 7.1 State Decisions for Creating Health Insurance Marketplaces, as of November 2014

Exchange Form	Number of States	State
State-Based Exchange	16 states and DC	CA, CO, CT, DC, HI, ID, KY, MD, MA, MN, NV, NM, NY, OR, RI, VT, WA
Federally Facilitated Exchange	20 states	AL, AK, AZ, FL, GA, IN, LA, MS, MO, NJ, NC, ND, OK, PA, SC, TN, TX, UT, WI, WY
State Partnership Exchange	7 states	AR, DE, IL, IA, MI, NH, WV
Marketplace Plan Management	7 states	KS, ME, MT, NE, OH, SD, VA

Source: Kaiser Family Foundation (2015)

Note: Idaho and New Mexico implemented a state-based exchange for 2015 enrollment, while the two states implemented a state partnership exchange for 2014 enrollment (Kaiser Family Foundation 2014). DHHS approved Mississippi and Utah to operate the SHOP marketplaces, with the federal government running the individual marketplaces for the two states (Kaiser Family Foundation 2015).

or less favored the Act made the least progress. This suggests that state government officials' choices on type of exchange were not solely a function of their partisan affiliation; state officials' choices were also affected by the partisan distribution of a state's citizenry. They also discovered that unexpected choices (findings that did not conform to their main result) were associated with "purple" states (i.e., governors and legislatures of different political parties).

Negotiated Choices

These early studies highlighted the partisan polarization bedeviling the ACA's implementation, but their findings were preliminary and incomplete. Lischko and Waldman (2013: 112) point out "because the law is so complex and far-reaching, such a simple partisan dichotomy does not fully explain state resistance and implementation strategy." Officials in many states waited until the outcome of the legal challenge to the Act and/or for the results of the 2012 presidential election, so decisions about exchange type were put on hold. Furthermore, the creation of state–federal partnership exchanges as well as DHHS's willingness to induce state participation by approval of state specific arrangements occurred after these initial studies were conducted. DHHS in its efforts to encourage more states to take responsibility for ACA implementation pursued a strategy of negotiation with the states. This strategy of national-state bargaining over the terms of program administration is a fundamental feature of American intergovernmental relations as explained by Wright's (1988: 49) overlapping-authority model. Both national and state governments bargain because each level is interdependent; simply put, each can lose from non-negotiation and each can gain from negotiation. The formal either-or choice in the Act has given way to a series of compromises between DHHS and several states. Any effort to gauge the degree of state or federal responsibility for administration of a state's insurance exchange must take into account the results of the intergovernmental negotiations.

As seen on Table 7.2, exchange options differ primarily based on the number of core functions, for which the federal or state governments are responsible: eligibility and enrollment, plan management, consumer assistance, and financial management. Eligibility and enrollment include determining or assessing eligibility for insurance affordability programs, and facilitating enrollment in appropriate coverage. Plan management includes certifying Qualified Health Plans for participation in the exchange, and monitoring for compliance. Consumer assistance, outreach, and education include assisting consumers with finding and enrolling in coverage, and operating a website, call center and Navigator program. Financial management includes generating financial support for continued operations (Dash et al. 2013). In terms of exchange functions, states with

Table 7.2 Forms of Health Insurance Exchange and State Responsibilities for Core Exchange Functions

Core Exchange Functions	Forms of Health Insurance Exchange			
	SBE	*SPE*	*MPM*	*FFE*
Eligibility and enrollment	State	—	—	—
Plan management	State	State (joint)	State (joint)	—
Consumer assistance, outreach, and education	State	State (joint)	—	—
Financial management	State	—	—	—
Total	4	2	1	0

Source: data from Dash et al. (2013)

a state-based exchange are responsible for all core exchange functions, but may have the federal government assist with determining eligibility for federal financial assistance, while other states with a federally-facilitated exchange conduct no core function. States with a state–federal partnership exchange take responsibilities jointly with the federal government for certain plan management functions, consumer assistance functions, or both. Other states with a marketplace plan management exchange are responsible for plan management jointly with the federal government. But the federal government can invite states with an FFE, an SPE and an MPM option to "incorporate, where possible, the results of certain reviews already conducted by state insurance departments into its certification decisions for qualified health plans wishing to participate in the federally facilitated exchange" (ibid.: 5).

The research presented here examines factors determining the number of core functions a state decided to administer. The number of core functions represents the degree of state control in the implementation of a health insurance exchange. The more exchange functions a state chose to operate, the more responsibilities the state accepted and the more control the state exercised. This dependent variable—the number of exchange functions administered by a state—offers a more discriminating measure of state implementation choices. By using the number of core exchange functions for individual plans and small employers, this analysis captures the diversity of state choices, rather than the original binary choice of exchange. Table 7.3 lists the states by number of core functions a state opted to administer, as of February 2014.

Explanation of State Choices

To explain variation in state choices to implement core exchange functions, the results of the initial studies need to be integrated more closely with the corpus of intergovernmental implementation analyses (e.g., Pressman and Wildavsky 1973; Pressman 1975; Van Meter and Van Horn 1975; Goggin et al. 1990; Winter 2003). Wright (1988: 22) taught us that "the participants in IGR are centrally concerned with 'getting things done'" and that "policy is generated by interactions among all public officials" (ibid.: 24). However, implementation of a new national program is not "automatic" (Leach 1970: 60) because policy implementation in the American federal union occurs within the matrix of multiple governments and power relationships characterized by fragmented authority and contending political interests. To "get things done" (implement policy) in a regime of shared governance, control over specific activities and functions becomes a critical component of understanding "who is responsible for it" and "how is it to be carried out" (Williams 1980: 65).

Control in implementation transcends the classic problem of clearances in a vertical "chain" between top and bottom (Pressman and Wildavsky 1973). The "chain of delegation" (Strom 2000: 267) entails creating commitment and capacity across a variety of agencies and jurisdictions. Factors such as a state's commitment to and capacity for program administration are equally important for analyzing state government choices. So, it can be hypothesized that *states with high commitment and high capacity will decide to implement more core exchange functions, while states with low commitment and low capacity will decide to implement fewer core exchange functions.*

State Commitment

State commitment to implementation of a new federal initiative is a function of state partisan configuration, political culture, ideological orientation, interest group influence, and severity of the

Table 7.3 State Decisions for Number of Core Exchange Functions, as of February 2014

	Total	Individual Plans				SHOP			
		Eligibility and Enrollment	Plan Management	Consumer Assistance	Financial Management	Eligibility and Enrollment	Plan Management	Consumer Assistance	Financial Management
AK	0	0	0	0	0	0	0	0	0
AL	0	0	0	0	0	0	0	0	0
AR	4	0	1	1	0	0	1	1	2
AZ	0	0	0	0	0	0	0	0	0
CA	8	1	1	1	1	1	1	1	4
CO	8	1	1	1	1	1	1	1	4
CT	8	1	1	1	1	1	1	1	4
DE	4	0	1	1	0	0	1	1	2
FL	0	0	0	0	0	0	0	0	0
GA	0	0	0	0	0	0	0	0	0
HI	8	1	1	1	1	1	1	1	4
IA	4	0	1	1	0	0	1	1	2
ID	4	0	1	1	0	0	1	1	2
IL	4	0	1	1	0	0	1	1	2
IN	0	0	0	0	0	0	0	0	0
KS	2	0	1	0	0	0	1	0	1
KY	8	1	1	1	1	1	1	1	4
LA	0	0	0	0	0	0	0	0	0
MA	8	1	1	1	1	1	1	1	4
MD	8	1	1	1	1	1	1	1	4
ME	2	0	1	0	0	0	1	0	1
MI	4	1	1	1	1	0	1	1	2
MN	8	1	1	1	1	1	1	1	4
MO	0	0	0	0	0	0	0	0	0
MS	2	0	0	0	0	0	1	1	2
MT	2	0	1	0	0	0	1	1	1
NC	0	0	0	0	0	0	0	0	0

(continued)

Table 7.3 State Decisions for Number of Core Exchange Functions, as of February 2014 (continued)

	Total	Individual Plans				SHOP			
		Eligibility and Enrollment	Plan Management	Consumer Assistance	Financial Management	Eligibility and Enrollment	Plan Management	Consumer Assistance	Financial Management
ND	0	0	0	0	0	0	0	0	0
NE	2	0	1	0	0	0	1	0	0
NH	4	0	1	1	0	0	1	1	0
NJ	0	0	0	0	0	0	0	0	0
NM	6	0	1	1	0	1	1	1	1
NV	8	1	1	1	1	1	1	1	1
NY	8	1	1	1	1	1	1	1	1
OH	2	0	1	0	0	0	1	0	0
OK	0	0	0	0	0	0	0	0	0
OR	8	1	1	1	1	1	1	1	1
PA	0	0	0	0	0	0	0	0	0
RI	8	1	1	1	1	1	1	1	1
SC	0	0	0	0	0	0	0	0	0
SD	2	0	1	0	0	0	1	0	0
TN	0	0	0	0	0	0	0	0	0
TX	0	0	0	0	0	0	0	0	0
UT	3	0	1	0	0	0	1	1	0
VA	2	0	1	0	0	0	1	0	0
VT	8	1	1	1	1	1	1	1	1
WA	8	1	1	1	1	1	1	1	1
WI	0	0	0	0	0	0	0	0	0
WV	4	0	1	1	0	0	1	1	0
WY	0	0	0	0	0	0	0	0	0

Source: authors' analysis using diverse sources: Centers for Medicare and Medicaid Services (2012–2013); Dash et al. (2013); Kaiser Family Foundation (2014)

problem. Divided government has been a feature of U.S. history and has had important effects on policy design and implementation (Fiorina 1992). Research on interstate policy diffusion demonstrates the importance of unified party control of state government for the achievement of a political party's policy objectives (Berry and Berry 1990; Volden 2006). The political configuration of a state—divided or unified—reflects the distribution of ideology among a state's citizens. Partisan polarization across the fifty states has become so extreme that observers of American culture and politics now label conservative/Republican states as "red" contrasted with "blue" liberal/Democratic states, and where partisan competition still exists the color designation is "purple." The spirit of federalism embodies the idea of "shared rule," but the intensifying partisan polarization of state and national politics trumps compromise. The initial studies of ACA implementation uniformly found the political configuration of a state was a strong determinant of state choice of exchange. Following suit, this research hypothesizes *states with unified Democratic political configuration will implement more core exchange functions, while unified Republican states will implement few or no exchange functions*. Three variables are used to categorize a state's political configuration:

- governor's party affiliation;
- party affiliation of the state legislature (Gray et al. 2013); and
- divided government (Berry and Berry 1990; Volden 2006).

Elazar (1984: 84) conceptualized political culture as "the particular pattern of orientation to political action in which each political system is imbedded," and identified three political cultures inside the larger American political culture: Moralist, Individualist, and Traditionalist. He hypothesized that the three cultures account for state-to-state differences in government and politics (ibid.: 100–101) because each culture varied as to government's role in society. As for the adoption of new programs, Elazar assumed that states with a moralistic political culture "will initiate without public pressure if believed to be in public interest," states with an individualistic political culture "will not initiate unless demanded by public opinion," and states with a traditionalistic political culture "will initiate if a program serves the interest of the governing elite" (ibid.: 100).

Implementation researchers after Elazar have included political culture as an important variable (Pressman and Wildavsky 1973; Goggin et al. 1990), so an examination of ACA implementation needs to address political culture because it can affect state officials' decisions. Olshfski and Cunningham (2008: 16) affirm the influence of political culture in their observations on how state government executives and middle managers make and administer policy: "A decision rarely strays far from the norms present in the environment. The culture does not readily acquiesce to change efforts by executives and middle managers." From this one can hypothesize that *states with moralistic political cultures will implement more ACA core functions, states with individualistic cultures will implement fewer functions (often by negotiating with DHHS), and states with traditionalistic cultures will implement few or no core functions*.

Two measures of political culture are used:

- Sharkansky's operationalization of Elazar's political cultures; and
- Lieske's updating of Elazar using the 2000 census and the Glenmary religious survey.

Elazar used eight variants of the three principal cultures (M, MI, IM, I, IT, TI, T, and TM) to describe the specific type found in the states and in 228 sub-areas of the states. Sharkansky

(1969: 71) quantified Elazar's judgments by using "the average numerical value of the several cultural designations made within each state" to construct a political culture continuum that ranged from a score of 1 for moralistic states to 9 for traditionalistic states.

Lieske (2010), using multiple measures of racial and ethnic origins, religious affiliations, and social structure in 2000, created an eleven-fold classification of political culture of all U.S. counties – his categories are: Nordic, Mormon, Anglo-French, Germanic, Heartland, Rurban, Global, Border, Blackbelt, Native American, and Latino – which he ultimately reduced to a three-fold categorization of moralistic, individualistic, and traditionalistic cultures. Lieske (2012) found that his classification was statistically significant in explaining state variations in government activities such as tax burden, per capita education spending, and per capita welfare spending. Our analysis uses both Sharkansky's and Lieske's approaches to test the respective effect of moralistic, individualistic, and traditionalistic political cultures, on federal–state control of core exchange functions.

Political ideology consists of beliefs and preferences about the types of policy government should make and implement, while political culture is related to the role of government (Lieske 2010). Policy diffusion literature reports a positive relation between liberal and progressive states and policy innovations, saying "liberal and progressive states are believed to be policy responsive, whereas conservative, traditional states are expected to oppose changes to the status quo" (Boushey 2010: 110). To examine the effect of political ideology, this study includes the distinction between citizen and government ideology as developed by Berry and associates (Berry et al. 1998, 2013), and as used by Soss et al. (2001) and by Nicholson-Crotty (2004). To test the effect of the divergence between citizen ideology and elected officials' ideology on state implementation of the ACA, ideological divergence is measured by subtracting citizen ideology from government ideology. The two types of ideology facilitate a comparative examination of citizen beliefs and preferences vis-à-vis those of elected officials as each may affect state ACA implementation. It can be hypothesized that *more liberal citizens and government officials will be associated with a state's implementation of more exchange functions (i.e., opt for an SBE). Conversely, conservative citizens and officials will be associated with a state's resistance to implementation of core exchange functions (i.e., opt for an FFE). The larger the divergence between citizen ideology and elected officials' ideology will be associated with state officials' deciding to negotiate with federal officials over which core functions the state will administer (i.e., opt for an SPE, MPM, or another variant).*

Political scientists have paid close attention to the role of interest groups in public policy areas with diverse perspectives on the extent of interest groups' influence (McFarland 2004). Interest groups at the state level have grown in terms of numbers, size, and diversity, and participate more actively in state policymaking. Interstate variation is considerable (Nownes and Newmark 2013)— for example, New York had 3,161 interest groups registered by the state in 2009, compared to 274 in Hawaii (National Institute on Money in State Politics 2014). Previous research has demonstrated the influence of interest groups in diverse aspects of state policymaking such as policy enactment (Bowling and Ferguson 2001; Yackee 2009), spending priorities (Jacoby and Schneider 2001), and administrative agency decision-making (Kelleher and Yackee 2009). Gray et al. (2010) found that states where Democrats are in charge and allied interests for the extension of health care coverage predominate, adopted universal health care coverage from 1988 to 2002. Other scholars confirm the power of interest group lobbying on state government policy-making (Goggin et al. 1990; Stephens and Wikstrom 2007). This study hypothesizes that *in a state where health related interest groups exert substantial influence, one can expect the state to implement more exchange functions.*

The influence of interest groups is measured with two indicators:

- Percentage of pro-reform groups' contribution to elections from 2010 to 2012 in a state (the National Institute on Money in State Politics 2014); and
- percent of health employment in a state (Kaiser Family Foundation 2012a).

In the examination of factors affecting universal health care adoption in states, Gray et al. (2013) categorized health organizations associated with the actual direct provision of health services and liberal advocacy organizations as allies for universal health care. Different from Gray et al., this study assumes that, in state implementation of the ACA, insurance companies can be regarded as allies because the individual requirement to purchase insurance and the extension of public insurance through Medicaid-expansion provide insurance companies an opportunity to enlarge the insurance market. So in this research, pro-reform groups include health professionals, health services, hospitals and nursing homes, pharmaceuticals and health products, health insurance companies, pro-choice groups, health welfare policy organizations, and liberal policy organizations. To estimate the number of interest groups related to health policy, we also use the percent of health employment in a state as a proxy because the number of interest groups in a state is related to how many constituents live there (Gray and Lowery 1996).

Legislators enact new programs to address needs and problems in a community or nation. The ACA's health exchanges are intended to enlarge citizen access to medical care by reducing the number of individuals without health insurance. However, the shared governance of U.S. federalism leaves open the possibility some state government officials may disagree with a national program's goals and instruments. In some states the number of uninsured may not be as large as in other states, therefore, it is likely elected officials in some states do not view health care access as a pressing problem. Consequently, it is necessary to examine *whether the size of the uninsured population in a state as well as the size of the eligible population is associated with state officials' decisions to implement more core functions*. To measure the severity of the health insurance coverage problem in a state, we use straightforward measures such as uninsured rate and unemployment rate. We assume that a state with more uninsured individuals and a higher unemployment rate will implement more exchange functions to respond to the lack of health care coverage for residents. For uninsured rate, the analysis uses Uninsured Estimates of Adults 18–64 from the American Community Survey (ACS) in 2010 (Kaiser Family Foundation 2012b). For unemployment rate, we measure it by the average of monthly unemployment rate from the U.S. Bureau of Labor in 2012 (U.S. Department of Labor 2015).

State Capacity

Public administration researchers have highlighted the importance of agency capacity for successful implementation. Capacity depends on agency resources, systems, and technologies (Williams 1980; Mazmanian and Sabatier 1989; Jennings et al. 1986; Goggin et al. 1990; Ingraham 2003). Typically, capacity is gauged by relying on a fiscal or personnel measure where it is assumed that an agency or organization gains or increases its capacity for action by acquiring or possessing comparatively higher levels of monetary and/or human resources. State budgetary conditions as well as the size and attributes of state government workforces vary considerably with a concomitant effect on program administration, so *one would expect the decision to adopt an SBE would be associated with higher levels of fiscal and personnel resources*. To measure state financial capacity, this study uses state government budget shortfall in 2013 and state per capita personal income in 2013. State budget shortfall is each state's estimation of a deficit or budget gap where revenues fall short of the amount necessary for sustaining current service levels for a given state fiscal year (Center on Budget and Policy Priorities 2012). Also, following previous research, to indirectly measure state financial capacity, the analysis includes state per capita personal income because more affluent states are expected to actively adopt innovations (Walker 1969; Volden 2006; Boushey 2010). Since the number of personnel available to implement a program positively impacts state implementation (Goggin et al. 1990), we measure the number of personnel by using (1) the number of full-time equivalent professional staff per capita, and (2) the number of full-time equivalent personnel per capita devoted to the program (ibid.: 183).

During the 1990s state governments across the country enacted "broad governing-for-results legislation" (Liner 2001: 1). This widespread movement toward performance-based management offers an additional way to conceptualize state administrative capacity (Brudney, Hebert, and Wright 1999; Aristegueta 1999). *The degree to which a state's administrative agencies practice results-oriented management can be hypothesized as making it more likely a state possesses the capacity to operate an SBE, while states which refrained from joining the performance movement will be more likely to opt for an FFE.* Comparative state studies of administrative capacity have been quite rare in public administration. One of the most recent and extensive efforts is the Government Performance Project (GPP) which evaluated state governments' performance in terms of people, money, information, infrastructure, and management systems (Ingraham 2003). The GPP study can be used to assess state administrative capacity because it focused on "effective maintenance, ongoing coordination, continual monitoring, and timely improvement to the management systems" (Heckman 2012). This analysis of ACA implementation gauges state administrative capacity with the GPP aggregate score, the GPP human resource management score, and the GPP financial management score.

The literature on intergovernmental implementation also directs attention to the role of communication between the federal government and states during program implementation (Goggin et al. 1990; Krane and Wright 1998; Thompson 2013). Governors, for example, by the nature of their office are in a position to express not just their own personal and partisan views, but also the preferences of their states' citizens. This positional advantage of governors also accrues to their efforts to negotiate with federal agencies (Krane 1993). Thompson's research on waivers (2013: 5) shows how "a congressional delegation of authority to the executive branch to permit states to deviate from the ordinary requirements of the law" creates a mechanism for state–national bargaining over a program's implementation. State application for waivers follows "extensive and time consuming negotiations with the federal government, not infrequently taking several years to obtain approval," enabling states to learn how to communicate effectively with the federal government (Callaghan and Jacobs 2013). This line of argument suggests that *states with more communicative capacity will be more likely to implement some or all core exchange functions and will be less likely to opt for an FFE.* To measure state communicative capacity, this study uses the number of Medicaid waivers for Section 1115 Research & Demonstration Projects, 1915 (b) Managed Care Waivers, and 1915 (c) Home and Community-Based Services Waivers (Centers for Medicare and Medicaid Services 2014).

Analysis of Data

A two-step analytical procedure was undertaken to determine factors which account for variation in the degree of state versus federal control of ACA core exchange functions, which were scored respectively for individual plans and for small business health options plans (SHOP) from 0 to 4. First, one-way ANOVA tests were conducted to identify any differences among the states in terms of political culture, political ideology, the influence of interest groups, severity of the problem, and state capacity, accompanied by post-hoc comparisons wherever the F ratios were statistically significant. To examine the relation between the dependent variables and political configuration, we utilized cross-tabulation tables because our measurements for political configuration are not continuous variables, and are not appropriate for ANOVA (Mertler and Vannatta 2001). Second, multivariate analysis of variance (MANOVA) was performed for variables statistically significant in the ANOVA analysis respectively for state commitment and state capacity (ibid.). As for test statistics for MANOVA, Wilks' lambda (λ) was used, followed by post-hoc comparisons.

Findings

Previous research emphasized the significant influence of partisanship on state government decisions as to the type of ACA insurance exchange to implement. Drawing from work on inter-governmental implementation of federal programs, we proposed that state government commitment to the national policy and state administrative capacity would also influence a state's decision to administer a particular type of health exchange. State commitment was operationalized in terms of political configuration, political culture, political ideology, interest groups, and severity of the problem, and state capacity was operationalized in terms of fiscal and personnel resources, use of performance management, and intergovernmental communication. Rather than posing state choice as a binary variable (state-based versus federally-facilitated exchanges) as previous studies have done, we operationalized state choice as the decision to take responsibility for a number of core exchange functions. States were assigned to one of four groups for analysis based on whether a state decided to implement 0, 1, 2, or 3 or more core functions for (1) individual plan exchanges and (2) SHOP exchanges. We also categorized states into four groups based on the combined number of individual and SHOP functions, scoring the groups as 0, 1–2, 3–4, and 5 or more functions. We also separately examined the state decisions first for individual plan exchanges, then for SHOP exchanges, and finally for the combined number of individual and SHOP functions. Because the results for the analysis of the SHOP exchanges and the combined individual and SHOP decisions on core health exchange functions essentially are the same as the results for state decisions on the individual plan exchanges, the following discussion of findings focuses primarily on the individual plan decisions. We do note any significant differences between individual, SHOP, and combined exchanges.

State Commitment

We hypothesized that states with unified Democratic political configuration would implement more core exchange functions, while unified Republican states would implement few or no exchange functions. Cross-tabulation results of governor's party affiliation and party affiliation of a state legislature with number of state exchange functions for individual plans are displayed on Table 7.4. Nineteen states chose to implement zero functions, of which 17 had a unified Republican

Table 7.4 State Political Configuration and Number of ACA Core Functions Implemented for Individual Plans

No. of functions	Governor	State Legislature			
		Democratic	Divided	Republican	Total
0	Democratic	0	0	1	1
	Republican	1	0	17	18
	Total	1	0	18	19
1	Democratic	0	0	1	1
	Republican	1	1	5	7
	Total	1	1	6	8
2	Democratic	3	1	1	5
	Republican	1	1	2	4
	Total	4	2	3	9
3 or more	Democratic	11	1	0	12
	Independent	1	0	0	1
	Republican	1	0	0	1
	Total	13	1	0	14
Total	Democratic	14	2	3	19
	Independent	1	0	0	1
	Republican	4	2	24	30
	Total	19	4	27	50

Source: authors' analysis using data from the National Conference of State Legislatures (2013) and data in Table 7.3
Note: Nebraska legislature is coded as Republican, following legislative composition in Congress.

government with a Republican governor and a Republican dominated legislature. Of the 14 states that opted to administer 3 or more core functions, 12 out of 14 had unified Democratic governments. These proportions on the relation between unified government and state choices for number of core functions confirm our hypothesis that states with unified Democratic political configuration would implement more core exchange functions, while unified Republican states would implement few or no exchange functions. State implementation of insurance exchanges follows the pattern of polarized politics in Washington.

It is necessary, however, to examine the choices made by officials in "purple" states (Krane 2007). As seen in Table 7.4, divided state governments do not follow the pattern of polarized politics in the implementation of ACA exchanges. For example, data for individual plan exchanges shows that among the 12 states with divided governments, two states decided to implement no core functions; three states, 1 function; four states, 2 functions; and three states, 4 functions. These results indicate that researchers need to pay attention to the dynamics of divided government in states and to avoid a reliance on measures of partisanship which are based on the party affiliation of a single official (e.g., governor) or a single institution (e.g., legislature).

Regarding political culture, we proposed that states with moralistic political cultures would implement more ACA core functions, states with individualistic cultures would implement fewer functions, and states with traditionalistic cultures would implement few or no core functions. To test the hypothesis, we performed serial one-way ANOVA tests for the three dependent variables and political culture as measured by Sharkansky (1969) and Lieske (2010). Values displayed on

Tables 7.5 indicate the serial one-way ANOVA tests found significant mean differences for Sharkansky's political culture measure among the four groups of states, with F (3, 44) = 8.82 for individual plans. Also, the means of political culture in states implementing zero core functions (6.62 for individual plans) is larger than the means for states with 3 and more core functions (3.89 for individual plans). Considering that moralistic culture is scored as 1 and traditionalistic culture is scored as 9, the above results support our hypothesis that states with moralistic political cultures

Table 7.5 Means and One-Way ANOVA Tests for Number of ACA Core Functions Implemented for Individual Plans

Variable	No. of Exchange Functions (N: States)				F-Score
	0 (19)	1 (8)	2 (9)	3 or More (14)	
State Commitment					
Political Culture					
Political Culture (Sharkansky)	6.62	3.14	4.88	3.89	8.82(W)**
Moralistic Culture (Lieske)	8.46	31.27	15.26	26.05	1.23(W)
Individualistic Culture (Lieske)	59.57	61.37	64.93	66.93	.12
Traditionalistic Culture (Lieske)	34.18	7.37	19.82	7.80	3.56(W)*
Political Ideology					
Citizen Ideology	39.79	40.55	49.59	60.34	7.54**
Government Ideology	32.68	42.94	75.53	73.46	10.00**
Ideological Divergence	−7.11	2.39	25.94	13.12	5.20**
The Influence of Interest Groups					
Interest Group Contribution Size	8.25	6.26	9.13	5.77	2.17
Health Employment	8.95	9.32	9.52	8.97	.38
Severity of the Problem					
Uninsured Rate	22.16	18.13	20.33	17.50	2.42
Unemployment Rate	7.55	5.80	6.86	8.25	4.66**
State Capacity					
State Administrative Capacity					
GPP Overall	2.35	2.46	2.19	2.17	.77
GPP Money	2.32	2.71	2.37	2.14	1.40
GPP People	2.21	2.29	1.93	1.95	.85
State Personnel Capacity					
Per Capita Full-time Personnel to Health	.88	.61	.79	.74	1.16(W)
Per Capita Full-time Personnel	17.30	16.86	18.46	17.78	.10
State Financial Capacity					
Budget Shortfalls	4.34	4.54	2.82	11.15	2.89*
Per Capita Income ($1,000)	40.62	40.81	39.04	45.90	3.46*
State Communicative Capacity					
Medicaid Waiver	9.53	9.25	8.44	8.57	.27

Note: For Political Culture, Moralistic Culture, Traditionalistic Culture and Per Capita Full-time Personnel to Health, Welch statistics are used because the variances of the variables violated the assumption of homogeneity of variance.

*$p < .05$; **$p < .01$.

would implement more ACA core functions, and states with more traditionalistic cultures would implement few or no core functions. However, the values using the Lieske measure of political culture did not produce significant mean differences among the states, except for individual plan exchange functions in traditionalistic states, F (3, 46) = 3.56.

These findings confirm the effect of political culture as a factor shaping state implementation of federal programs. Interestingly, Sharkansky's measure showed consistently significant mean differences among the four groups of states, while Lieske's did not. Since political cultures change slowly, we suspect that political culture continues to possess validity because of the way it was conceptualized and developed by Elazar. It may be that Lieske's measure, which is based on racial and ethnic origins, religious affiliations, and social structure in 2000, is susceptible to more rapid demographic changes which are not necessarily related to a state's political culture.

We hypothesized that those citizens and state government officials who are more liberal would be associated with a state's decision to implement more exchange functions. Conversely, where there is a large divergence between citizens' ideology and the ideology of elected officials, then it was hypothesized that those states would exhibit substantial variation as to the number of core functions officials chose to implement—some states would implement none, while others would implement one or two functions. Results on Table 7.5 show significant mean differences for citizen ideology among states with different numbers of core functions, with F (3, 46) = 7.54 for individual plans. We also found significant mean differences for government ideology among the four groups of states, with F (3, 46) = 10.00 for individual plans. Along the same line, the means for states implementing 3 and more core functions were consistently over 60 for individual plans, but the means of states with zero functions were less than 35. These findings support our hypothesis that more liberal citizens and more liberal government officials would be associated with a state's implementation of more exchange functions, corroborating previous research on policy innovation (Soss et al. 2001; Nicholson-Crotty 2004; Boushey 2010).

States showed significant differences for ideological divergence, with F (3, 46) = 4.06 for individual plans. State officials with more liberal ideology than their residents, as indicated by the positive values for ideological divergence on Table 7.5, tended to implement more functions, while other state officials with less liberal ideology than their citizens, as indicated by negative values of ideological divergence, tended not to implement core functions. This means ideological divergence between citizens and government officials is an important factor shaping state implementation of insurance exchanges. Where the gap between the ideological stance of citizens and that of state government officials is great, it is more likely the ideological policy preferences of elected officials will prevail over the preferences of citizens.

Regarding the role of interest groups in a state, it was hypothesized that in a state where health related interest groups exert substantial influence, one would expect the state to implement more exchange functions. To test this hypothesis, we used ANOVA tests for two measurements, size of interest group contributions in elections and percent of health employment in a state. The ANOVA tests reported on Table 7.5 did not yield mean differences of interest groups' influence among the four groups of states for individual plans, thus the hypothesis on the influence of interest groups is not supported. These results are not consistent with previous research on the role of interest groups in state policymaking and implementation (Gray and Lowery 1996; Bowling and Ferguson 2001; Jacoby and Schneider 2001; Kelleher and Yackee 2009; Yackee 2009).

Although the influence of interest groups is not statistically significant in this research, it is still necessary to consider the role played by health interest groups. Data from the National

Institute on Money in State Politics during 2010–2012 attests to the influence of health-related interest groups such as health professionals, health services, hospitals and nursing homes, pharmaceuticals and health products, health insurance companies, pro-choice groups, health welfare policy organizations, and liberal policy organizations. According to the National Institute data, health interest groups contributed considerable funds during state elections, amounting to over 8 percent of total contributions of all interest groups in the states that decided not to implement any core functions. Our data show that health-related interest groups spent more in states with state–federal partnerships, followed by states using federally-facilitated exchanges. By contrast, in the states implementing 3 and more functions, health-related interest groups spent less than 6 percent of total contributions of all interest groups in state elections. Statistical analysis found no significant relationship between health interest group spending and choice of health exchange, thus there is no support for the hypothesis that health-related groups exercised substantial influence over a state's selection of exchange type. Our data leads us to speculate that where a state's political configuration and its political culture (including citizen ideology) were supportive of a state-based exchange, health interest groups did not need to expend large amounts of funds to influence the state's decision, and where the opposite was the case, health groups were impelled to spend more in their effort to overcome the opposition of state officials and/or state citizens.

In examining whether state officials considered severity of the health coverage problem in their states, we hypothesized that the size of the uninsured population in a state as well as the size of the population eligible for ACA coverage would be associated with state officials' decisions to implement more core functions. Table 7.5 shows significant mean differences of the unemployment rate among states with different numbers of core functions, with F (3, 46) = 4.66 for individual plans. The analysis found significant differences for the total number of individual plus SHOP functions. For individual plus SHOP functions, states with 1 or 2 core functions had lower means for the unemployment rate (6.25) compared to the other three groups of states (respectively: 7.47, 6.67, 8.17). But there was no significant difference for the uninsured rate among the four groups of states. So, the hypothesis on the relation between severity of the problem and state responsibility for exchange functions is only partially confirmed. Also, for individual plans and SHOP, states implementing 1 function had a lower unemployment rate than the other three groups. We suspect in the states with lower unemployment rates state officials did not encounter much pressure from their citizens about decisions related to the choice of exchange functions.

State Capacity

To examine the role of state administrative capacity in state decisions for the number of core exchange functions, we proposed three hypotheses:

* higher levels of fiscal and personnel resources are related to more core functions;
* states practicing performance management would choose to operate more core functions; and
* states with more communicative capacity would be associated with more core exchange functions.

To test state personnel capacity, we used serial one-way ANOVA tests respectively for per capita full-time health personnel and for per capita full-time administrative personnel. As shown on

Table 7.5, the tests indicate that the four groups of states did not have significant mean differences in terms of state personnel capacity. To examine the effect of state administrative capacity as gauged by a state's use of performance management, we computed mean differences using state aggregate GPP ratings, state GPP financial management ratings, and state GPP human resource management ratings among the four groups of states, but found no statistically significant differences. States with different numbers of core functions did not have statistically significant mean differences on state personnel capacity or on state communicative capacity, measured by number of Medicaid waivers. But interstate variation on state financial capacity, as measured by budget shortfalls and by per capita income, is associated with interstate variation in the number of core functions. The four groups of states showed statistically significant mean differences for budget shortfalls, with $W(3, 46) = 2.89$ for individual plans. Also, we observed significant differences on per capita income among the four groups of states, with $F(3, 46) = 3.46$ for individual plans.

These findings indicate that states with more wealth and with larger fiscal problems decided to implement more core exchange functions. This is partly consistent with previous research reporting that states with more affluent resources are expected to actively adopt innovations (Walker 1969; Volden 2006; Boushey 2010). However, that states with larger budget shortfalls also chose to administer more exchange functions is perhaps an unexpected finding. Three possible situations may account for the apparent deviant result:

- the lure of large amounts of ACA money;
- partisan affiliation of state officials; and/or
- citizen demands.

The absence of positive effects for several aspects of state administrative capacity on state choice of exchanges runs counter to established models of implementation (Williams 1980; Mazmanian and Sabatier 1989; Jennings et al. 1986; Goggin et al. 1990; Brudney, Hebert, and Wright 1999; Aristegueta 1999; Ingraham 2003). This finding implies that states which have implemented 3 or more core functions do not necessarily possess a superior administrative capacity to states implementing fewer functions. Future research will be required to explore whether differences in state administrative capacity will account for differences in the success of state implemented health exchanges.

State Commitment and State Capacity

The final hypothesis we examine is: states with high commitment and high capacity would decide to implement more core exchange functions, while states with low commitment and low capacity would decide to implement fewer core exchange functions. As discussed above, state commitment is a function of political configuration, political culture, political ideology, and severity of the problem. Through serial ANOVA tests, we found that states implementing more functions were associated with moralistic political culture, liberal citizen and government ideology, and more liberal government ideology than citizen ideology, all contributing to state commitment. Also, in terms of state capacity, the findings showed that states with more affluence and with larger fiscal problems tended to implement more functions.

Since serial one-way ANOVA tests lead to a greatly inflated Type I error rate (Mertler and Vannatta 2001), there is a greater likelihood of rejecting the null hypothesis when it is true. So, we

Table 7.6 MANOVA Tests for Number of ACA Core Functions

Variable	Marketplaces		
	Individual plans	*SHOP*	*Combination*
State commitment			
Political culture (Sharkansky)	5.91**	4.07*	3.44*
Citizen ideology	6.82**	6.23**	6.51**
Government ideology	9.55**	6.79**	7.44**
Ideological divergence	4.09*	3.45*	3.76*
State capacity			
Per capita income	3.55*	2.97*	2.56
Budget shortfall	2.71	2.22	2.12

*$p < .05$; **$p < .01$

used multivariate analysis of variance (MANOVA) tests for the variables statistically significant in the ANOVA tests. In Table 7.6, we found that the four groups of states showed significant mean differences in terms of political culture, citizen ideology, government ideology, ideological divergence, per capita income, and budget shortfall, after controlling for the inflated Type I error rate. One can conclude that state commitment to the national policy and some attributes of state capacity explain the observed differences in state choice of core exchange functions to implement.

Without a doubt this research has its limitations. First, the posttest comparison group design in the context of U.S. states provides a basis for credible results (Spector 1981; Langbein 2012). But at best the conclusions are preliminary because decisions about core exchange functions are ongoing. Since the study captures only the initial implementation decisions, a longitudinal analysis would impart additional confirmation (or rejection) of our findings. For future research, multiple comparison group time series design could be employed to improve statistical validity. This would permit researchers to capture the dynamics of state implementation. Also, panel data gathered at several different points in time could enhance the understanding of state health exchange choices.

Conclusion

Deil Wright, in the third edition of his magisterial *Understanding Intergovernmental Relations* (1988), closed his text with a discussion of future directions in intergovernmental relations. His projections included both conflict and cooperation, and he pointedly explained he used the word *and* "deliberately" (ibid.: 458). In many ways, the adoption and initial implementation of the Affordable Care Act exemplify Wright's prediction of conflict *and* cooperation. The politically rancorous passage of the ACA is well-known and has been chronicled by many. The findings presented here replicate the previous studies that found that conflict in the form of partisan opposition or support for the new national health policy directly affected state implementation choices. Party affiliation in unified Republican state governments motivated state officials to oppose the ACA, and ironically to prefer leaving the operation of health insurance exchanges, especially for individual plans, to the federal government. The converse situation characterized states with unified Democratic governments (also see Posner and Conlan 2014). Partisan divisions between governor and legislature or between legislative chambers in politically divided states created an "approach-avoidance" dilemma for officials which they sought to resolve through negotiation with the federal government over the division of responsibility for health exchange functions.

Our findings offer evidence that state government discretionary choices to implement all, none, or some of the health exchange core functions were also associated with a state's commitment to the national policy, which was shaped in turn by the state's political culture, the ideology of its citizens and elected officials, the severity of the health coverage problem in the state, and the level of state affluence. Unexpectedly, certain aspects of state administrative capacity did not account for differences in state choices. Considering that much implementation research argues for the importance of state administrative capacity, future researchers will want to examine whether the successful implementation of health exchanges will vary widely with state administrative capacity. They will also want to examine whether different types of exchanges affect the enrollment of citizens in health insurance plans.

That the implementation of ACA health insurance exchanges exhibits substantial variation comes as no surprise to those familiar with American intergovernmental relations. Well established propositions predict the extant variation. For example, Elazar (1984: 14–18) pointed out that the degree of cooperation or conflict in national-state relations is a function of "overall state deviation from national patterns and norms" as well as from "national policies and interests" and of "intrastate sharing of common patterns and norms." That is to say, as national and state norms and preferences diverge, the likelihood of conflict between a state and the national government will increase. Similarly, Derthick's (2001: 158–159) emphasis on the norms governing American intergovernmental relations explains the "pushback" by state officials and their negotiations with DHHS over health exchange implementation. As Derthick would say, if "orders" from the national government impose national objectives at odds with important constituencies at the state level, eliminate substantial state discretion, and require states to bear significant costs of a new policy or program, then it is highly likely state officials would resist the new initiative.

The 2012 Supreme Court decision in *National Federation of Independent Business v. Sebelius*, as Dinan (2014: 409) noted, changed the bargaining position of federal and state officials. This decision coupled with the Obama Administration's efforts to induce states to implement the ACA altered the original "either-or" choice to one where states could choose to administer fewer or more core exchange functions, thus producing meaningful variation in the degree of state administrative control in health exchanges. Having failed to overturn the ACA in the 2012 *NFIB* case, opponents of Obamacare filed a lawsuit challenging a key feature of the Act: the provision of tax subsidies to low income persons in states using the federally facilitated exchange because the Act appears to say subsidies are available only to persons buying insurance through "an exchange established by the state," that is, a state based exchange. The Supreme Court on 25 June 2015 ruled 6–3 in *King v. Burwell* that eligible health insurance consumers nationwide could receive the tax subsidy. The Court's affirmation of the ACA's subsidies meant health insurance markets would not be thrown into turmoil and more than 6 million people would not lose their insurance (Liptak 2015).

Since the ACA's enactment in 2010 congressional Republicans have tried sixty-two times to repeal the law, but were stymied by President Obama. Republicans made the promise to "repeal and replace Obamacare" a central theme of their 2016 campaign. The election of President Donald Trump coupled with the continued majority control of Congress seemingly meant nothing could prevent Republicans from fulfilling their pledge, including Trump's declaration that the "beautiful" replacement would provide "insurance for everybody." Factional feuding among House

Republicans over whether to fully repeal the ACA or to retain several of the Act's provisions was resolved by May 2017 with the passage of the American Health Care Act (AHCA) on a vote of 217–213. The repeal bill retained popular elements of Obamacare, ended the individual and employer mandates, ended Medicaid expansion and converted it to a block grant, gave states more flexibility on age-based pricing, allowed states to waive some or all of the ACA essential health services, and repealed most ACA taxes (Ehley 2017; Pear 2017). Analysis by the Congressional Budget Office (CBO) estimated by 2026 the bill would result in about twenty-four million more uninsured persons. Public opinion panned the AHCA as fifty-five percent of Americans viewed it unfavorably (Kirzinger et al. 2017).

The factional divisions among Republicans in the narrowly divided Senate posed a serious challenge to the leadership's ability to craft a bill since any three Republican Senators could block a majority vote. An initial bill, the Better Care Reconciliation Act (BCRA), failed to gain majority support, so a revised version sought to attract conservatives who pushed to repeal Obamacare regulations by allowing insurers to offer plans with or without the ACA's essential health benefits, while mollifying moderates with more funds to cope with the opioid crisis and to help states reduce premiums. As of July 15, 2017, the Senate had not passed a repeal bill, and President Trump publicly declared he would be "very angry" if they failed (Eliperin and Cunningham 2017).

It is worth noting some of the federalism impacts of each chamber's repeal and replace bills. First, both bills would significantly alter Medicaid by changing its open-ended federal funding to a per capita amount or transforming the program into a block grant with lump sum funding. The CBO estimated states would have received nearly $880 billion less, or 25 percent, over ten years, and lose about $400 billion in ACA marketplace tax credits. States that expanded Medicaid under Obamacare would lose more funding due to a roll back in expansion monies. Both repeal bills attempted to stabilize state health marketplaces by funding high risk pools with between $130 and $182 billion over ten years. While the Senate proposal included $45 billion for the opioid epidemic, both bills imposed a one-year freeze on monies to Planned Parenthood. Overall, the worry was state governments would be forced to choose between increasing or decreasing their own expenditures on health care as federal funds diminish (Soffen and Cameron 2017).

Second, both repeal bills would increase the number of uninsured persons by over twenty million—in effect returning the number to its pre-ACA level of about 50 million. The loss of coverage would impact states differently: those that expanded Medicaid and/or have large poverty populations would be hit hardest especially because the Obamacare cost-sharing subsidies would end in 2020. Both bills also would allow insurance companies to raise the cap on the ACA's community rating limits on charges to seniors from no more than three times what younger persons pay for the same coverage to five times as much (Pear 2017). As premiums rise, older Americans may drop coverage, which would increase the burden of uncompensated care on hospitals and clinics.

Third, the AHCA would allow states to request waivers permitting insurance companies to offer plans that do not provide the full set of essential health services required by the ACA, while the BCRA includes an amendment by Senator Cruz (R-TX) which would permit insurance companies to sell low cost "skinny" plans that do not offer the ACA's essential benefits as long as companies also sell a plan with the ACA benefits. Many health care organizations fear this proposal would create a two-tier marketplace – one for healthy people paying lower costs and one for sick and older persons paying much higher prices – despite the bill's additional funding to offset higher premiums (Pear and Kaplan 2017). Politically, giving states flexibility shifts the blame for higher prices and/or the loss of health care protections from Washington DC to governors and state legislators.

Fourth, both bills include tax credits to aid in the purchase of health insurance, while also terminating the individual mandate to buy insurance. However, the bills allow insurance companies to charge more if persons let their coverage lapse. The individual mandate will disappear, but will reappear as a requirement of insurance policies.

The House and Senate efforts to repeal and replace Obamacare transfer numerous health care policy decisions to state governments, which raises the classic federalism issue of unity versus diversity. For example, states with less wealthy populations may well decide to limit the type of essential services insurance policies must include so as to make coverage affordable but narrow. "State flexibility" creates the possibility that a citizen in one state may not be afforded one or more essential health services which are available to citizens in another state, or that the cost for the same service will be more or less expensive. Fiscal disparity among the states will likely increase as health care costs are shifted to the states, which will face not just decisions related to health care but also in other areas of their budgets. Politically, the impacts on state governments do not account for the positions different congressional Republicans have taken on specific provisions. While negative effects on their constituents motivated some in each chamber to defect from the leaderships' proposals, others strongly supported the bills even though citizens in their states would be harmed (Soffen 2017). A "Trumpcare" replacement of the ACA most likely will not be a radically new plan but rather an amalgamation of elements drawn from Obamacare and the compromises among congressional Republicans.

References

Aristegueta, Maria. 1999. *Managing for Results in State Government.* Westport, CT: Quorum Books.
Barr, Donald A. 2011. *Introduction to U.S. Health Policy: The Organization, Financing, and Delivery of Health Care in America.* Baltimore, MD: Johns Hopkins University Press.
Berry, Frances S., and William D. Berry. 1990. "State lottery adoptions as policy innovations: An event history analysis." *American Political Science Review* 84(2): 395–415.
Berry, William D., Evan J. Ringquist, Richard C. Fording, and Russell L. Hanson. 1998. "Measuring citizen and government ideology in the American states, 1960–93." *American Journal of Political Science* 42 (1): 327–348.
Berry, William D., Richard C. Fording, Evan J. Ringquist, Russell L. Hanson, and Carl Klarner. 2013. "A new measure of state government ideology, and evidence that both the new Measure and an old Measure are valid." *State Politics and Policy Quarterly* 13(2): 164–182.
Boushey, Graeme T. 2010. *Policy Diffusion Dynamics in America.* Cambridge: Cambridge University Press.
Bowling, Cynthia J., and Margaret R. Ferguson. 2001. "Divided government, interest representation, and policy differences: Competing explanations of gridlock in the fifty states." *Journal of Politics* 63(1): 182–206.
Bowling, Cynthia J., and J. Mitchell Pickerill. 2013. "Fragmented federalism: The state of American federalism 2012–13." *Publius: The Journal of Federalism* 43(3): 315–346.
Brudney, Jeffrey L., F. Ted Hebert, and Deil S. Wright. 1999. "Reinventing government in the American states: Measuring and explaining administrative reform." *Public Administrative Review* 59(1): 19–30.
Burke, Sheila, and Elaine Kamarck. 2013. *The Affordable Care Act: A User's Guide to Implementation.* October. Washington, DC: Center for Effective Public Management, The Brookings Institution.

Callaghan, Timothy and Jacobs, Lawrence. 2013. "Dynamic federalism and the implementation of the Affordable Care Act." Paper presented at the annual meeting of the American Political Science Association, Chicago, August 29–September 1.

Carey, Mary A. 2014. "States get extra time to decide on health exchanges." *Kaiser Health News* (March 6). Retrieved from www.governing.com/headlines/khn-states-get-extra-time.html.

Center for Consumer Information and Insurance Oversight. 2012. "General guidance on federally facilitated exchanges." Retrieved from www.cms.gov/CCIIO/Resources/Fact-Sheets-and-FAQs/Downloads/ffe-guidance-05-16-2012.pdf.

Center on Budget and Policy Priorities. 2012. "States continue to feel recession's impact." Retrieved from www.cbpp.org/cms/index.cfm?fa=view&id=711.

Centers for Medicare and Medicaid Services. 2012–2013. "Letters." Retrieved from www.cms.gov/CCIIO/Resources/Letters/index.html.

Centers for Medicare and Medicaid Services. 2014. "Waivers." Retrieved from www.medicaid.gov/medicaid-chip-program-information/by-topics/waivers/waivers_faceted.html.

Congressional Budget Office. 2011. "CBO's analysis of the major health care legislation enacted in March 2010." Retrieved from http://cbo.gov/sites/default/files/cbofiles/ftpdocs/121xx/doc12119/03-30-healthcarelegislation.pdf.

Conlan, Timothy J., and Paul Posner. 2011. "Inflection point? Federalism and the Obama administration." *Publius: The Journal of Federalism* 41(3): 421–446.

Dash, Sarah, Christine Monahan, and Kevin Lucia. 2013. *Implementing the Affordable Care Act: State Decisions about Health Insurance Exchange Establishment*. Washington, DC: Georgetown University Health Policy Institute.

Derthick, Martha. 2001. *Keeping the Compound Republic*. Washington, DC: Brookings Institution Press.

Dinan, John. 2014. "Implementing health reform: Intergovernmental bargaining and the Affordable Care Act." *Publius: The Journal of Federalism* 44(3): 399–425.

Donahue, John D. 1997. *Disunited States*. New York: Basic Books.

Doonan, Micahel. 2013. *American Federalism in Practice: The Formulation and Implementation of Contemporary Health Policy*. Washington, DC: Brookings Institution Press.

Ehley, Brianna. 2017. "What's actually in the GOP health care bill." *Politico* (May 4). Retrieved from www.politico.com/story/05/04/what's actually in the gop health care bill.

Elazar, Daniel J. 1966. *American Federalism: A View from the States*. New York: Thomas Crowell Company.

Elazar, Daniel J. 1984. *American Federalism: A View from the States*, 3rd edition. New York: Harper & Row.

Eliperin, Juliet, and Paige Winfield Cunningham. 2017. "From hospitals, doctors and patients, a last gasp of opposition to the Senate health-care bill." *Washington Post* (July 14). Retrieved from www.washingtonpost.com/powerpost/from-hospitals-doctors-and-patients.

Feeley, Malcolm M., and Edward Rubin. 2008. *Federalism: Political Identity and Tragic Compromise*. Ann Arbor, MI: University of Michigan Press.

Fiorina, Morris. 1992. *Divided government*. New York: Macmillan.

Goggin, Malcolm L., Ann O'M Bowman, James P. Lester, and Laurence J. O'Toole, Jr. 1990. *Implementation Theory and Practice: Toward a Third Generation*. Glenview, IL: Scott, Foresman/Little, Brown Higher Education.

Gray, Virginia, and David Lowery. 1996. *The Population Ecology of Interest Representation: Lobbying Communities in the American States*. Ann Arbor, MI: The University of Michigan

Gray, Virginia, David Lowery, James Monogan, and Erik K. Godwin. 2010. "Incrementing toward nowhere: Universal health care coverage in the states." *Publius: The Journal of Federalism* 40(1): 82–113.

Gray, Virginia, David Lowery, and Jennifer K Benz. 2013. *Interest Groups and Health Care Reform across the United States*. Washington, DC: Georgetown University Press.

Grodzins, Morton. 1966. *The American System: A New View of Government in the United States* (ed. Daniel J. Elazar). Chicago, IL: Rand McNally.

Haeder, Simon, and David L. Weimer. 2013. "You can't make me do it: State implementation of insurance exchanges under the Affordable Care Act." *Public Administration Review* 73(S1): S34–S47.

Heckman, Alexander C. 2012. "Desperately seeking management: Understanding management quality and its impact on government performance outcomes under the Clean Air Act." *Journal of Public Administration Research and Theory* 22(3): 473–496.

Ingraham, Patricia. 2003. "Methodology and criteria." *Pathways to Performance in State and Local Government: A Final Assessment from the Maxwell School of Citizenship and Public Affairs*, 27–34. Alan K. Campbell Public Affairs Institute, Syracuse University.

Jacoby, W.G., and Schneider, S. K. 2001. "Variability in state policy priorities: An empirical analysis." *Journal of Politics* 63(2): 544–568.

Jennings, Edward T., Jr., Dale Krane, Alex N. Pattakos, and B. J. Reed. 1986. *From Nation to States: The Small Cities Community Development Block Grant Program*. Albany, NY: SUNY Press.

Kaiser Family Foundation. 2010. "Explaining health care reform: Questions about health insurance exchanges." Retrieved from https://kaiserfamilyfoundation.files.wordpress.com/2013/01/7908-02.pdf.

Kaiser Family Foundation. 2012a. "Health care employment as a percent of total employment." Retrieved from http://kff.org/other/state-indicator/health-care-employment-as-total.

Kaiser Family Foundation. 2012b. "Uninsured estimates of adults ages 18-64." American Community Survey (ACS). Retrieved from http://kff.org/uninsured/state-indicator/adults-18-64.

Kaiser Family Foundation. 2014. "State decisions for creating health insurance marketplaces."

Kaiser Family Foundation. 2015. "State health insurance marketplace types, 2015." Retrieved from http://kff.org/health-reform/state-indicator/state-health-insurance-marketplace-types/view.

Kelleher, Christine A., and Susan Webb Yackee. 2009. "A political consequence of contracting: Organized interests and state agency decision making." *Journal of Public Administration Research and Theory* 19(3): 579–602.

Kirzinger, Ashley, Bianca DiJulio, Liz Hamel, Elise Sugarman, and Molly Brodie. 2017. "Kaiser health tracking poll—May 2017: The AHCA's proposed changes to health care." Retrieved from www.kff.org/health-costs/report/kaiser-health-tracking-poll-may-2017.

Krane, Dale. 1992. "Mississippi in the federal union: An 'approach-avoidance' dilemma." In Dale Krane and Stephen D. Shaffer (eds), *Mississippi Government and Politics: Modernizers versus Traditionalists*, 249–269. Lincoln, NE: University of Nebraska Press.

Krane, Dale. 1993. "State efforts to influence national policy." In Edward T. Jennings, Jr. and Neal S. Zank (eds), *Welfare System Reform: Coordinating Federal, State, and Local Public Assistance Programs*, 143–156. Westport, CT: Greenwood Press.

Krane, Dale. 2007. "The middle tier in American federalism: State government policy activism during the Bush presidency." *Publius: The Journal of Federalism* 37(3): 453–477.

Krane, Dale, and Wright, Deil S. 1998. "Intergovernmental relations." In Jay M. Shafritz (ed.), *International Encyclopedia of Public Policy and Administration*, 1168–1175. New York: Henry Holt.

Langbein, Laura. 2012. *Public Program Evaluation: A Statistical Guide*, 2nd edition. Armonk, New York: M. E. Sharpe.

Leach, Richard H. 1970. *American Federalism*. New York: W.W. Norton.

Lieske, Joel. 2010. "The changing regional subcultures of the American states and the utility of a new cultural measure." *Political Research Quarterly* 63(3): 538–552.

Lieske, Joel. 2012. American state cultures: Testing a new measure and theory." *Publius: The Journal of Federalism* 42(1): 108–133.

Liner, Blaine. 2001. *Making Results-Based State Government Work*. Washington, DC: The Urban Institute.

Liptak, Adam. 2015. "Supreme court allows nationwide health care subsidies." *The New York Times* (June 25). Retrieved from https://nyti.ms/2j003A1.

Lischko, Amy, and Beth Waldman. 2013 "Understanding state resistance to the Patient Protection and Affordable Care Act: Is it really just politics as usual?" *Journal of Health and Biomedical Law* IX(1):101–134.

McFarland, Andrew S. 2004. *Neopluralism: The Evolution of Political Process Theory*. Lawrence, KS: University Press of Kansas.

Mazmanian, Daniel. A., and Paul. A. Sabatier 1989. *Implementation and Public Policy*, 2nd edition. Glenview, IL: Scott, Foreman & Company.

Mertler, Craig A., and Rachel A. Vannatta. 2001. *Advanced and Multivariate Statistical Methods: Practical Application and Interpretation*. Los Angeles, CA: Pyrczak Publishing.

Mitchell, Tia. 2014. "After 6 years, Florida might finally have a health insurance exchange: Florida health choices at last ready to launch." *McClatchy News* (February 4). Retrieved from http://governing.com/news/headline/after-6-years-florida-mght-have-a-health-insuranceexchange.html.

National Conference of State Legislatures. 2012. "2012 state and legislative partisan composition." Retrieved from www.ncsl.org/documents/statevote/legiscontrol_2012.pdf.

National Conference of State Legislatures. 2013. "2012 election results state and legislative partisan composition." Retrieved from www.ncsl.org/documents/statevote/legiscontrol_2013.pdf.

National Institute on Money in State Politics. 2009. State overviews. Retrieved from www.followthemoney.org/our-data/state-oveviews.

Nicholson-Crotty, Sean. 2004. "Goal conflict and fund diversion in federal grants to the states." *American Journal of Political Science* 48(1): 110–122.

Nownes, Anthorny J., and Adam J. Newmark. 2013. "Interest groups in the states." In Virginia Gray and Russell L. Hanson (eds), *Politics in the American states: A Comparative Analysis*, 10th edition, 105–131. Thousand Oaks, CA: Sage.

Nugent, John D. 2009. *Safeguarding Federalism: How States Protect Their Interests in National Policymaking*. Norman, OK: The University of Oklahoma Press.

Olshfski, Dorothy F, and Robert Cunningham. 2008. *Agendas and Decisions: How State Government Executives and Middle Managers Make and Administer Policy*. Albany, NY: State University of New York Press.

Pear, Robert. 2017. "Major provisions of the Republican health care bill." *The New York Times* (May 4). Retrieved from www.nytimes.com/2017/05/04/us/politics/major-prov-republican.

Pear, Robert, and Thomas Kaplan. 2017. "Senate Republicans unveil new health bill but divisions remain." *The New York Times* (July 13). Retrieved from www.nytimes.com/2017/07/13/us/politics/senate-republicans-health-bill.

Posner, Paul L., and Timothy J. Conlan. 2014. "The future of federalism in a polarized country." *Governing* (February 5). Retrieved from www.governing.com/columns/smart-mgmt/col-states-polarized-politics-variable-speed-federalism-html.

Pressman, Jeffrey L. 1975. *Federal Programs and City Politics: The Dynamics of the Aid Process in Oakland*. Berkeley, CA: University of California Press.

Pressman, Jeffrey L., and Aaron B Wildavsky. 1973. *Implementation*. Berkeley, CA: University of California Press.

Reagan, Michael. 1972. *The new federalism*. New York: Oxford University Press.

Rigby, Elizabeth, and Jake Haselwerdt. 2013. "Hybrid federalism, partisan politics, and early implementation of state health exchanges." *Publius: The Journal of Federalism* 43(3): 368–391.

Sharkansky, Ira. 1969. "The utility of Elazar's political culture: A research note." *Polity* 2(1): 66–83.

Soffen, Kim. 2017. "See which states would be hit hardest by the Senate's Obamacare repeal bill." *The Washington Post* (June 30). Retrieved from https://washingtonpost.com/graphics/2017/politics/obamacare-repeal-bill.

Soffen, Kim, and Daria Cameron. 2017. "What the Senate bill changes about Obamacare." *The Washington Post* (July 13). Retrieved from https://wapo.st/senate-heaalth-care?tid=ss.

Soss, Joe, Sanford F. Schram, Thomas P. Vartanian, and Erin O'Brien. 2001. "Setting the terms of relief: Explaining state policy choices in the devolution revolution." *American Journal of Political Science* 45(2): 378–395.

Spector, Paul E. 1981. *Research Design*. Thousand Oaks, CA: SAGE Publications.

Starr, Paul. 2013. *Remedy and Reaction: The Peculiar American Struggle over Health Care Reform*, revised edition. New Haven, CT: Yale University Press.

Stephens, G. Ross, and Nelson Wikstrom. 2007. *American Intergovernmental Relations: A Fragmented Federal Polity*. New York: Oxford University Press.

Strom, Kaare. 2000. "Delegation and accountability in parliamentary democracies." *European Journal of Political Research* 37(3): 261–290.

Sundquist, James L., and David W. Davis. 1969. *Making Federalism Work: A Study of Program Coordination at the Community Level*. Washington, DC: The Brookings Institution.

Thompson, Frank J. 2012. *Medicaid Politics: Federalism, Policy Durability, and Health Reform*. Washington, DC: Georgetown University Press.

Thompson, Frank. 2013. "The rise of executive federalism: Implications for the picket fence and IGM." *The American Review of Public Administration* 43(1): 3–25.

U.S. Department of Labor. Bureau of Labor Statistics. 2015. "Unemployment rate for states." Retrieved from www.bls.gov/lau/lastrk12.hmt.

U.S. Government Accountability Office. 2013a. *Health Insurance: Seven States' Actions to Establish Exchanges under the Patient Protection and Affordable Care Act*. GAO-13-486. April.Washington, DC: Government Accountability Office.

U.S. Government Accountability Office. 2013b. *Patient Protection and Affordable Care Act: Status of CMS Efforts to Establish Federally Facilitated Health Insurance Exchanges*. GAO-13-601. June. Washington, DC: Government Accountability Office.

U.S. Government Accountability Office. 2013c. *Patient Protection and Affordable Care Act: Status of Federal and State Efforts to Establish Health Insurance Exchanges for Small Businesses*. GAO-13-614. June. Washington, DC: Government Accountability Office.

Van Meter, Donald S., and Carl E. Van Horn. 1975. "The policy implementation process: A conceptual framework." *Administration and Society* 6(4): 445–488.

Vestal, Christine. 2011. *Setting Up Health Insurance Exchanges, States Face Big Decisions*. January 26. Philadelphia, PA: Pew Charitable Trusts.

Vestal, Christine . 2012. *GOP Governors Stall Health Insurance Exchange Plans*. March 1. Philadelphia, PA: Pew Charitable Trusts.

Volden, Craig. 2006. States as policy laboratories: Emulating success in the Children's Health Insurance Program." *American Journal of Political Science* 50(2): 294–312.

Walker, Jack L. 1969. The diffusion of innovations among the American states. *American Political Science Review* 63(3): 880–899.

Williams, Walter. 1980. *The Implementation Perspective: A Guide for Managing Social Service Delivery Programs*. Berkeley, CA: University of California Press.

Winter, Soren C. 2003. "Implementation perspectives: Status and reconsideration." In Peters, B. Guy and Jon Pierre, eds. *Handbook of Public Administration*, 221–222. Thousand Oaks, CA: Sage Publications.

Wright, Deil S. 1988. *Understanding Intergovernmental Relations*, 3rd edition. Pacific Grove, CA: Brooks/Cole Publishing.

Yackee, Susan Webb. 2009. "Private conflict and policy passage: Interest-group conflict and state medical malpractice reform." *Policy Studies Journal* 37(2): 213–231.

8 The Diffusion of Federal Regulation through Contracts

The Case of Food Safety Policy

Jocelyn M. Johnston and Rebecca Yurman

Intergovernmental programs, administered jointly by the federal government and states, generate significant contracting and outsourcing activity. Much of this manifests in the area of social welfare policy when states contract with nongovernmental organizations to provide services and case management for welfare to work programs, child welfare, Medicaid, and the State Children's Health Insurance Program ("CHIP"). The Affordable Care Act—the largest social welfare innovation in decades, the future of which remains uncertain—relied heavily on contracts, including those for the notorious health exchange problems experienced by the federal government and several states. Thus, for many federal programs, authority and responsibility are granted to the states in combination with program frameworks and requirements; states may then "stretch" the program by outsourcing service delivery.

Our research focuses on a fundamentally different emerging phenomenon in the intergovernmental arena: the contracting out of core federal *regulatory* duties to states. Regulatory activity related to food safety—specifically, food safety inspections—is diffusing from the U.S. Food and Drug Administration (FDA) to states via contracts in a phenomenon that is similar to, but distinct from intergovernmental social welfare "contractual devolution" (Nathan and Gais 1998). In the food safety case, the contractual devolution involves federal contracts for regulation, which has traditionally been a federal government function.

Reliance on contracts with states to carry out core regulatory duties is therefore a new and noteworthy strategy in what Deil Wright (1990) referred to as the "complex configuration" of intergovernmental relations and federalism (see also Agranoff and Radin 2014 for a contemporary discussion of Wright's work). We view this development in intergovernmental devolution as one that is important from a variety of perspectives—political, legal, administrative, and economic. We explore the phenomenon here with a focus on the responses of federal and state managers charged with ensuring the safety of the nation's food supply. The diffusion of food safety regulation provides an opportunity for a fresh look at the costs and benefits of decentralized governance and reliance on third party delivery.

Overview and Methods

News about the latest high-profile food-borne illness outbreak seems to abound. In 2016, Dole issued a recall of bagged salad after at least 19 people spanning nine states and Canada were seriously sickened by Listeria. This outbreak ultimately resulted in one death and highlighted both the increasingly consolidated nature of the food industry and the interconnected nature of the food supply, in which a single processing plant's food safety problems related to a highly perishable product—salad—could rapidly harm people many states away. In 2015, Blue Bell, the nation's third largest ice cream company, was forced to recall all of its products from the market when it was discovered that people were being sickened by Listeria linked to the company's ice cream. Ultimately, 10 people were seriously sickened and three people died; thousands of workers were left unemployed or furloughed. The central role of state food safety agencies is demonstrated by this case, as the handful of nominal FDA inspections that occurred at the implicated Blue Bell plants over the last several years were in fact conducted by state agencies under contract with FDA.

We rely on data from 52 semi-structured interviews with actors in the food safety policy arena, supplemented by document reviews. We interviewed directors and staff from food safety programs in twenty states that contract with FDA and one state that has elected not to contract with FDA. Additional interviews were conducted with six federal FDA managers responsible for managing contracts and other partnerships with state counterparts, two senior FDA officials responsible for shaping policy, and a senior investigator in the U.S. Department of Health and Human Services (HHS) Office of the Inspector General (OIG) involved in their investigation of FDA's contracts with states. We extended beyond FDA and state officials, interviewing senior food safety officials at the Centers for Disease Control and Prevention (CDC), stakeholders from national consumer protection groups, experts in food safety and government contracting from the U.S. Government Accountability Office (GAO), a senior executive of a large multinational third party inspection and auditing firm, and the executive director of a nongovernmental professional organization whose membership is comprised mostly of state-level food safety officials, which represents the interests of food regulatory agencies in Congress and elsewhere.[1]

Thus, we have data on the perspectives of federal and state officials and a range of stakeholder groups. These individuals and organizations are for the most part technical experts in food safety. The federal and state officials work along the "picket fences" (Sanford 1967: 80) that frame inter-governmental management and that serve as a conduit for a common professional orientation to "grease the wheels" of these contractual arrangements. While the picket fence metaphor invokes the currency of common language and culture shared by professionals from a particular back-ground, we will see that the governmental "rails" of the fence nonetheless persist. Thus, as in other intergovernmental arenas, we can conceive of the food safety regulation "fence" as based on federal, state, and local government "rails" that are bound by "pickets" comprised of similarly trained professionals charged with food safety—pickets that may help to reduce political conflict among the rails and help hold the fence together structurally and operationally.

As states assume the primary responsibility for federal *domestic* food safety inspections, the FDA's role has become increasingly confined to oversight and policymaking as opposed to direct regulatory activity. At the same time, Congress, responding to growing concerns about the safety of *imported* food, has recently adopted legislation authorizing the FDA to rely on third parties—mostly private companies—for inspections and certifications of foreign firms. In short, in both the domestic and international arenas, federal food safety regulation is increasingly outsourced to states and nongovernmental entities, with FDA managing these relationships from a distance. We see this new system as one that comports with Provan and Milward's (2000: 362) hollow state and their concept of a "systems integration function," which emerges when government has contracted out most of its core functions and shifts primarily to a focus on monitoring and evaluating contracts.[2]

Although Provan and Milward were describing the contracting out of government services to the private sector, we believe their description lends insight into the dynamics of contracting out regulatory inspections to states. As FDA relies more and more on states to conduct regulatory inspections, the agency function in this area has narrowed to two primary functions:

1   managing contracts; and
2   setting and implementing policies that attempt to establish consistency among states (an activity very familiar to students of federalism).

Several states in turn contract out all or some portions of their federal food inspection contracts to nongovernmental organizations, adding complexity to the accountability process for this regulatory function.

We began the interview and data collection process with the goal of learning how federal and state actors responded to a 2011 HHS OIG report on major gaps in FDA's oversight of its food safety inspection state contracts (discussed below). Our interview respondents consistently cited these contracts as a central concern, for a variety of reasons. In addition to the OIG report background, actors frequently discussed the mandate contained in recent federal legislation that requires FDA to dramatically increase the number of annual domestic food safety inspections. The FDA, according to our interviews and other documents, intends to meet this mandate primarily through state contracts.

Our research is clear on one conclusion: the devolution of regulation via contracts to states is a significant phenomenon that is changing the landscape of food safety and national regulatory policy. It is our goal to identify and describe this development, and its implications for contracting, regulatory policy, and the relationship between federal and state level actors. NVivo analysis highlights key details of our interviews, and allows us to offer some insights about how and why federal and state officials are both driving and responding to this regulatory decentralization.

States as Contractual Agents: Contributions from the Literature

A review of the analytic frameworks in literatures on contracting, federalism, and networks lend insights into contractual devolution in the context of food safety regulation. These themes include the familiar: the "hollow" state and its impact on accountability; the role of intergovernmental, network, and contract management in service delivery; the "price" of federalism; and states as laboratories of democracy. But the case of contracting out regulatory authority to state agencies is decidedly not familiar. It invokes elements of these frameworks, but the fit is not neat. In the sections that follow, we address selected themes that help to guide our analysis.

The Hollow State

Provan and Milward (2000) used the phrase "hollow state" to describe both the "increasing reliance of the public sector on contracting with nonprofit agencies and for-profit firms for the delivery of taxpayer funded goods and services," as well as the "degree of separation between a government and the services it funds—i.e. the number of layers between the source and the use of funds" (ibid.: 362). Furthermore, "carried to an extreme it refers to a government that as a matter of public policy has chosen to contract out all its production capability to third parties, perhaps retaining only a systems integration function that is responsible for negotiating, monitoring, and evaluating contracts" (ibid.).

Growing reliance on contracting has created a situation in which managers at all levels of government are increasingly responsible for managing and overseeing contracts and the contracting process, rather than carrying out service-oriented work (Durant et al. 2009). Perhaps more importantly, these managers must help mitigate the elongated chains of accountability that result with the growing distance between the policymaker and the citizen (Johnston and Girth 2012; Romzek and Johnston 2005). In the case of food safety, contracts between FDA and the states have begun to take on the familiar traits of intergovernmental programs in which discretion is granted, then reduced through the tightening of legislation designed to enhance accountability (not unlike the "recategorization" of grants discussed by Posner and Wrightson 1996). Writing about the challenges associated with managing contracts and other indirect relationships, Kettl (2002: 492) reminds us "government's performance is only as good as its ability to manage its tools and hold its tool users accountable."

Contract and Network Management

Scholars of network management highlight the lessons that can be drawn from the literatures on federalism and devolution (Agranoff and McGuire 2004; Bird 1993; Soss et al. 2001; Krane et al. 2004), and they help to articulate the transaction costs inherent in network management (Williamson 1999; Frederickson and Stazyk 2010; Johnston and Romzek 2010; Romzek and Johnston 2005). At the same time, a substantial body of research highlights and examines various challenges in managing contract-based networks in a variety of areas such as non-profit nursing homes (Amirkhanyan et al. 2008; Amirkhanyan 2008), local transit systems (Zullo 2008), child welfare and other social welfare systems (Johnston and Romzek 2008; Romzek and Johnston 2005), and mental health systems (Milward et al. 2010). While noncompetitive contract markets can increase contract monitoring costs and diminish the power of the "purchaser" (Girth et al. 2012; Johnston and Girth 2012), "relational" contracting and/or collaborative service delivery can help to overcome some of these costs (Van Slyke 2003; Romzek et al. 2013). Regardless of the structural arrangement at work, interactions with other organizations entail investments in the mechanics of the agreement, whether it is a contract, a network, or something in between.

Outsourcing Regulatory Policy?

There is comparatively little research that examines these issues in the arena of federal regulatory policy. One exception is the area of environmental policy. We know, for instance, that the federal government has devolved significant environmental responsibilities to the states through partnerships, including the implementation and enforcement of key federal statutes such as the Clean Water Act. This decentralization has taken a variety of forms (Radin 2000). Sigman (2003) describes "authorization," a status granted to states by the Environmental Protection Agency (EPA) that gives states the legal authority—and responsibility—to implement, monitor, and enforce federal environmental regulations. She argues that this practice represents the most significant form of decentralization of environmental policy. Accordingly, federal environmental programs should not be treated (or evaluated) as uniform, since the practice of granting states authorization conveys discretion that can result in significant differences across programs and regulatory regimes.

Decentralization of regulatory responsibilities can therefore lead to substantial variation in the enforcement of federal environmental statutes (Flatt 1997; Farber 1999), with potentially weaker enforcement in states with close ties to industry. Potoski and Woods (2002) remind us that political priorities and existing state environmental and regulatory policies are likely to be important determinants of a given state's post-devolution environmental policy decisions; Soss, Fording and Schram (2008) and others have observed similar dynamics in the area of social welfare policy. As Plotnick and Winters (1985) explain with their comprehensive model, state policy decisions are driven by a large and complicated set of factors related to economic, political, and demographic profiles.

One school of thought suggests that granting states greater authority leads to more robust enforcement of regulations (Revesz 2001). Empirical investigations into this question are mixed in their conclusions: for instance, Helland (1998) finds a weak but statistically significant positive correlation between authorization and outcomes of environmental inspections, wherein states with greater authorization authority tended to have better inspections outcomes (i.e. more firms passing inspections). However, Helland also concluded that the stringency of compliance inspections conducted by state agencies may be moderated by budgetary and political forces, such as a state agency's "industry friendliness," calling into question the conclusions that one should draw from higher inspection "pass" rates. Sigman (2003) reminds us that empirical studies are limited in their ability to make causal claims; for example, it could be that states with stronger environmental programs are those that are in fact granted more authorization authority. More troubling is the prospect that some states may take a more lax approach to inspections and enforcement, resulting in the false appearance of compliance.

These literatures and frameworks lead us to the following questions: In view of environmental regulation and the increasing levels of discretion granted to states, is there reason to believe that states can strengthen food safety regulation? What actions are federal and state managers adopting in response to the devolution of food safety regulation activities? Do their responses mitigate the accountability deficits in the increasingly "hollow state" of food safety? Does the inevitable inter-state variation in food safety enforcement practices threaten the integrity of our increasingly mobile food supply? Our study begins to shed some light on these areas of inquiry.

Federal Regulation, Food Safety, and the States

There is no doubt that in a global context, Americans enjoy a relatively safe food supply. Nonetheless, the Centers for Disease Control and Prevention (CDC) estimate that each year food-borne diseases sicken roughly 1 in 6 Americans (or 48 million people), hospitalize 128,000, and kill 3,000 (Centers for Disease Control and Prevention 2011). And the number and scale of multi-state outbreaks of food-borne illness is increasing. These incidents impose significant economic impacts: a 2012 study estimates that, accounting only for the health-related costs associated with food-borne illnesses, totals exceed $75 billion per year (Scharff 2012).

The FDA is responsible for ensuring the safety and quality of 80 percent of the American food supply, representing an annual value of over $465 billion, including domestic and imported food (U.S. Government Accountability Office 2008). Federal regulation of food safety was non-existent until the early part of the twentieth century when Upton Sinclair's famous 1906 book,

The Jungle, exposed horrific and unsanitary conditions in the Chicago meatpacking industry, inducing progressive-era food safety reform efforts. The Pure Food and Drugs Act was passed within the same year, with the primary aim of enabling the government to act "after the fact, against blatant, reckless deception" by food suppliers. It also established the Bureau of Chemistry, which became the FDA in 1938, with the passage of the Food, Drug, and Cosmetics Act.

The FDA's statutory responsibilities include the enforcement of food safety laws and regulations via inspections and other activities. FDA is required by law to conduct a certain number of domestic food facility inspections per year. Though hard-won, federal regulation of food safety has been subject to much criticism, often from within the food industry, but also from members of Congress who censure FDA variously for doing too much—or not enough. In his history of the agency, Quirk observes:

> The balance of external forces impinging on the FDA is not a constant. It fluctuates with events, with the rise and decline of social movements and political organizations, with experience of the impact of previous regulatory decisions, and with broad changes of public attitude . . . There are significant pressures on the FDA to regulate both strictly and leniently.
>
> (Quirk 1980: 193)

In the years since 2005, the majority of FDA inspections have typically been conducted by state agencies acting under contract with FDA. This number and proportion has been steadily increasing, a trend which is expected to continue. According to our interview data, FDA officials began pursuing contracts with states in the 1970s as a way to meet new annual inspections requirements (performance standards) set by Congress but typically unaccompanied by new resources. Over the years, Congress informed the agency that if it did not complete stipulated number of annual inspections, its budget would be cut. Some states have been performing contract inspections for well over a decade, while others have only begun doing so in the last few years. As of 2013, FDA contracted with 43 states, with contract work totaling $11.75 million of FDA's budget, according to FDA budget documents. States typically do not perform all FDA inspections within their borders, but rather take responsibility for some proportion of FDA's inspections through their contracts.[3]

Why Outsource Food Safety Regulation?

Our interview respondents reported consistently that the costs of food safety inspections are much lower for states, in part because of comparatively low state costs for travel and personnel. For example, a food safety official from a large Western state pointed out that his state inspectors are located throughout the state and can reach a facility faster—and at lower cost—than an FDA inspector who may be based much farther away. Additionally, a key determinant of the cost per inspection is personnel costs, and state inspectors are paid less than FDA inspectors on average, according to our interview data.

But food safety costs vary across states, as do the value of the federal food inspection contracts. FDA does compensate states for higher costs associated with a unionized inspector workforce, but some state officials reported to us that the compensation does not always fully cover all costs. In addition, states need to invest in contract management capacity if they sub-contract inspection work, and that is not necessarily funded through the FDA contracts. Despite these complications for the states, our respondents generally agreed that lower cost per inspection is one of the primary drivers behind FDA's food inspection contracts.

Another important cost difference between federal and state inspections relates to the time and amount of documentation involved. All state officials we interviewed remarked that inspections conducted by FDA tend to be very time-intensive, particularly with regard to the required paperwork after the actual physical inspections are conducted; they stress that it takes weeks for an FDA inspector to prepare an inspection report, compared to one or two days for a state inspector. Several described the FDA process using terms such as "burdensome," "overly bureaucratic, and "unnecessary paperwork."

Importantly, this differential in processing costs relates to reduced reporting requirements for states: when states conduct inspections for FDA under contract, they are not required to follow the exact FDA process or its documentation protocols. As one food safety administrator put it, states are "basically doing our own inspections," but getting paid by FDA. The result is far less time spent per inspection, which drives costs down even further. According to FDA officials, differences in federal and state law mostly exempt state agencies from having to document inspections results at the same level of detail as FDA.

States tend to have far more stringent food safety laws than FDA, an explanation that may appear counterintuitive; however, in this case, greater legal authority comes with reduced red tape. For example, most states are able to place an immediate embargo (or "stop sale") on a company if a state inspector has credible belief that there may be contamination in a food production facility, while federal law requires FDA to obtain a court order to do so. The court order involves a time- and paperwork-intensive process, with all of the accompanying rules of evidence, and is the main reason that FDA inspectors must spend so much time documenting their inspections. As one interviewee put it, the FDA inspectors are essentially "building a hypothetical legal case" every time they conduct an inspection, even if no such case ever arises. However, as emphasized by another FDA official, this difference also means that federal inspectors take more time conducting inspections, collecting evidence and extensive data that may prove invaluable in the event of an outbreak of food-borne illness and ensuing court case.

Thus, from FDA's perspective, these state contracts deliver lower inspection costs and adherence to state food safety standards that tend to be as high or higher than federal standards.[4] State and FDA officials cited advantages and reasons beyond cost savings for outsourcing inspections to states. Key among these was the observation—familiar to students of federalism and decentralization—that state inspectors tend to be more familiar with the industries within their states, and hence bring greater knowledge to the table than FDA inspectors who may not even be located in the state where the inspections take place. One state inspector told us that it is very common for FDA to request inspections of facilities that are no longer in operation, or that have been sold or relocated; hence, state inspectors have "institutional knowledge" that FDA inspectors lack. Furthermore, FDA is organized into numerous regional and district offices, some of which span several states. An FDA inspector whose office is in one state may be responsible for inspections in a neighboring state. This not only contributes to costs (e.g. time spent traveling and related expenses), but also often means that FDA inspectors must have knowledge of the food industries and firms within several states. State inspectors, on the other hand, are only responsible for the firms within their state and hence are likely to be more knowledgeable about them (though this knowledge should be balanced against the dangers of shorter than arms-length relationships with entities to be inspected).

State officials and consumer advocates pointed out to us that state innovation is also beneficial to food safety. Some states have very sophisticated food safety programs due to unique circumstances that might be difficult to replicate elsewhere. For example, the University of Minnesota has a very strong, internationally recognized program in epidemiology, and the state benefits from a close partnership with the university. New York has historically had a large immigrant community and many retail establishments catering to this population, and hence state health officials focused on imported food safety decades before this became a national issue—in fact, New York is serving as a model for FDA as the agency restructures its approach to regulating imported food. These dynamics invoke the concept of states as "laboratories of democracy," and offer the opportunity for other states and the federal government to learn from the discretionary practices of innovators.

Such state-specific innovations and practices are consistent with the common theoretical arguments for devolution: the level of government that best understands a jurisdiction's needs and contexts is best suited to deliver more efficient services. As one state inspector put it, reflecting a common theme, "It's better to do things locally;" another argued that states can do the "same work more effectively and cheaper" than FDA. Similarly, senior CDC officials highlighted the critical, front-line role of local public health departments during investigations of food-borne illness outbreaks, while citing the drawbacks of an often fragmented food safety system, which prompts their agency to promote uniformity across state and local health departments. And innovation among the states, inherent in the discretionary behavior implicit in decentralization, can offer benefits that extend beyond state borders.

Cost Savings are not Costless

As noted, states have their own laws and regulations pertaining to food safety, and they conduct their own regulatory inspections to enforce them. They are also responsible for ensuring state food safety policy compliance with federal regulations. At the same time, as our interview respondents point out, there are significant differences in states' regulatory capacities, and that variation could undermine the benefits of assigning states primary responsibility for regulatory inspections. Concerns have been raised in recent years by FDA officials and consumer groups regarding the rigor of some state inspections. As one FDA official put it, state inspectors "should not leave their state inspector hats on when they go do an FDA inspection" because a federal FDA inspector would approach the same inspection with higher standards.

These concerns were heightened following the infamous 2009 outbreak of salmonella in peanut butter that originated in a Georgia peanut plant. Congress learned that a state agency working under contract with FDA had inspected the peanut plant multiple times and awarded it a clean bill of health. This peanut incident prompted Congress to mandate a review by the Department of Health and Human Services' Office of the Inspector General (HHS OIG) of FDA's contractual relationships with states, noting that "this outbreak . . . leads to serious questions about the effectiveness of state food facility inspections and FDA's ability to oversee its contracts with states" (U.S. Department of Health and Human Services Office of Inspector General 2011: 194). Recognizing the disparity between federal and state inspection protocols, FDA took steps to oversee its state contracts more closely, and enacted policies aimed at addressing discrepancies between state and federal inspections, as well as differences between states. For example, following the 2011 OIG report, FDA hired a small cadre of federal–state liaisons to work with states on meeting their contract requirements. FDA also began requiring states to submit quarterly, rather than annual, inspections reports. However, these reports do not include details about how the inspections were conducted—only that they were conducted and the results of the inspections. The agency also strengthened its Contract Audit Program; seven percent of state inspections are now accompanied by an FDA state liaison who observes the inspection as it is conducted and provides feedback to the state. However, as one FDA liaison observed, inspectors might behave differently if they are being audited, so there is no guarantee that these inspections represent the norm.

Differences in state food safety policies can create a range of complexities for both FDA and the states. For example, one interviewed state official cited policies related to raw, unpasteurized milk; certain states, such as Oregon and Pennsylvania, permit the selling of this product, but federal law prohibits its interstate trade. Hence, state-level inspections must take both sets of regulations into account, depending on where the product is to be sold, and its destination is not always known; transaction costs to states rise as a result. In some states, food safety authority is dispersed across several agencies, typically because of decades-old structural arrangements, further confounding state food safety management.

Regardless of these complications and implicit costs, the trend to outsource more regulation is entrenched and indeed endorsed by federal statute, as described in the next section. Data from the OIG report and FDA's annual performance reports to Congress indicate that the overall number of domestic food facilities inspected directly by FDA decreased from 10,354 in FY 2004 to 7,133 in FY 2014. This trend is directly correlated with a significant increase in the percentage inspected by states under contract with FDA, from 42 percent in fiscal year (FY) 2004 to 58 percent in FY 2014, according to FDA.

Our interview data further confirmed this rapid acceleration; one state official noted that his state had moved from conducting "2 or 3" contract inspections in 2009 to more than 50 in 2012–2013.[5] The data are also firmly consistent: each respondent fully expects this trend to continue.

Congress Reacts: The FSMA Solution

At about the same time that the OIG was finalizing its investigation of these concerns, Congress enacted the 2011 Food and Drug Modernization Act (FSMA), which significantly increases federal reliance on states for food safety regulation.[6] FSMA mandates that FDA must raise the frequency of annual food safety inspections—though an exact number is not specified in the Act itself—and explicitly authorizes the agency to utilize counterpart agencies, including states, to meet this requirement.

According to interviewed FDA officials, this mandate will be met primarily by expanding the number and scope of state contracts. In addition to increasing inspections of domestic facilities, FSMA mandates an exponential increase in inspections of overseas facilities; the number of foreign facilities inspected must double each year. Several high-profile incidents of food-borne illness traced back to imported food motivated this mandate.

FDA and state officials explained in interviews that the FDA is shifting the majority of its domestic inspection responsibilities to states in large part to free FDA inspectors to focus their attention abroad. Concerns about the safety of imported food have renewed pressure on FDA to increase the number of overseas inspections. While this intensification is central to the new legislation, FDA has struggled to implement it because no new resources have been allocated to the agency to support the required work. Indeed, a recurring theme across our interviews is the persistent gap between mandates to the agency and the resources needed to meet the mandates. The new FSMA imported food requirements were repeatedly cited as an unrealistic expectation—if no new resources are provided—on the part of Congress.

It remains to be seen how FDA will meet this challenge, but it seems certain that heavy reliance on states to meet domestic inspection requirements is here to stay, at least in the coming years. The agency requested that Congress fund an additional 1,000 full-time equivalent (FTE) employees to meet the new inspections mandate. Because Congress denied the request, the FDA is all but forced to outsource the inspections. As one senior state official put it, FDA is "never going to get enough money to do the work (mandated by FSMA) themselves" and will have to rely on states, and in the case of imported food, private third parties. A senior FDA official similarly cautioned that, "FSMA is a huge step forward, but we need the money to implement it;" another refers publicly to "the FSMA funding gap," estimated at $225 million. The lack of resources for contract management is a familiar theme in scholarship on government outsourcing; without adequate contract management capacity, it becomes difficult to ascertain contractor performance and to articulate the benefits and costs inherent in the contract. In other words, low resource levels correspond with reduced accountability.

Back to the Future? The "Price of Federalism"

Emergent patterns in our interview data reveal that states vary considerably on a number of other dimensions related to regulating food safety, including historical and structural features, regulatory and political culture, resource and budget constraints, and economic and industry contexts and their consequent incentives. In this section we address selected identified patterns and their relationship to food safety regulation.

Structure and Regulatory Culture

The structures of states' regulatory systems may be especially important to ensuring food safety. Most states' food safety programs are housed either in departments of agriculture or health. This distinction can have important implications for food safety, regulatory policy, and contract management.[7]

Consumer advocates expressed concerns in interviews that state agriculture departments have historically focused on the promotion of trade, and may not prioritize food safety. The food programs within many state agriculture departments are primarily tasked with marketing and promoting state industries and commodities. By comparison, state health departments tend to have greater expertise related to epidemiology and other food-safety areas. A senior state health department manager told us that his department is essentially a "mirror image" of FDA, and that, in his experience, there tends to be a "clear conflict of interest" in state agriculture departments charged both with promoting agriculture and regulating food safety. He also observed that while this conflict is not necessarily evident at the "ground level" (i.e. in the quality and rigor of inspections), there are competing interests that play out at the level of state policymaking and politics, where the influence of industry can dominate.

Officials from state agriculture departments disagree, although their own characterization of how they approach food safety regulation suggests a difference between their approach and that of FDA. As officials from one state agriculture department put it, "we educate before we regulate," preferring to avoid the punitive measures sometimes used by the FDA, but instead working with industry to help companies come into compliance with regulations. Another state official said that industry views the FDA as akin to "the police," and that many state agencies tend to take a much more collaborative approach to regulation. Some state agriculture department officials told us that if a state inspector suspects a firm is going to fail an inspection, it is common practice for the inspector to reschedule the inspection, giving the firm extra time to come into compliance in order to avoid the costs involved with failing an inspection. Consumer safety groups have noted this practice and cite their concern that companies use this time to offload potentially hazardous products into the marketplace.

A retired FDA official who worked extensively with states agreed that agriculture departments tend to focus on promotion of state commodities, but pointed out that food safety is not necessarily prioritized in state health departments; other public health concerns such as hospital safety inspections, or limited budgets, might reduce attention to food safety inspections. He and several other interviewees argued that the quality of a state's food safety program is affected as much or more by its political climate and fiscal conditions relative to other factors. One state official lamented the deleterious impact the current state legislature was having on his department's ability to carry out its basic oversight functions, citing several examples of political ideology influencing regulatory policy decisions. Even absent overt political influence, most state interviewees cited ongoing fiscal constraints as significant impediments to their food safety work. One veteran of FDA with a background in a state health department told us that large manufacturers carry enormous clout in states, regardless of whether the primary food safety agency is housed in an agriculture or health department, and that he was aware of cases where state agencies were pressured by the industry and state leadership to release bad food into commerce.

State officials also expressed awareness of the costs of weakened food safety regimes. It is important to remember that, in addition to affecting public health, outbreaks of food-borne illness can have significant economic ramifications for individual states. For example, the Georgia peanut industry was greatly damaged by the 2009 outbreak, representing a significant economic loss for the state; FDA estimates that the total cost to the food industry in the ensuing nationwide recall exceeded $1 billion. In other words, economic interests could benefit from stronger—not weaker—regulatory actions. In fact, this very dynamic is what scholars such as Quirk (1980) have argued led to the creation of the FDA in the first place. Interestingly, one change that resulted from the 2009 outbreak was that the Georgia Department of Agriculture was granted far greater punitive authority, including the ability to levy civil penalties on companies that do not comply with certain state reporting requirements, exceeding authority possessed by the FDA at that time. While they have not yet exercised this particular authority, Georgia officials we spoke to said it plays an important deterrent effect on would-be "bad apples," and a consumer safety group representative we interviewed cited great strides in the Georgia food safety regime overall.

State Constraints

Fiscally strained states often struggle to generate adequate resources to develop robust food safety programs. In addition, some interviewed state officials underscored the unseen costs of doing business with FDA, citing the amount of time required to complete necessary paperwork and engage in FDA's increasingly robust oversight of state contracts. Another source of frustration among state officials is the fact that some states' budget structures prevent direct disbursement of federal funds into food safety programs. For example, several interviewed state officials pointed out that their agency's budgets are financed through state general funds; state decisions against dedicated funds for federal contract payments hinders the ability of food safety officials to make out-year budget projections.[8]

One contract-state official emphasized the impact of internal FDA fragmentation between offices that plan and oversee contracts and those that pay states for their contract work. One consequence is long wait periods for payment, supplemented by "onerous" state efforts spent pursuing these payments. When states are more fiscally constrained, these delays are especially burdensome, as are other, less explicit contract compliance costs.

Industry

Some states do not have a large food manufacturing industry and hence their regulatory framework for food is minimal. Others have food-related industries that dominate state economies. In this latter situation, we should expect anti-regulatory pressures, which often succeed, according to much of the scholarship on federal regulation (particularly in the area of environmental regulation—see Potoski and Woods 2002; Ringquist 1993).

Related to this is the role of industry fees at the state and federal levels. Most state departments of agriculture collect fees from industry for market grading services. To illustrate, the egg industry pays for a "Grade A" designation, which is based mostly on market-based criteria such as appearance and size, but with some considerations of safety and "good manufacturing practices" taken into account. But most states cannot collect industry fees for regulatory safety inspections.

Historically, while FDA has collected industry (user) fees for certain services, most inspection costs have been borne by the agency.[9] The Food Safety Modernization Act changes this by granting FDA authority to require firms to pay for inspections in cases where the firms have failed initial routine inspections. FDA sees these re-inspection fees as an important step toward shifting the cost of high risk inspections to industry and acting as a potential deterrent to safety violations. According to some officials we interviewed, it also makes it more likely that a state will turn over an investigation to FDA if the state believes a firm should be held liable for the cost of inspections—rather than using state resources, states have a new incentive to collaborate with FDA. However, in spite of the demonstrable benefits of this new authority, Congress remains staunchly opposed to granting FDA the ability to collect industry fees for routine regulatory inspections, a common practice and vital source of revenue for agencies such as USDA, EPA, and others.

Overall, these patterns in our data, as observed in interviews and official documents, suggest that, as in other policy arenas, the "price of federalism" (Peterson 1995) emerges—in this case, as variations in the protection of citizens from unsafe food. State officials cited numerous examples of unique challenges within their states, but emphasized that resources, including training, are the key factors that determine a state's ability to effectively carry out food safety inspections. States will of course vary with regard to their willingness to fund robust food safety programs and their tolerance for regulatory activity. But there is little doubt that the safety of food production practices— and the consequent effects on the public health of citizens—vary across states. As in the area of environmental policy, spillovers across states are not uncommon, particularly because food has become increasingly mobile.

Familiar Centralization Woes, Even in a Contracting Context: the Manufactured Food Regulatory Program Standards

According to FDA officials, the agency is making a concerted effort to address food safety discrepancies between states, primarily through a program called the Manufactured Food Regulatory Program Standards (MFRPS). This program was raised in nearly every interview as a source of both promise and consternation for states. MFRPS is a voluntary program in which states opt to enroll if they contract with FDA; in doing so, they agree to implement numerous FDA standards and submit to periodic audits by FDA to ensure that these standards are being properly implemented. FDA, however, sees MFRPS as a way to ensure a baseline national standard across states' food safety programs.

The program is in some ways analogous to the "primacy" movements in environmental policy that increased autonomy to those states willing to craft state implementation plans (SIPs) consistent with federal standards. Enrollment in MFRPS also generates some federal grants, and includes both opportunities and requirements for state officials to receive training from FDA. At present, according to FDA, 41 contract states are enrolled in MFRPS, although they vary widely in terms of implementation progress. Officials from several states cited their participation in MFRPS as key in the development and improvement of their food safety program, and described the FDA audits as useful and welcomed.

While FDA characterizes enrollment in MFRPS as a requirement for all states that wish to contract with FDA, the formality of the requirement is not clear. One interviewed state official contradicted the new policy's mandatory feature, while expressing doubt that MFRPS (mostly "busy work") will actually lead to improvements in state programs. Some states are highly resistant to MFRPS, citing the loss of autonomy as a primary reason, along with an increased workload and training requirements that they view as unnecessary and onerous. One state official told us that his state avoided enrolling in MFRPS since it seemed like it would be "a lot of work" requiring a large amount of documentation and report reviews.

By contrast, an FDA official stressed that the goal of the program is not to create "cookie-cutter" uniformity across states, but to encourage states to build comparably robust food safety programs that, at a minimum, meet FDA regulatory standards. In other words, FDA recognizes that while it is tapping into state innovation, there are also benefits to some uniformity. Another FDA official described the purpose of MFRPS as the gradual establishment of a minimum level of consistency, with the ultimate aim of achieving a national integrated food safety system.

But as often happens when the national government attempts to improve performance in some states, resentment emerges about a one size fits all policy to foster uniformity. One state official argued that FDA should focus on bringing weaker and higher risk states up to par because "strong states aren't the issue." Another state official argued that FDA would not be able to meet its own standards as laid out in MFRPS and expressed resentment that states are being forced into participating. MFRPS enrollment may include grants for states, but not necessarily, and some state officials complained about the additional non-remunerated costs they incur though participation in the program. Still in its early stages, it remains to be seen how effective the program will be and whether it will achieve its goals.

Impacts and Future Directions

Federal government reliance on state contracts for regulatory enforcement adds a new dimension to Deil Wright's articulations of IGR and IGM. First, this practice incorporates a new intergovernmental regime in a regulatory policy arena that, like environmental protection, relies on the overlapping elements of the federal system to accomplish a policy objective and solve spillover problems. However, unlike environmental protection, federal–state food safety relations are comparatively conflict-free—so far.

Second, these contracts introduce a new IGM strategy. Unlike grants or mandates, which are widely recognized tools used to induce state cooperation, contracts imply state discretion on whether or not to cooperate. The history of the FDA contracts as reflected in our interview data seems quite benign and cooperative relative to conflict levels in the area of environmental protection. The management costs of these contracts as currently observed appear to be substantially lower than costs implicit in the use of traditional IGR tools, particularly in terms of the transaction costs associated with bargaining and negotiation. They may be lower because of inadequate attention to contract management, but nonetheless, conflict seems to be comparatively manageable.

But we must consider a large caveat. These contracts are atypical. They do not seek to tap into competitive supply environments to reduce costs and improve quality and are therefore not consistent with the rationale typically embedded in new public management market-based reforms. The contracts are completely voluntary for states—a critically important distinction. States are free to say no; that is simply not the case with mandates or grant conditions. Food safety incentives for all governments are therefore unlike grant/mandate incentives. If and when the FDA becomes even more dependent on states to conduct inspections, as FSMA recommends, and if and when states become more dependent on FDA revenues associated with these contracts, a reasonable expectation is that the contract strategy will grow to resemble traditional IGR tools and will engender similar levels of conflict. As is typical, such conflicts would be likely to stem from the familiar and inherent differences between federal approaches to nationwide problems and state incentives driven by pressure from state-based economic interests.

As with other intergovernmental policies, federal organizations are fundamentally altered through devolution. Administrative capacity for effective contract oversight is hardly a new worry (Romzek and Johnston 2005; Van Slyke 2003), and FDA is clearly adjusting to capacity issues as it faces the new demands on its workforce. By embracing the delegation of regulatory responsibility through contracts, the FDA is taking on an increasingly systems integration and oversight role, with states becoming the primary regulatory actors. One senior state official framed it as an identity crisis, with FDA finding itself in the position of having to decide what kind of agency it wants to be: "an inspection agency, or an oversight, training, evaluation, auditing agency." In other words, as he put it, "is FDA willing to relinquish control over regulation and shift to an auditing approach?" If the latter is the case—as our initial research suggests—then, according to this official, the central challenge becomes ensuring—and being able to demonstrate—that states are delivering inspection quality equivalent to that of FDA and other states. As he asked, "how do we know we [states and feds] are on the same page?"

As our research continues, our intent is to dig deeper to further define the implications of this new intergovernmental regime. In addition to shedding light on how and why federal and state managers are responding to this evolving situation in regulatory policy, we will make use of newly acquired food outbreak data to identify state strategies that are deemed most effective in protecting food supplies and why, and to help inform policymakers responsible for these matters. In addition, several related lines of inquiry emerge, all related to the IGR and IGM models articulated by Deil Wright.

One important question has to do with determining whether food safety outsourcing results are equal to or better than results from traditional IGR/IGM tools such as grants and mandates, even in a regulatory policy area. If so, what factors help to explain differences in results? What data would be required to answer these questions? The measurement of food safety results has not developed to the point achieved in environmental protection. Will intensification of state contracting help push food performance safety data forward as the federal government becomes more dependent on, and possibly demanding of states?

A legitimate concern, as described earlier, has to do with the relative impact of contracts on the "price" of federalism and interstate variations in food safety protections. The salience of food safety failures is high, and the impact of failures is swift and often widespread. Food safety is a fundamentally different problem from the slow encroachment of environmental toxins or shifts in welfare benefits. To some extent, these patterns resemble those observed in earlier versions of devolution. Like welfare devolution, this FDA policy cedes significant authority to the states in order to facilitate tailored oversight by agencies closest to the jurisdictional policy problem, and to generate innovation from which other states and the federal government can learn. Our data document variations in the willingness and capacities of states to fully assume their new responsibility as food safety contractors. These findings are especially important as FDA takes steps to implement FSMA's expansion of the role of third parties in imported food safety inspections. Thus, will the familiar regional patterns of government protection and social safety-net infrastructure hold on the American map? Could contracts help mitigate these variations—which pose direct threats to individuals—and perhaps reduce state-based actions that might undermine federal collective goals? More simply, might contracts improve equity outcomes relative to traditional IGR/IGM tools?

Could contracts replace traditional IGR/IGM tools in other policy areas? Will the development of FDA-state contracts prompt interest from policy makers responsible for other programs? Although the long histories of intergovernmental efforts suggest otherwise, it is possible - at the margins and for new program components and new programs—that the contract approach might be attractive to all levels of government. If federal–state contracts do become established intergovernmental strategies, how might the politics of IGR change? Could the adoption of this tool, which smacks of discretion, alter and/or reduce intergovernmental conflict? How might this tool alter the relative power of the federal government and the states, and how could such power shifts affect program success?

Is it more likely that as federal and state food safety interdependencies evolve, contracts will simply take on the trappings of traditional IGR/IGM tools? Will contracts become a new tool of coercion? If so, how might intergovernmental deployment of contracts affect contract management throughout government, as well as the trajectory of New Public Management and market-based strategies?

From the perspective of regulatory enforcement, consumer protection, and IGR, will food safety devolution, through its use of contracts, follow a path that differs substantially from environmental regulation? If so, how might environmental protection respond? Over time, will regulatory contracting become preferable to the use of traditional IGR/IGM tools for the federal government and/or the states? Could direct federal–state contractual devolution mute the traditionally conflicted grant/mandate politics of federal regulatory enforcement, and federalism?

These questions and others motivate our continued research. More questions will arise, but we hope that some answers will emerge as well—answers that can help guide policy makers responsible for leveraging other governments in the context of protecting citizens. Ultimately, we hope to build knowledge about what we should expect from this new strategy in terms of its larger impacts on federalism, intergovernmental relations and management, regulatory enforcement, and the improvement of services to citizens.

Notes

1   We followed a purposive sampling approach (Patton 1990), a nonrandom sampling technique, which inherently entails a threat of bias. However, purposive sampling is indicated when information sought for analysis is restricted to a limited group of individuals that are selected *on purpose*; without its use, the information necessary for analysis would not be obtained. In our case, it is used to explore a relatively new phenomenon that has received no scholarly attention of which we are aware. We used the snowball technique as well, in order to identify key informants as the research progressed. These sampling approaches also helped us obtain the "thick description" (Geertz 1973) that facilitates external validity (Lincoln and Guba 1985) and the development of a knowledge base to shape hypotheses to test more systematically. We do not claim that our interview data is free of bias; however, we did interview individuals that could help validate our data—interest group individuals, for instance, as a check on government officials, and vice-versa—and we also reviewed government and interest group documents.
2   Contracting with nongovernmental entities merits attention, and is the subject of some of our related research but the primary focus of this paper is on FDA contracts with states.
3   The states that had not contracted with FDA are North Dakota, South Dakota, New Mexico, Arizona, Oklahoma, New Hampshire and Delaware. The allocation of inspections in each state—which inspections are inspected by FDA directly and which by the state under contract—is not yet known. Interview data indicate that this breakdown may be available in some of the states that more recently agreed to contract for inspections. State officials we interviewed were not aware of exactly how many FDA inspections occur in their jurisdictions. Unfortunately, our data do not yet include dollar values of individual state contracts with FDA.
4   A mapping of standards for FDA and the individual states, and an analysis of the impact of those differences on food safety performance, is planned for future stages of this research.
5   Precise data on the current number of contracts has been requested from FDA but is not yet available.
6   The IG investigation and the development of FSMA were happening concurrently. The IG investigation was nearing completion, and it is highly likely that Congress was aware of developments in the investigation as it crafted the law.
7   The decision about structure is historical, and usually is not even known by people currently working for the state, unless it has recently changed. Essentially, whichever state department has jurisdiction over manufactured food regulations in that state is automatically the department with which FDA will contract. FDA contracts only cover manufactured food (e.g. food processing firms), not restaurant and retail inspections. It is very common for a state agriculture department to perform manufactured food inspections (and contract with FDA), and for health departments to do the retail/restaurant inspections (these are under complete state authority). These practices are not concrete—in some states, for example, the department of health performs all inspections.
8   The rationale for these fund structure arrangements are unknown but will be explored in later research.
9   While user fees fund over half of the FDA's annual budget, these overwhelmingly come from the pharmaceutical, cosmetics, and medical devices industries.

References

Agranoff, R. and M. McGuire. 2004. *Collaborative Public Management: New Strategies for Local Governments*. Washington, DC: Georgetown University Press.

Agranoff, R. and B. A. Radin. 2014. "Deil Wright's overlapping model of intergovernmental relations: The basis for contemporary intergovernmental relationships." *Publius: The Journal of Federalism* 45(1): 139–159.

Amirkhanyan, A. A. 2008. "Privatizing public nursing homes: Examining the effect on quality and access." *Public Administration Review* 68(4): 665–680.

Amirkhanyan, A., J. Kim, and K. Lambright. 2008. "Does the public sector outperform the nonprofit and for profit sectors? Evidence from a national panel study on nursing home quality and access." *Journal of Policy Analysis and Management* 27(2): 326–353.

Bird, Richard M. 1993. "Threading the fiscal labyrinth: Some issues in fiscal decentralization." *National Tax Journal* 46(2) (June): 207–227.

Centers for Disease Control and Prevention. 2011. *CDC Estimates of Food-borne Illness in the United States*. Atlanta, GA: Centers for Disease Control and Prevention.

Durant, R. F., A. M. Girth, and J. M. Johnston. 2009. "American exceptionalism, human resource management, and the contract state." *Review of Public Personnel Administration* 29(3): 207–229.

Girth, A. M., A. Hefetz, J. M. Johnston, and M. E. Warner. 2012. "Outsourcing public service delivery: Management responses in noncompetitive markets." *Public Administration Review*, 72(6): 887–900.

Farber, Daniel. 1999. "Taking slippage seriously: Noncompliance and creative compliance in environmental law." *Harvard Environmental Law Review* 23(2): 297–325.

Flatt, Victor B. 1997. "A dirty river runs through it: The failure of enforcement in the clean water act." *Boston College Environmental Affairs Law Review* 25: 1–45.

Frederickson, H. G. and E. C. Stazyk. 2010. "Myths, markets and the 'visible hand' of American bureaucracy." In R. F. Durant (ed.), *The Oxford Handbook of American Bureaucracy*. New York: Oxford University Press.

Geertz, C., 1973. *The Interpretation of Cultures*. New York: Basic Books.

Helland, Eric. 1998. "The Revealed Preferences of State EPAs: Stringency, Enforcement, and Substitution." *Journal of Environmental Economics and Management* 35(3): 242–261.

Johnston, J. M., and A. M. Girth. 2012. "Government Contracts and 'Managing the Market': Exploring the Costs of Strategic Management Responses to Weak Vendor Competition." *Administration and Society* 44(1): 3–29.

Johnston, Jocelyn M., and Barbara S. Romzek. 2008. "Social welfare contracts as networks: The impact of network stability on management and performance." *Administration and Society* 40(2): 115–146.

Johnston, Jocelyn M., and Barbara S. Romzek. 2010. "Contracting: Promise, Performance, Perils, Possibilities." In Robert F. Durant (ed.), *The Oxford Handbook of American Bureaucracy*, Oxford University Press.

Kettl, D. F. 2002. Managing indirect government." In Lester M. Salamon (ed.), *The Tools of Government: A Guide to the New Governance*, 490–510. New York: Oxford University Press.

Krane, Dale, Carol Ebdon and John Bartle. 2004. "Devolution, fiscal federalism, and changing patterns of municipal revenues: The mismatch between theory and reality." *Journal of Public Administration Research and Theory* 14(4): 513–534.

Lincoln, Y. S. and E. G. Guba. 1985. *Naturalistic Inquiry*. Thousand Oaks, CA: Sage.

Milward, H. B., K. G. Provan, A. Fish, K. R. Isett, and K. Huang. 2009. "Governance and collaboration: An evolutionary study of two mental health networks." *Journal of Public Administration Research and Theory* 20(suppl_1): i125–i141.

Nathan, Richard P., and Thomas L. Gais. 1998. "Early findings about the newest new federalism for welfare." *Publius* 28(3): 95–103.

Patton, M. Q. 1990. *Qualitative Evaluation and Research Methods*. Thousand Oaks, CA: Sage.

Peterson, Paul E. 1995. *The Price of Federalism*. Washington, DC: Brookings Institution Press.

Plotnick, R. D., and R. F. Winters. 1985. "A politico-economic theory of income redistribution." *American Political Science Review* 79(2): 458–473.

Posner, P. L. and M. T. Wrightson. 1996. "Block grants: A perennial, but unstable, tool of government." *Publius: The Journal of Federalism* 26(3): 87–108.

Potoski, M., and N. D. Woods. 2002. "Dimensions of state environmental policies." *Policy Studies Journal* 30(2): 208–226.

Provan, K. and H. Milward. 2000. "Governing the hollow state." *Journal of Public Administration Research and Theory* 10: 359–380.

Quirk, Paul. 1980. "Food and Drug Administration." In James Q. Wilson (ed.), *The Politics of Regulation*. New York: Basic Books.

Radin, B. A. 2000. "The Government Performance and Results Act and the tradition of federal management reform: Square pegs in round holes?". *Journal of Public Administration Research and Theory* 10(1): 111–135.

Revesz, R. L. 2001. "Federalism and environmental regulation: A public choice analysis." *Harvard Law Review* 115: 553–641.

Ringquist, E. 1993. *Environmental Protection at the State Level: Politics and Progress in Controlling Pollution*. Armonk, NY: M. E. Sharpe.

Romzek, Barbara S., and Jocelyn M. Johnston. 2005. "State Social Services Contracting: Exploring Determinants of Effective Contract Accountability." *Public Administration Review* 65(4): 436.

Romzek, B., K. LeRoux, J. Johnston, R. J. Kempf, and J. S. Piatak. 2013. "Informal accountability in multisector service delivery collaborations." *Journal of Public Administration Research and Theory* 24(4): 813–842.

Sanford, Terry. 1967. *Storm Over the States*. New York: McGraw-Hill.

Scharff, R. L. 2012. "Economic burden from health losses due to food-borne illness in the United States." *Journal of Food Protection* 75(1): 123–131.

Sigman, H. 2003. *Letting States Do the Dirty Work: State Responsibility for Federal Environmental Regulation*. Washington, DC: National Bureau of Economic Research.

Sinclair, Upton. 1906. *The Jungle*. New York: Doubleday, Jabber & Company.

Soss, Joe, Richard C. Fording, and Sanford F. Schram. 2008. "The color of devolution: Race, federalism, and the politics of social control." *American Journal of Political Science* 52(3): 536–553.

Soss, Joe, Sanford F. Schram, Thomas P. Vartanian, and Erin O'Brien. 2001. "Setting the terms of relief: Explaining state policy choices in the devolution revolution." *American Journal of Political Science* 45(2): 378–395.

U.S. Department of Health and Human Services Office of Inspector General. 2011. *Vulnerabilities in FDA's Oversight of State Food Facility Inspections*. OEI-02-09-00430. December. Washington, DC: U.S. Department of Health and Human Services Office of Inspector General.

U.S. Government Accountability Office. 2008. *Federal Oversight of Food Safety: FDA has Provided Few Details on the Resources and Strategies Needed to Implement Its Food Protection Plan*. GAO-08–909T. Washington, DC: U.S. Government Accountability Office.

Van Slyke, David M. 2003. "The mythology of privatization in contracting for social services." *Public Administration Review* 63 (May/June): 296–315.

Williamson, Oliver E. 1999. "Public and private bureaucracies: A transaction cost economics perspective." *Journal of Law, Economics, and Organization* 15(1): 306–42.

Wright, Deil S.1990. "Federalism, intergovernmental relations, and intergovernmental management: Historical reflections and conceptual comparisons." *Public Administration Review* 50(2): 168–178.

Zullo, Roland. 2008. "Transit contracting reexamined: determinants of cost efficiency and resource allocation." *Journal of Public Administration Research and Theory* 18: 495–515.

9 Clean Energy and Growth through State and Local Implementation

Benjamin H. Deitchman

Today's state and local governments are seeking to drive employment opportunities through a cleaner, greener economic engine within the contemporary intergovernmental framework. Federal proposals to mitigate greenhouse gas emissions recognize the importance of the implementation of relevant policies and practices at the state and local levels of government. Over the last two decades, states, cities, and counties have emerged as leaders in the expansion of the low-carbon economy as part of the competition of ideas in the laboratories of democracy and, in particular, as part of the competition for economic development opportunities through energy efficiency and renewable energy projects. Although governors have focused on the green jobs potential of renewable technologies, energy efficiency has also served as an effective and equitable engine of financial and employment opportunities. This chapter will address intergovernmental tensions in priorities for clean energy policy, focusing on how state and local understanding of the economic opportunity of clean energy technologies can meet multiple dimensions of energy policy.

Green jobs are a key co-benefit of actions to mitigate climate change and promote the deployment of clean energy resources. Replacing capital-intensive industries—such as fossil-fuel based power production—with labor-intensive efforts—such as renewable energy installation or energy efficient building retrofitting—and shifting expenditures towards more productive sectors can improve the economic outlook. Understanding these shifts is fundamental to understanding policy-induced employment from climate and clean energy policy in the American states and localities.

Successful policies, programs, and regulations in clean energy in the United States have required state and local implementation. While competition and diffusion in federalism have existed for centuries, the twenty-first century energy and environmental challenges are a modern dilemma for American society. The energy challenges today are "wicked" problems, in that they lack simple, clearly correct solutions to the on-going issues requiring action under conditions of uncertainty (Rittel and Webber 1973). The Intergovernmental Panel on Climate Change (IPCC 2014) for the United Nations disseminates comprehensive and rigorous studies on the global anthropogenic causes and global risks to the health, welfare, and the economy of the planet and human society from energy consumption of carbon-emitting fuels. The additional dimensions of energy prices and energy security add to this global challenge beyond just the environmental impacts (Brown and Sovacool 2011). Hirsch and Norton (2012), borrowing from the philosophy of nature of Aldo Leopold, argue that climate change efforts require policymakers to be "thinking like a planet," in this collective undertaking by working outside traditional geopolitical boundaries. Achieving meaningful action in the American states is institutionally vexing but also a significant opportunity to improve politicians' standing, the functionality of federalism, and maximize benefits and co-benefits of stringent and effective public policies.

In the wake of the global financial crisis and the difficulty of generating enough high-quality middle-class jobs, employment has become a defining issue in states and localities across the country. While many communities have turned to hydraulic fracturing and other extraction industries to improve local economic conditions, the opportunity to promote and develop renewable resources and energy efficiency technologies exists across the United States. How states, cities, and counties use their federalist authority in this context can impact the next generations of competition in energy, environmental, and economic policies. The Trump Administration's policies on the environment will impact this policy realm.

Federalism and Energy Policy

Economic development is the purview of the state and local levels of governance (Peterson 1995). The co-benefit of jobs and economic growth has emerged as the most important rationale for state and local energy efficiency programs. There are also a multitude of barriers towards developing clean energy policies and addressing climate change. The Committee on Climate Change Science and Technology Integration (CCCSTI 2009) recognizes cost effectiveness of technology, fiscal barriers, regulatory barriers, statutory barriers, intellectual barriers, and other informational barriers to managing the emissions, supply, and demand of energy. Brown and Chandler (2008) note the difficulty of mismatched and incongruent policies among multiple jurisdictions. Academics, policymakers, firms, and consumers, however, continue to research, develop, and deploy mechanisms to advance new technologies and actions and overcome the market failures.

The United States has experience with a diverse array of energy and environmental policies. The Clean Air Act, for example, has led to decreasing pollution across the country through regulation of National Ambient Air Quality Standards (Portney 2000). Stavins (2000) highlights the success of market-based mechanisms that encourage beneficial behaviors for the environment through the correction of externalities, including the acid rain reduction program. These programs suffer when there are inaccurate predictions about the pollutants or emissions, design problems, or limitations in the firms. Benefits, cost, and uncertainty are important in the design of climate change policies. Norton (2005) encourages policy experimentation to tackle wicked problems. While the institutional setting may not follow Norton's theory of adaptive management, the states have adopted command-and-control and market-based policies to meet climate and energy challenges, learning from themselves and each other within the context of the federalist system.

Federalism has been a constant driver of progress and source of tension throughout the history of the United States. *Federalist* no. 46 notes the limitation of federal authorities but also indicates an opportunity for expansion of federal power where voters and politicians find it prudent (Madison 1788). Federalism can be unequal and inefficient, but it can also suit local resources and needs and foster effective competition (Tiebout 1956; Gray 1973; Polsby 1984; Peterson 1995; Wildavsky 1998). Global commons problems, such as climate change and energy security, further confound these issues with debate over responsibilities from the local to the international levels. Whether the United Nations Framework Convention on Climate Change (UNFCCC) has or can ever provide an effective global regime, it will always require sub-national buy-in and policy action to meet carbon mitigation goals and a polycentric approach in which overlapping jurisdictions handle problems at the optimal governance level (Andersson and Ostrom 2008; Brown and

Sovacool 2011). Although Stone (2002) comments, "arguments about federalism tend to be abstract and metaphorical," the federalist structure is a critical political structure for how the world's largest economy will meet, or fail to meet, the challenges of the climate and energy future.

Economic competition under functional federalism considers the idea that localities and states—with federal cooperation—aim to formulate effective policy at the most appropriate institutional level while competing with one another in the political, policy, and economic development marketplaces (Peterson 1995; Wildavsky 1998). While competitive federalism scholarship has often centered on fiscal federalism, current political dynamics require incorporation of partisan federalism into the theory (Bulman-Pozen 2014).

One challenge for governors involved in vertical federalist competition is achieving credit for innovations and accomplishments in the federal system (Nicholson-Crotty and Theobald 2011). As an example, the debate over the economic stimulus bill in 2009 revealed tensions between federal and state elected officials, particularly from the Democratic Congress and Republican governors (Grunwald 2012). State and local governments chose climate and energy as an area of opportunity for legislation, litigation, and action in part due to a lack of federal policy adoption (Engel 2009). Rabe (2008) noted that most analysis of American climate policy focuses on the failure of the Senate to ratify the Kyoto Protocol and the lack of significant proposals to reduce greenhouse gas emissions from the administration of George W. Bush. The contemporary wisdom focusing on the United States' climate policy exclusively at the federal level misses the significance of the "bottom-up" efforts of the states, with the leadership of almost every state passing or at least proposing significant actions.

Rabe (2011) highlights the history of climate change federalism. From 1975 to 1997 both federal and state policies for mitigating greenhouse gas emissions were largely "symbolic," lacking in useful action towards handling this problem. For the decade afterwards, however, there was state domination in this subsystem with regional compacts and other policy mechanisms. With the Supreme Court decision about greenhouse gas regulation in 2007 and changes in Congress and the White House, the current situation in Rabe's typology is "contested federalism," as the different units of government explore different governing mechanisms. Derthick (2010) uses the term "compensatory federalism" for the preferred system in environmental policy. She declares, "federalism works when governments at one level of the system are able to compensate for weaknesses or defects at another level." Posner (2010) says that through vertical diffusion state-level policy adoptions are spurring federal action. The roles of the state and federal governments are in flux not just in the academic literature, but in the public policy discourse of political leaders at all levels of government. There is a competition in the policy arena for the local, state, and federal governments and this study can show how the competition and cooperation facilitated opposition and change.

Laboratories of democracy have provided significant leadership in the development of innovative tools to overcome the difficulty of obtaining financial resources to support energy efficiency and renewable energy projects, even where the long-term discounted benefits outweigh the initial costs (Deitchman, Brown, and Wang 2012). Revolving loan funds provide the upfront costs to energy consumers to pay for energy-efficiency retrofits or renewable energy systems and recycle the repayments through energy savings to continue the financing in perpetuity. The National Association of State Energy Officials (NASEO) database shows that states operate over $925 million in revolving loan funds for all sectors. While some of these programs are new, others have existed since the 1970s. The LoanSTAR program in Texas, for example, has made loans for over two decades using resources from the petroleum violation escrow (PVE), financing 202 projects, none of which have defaulted (NASEO 2012).

Other traditional sources of energy efficiency financing are public benefits funds and direct tax incentives or rebates (Carley 2011). The Center for Climate and Energy Solutions (C2ES 2013) notes that public benefits funds, also known as systems benefits funds, "are collected either through a small charge on the bill of every electric customer or through specified contributions from utilities." As with tax deductions or direct financing appropriations, these resources can help the procurement of energy efficiency or renewable energy systems (as well as research, development, and demonstration projects).

Cities and states have also developed a variety of innovative financing tools in recent years. They have worked with utilities on on-bill financing efforts, where customers can pay for clean energy upgrades over time on their regular electricity or natural gas bill. In addition, they have worked with lending institutions to buy down loan rates through loan loss reserves (Deitchman, Brown, and Wang 2012). The most prominent effort, however, has been in the authorization of policy assessed clean energy (PACE) financing activities. Tax lien financing through PACE taxation districts allows property owners to finance energy-related upgrades through debt assessed to real estate. This debt is repaid through the property taxes collected by municipal governments. PACE financing operates through municipal bond sales, the proceeds of which go to finance energy upgrades. PACE programs have faced federalism-related regulatory challenges due to concerns of Fannie Mae and Freddie Mac about the seniority of loan repayments, but these programs serve as an important indicator of state and local interest in overcoming financing barriers.

The federal government recognized the financial leadership of cities and states with the American Recovery and Reinvestment Act's (ARRA) investment of $2 billion in the city and county level Energy Efficiency and Conservation Block Grants (EECBG) Program and $3.1 billion to the federally funded State Energy Program (SEP). The Recovery Act altered the relationship of the U.S. Department of Energy (DOE) with the State Energy Offices (SEOs). The states and localities, in turn, used this program to further subsidize and expand renewable energy and, in particular, energy efficiency financing programs. Even after the expiration of the Recovery Act period in 2012, leveraging of resources through loan programs and public-private partnerships has stimulated further state-level innovation and policy implementation in energy efficiency and renewable energy financing.

The carrot of the stimulus funding was enough to get 49 state governors to agree to consideration of federalization of building codes and utility rate structuring. In accepting the funding each year, states had agreed to the limitations on the funding outlined in the Code of Federal Regulations (10 CFR 420): including cost-sharing, development of a state energy plan, and various energy provisions such as allowing right turns on a red light where it is safe to reduce gasoline consumption. While ARRA removed the cost share requirement, governors expressed concern about onerous burdens that came with the windfall. In accepting the money, Governor Perry of Texas wrote as part of Texas's application for ARRA SEP to U.S. Secretary of Energy Steven Chu:

> I must express concern, however, that your agency puts the state in a precarious position by announcing that it will publish additional rules on permissible uses of the money after a state accepts the money. . . . Imposing unnecessary restrictions on the development of our domestic energy resources and implementing draconian carbon regulations and new taxes on our

energy supply at a time when American families and businesses are struggling to make ends meet will only prolong the nation's recession and irreparably damage America's competitiveness.

Only Governor Sarah Palin refused to accept the money due to the building code requirements (Galbraith 2009), and with her resignation and the approval of the Alaska legislature, every state approved the SEP requirements under the ARRA restrictions.

The idea of the Recovery Act SEP programs was that they would support states in climate and clean energy policy and serve as a first step towards a greater greenhouse gas mitigation effort (Grunwald 2012). President Obama, in fact, continued to make states a central player in his climate and clean energy programs: his proposal to regulate greenhouse gas emissions under Section 111(d) of the Clean Air Act through executive action relied on state-level implementation to meet federal mitigation targets outlined for each state. For the ARRA SEP, as with all recovery programs, job creation, in this case green jobs, was key.

Green jobs and the green economy are a relatively new concept in the policy discourse. The Obama Administration focused its climate policy proposals on the potential co-benefit of green jobs from the research, development, and deployment of clean energy technology as a means to improve the domestic economy (Jones 2008). Vice President Joseph Biden (2009) defined green jobs as careers that "provide products and services that use renewable energy resources, reduce pollution, and conserve energy and natural resources." Employment growth, however, is one of many justifications for energy policy at the Federal, state, or local levels of governance.

Dimensions of Energy Policy

Energy policies must meet the needs of multiple stakeholders at multiple levels of governance. A survey of 884 energy professionals found a desire for a balanced approach on the goals of energy supply security, environment and climate, and economics and job creation. The study notes that among the general public in polls "Americans can simultaneously have a preferred policy goal and support policies that may undermine that goal" (Jordan et al. 2012: 4), indicating the difficulty of climate and energy policy in meeting multiple critical challenges. With rare exceptions, such as the oil supply disruptions from Hurricane Katrina in 2005 or the Northeast Blackout of 2003, Americans can generally expect that their gas station will have fuel and the lights will go on when they flip the switch. The price of gasoline in the United States can vary based on geopolitical events and the financial situation, but energy is reliable and affordable compared to the developing world or nations with scarcer resources and higher sumptuary taxes. The expansion of natural gas exploration and energy assurance issues from accidents, natural disasters, and because of utility deregulation, however, are still a backdrop in the current primarily fossil fuel based economy.

The National Renewable Energy Laboratory (NREL 2012) characterizes the policy drivers for state and local activities as environmental policy, economic development, and energy security. Table 9.1 shows the priorities by driver type. These characteristics are useful for identifying policy priorities. World events helped shape these priorities from 2001 to 2012. In the early part of this period, national security after the attacks of September 11, 2001 and the California deregulation debacle pushed energy supply security. Environmental priorities gained prominence mid-decade with the growing public attention towards climate change, while the economic crisis has dominated all policymaking since the start of the downturn.

Table 9.1 Assessment of State Clean Energy Policy Effectiveness: Policy Drivers

Environmental Policy	*Economic Development*	*Energy Security*
Clean air benefits	Job creation	Abundant energy supply
GHG emissions reductions	State economic growth	Affordable energy supply
Reduced water use	Minimize energy variations	Reduce transfer of wealth outside the U.S.
Reduce water pollution	Minimize consumer impacts	Net export of energy
Reduced fuel extraction impacts	Energy price stability	Diversify energy resources
Preserve sensitive areas	Revitalize rural areas	Peak demand reduction
Protected species	Attract new investment	Resilient grid system
Minimize human impacts	Develop locally owned assets	Encourage distributed energy generation

Source: NREL (2012)

The Governors on Climate and Clean Energy

Through their words and actions, American governors have provided leadership in climate and clean energy across its multiple dimensions. A rigorous analysis of State of the State Addresses provides data towards understanding trends in energy politics and policy. Coding of the gubernatorial statements is an iterative process to identify the proposals and trends for the justification of climate and clean energy policies based on the codebook of the Policy Agendas Project at the University of Texas at Austin (2013) and the policy drivers in Table 9.1 (NREL 2012). Heidbreder (2012), for example, adapted her study from this codebook to analyze trends in State of the State Addresses on social welfare and healthcare policy from 2000–2007, providing a model for this effort. Coffey (2005) also used State of the State Addresses to analyze ideology through computer-assisted content analysis. State of the State Addresses are a useful window into gubernatorial initiatives, as they serve as a key indicator at the start of the legislative session into gubernatorial priorities (Morehouse and Jewell 2004). There were 536 State of the State or similar (such as State of the Commonwealth) addresses from 2001–2012, as some states do not have such a speech each year.

This analysis focuses on governors. Morehouse and Jewell (2004) indicate that the "governor is responsible for defining the issues and making the commitments that form the basis of his or her legislative program." Their review, however, also indicates that formal gubernatorial powers vary across the nation based on tenure in office, separately elected executive-branch officials, appointive power, budgetary power, and veto power. Gubernatorial decision-making and internal and external factors of state policies are a vibrant area for research and analysis. Governors, individually and collectively through the National Governors Associations, pushed for additional state authorities in this arena. While each governor's office and its occupant are unique, governors are policy leaders and internal and external advocates for their states (Brooks 1961; Ransone Jr. 1982; Beyle and Munchmore 1983). Stone (2002) notes that all politicians must meet the dual goals of successful policy and successful politics; this is particularly true in a policy domain such as climate and clean energy that is both politically contentious in adoption and highly technical in implementation.

Using gubernatorial statements is a simplifying assumption for this research. Legislatures are critical to policy adoption, but it is the governor who is at the top of the hierarchy and is the most visible official in the political hierarchy (Rosenthal 1990). Within the executive branch there are a variety of officials involved in energy decisions. State energy offices (SEOs) occupy different positions in the internal governance structure and often change. The departments responsible for different energy policy functions also vary across the different state bureaucracies. For example, in some states housing departments manage low-income weatherization programs and administration departments may run lead-by-example activities, in which the state adopts energy management best practices to encourage other organizations and firms to learn and follow these energy conservation blueprints. The fact that this chapter centers on governors is a limitation, but it will also provide targeted insight into these key policymaking actors internally and externally to their respective states. The focus on states also is a simplifying assumption for both state and local government, as state officials often dictate the policy environment for energy efficiency within all jurisdictions.

Leaders do not risk political or economic capital for public policies simply because they seem like a good idea; they need to find justification in the policy environment for their proposals. Rabe (2008) differentiates the different strategies of state politicians in handling the impending climate crisis. Prime-time strategies are those that directly address climate mitigation or adaptation, such as carbon cap-and-trade. Opportunistic strategies, such as renewable energy development, are policy plans that have additional benefits beyond climate change solutions. Finally, stealth strategies attack climate change without framing them as climate change related actions. Co-benefits of climate change regulation are the environmental, public health, and economic benefits (IPCC 2007) that can facilitate opportunistic and stealth strategies, as well as provide additional justification for prime-time options.

A thorough analysis of the 536 State of the State Speeches between 2001 and 2012 found support for clean energy initiatives within 207 of the speeches (39 percent). Renewable energy topics appeared in 129 speeches, while energy efficiency only received agenda setting mentions in 72 speeches, and the energy efficiency and renewable energy encompassing "clean energy" getting 50 mentions. Climate change efforts appeared 84 times when the governor made the State of the State address. Consistent with the broader public policy dialogue, "green jobs" as a discussion point first appeared in 2008 and received 17 mentions in this study. While Republicans mentioned energy security and nuclear energy issues more than Democrats, Democrats mentioned all climate and clean energy topics significantly more often than Republican governors. There were limited regional or cultural differences, with political party of the leadership serving, with several notable exceptions, as the primary differentiating factor in the data analysis.

Renewable Portfolio Standards (RPS), which mandate a certain percentage of electricity sales through renewable energy technologies, and Energy Efficiency Resources Standards (EERS), which mandate a displacement of a percentage of electricity sales through energy efficiency, provide a useful comparison point for understanding differences in the popularity of renewable and efficiency energy policies. While Members of Congress have considered a national RPS and national EERS, this legislation has never moved in the House or Senate. The state level RPS and EERS have served and will continue to serve as a model in the laboratories of democracy for federal proposals. They are both regulatory policies that essentially serve a similar function through direct requirements on utilities and power producers. In some cases, the RPS and EERS are enacted in the same piece of legislation. Based on the broad definition of EERS and RPS from the Center for Climate and Energy Strategies (C2ES 2013), 33 states had an EERS and 38 states had an RPS at the end of 2012. From wind and solar to biofuel from swine feces, these standards are as varied as the states that are implementing them. While there has been discussion in North

Carolina and Maine among other states of repealing these standards based on recommendations of the American Legislative Exchange Council (ALEC), a free market interstate lobbying group, no state repealed an EERS or RPS within the 2001 to 2012 time frame.

Finally, to understand intra-state dynamics, the entity adopting an EERS or RPS matters. In 2008, Governor Eliot Spitzer of New York stated in his State of the State Address:

> On the demand side, we are committed to 15% by '15, the most progressive and attainable energy efficiency target in the country, which sets a goal of reducing statewide electricity use by 15 percent from projected levels by 2015. We approach this goal the way a business would, with a requirement that our energy investments produce savings well in excess of the cost of achieving them.
>
> (Spitzer 2008: n.p.)

He was the only American governor of this period to address this topic in a State of the State Address. In New York, however, it was not the governor or the legislature that adopted the standard. The New York Public Service Commission (PSC) established the energy efficiency, as well as renewable energy, standards in that state. In New York, the governor appoints the commissioners, while in states such as Georgia, for example, the public votes for the members of the quasi-judicial utility regulatory authority that sets standards and electricity prices. In different states different authorities, be they the governor, legislature, or a judicial or semi-judicial branch of government or a combination of branches, play different roles in setting utility standards and shaping rules and regulations for the energy portfolio.

Unlike EERS policies, RPS policies have garnered more attention of governors, but have not shown the same level of partisan differentials based on the governors' parties for adoption. Also in contrast to EERS only two states went through utility commissions rather than the legislative process to establish rules and regulations mandating renewable and alternative electricity technologies. That said, there is a strong correlation between adoptions of the two policies and, in fact, several states established EERS and RPS requirements in the same legislation. The states with an RPS or RPS Goal are six times more likely to adopt an EERS or EERS Goal in a given year. By 2012, 38 states had adopted an RPS, RPS goal, or Alternative Portfolio Standard, a number that has remained stable.

Governors of both major parties have touted RPS policies in State of the State Addresses. Alaska Governor and 2008 Republican Vice Presidential Candidate Sarah Palin was one of nine governors (three Republican and six Democrat) to support such a policy before it became law in his or her state. She said in 2009, "This includes meeting my goal of generating 50 percent of our electric power with renewable sources. That's an unprecedented policy across the U.S, but we're the state that can do it with our abundant renewables, and with Alaskan ingenuity" (Palin 2009: n.p.). She was not the only governor to bring local resources into the discussion. Maine Governor John Baldacci argued in his 2008 State of the State Address, "In this energy crisis, we will develop renewable sources of energy made in Maine, by Maine businesses for Maine people" (Baldacci 2008: n.p.). Several governors spoke about the policy after its passage, including Governor Palin's successor Sean Parnell who proposed financial incentives to support the RPS in 2011:

> This comprehensive plan puts us on track to achieve the renewable energy goal we established, together, that Alaska will derive 50 percent of our electrical power from renewable sources by

2025. To get there, I'm asking you to move decisively and aggressively with me. Let's work together this year to invest at least $65 million to jump start planning, design, and permitting for the Susitna Hydro Project; provide at least $25 million for renewable energy grants; $10 million for a Southeast [Alaska] Energy Grant Fund; and $25 million for weatherization.

(Parnell 2011: n.p.)

Overall, 26 speeches of this era referenced the RPS in a supportive manner in 17 states, with Governor Baldacci's Republican successor Paul LePage being the only governor to urge repeal of the policy in a State of the State Address for the 2001–2012 period. The data show that there is not a statistical significance in the event history analysis of the likelihood of adoption with a Democratic versus a Republican governor or based on region or political culture.

The RPS was infused with economic development policy justifications, as governors were able to connect resources in state goals. One can talk about Minnesota's fuel crops or Texas's wind with pride in the local parlance, but it is difficult to specifically cite or show a comparative advantage on energy intensity improvements. While efficiency is often the cheapest, most cost effective, and consumer friendly improvement to mitigate emissions and reduce dependence on fossil fuels and—this research will later show—more prudent from an economic development perspective, local politics and resources appear more politically feasible. It appears that RPS policies are effective at promoting development and deployment of chosen alternative technologies, but they also face challenges with competing resources, including cheaper energy efficiency resources.

Figure 9.1 shows the trends in climate and clean energy topics in State of the State addresses. Green jobs were a new idea to enter the political lexicon in 2009. Green jobs topics did in fact rise as discussion of climate change dropped from its peak in 2009. Figure 9.2 shows that despite

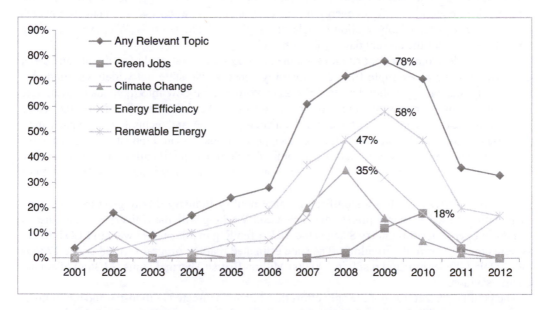

Figure 9.1 Gubernatorial Topics Related to Climate and Clean Energy in State of the State Address by Percentage of Speeches, 2001.

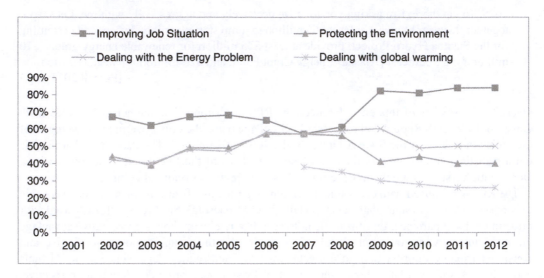

Figure 9.2 Public's Federal Policy Priorities.

Source: Pew Research Center (2013)

the broad shift for governors, public opinion on this issue for the relevant policy areas remained relatively steady throughout the period under consideration. Although the Pew Research Center's (2013) surveys focused on the federal level and were not complete for every topic across the time period, it shows some degree of stability in public opinion about energy, the environment, and climate change, despite shifts in energy prices, environmental awareness, and changing beliefs about the importance of job creation in light of the global financial crisis. Whatever the policy area, the agenda for the present day is jobs, jobs, jobs.

Economic development opportunities are the most prominent rationale for climate and clean energy policy. As an example from a historically conservative state not widely credited as a climate or clean energy policy leader, Arkansas provides a window into methods to overcome policy inertia in clean energy policy. Arkansas's Recovery Act SEP plan illuminates the state's strategy on the deployment of climate and clean energy policies and technologies. In particular, Arkansas focused on "stealth" strategies and support for business and industry in its programming. The state serves as a model of economic development justifications for clean energy investments. Arkansas paid close attention to local resources and interests. In its description of its $1.6 million for the Advanced Lighting Technology for Poultry Growers the Arkansas Energy Office wrote, "Arkansas has a significantly large poultry industry. Many growers have been financially stressed as energy prices have increased." Working with the University of Arkansas's Center of Excellence for Poultry Science the ARRA funding in this project went to LED lighting systems for this form of agriculture. The state estimated that the program would create 17 jobs (about $95,000 per job) and result in 300,000 Million British Thermal Units (MBtus) of annual energy savings.

The poultry project was not the only effort that Arkansas directed at industry and agriculture, as the state devoted $11 million to these sectors, much of it in cooperation with local universities including through the Arkansas Industry Clearinghouse. Beyond universities, the State of

Arkansas also partnered with the Clinton Climate Initiative on the Employer Assisted Home Energy Assistance Loan (HEAL) Program. Not only does HEAL diffuse and adapt an established model for the financing and deployment of energy efficiency, but it is a sustainable mechanism for continued disbursement of funds without continued windfall federal appropriations that will help the State of Arkansas to remain in its new leadership position beyond the Recovery Act period.

The goal of the SEP under ARRA was to expand clean energy programs in the states for job creation; and the states responded with programs laden with job creation and retention goals. Not all states maximized the immediate employment potential of clean energy investments. Tennessee, for example, invested all of its approximately $62.5 million share of ARRA SEP into the state's solar initiative. Despite the lack of immediate optimization in employment opportunities through the funding, the Tennessee plan was bullish on its economic development potential. Collaborating with Oak Ridge National Laboratory and the University of Tennessee, the state energy office hoped to rapidly develop a mature solar energy industry that could support in-state generation and become a leader in this technology. While the majority of Recovery Act funding under SEP went towards energy efficiency projects, ranging from Tennessee's Volunteer State Solar initiative to Pennsylvania's Clean Energy Works and other programs across the country, the economic development potential of clean energy was evident in the plans.

The Opportunities Ahead

In comparing the political and economic analysis, political leaders seek to drive green jobs through renewable energy even as the strongest economic opportunity is in energy efficiency. Not only does energy efficiency have direct green jobs benefits, but it supports consumers through long-term bill savings, ripe for reinvestment into the local economy. Regardless, the federalist environment continues to support states and localities in their efforts to advance the clean energy agenda. In the current state of affairs, any effort to tackle climate change and improve energy efficiency of the American electricity and natural gas systems will require an approach that focuses on the economic potential of these technologies and services.

The federal government is an enabler of this system not just in its own failures to pass comprehensive (or even partial) legislation on energy efficiency, but also as a purposeful strategy. Washington learns from the states and when leaders in Washington recognize their shortcomings or want to oppose their own status quo, the states and localities are a venue to create new opportunities. At the federal level, policy proposals for climate and clean energy support a critical state and local role. With Washington unable to move legislation to improve these technologies and services, there remains a vibrant and vital opportunity for state and local leaders to achieve economic development in this domain. Calls for a polycentric approach to international climate change efforts also require a locally-based approach across the globe. Climate change and energy security are a worldwide problem requiring localized solutions. Remaking economies to take advantage of efficiencies in energy and other facets of economic development can have positive environmental and—politically more important—economic impacts on all jurisdictions in the country.

With the Republican Party controlling the White House, Congress, the majority of governors' mansions and state legislatures, a devolutionary philosophy could drive policy decisions. As stated in the 2016 Republican Party's platform, "Federalism is a cornerstone of our constitutional system.

Every violation of state sovereignty by Federal officials is not merely a transgression of one unit of government against another; it is an assault on the liberties of individual Americans." Democratic Party leaders, however, may also strengthen state institutions in pursuit of their visions of the future of the United States.

After the U.S. Environmental Protection Agency (EPA) promulgated regulations during the Obama Administration to mitigate climate change—the Clean Power Plan (CPP)—it was state-level elected officials who led the legal opposition to the executive action. In fact, the EPA's authority to regulate greenhouse gases as a pollutant under the Clean Air Act derives from a state-initiated Supreme Court decision in 2007's Massachusetts vs. EPA. One of the most notable litigants against the CPP, as well as the Affordable Care Act and other politically polarizing Federal policies, was Oklahoma attorney general Scott Pruitt. In the Trump Administration, Attorney General Pruitt is now a likely defendant against state plaintiffs encouraging stringency in environmental policies and enforcement as the President's selection for EPA Administrator after President Trump overturned the CPP.

It is no surprise that today's debates require rethinking federalist roles and responsibilities in a growing, complex, and ever-changing American society. With the repeal of the Paris Agreement on Climate Change, cities and states are also engaging the international community to protect the UNFCC and worldwide efforts at clean energy development and climate change mitigation and adaptation. Although the exact role of cities, states, regions, and other subnational units remains uncertain and the globalized policy environment is volatile, clean energy and growth remain central points of debate for our planetary future.

References

Andersson, K. P., and Ostrom, E. 2008. "Analyzing decentralized resource regimes from a polycentric perspective." *Policy Sciences* 41(1): 71–93.

Baldacci, John. 2008, Jan 9. "Maine State of the State Address 2008." Retrieved from http://stateofthestate.com/content.aspx?state=MEanddate=01/09/2008.

Beyle, Thad, and Roy Munchmore. 1983. "Governors and intergovernmental relations: Middlemen in the federal system." In Thad Beyle and Roy Munchmore, eds. *Being Governor*. Durham, NC: Duke Press Policy Studies.

Biden, Joseph. 2009, Feb 27. "Green jobs are a way to aid the middle class." *Philadelphia Inquirer* (February 27). Retrieved from https://en.wikisource.org/wiki/Green_jobs_are_a_way_to_aid_the_middle_class (accessed October 29, 2017).

Brooks, Glenn. 1961. *When Governors Convene*. Baltimore, MD: Johns Hopkins University Press.

Brown, Marilyn, and Benjamin Sovacool. 2001. *Climate Change and Global Energy Security*. Cambridge, MA: MIT Press.

Brown, Marilyn, and Sharon Chandler. 2008. "Governing confusion: How statutes, fiscal policy, and regulations impede clean energy technologies." *Stanford Law and Policy Review* 19(3): 472–509.

Bulman-Pozen, Jessica. 2014. "Partisan federalism." *Harvard Law Review* 127(4): 1077–1146.

C2ES. 2013. *U.S. States and Regions*. Arlington, VA: Center for Climate and Energy Solutions (C2ES).

Carley, Sonya. 2011. "The era of state energy policy innovation: A review of policy instruments." *Review of Policy Research* 28(3): 265–294.

CCCSTI. 2009. *Strategies for the Commercialization and Deployment of Greenhouse Gas Intensity-Reducing Technologies and Practices*. Washington, DC: Department of Energy.

Coffey, Daniel. 2005. "Measuring gubernatorial ideology: A content analysis of state of the State speeches." *State Politics and Policy Quarterly* 5(1): 88–103.

Deitchman, Benjamin H., Marilyn Brown, and Yu Wang. 2012. *Making Industry Part of the Climate Solution Through Flexible Innovative Financing*. Georgia Institute of Technology School of Public Policy Working Paper no. 73. Atlanta, GA: Georgia Institute of Technology.

Derthick, Martha. 2010. "Compensatory federalism." In Barry Rabe, ed. *Greenhouse Governance*. Washington, DC: Brookings Institution Press.

Engel, Kirsten. 2009. "Whither subnational climate change initiatives in the wake of federal climate legislation?" *Publius: The Journal of Federalism* 39(3): 432–454.

Galbraith, Kate. 2009. "Gov. Palin on energy money: No, thanks." *The New York Times* (May 1). Retrieved from https://green.blogs.nytimes.com/2009/05/01/gov-palin-on-energy-money-no-thanks/?_r=0.

Gray, Virginia. 1973 "Innovation in the states: A diffusion study." *The American Political Science Review* 67(4): 1174–1185.

Grunwald, Michael. 2012. *The New New Deal*. New York: Simon & Schuster.

Heidbreder, Brianna. 2012. "Agenda setting in the states: How politics and policy needs shape gubernatorial agendas." *Politics and Policy* 40(2): 296–319.

Hirsch, Paul D, and Bryan G. Norton. 2012. "Thinking like a planet." In Allen Thompson and Jeremy Bendik-Keymer, eds. *Ethical Adaptation to Climate Change: Human Virtues of the Future*. Cambridge, MA: MIT Press.

IPCC. 2007. *Climate Change 2007*. Geneva: Intergovernmental Panel on Climate Change.

IPCC. 2014. *Climate Change 2014*. Geneva: Intergovernmental Panel on Climate Change.

Jones, Van. 2008. *The Green Collar Economy*. New York: HarperOne,

Jordan, Matt, Dawn Manley, Valerie Peters, and Ron Stoltz. 2012. *The Goals of Energy Policy*. Washington, DC: Sandia National Laboratories and OurEnergyPolicy.org.

Madison, James. 1788. *The Federalist Papers* 46.

Morehouse, Sarah M., and Malcolm E. Jewell. 2004. "States as laboratories: A reprise." *Annual Review Of Political Science* 7: 177–203.

NASEO. 2012. "State Energy Loan Fund (SELF) database." NASEO. Retrieved from www.naseo.org (December 1, 2012).

Nicholson-Crotty, Sean, and Nick Theobald. N. 2011. "Claiming credit in the US federal system: Testing a model of competitive federalism." *Publius: The Journal of Federalism* 41(2): 232–256.

Norton, Bryan G. 2005. *Sustainability: A Philosophy of Adaptive Ecosystem Management*. Chicago, IL: University of Chicago Press.

NREL. 2012. *Assessment of State Clean Energy Policy Effectiveness*. Golden, CO: NREL.

Palin, Sarah. 2009. "Alaska State of the State Address 2009." January 22. Retrieved from http://stateofthestate.com/content.aspx?state=AKanddate=01/22/2009.

Parnell, Sean. 2011. "Alaska State of the State Address 2011." January 19. Retrieved from http://stateofthestate.com/content.aspx?state=AKanddate=01/19/2011.

Peterson, Paul E. 1995. *The Price of Federalism*. Washington, DC: The Brookings Institution.

Pew Research Center. 2013. *Public's Policy Priorities: 1994–2013*. Washington, DC: Pew Research Center.

Polsby, Nelson W. 1984. *Political Innovation in America*. New Haven, CT: Yale University Press,.

Portney, Paul R. 2000. "Air pollution policy." In Paul R. Portney and Robert N. Stavins, eds. *Public Policies for Environmental Protection*, 2nd edition. Washington, DC: Resources for the Future Press

Posner, Paul. 2010. "The politics of vertical diffusion: The states and climate change." In Barry Rabe, ed. *Greenhouse Governance*. Washington, DC: Brookings Institution Press.

Rabe, Barry. 2008. "States on steroids: The intergovernmental odyssey of American climate policy." *Review of Policy Research* 25(2): 105–128.

Rabe, Barry. 2011. "Contested federalism and American climate policy." *Publius: The Journal of Federalism* 41(3): 494–521.

Rittel, Horst and Melvin Webber. 1973. "Dilemmas in a general theory of planning." *Policy Sciences* 4(2): 155–169.

Ransone Jr., Coleman B. 1982. *The American Governorship*. Westport, CT: Greenwood Press.

Rosenthal, Allan. 1990. *Governors and Legislatures: Contenting Powers*. Washington, DC: CQ Press.

Spitzer, Eliot. 2008. "New York State of the States Address 2008." January 1. Retrieved from http://stateofthestate.com/content.aspx?state=NYanddate=01/09/2008.

Stavins, Robert. 2000. "Market-based environmental policies." In Paul R. Portney and Robert N. Stavins, eds. *Public Policies for Environmental Protection*, 2nd edition. Washington, DC: Resources for the Future Press.

Stone, D. 2002. *The Policy Paradox*, 3rd edition. New York: W. W. Norton and Company.

Tiebout, Charles M. 1956. "A pure theory of local expenditures." *The Journal of Political Economy* 64(5): 416–424.

Wildavsky, Aaron. 1998. *Federalism and Political Culture*. New Brunswick, NJ: Transaction Publishers.

10 Bottom-Up Federalism

An Examination of U.S. Local Government Climate Change Policy and Practice

Benoy Jacob, Brian J. Gerber, and Samuel Gallaher

The American federal system ensures that public policy and management are shaped through the distinct powers of each level of government. As it relates to local governments, the nature of this power, and subsequent responsibility, varies depending upon ones' perspective. On the one hand, cities are often considered "mere creatures of the State" (Dillon 1868). This suggests that cities can only undertake activities that a state government specifically authorizes. Thus, even in states with home-rule provisions, which provide for greater local policy-making autonomy, the responsibilities of cities are proscribed by the state (Krane, Rigos, and Hill 2001). From this perspective, policy-making in America is an inherently top-down system.

On the other hand, an important body of work offers a different perspective suggesting that the top-down characterization of policy-making is, with respect to cities, unduly narrow. As noted by Berman, there "is a considerable gap between . . . what state governments under prevailing legal theories might do to local governments and what they have actually done" (Berman 2003: 5). This is particularly true when it comes to the implementation of public policy. Even where a state government actively defines the policies and programmatic activities of local governments, the locality often bears many critical administrative responsibilities. In turn these responsibilities have afforded local governments a larger role in shaping public policy. This perspective, in short, suggests policy is developed through a process of interdependent bargaining among national, state, and local governments (Agranoff and Radin 2014; Sbargia 1996; Wright 1988).

While both perspectives—cities as limited policy actors by being creatures of state government versus cities as key partners in negotiated policy actions—offer important insights into the role of local governments in American policy-making, neither provides much room for considering a third alternative: the ability of local governments to *lead* public policy efforts. That is, neither perspective fully considers the ability of a local government to proactively and independently create innovative policy options that influence higher orders of government. Simply stated, the extant views of local governments fail to adequately consider the possibility of a federal system of government where policy is shaped from the bottom-up under certain circumstances.

Such an omission of a bottom-up view of important agents of policy-making or policy change is problematic. Recent observations of local governments suggest cities are, in fact, leading policy efforts on a wide range of issues (Katz and Bradley 2013; Shipan and Volden 2006). However, such studies treating cities as a locus of policy innovation are relatively recent and relatively limited in quantity. This disconnect between the prevailing academic literature on what cities can or cannot do and the reality of the current proactive policy initiative of cities, suggests that the idea of bottom-up federalism is worthy of increased scholarly attention.

To be clear, despite the fairly limited amount of work on the topic, some have argued that bottom-up efforts are a portent to some form of restructured federalism (Brenner 2004). While this might be true, our position is that the idea of bottom-up policy-making remains too under-developed theoretically and empirically to make such claims—in either direction. Thus, in this chapter, we advance the scholarly work by establishing a coherent conceptual framework that is grounded in the extant, though disparate, literature. The framework we put forward will help scholars and practitioners better understand bottom-up federalism by providing a strong foundation by which to: (1) assess the extent to which bottom-up efforts are driving public policy; (2) identify causal factors that lead to or support bottom-up efforts; and (3) understand the potential conditions where bottom-up efforts are more, or less, likely to succeed.

Following this introduction, our chapter is divided into four sections. The first two sections develop our framework around three key factors—devolution, intentionality and innovation. The next section provides an overview of climate change efforts at the local level, which is the policy context in which we apply our framework and outlines key insights garnered from a pilot survey of local government activity on climate change and hazard management. The final section offers a discussion of bottom-up federalism in the current Federal policy context and some concluding thoughts.

Bottom-Up Federalism: Devolution, Intentionality, and Innovation

Despite the aforementioned gap between existing academic arguments on cities and federalism and the observed practice of cities as policy innovators, there are several important streams of work that provide a basis from which to begin our inquiry. This existing theoretic and empirical work, however, suffers from two key shortcomings. First, much of the literature in this area is focused on understanding federalism, or intergovernmental relationships, in general. The particular role of local governments is rarely the primary unit of analysis and thus, insights about local policy efforts *vis-à-vis* other levels of government are often underdeveloped. Second, while there is a relatively recent set of studies that do focus on bottom-up federalism, these works have something of a disadvantage of spanning several distinct disciplinary traditions. Given the different perspectives, approaches, and points of emphasis from the fields, our understanding of bottom-up federalism is, at best, inchoate. Thus, to move the extant work forward, we begin by establishing a conceptual framework for bottom-up federalism that is based upon a synthesis of disparate arguments about the policy-making role of local governments (cities in particular).

An initial challenge in synthesizing prior federalism studies to offer a more precise characterization of bottom-up federalism is that the term and key associated concepts are rarely well-defined. Rather, the term "bottom-up federalism" is often employed somewhat casually to describe various forms of local policy-making. Based on our review, however, bottom-up federalism seems to require the following three conditions: (1) policy efforts that are outside the traditional responsibilities of local governments; (2) reflect deliberate efforts to influence higher orders of government; and (3) are driven by local policy innovations. This conceptualization suggests that bottom-up policy efforts can be understood through the integration of three key factors—devolution, intentionality, and innovation.

Devolution

American federalism is highlighted by the ongoing give-and-take between state and local authorities over areas of programmatic responsibility—what Krane, Ebdon, and Bartle (2004: 514) describe as the "thrust and counterthrust" between state and local government interactions. This give-and-take has been highlighted by episodic periods of devolution; the "transfer of governmental functions and responsibilities from higher to lower levels of government" (Bowman and Kearney 2011).[1] As it relates to bottom-up federalism, these periods of devolution have been fundamental to expanding the policy and programmatic issues addressed by local governments. The extent to which devolution has expanded the bounds of local policy efforts, however, is somewhat unclear.

In the early 1980s, Ronald Reagan instituted a series of reforms that would "curb the size and influence of the Federal establishment and to demand recognition of the distinction between the powers granted to the Federal government and those reserved to the States [and localities]."[2] Scholars and policy-makers viewed the coinciding devolution of programs to be leading a "devolution-revolution" in the organization of policy-making authority and programmatic responsibility. For example, Richard Nathan argued that it might represent a "historic long-term realignment for American federalism" (1996: 5). Others, however, were less certain of the impacts. John Kincaid, for example, argued that devolution was "plodding along at a turtles pace, while centralization is still racing ahead at a rabbits pace" (Kincaid 1998: 38; see also Chapter 3, this volume). Specific to cities, the tangible impacts—positive or negative—have also been particularly hard to identify. On the one hand, for example Peter Eisenger (1998) anticipated that devolution would affect local government finances, shift functional responsibilities, and change the nature of local and state leadership. On the other hand, empirical research has found surprisingly few local effects from devolution (Cole, Hissong, and Arvidson 1999).[3]

Despite ambiguity around the extent of the impacts of devolution, particularly with respect to the expansion of local policy efforts, two key insights are worth noting. First, it is clear that, while the particular effects are hard to quantify, devolution has impacted local government in varied ways (Bowman and Kearney 2011). Second, regardless of the extent of the programmatic effect on local governments, devolution has reshaped the nature of intergovernmental relationships, particularly between states and localities. It empowered and emboldened cities to take action in new policy domains, and to do so in innovative ways (Herbers 1987).

Taken together, these insights suggest that devolution, as a catalyst for bottom-up effort, resides on a continuum; some cities are highly affected by devolutionary pressures, while others are less so. Highly impacted cities will, by definition, have seen their responsibilities expand, while those that have been less affected will, most likely, pursue policy efforts in concert with the status quo.

The devolutionary pressures outlined above, and typically described in the literature, can be thought of as 'explicit' in nature. The expansion of local policy efforts, due to devolution, was driven by states explicitly shifting programmatic responsibilities to local governments. However, more recent observations of bottom-up federalism, suggest that local government policy domains are responding to something more akin to *de facto* devolution. Bowman and Kearney (2011) refer to *de facto* devolution as a process whereby higher orders of government do not fully weigh the pros and cons of devolved programmatic responsibilities. Thus, it may "involve a mandate . . . without adequate authority or fiscal capacity . . . It is, in effect, an action devoid devolutionary intent" (ibid.: 565). In contrast, we are defining *de facto* devolution as policy inactivity. By this we mean, that the State has simply stopped providing a program or refused to take action on a particular issue. Faced with this policy void, local governments 'step in' to address the issue. This idea is highlighted in recent work by Bruce Katz and Jennifer Bradley from the Brookings Institution.

Katz and Bradley (2013) argue that local governments have had to expand their policy efforts to address the policy void left by inactivity from higher orders of government. In their own words, "with each illustration of partisan gridlock and each indication of federal, and also state, unreliability, metros have become more assertive in their advocacy, more expansive in their reach . . . metro leaders have met the solution, and it is them" (ibid.: 4). For Katz and Bradley, then, shift in policy activity by local governments is not due to the downward pressure from higher orders of government, but rather a recognition that if they do not address a particular issue, than no one will. This, they argue, is leading to a restructured form of federalism:

> In traditional political science textbooks, the United States is portrayed neatly as a hierarchical structure—the federal government and the states on top, the cities and metropolitan areas at the bottom. The feds and the states are the adults in the system, setting direction; the cities and metropolitan areas are the children, waiting for their allowance. The metropolitan revolution is exploding this tired construct. Cities and metropolitan areas are becoming the leaders in the nation: experimenting, taking risk, making hard choices, and asking for forgiveness, not permission.
>
> (Katz and Bradley 2013: 2)

Our review of the devolution literature, then, suggests that American local governments have had to address policy issues stemming from devolutionary pressures, *de facto* or otherwise. Certainly, the nature and extent of these effects varies across regions. Given our definition of the concept, however, these new policy efforts do not necessarily reflect bottom-up federalism.[4] Bottom-up federalism not only requires the expansion of policy issues, but also a degree of intentionality with respect to influencing higher orders of government.

Intentionality

The second component to our conceptualization of bottom-up federalism is intentionality. By this we mean, local policy efforts that are specifically undertaken to lead on some form of policy initiative and thereby influence higher orders of government. Scholars that describe bottom-up federalism have paid little heed to the role of intentionality, yet it seems fundamental to any reasonable conceptualization of bottom-up federalism. To clarify the idea of intentionality we turn to Lori Riverstone-Newell's work on local activism, which provides, as best we can tell, the only explicit description of bottom-up intentionality.

Riverstone-Newell argues that cities are not merely responding to policy voids left by inactive, or otherwise uninterested, higher levels of government. Rather, some cities are actively challenging the policies of higher orders of government. Such local activism "represents a category of political behavior reserved to local officials who use their positions of authority to purposefully challenge higher governments . . . to *compel* higher governments to defend their policy positions or to change them, voluntarily or through the Courts" (Riverstone-Newell 2012: 404; emphasis added). Such activism occurs when local leaders deem the status quo to be unacceptable and subsequently, "force themselves into policy arenas where they have no formal role" (ibid.: 405). One example, highlighted in her work is the case of San Francisco's licensing of same-sex marriages in 2004. In this case, the city's mayor at the time—Gavin Newsome—issued an executive order that allowed same-sex couples to legally marry. This local act, which was in opposition to state law, resulted in the legal recognition of thousands of same-sex marriages as well as a judicial examination of same sex marriage bans. Riverstone-Newell notes that, while this case may be "unusual in its impact and visibility," it is "not an isolated event. Across the nation, localities large and small have enacted thousands of ordinances, resolutions, and executive orders in policy areas reserved to state and/or federal purview" (Riverstone-Newell 2012: 402).

As it relates to bottom-up federalism, Riverstone-Newell's work is important. It demonstrates that not only are local governments engaged in a broader range of policies than traditional perspectives would lead us to believe, but also that they are engaged *specifically* to "compel higher governments." This is the clearest example of intentionality that we can find in the literature. However, it is also likely that it represents a fairly heightened, or atypical, or perhaps even "extreme" example of intentionality. Much like the idea that there can be *de facto* forms of devolution, we can also observe *de facto* intentionality; where the policy action of the local government is not developed to deliberately compel higher orders of government, but, because of the potential for positive impacts, are likely to be compelling. An example of such *de facto* intentionality is described in Shipan and Volden's work on vertical diffusion (2006).

Shipan and Volden (2006) consider whether or not local laws—specifically anti-smoking policies—influence statewide policy adoptions. In their work, they find empirical evidence that local policies do, in fact, 'diffuse' upward. This diffusion, however, is contingent on a series of state level factors; in particular, the level of legislative professionalism. Their explanation is that state-level professionalism provides a vehicle by which state agencies are more likely to 'learn' from local action and to proactively shape state policy. Where such professionalism is not present, local laws will serve as a substitute for state legislation, as opposed to diffusing upward.[5]

While the work on local activism and vertical diffusion offer several important insights that could drive future research and help understand the causal drivers of bottom-up federalism, the important take-away for us, is that—like devolution—intentionality resides along a continuum. In terms of bottom-up federalism, the key point is that local policy efforts must be pursued with some deliberate intention, or at least potential, for upward influence.

Innovation

The third element in our conceptualization of bottom-up federalism is policy innovation; "the adoption of a policy or program by a government entity that had never before utilized it;. . .but is not necessarily an altogether new idea" (Krause 2010: 47). Innovation and experimentation is one of the hallmarks of the American federal system. As eloquently described by Supreme Court Justice Louis Brandeis (1932):

> It is one of those happy incidents of the federal system that a single courageous State may, if its citizen's choose, serve as a laboratory; and try novel social and economic experiments without risk to the rest of the country.
>
> (*New State Ice Co. v. Liebmann*, 285 U.S. 311, 1932)

While Brandeis was, of course, describing the innovative potential of the America's 50 states, others have suggested that the true laboratory for policy innovations rests in the country's local governments. As noted by Briffault (2004: 259), "if the fifty states are laboratories for public policy formation, then surely the 3,000 counties and 15,000 municipalities provide logarithmically more opportunities for innovation, experimentation, and reform." Indeed, a large body of literature has developed that describes the extent and impacts of policy innovation, particularly as part of local policy efforts, such as: school choice (Mintrom 2000); gun control ordinances (Godwin and Schrodel 2000); and environmental policies (Krause 2010).

As it relates to bottom-up federalism, innovation is a key component. The first factor in our conceptualization—devolution—is important to bottom-up federalism in that it may expand the policy domains of local governments. As local governments engage in these new domains they will, by necessity, be forced to innovate. Thus, to the degree that bottom-up efforts are shaped by devolutionary pressures, we expect local policy to reflect local capacities to innovate. Additionally, innovation is also a part of the second defining characteristic of bottom-up federalism—intentionality. For instance, from Shipan and Volden's (2006) point of view, local policy innovation is a key component of vertical diffusion (a passive form of intentionality). States that have the capacity will learn from local policy efforts and successful policies may diffuse upwards. Thus, innovation is critical to, ultimately, defining bottom-up policy efforts. More precisely, local governments that have capacity for innovation, may be more likely to pursue bottom-up efforts. Scholars of policy innovation point to three factors that shape the innovative capacity of local governments; in particular, the presence of policy entrepreneurs; local autonomy; and local capacity.

The first characteristic of successful policy innovations is the presence of a policy entrepreneurs. Policy entrepreneurs, "distinguish themselves through their desire to significantly change current ways of doing things in their area of interest" (Mintrom 2000: 650). They recognize, and take advantage of, "windows of opportunities" to advance their interest. Thus, from the perspective of our framework, one can imagine such windows of opportunity emerging from devolution, in particular, de facto devolution. The inactivity from higher orders of government, provides a ripe opportunity for policy entrepreneurs to step in and shape the policy domain.

The second characteristic that influences local innovation is the presence of autonomy. Given that autonomy, to some degree, defines the power of a division of government-to-government, it is clearly a central focus of federalism studies, particularly with respect to cities. That said, autonomy can be understood to mean different things. For our purposes, we draw on Clark's (1984) classic distinctions on local autonomy.[6]

For Clark, autonomy can be considered in terms of initiative and immunity. Initiative refers to the power to create policies that are in their own interest, while immunity refers to the localities' ability to act without review or oversight by higher orders of government. As it relates to innovation—and bottom-up federalism—initiative autonomy is central. Simply stated, to be innovative local governments must be able to have adequate discretion to pursue novel ideas. As noted in *City of New Orleans v. Board of Commissioners of the Orleans Levee District 1994*, the court explained initiative as "a local government's ability to initiate legislation and regulation in the absence of express state legislative authorization" (Richardson 2011).

The final, and related factor defining innovation in bottom-up federalism is local capacity. Capacity is, for many scholars, closely related to autonomy (Jacob et al. 2008). For example, to the degree that devolution has expanded the policy domains of local governments, in some instances it has also limited the capacity to effectively act in those domains because they have not been adequately supported (Bowman and Kearney 2011). Thus, having autonomy to make decisions is inconsequential without the capacity (i.e. resources) to act on those decisions. This is particularly true with respect to policy innovation. Simply stated, then, to the degree that bottom-up efforts are defined by local autonomy, they will also reflect local capacity, in terms of the fiscal, human, and other resources required to support the creation and likely implementation of novel policies.

A Bottom-Up Policy Framework

As explained in our introductory comments, our motivation in considering the question of the possibility of meaningful bottom-up federalism phenomena is rooted in the disconnect between traditional scholarly descriptions of local policy efforts in the American federal system and what seems to be observable instances of significant bottom-up policy efforts by local governments (cities in particular). To help bridge this divide, we have synthesized various streams of literature around the foundational elements of devolution, intentionality, and innovation in defining the concept of bottom-up federalism. In this section, then, we further integrate these three concepts to fully articulate a proposed analytic framework.

To integrate our concepts, we employ devolution and intentionality as the *x, y*-axis of a Cartesian Plane (Figure 10.1) upon which to map local policy efforts.[7] Policy efforts that are characterized by lower devolutionary pressures will be mapped in the quadrants on the left side of the figure (quadrants 1 and 3) while those with higher pressures will be mapped in the quadrants on the right side of the figure (quadrants 2 and 4). Similarly, policy efforts that are characterized by higher or lower levels of intentionality will be mapped to the top quadrants (quadrants 3 and 4) or the lower quadrants (quadrants 1 and 2), respectively. This representation suggests that local policy efforts

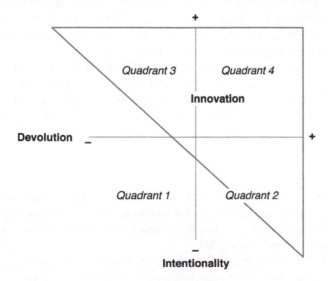

Figure 10.1 Bottom-Up Federalism Interpretative Heuristic.

Triangle overlay represents more innovative policies.

can be organized into one of four categories depending on the joint characteristics of devolution and intentionality.

Innovation, as both a component of devolution and intentionality, and a further defining characteristic of local policy efforts in general, and bottom-up federalism in particular, overlaps each quadrant in varying degrees. For example, policies in quadrant 1 (bottom-left) are less likely to be defined as innovative as they are more likely to reflect the traditional range of local policy efforts. As devolutionary and intentionality pressures increase, policy efforts are bound to be more innovative, hence, innovation is a key characteristic of quadrant 2, 3, and 4. To further understand how this conceptual framework informs our thinking of bottom-up federalism, we consider each quadrant with respect to the policy efforts they represent, in turn.

Quadrant 1: Traditional Local Policy Effort

First, the bottom left quadrant (quadrant 1) reflects policy efforts that are characterized by 'low levels' of devolution and intentionality. So at the bottom-left corner, one might map policy efforts that conform to the traditional political-economy and legal perspective of federal policy responsibility. This reflects a top-down perspective of policy effort, which we have referred to as the "mere creatures of the state" perspective.

The basis for the 'creatures of the state' perspective originates within the field of political economy. Theories from this perspective assert that policy-making authority and responsibility should be based upon the nature of the externalities associated with the underlying policy issue being addressed. Accordingly, as issues are characterized by a broader 'geographic' range of externalities, or spillover effects, the higher the order of government that should be responsible for the development of the associated public policy. So, for example, policies directed at the quality and protection of the natural environment would be best pursued at the federal or state level because environmental issues spillover local jurisdictional boundaries, e.g. rivers and air sheds move beyond state lines (Butler and Macey 1996). Thus, local policy efforts should be directed toward those issues whose impacts are felt exclusively within the local jurisdiction, such as local economic development policies, land-use regulations, and local public works.

The traditional set of policy efforts, however, represent one type of policy effort that can be mapped to this quadrant. Certainly as devolutionary pressures increase—and the policy responsibilities expand—local policy efforts might be mapped more closely to the right side of this quadrant. Additionally, as this expansion leads to innovative policies these would be mapped closer to the top of the quadrant.

Quadrant 2: Metropolitan Revolution

Local government policy efforts in the second quadrant in our framework (bottom-right) are characterized by higher levels of devolution than quadrant 1, but equally low levels of intentionality. Thus, in this quadrant, we would map many of the policy and programmatic activities described in Katz and Bradley's *The Metropolitan Revolution* (2013).

As described above, Katz and Bradley's argument for bottom-up federalism is based on a description of *de facto* devolution. To be clear, *de facto* devolution on its own does not necessarily dictate a higher degree of devolution than first and second order devolution described as part of quadrant 1. Katz and Bradley's description, however, seems to suggest that cities are responding not only to political stagnation at higher orders of government, but also past devolutionary pressures. Thus, to the degree that this is reasonable interpretation of the local policy efforts they describe, then they should, indeed, be mapped to quadrant 2.

Another defining feature of policies that are mapped to this quadrant—such as efforts examined in the *The Metropolitan Revolution*—are those that are characterized by higher levels of innovation than those in quadrant 1. Thus, policies in this quadrant reflect policy efforts, whereby the devolutionary pressures have led to an emboldened local government—one that is willing and able to innovate, as well as proactively engage with higher orders of government. An example of policy efforts at this point on the figure, is Shipan and Volden's (2006) "pressure valve" bottom-up efforts. Recall that these efforts are innovative local policies, that are not designed to trickle-up, but could if not for limited professional capacities in the State.

Quadrant 3: Diffusion and Local Activism

Local policy efforts mapped to the third quadrant are characterized by high levels of intentionality. As such, this quadrant would include the policy efforts defined by local activism *and* vertical diffusion, i.e. snowball effect. First, policies such as Shipan and Volden's anti-smoking policies that actually diffuse upwards would be mapped to this quadrant, in particular, the bottom-right of quadrant 3. The policy efforts are not expressly devolved to local governments, but local efforts are innovative enough that they have the potential to influence higher orders of government *and* the state has the professional capacity to implement successful local efforts. In contrast, Riverstone-Newell's local activism would be mapped to the top section of this quadrant where intentionality is the highest. Then, depending on the underlying devolutionary pressures, which might be 'zero,' the local activism efforts could be mapped more to the left or right of the quadrant.

Quadrant 4: Bottom-up Federalism

The final quadrant at the top right of the figure, represents what we would argue is the local government policy effort conforming to the definition of bottom-up federalism we have offered here. The high levels of devolution in this quadrant suggest that local governments are taking responsibility and initiative for policy-making in a given domain than traditional expectations would suggest, especially political economy and certain legal perspectives on federalism. A critical distinction in this quadrant is that the local governments are also doing so with an eye toward compelling higher orders of government toward modification or reprioritization of policy at those levels. In other words, through their initiative, local governments would intentionally seek to influence or drive the direction of state and federal policy toward a preferred end. Local policy efforts in this space will be highly innovative, and subsequently characterized by policy entrepreneurs that take advantage of a wide breadth of local autonomy and capacity to shape and implement public policy.

Bottom-up Federalism in the Context of Climate Change Policy

Climate change policy offers a unique context in which to consider the possibility of bottom-up federalism, as defined here, in practice. First, the issues associated with climate change are characterized by large externality or spillover effects. Thus, the potential negative impacts of climate change are not restricted to any particular jurisdiction. It is a traditional global commons problem (Engel 2006). Theoretical expectations for climate policy are that it is appropriately developed and implemented by higher order governments, including at an international regime level as seen by the 2016 Paris climate accord. Yet, local governments, particularly in the United States, have been actively involved in this policy domain (Gerber 2015; Goggin et al. 2014; Krause 2011). Indeed, some argue that American climate change policy "has shifted decidedly toward local-level government action" (Lutsey and Sperling 2008: 673). Given the contrast between theoretical expectations of climate policy and the actions of local governments, some scholars have suggested that climate policy reflects the emergence, or likely emergence, of a restructured American federalism. Within this context, where local action runs counter to the traditional expectations of policy effort, the questions are: what does our framework suggest and how does it hold up under analytical scrutiny?

First, consider the devolution element of our framework. Climate change policy, it seems reasonable to assert, has not been undertaken by local governments as a result of explicit devolutionary pressures. That said, there is some evidence that suggests that local action is a response to constituents' perception that higher levels of government, the federal government in particular, are not taking adequate action on climate change (Engel 2006). Administrators in cities have explicitly been proactive in seeking out techniques for climate hazard adjustment in that very context (Gerber 2015). Thus, our expectation is that climate change policy would be fairly low along the devolution axis (i.e. mapped to either quadrant 1 or 3).

Second, consider the issue of intentionality. There are clear indications in the empirical literature that cities in the United States have attempted to exert leadership on climate issues (Krause 2010, 2011). The networked form of governance described by policy scholars (e.g. the Mayors Climate Action Protection Agreement), leads some to argue that "the long-term significance of state and local action on climate change may lie in its impact in triggering action at higher levels of government" (Engel 2006: 1026). Others similarly argue that state and regional efforts will help promote the development of federal climate policy from the bottom-up (Rabe 2004; Selin and VanDeever 2009). Local efforts on climate policy, then, likely represents a *de facto* form of intentionality. The potential for upward diffusion is possible, but it depends mostly on the capacity of the state, as opposed to local efforts.

Finally, local climate change policy is inherently innovative. The nature of this innovation is described in a series of scholarly works (Gerber 2015; Goggin et al. 2014; Krause 2011; Lutsey and Sperling 2008; Jacob, Welch, and Simms 2009). Others have noted the importance of innovative factors such as policy entrepreneurs, local autonomy, and capacity for facilitating local climate policy action. Thus, it seems reasonable to characterize local climate policy efforts as highly innovative.

Taken together then, local government climate policy and management efforts (again, cities specifically) from our perspective are not particularly influenced by devolutionary pressures. They are also characterized by some intentional (albeit *de facto*) efforts to influence higher levels of government, and can further be defined as highly innovative. Based on our framework then, local climate policy is reflective of efforts that map to quadrant 3—local activism or diffusion. This mapping runs counter to at least some of the literature that describes local climate policy as representative of a restructured bottom-up federalism.

We consider our characterization of local climate policy using a survey we conducted in 2015 of local government administrators in the United States. The goal of this survey was to consider how local governments are addressing natural hazard management challenges, including potentially engaging in climate change mitigation and adaptation innovations. Several items from the survey instrument permit us to gain some insights into the three factors—devolution, intentionality, and innovation—that define our framework and subsequently test our expectations about bottom-up federalism in this policy domain.

Bottom-up Federalism in Climate Policy: Assessing Local Government Actions

Those survey data we use here came from an original sample frame composed of a stratified random selection of cities with populations greater than 50,000 (based on 2010 U.S. Census Data) and the county in which the city resides. Sample stratification groups were based on city populations and included three groups: cities with populations greater than 250,000; cities with populations between 100,000 and 249,999; and cities with populations between 50,000 and 99,999. Large cities were slightly oversampled to provide a large enough sample from which to receive responses. Otherwise, all sampling across the size stratum was proportional to the distribution in the population for those city size categories. Once the cities and counties were identified, the email addresses of city or county officials involved in, or knowledgeable of, hazard management and climate change activities were collected. A sample frame of individual administrators was drawn from city or county departments or offices of planning, emergency management, public health, fire response services, economic development, public works, or the executive office of the city or county. The sampling frame resulted in $N = 778$ individuals with valid emails. An electronic survey was administered via email in the fall of 2015 with each potential respondent receiving an initial invite and two follow-up email reminders. A total of 256 surveys were completed, resulting in a survey participation rate of 32.9 percent. Of those respondents, 142 (or 55.5%) were city administrative personnel in the departments mentioned above; the other 114 (45.5%) were individuals from county-level government and those same corresponding categories.

With respect to our assessment of bottom-up federalism in the climate mitigation and adaptation domain, the first issue we need to consider is the degree to which climate action plans are developed in response to devolutionary pressures. Of the 256 respondents in the survey approximately a quarter of them ($N = 105$) had developed a climate action plan. This response is important in itself, as it offers support for the extant insights that—despite the externality issues associated with climate policy—local governments at the city and county level are actively moving into a "nontraditional" policy domain. Or to put it another way: traditional political economy and legal theory generally would not anticipate such local effort on a transboundary problem of global scale.

To assess the devolutionary pressures that might be driving local climate policy action, we consider responses to a question about the underlying reasons for the climate action plan. More specifically, the 105 respondents who noted the presence of a climate action plan in their jurisdictional government were asked to consider why they had adopted such a plan. Was it because: (1) their constituents desired a plan; (2) their peers in other local governments were taking similar action; and/or (3) no other level of government was taking effective action. We interpreted positive responses to the latter—no other level of government was taking effective action—as an indication of devolutionary pressure.[8] The responses are summarized in Table 10.1.

As shown in Table 10.1, of the 105 respondents that indicated having a climate action plan, 29 percent answered that *one* of their reasons for having such plan is that other levels of government were not taking effective action. This provides some indication that devolutionary pressures—particularly *de facto* forms of devolution—are, as anticipated, a key motivating factor for local

Table 10.1 Reason the City has Climate Action Plan

Reasons the City Has a Plan N = 105	Agree	Disagree
Constituents desired a plan	68%	32%
Peers in other local governments are taking similar action	61%	39%
No other level of government is taking effective action	29%	71%

action. However, it is equally telling that much of the motivation for cities taking on climate change issues originates from local constituents or peer communities. This is consistent with the 'story' of climate change found in the extant literature. Local citizens tend to feel the effects of climate change quite acutely. They are directly impacted by flooding, heat waves, changes in air quality, and other environmental changes associated with climate change. Local constituents, however, would *not* demand local action on the issue if they felt that their concerns were being adequately addressed by other levels of government. While there has not been an explicit federal policy shifting climate hazard adjustment to local governments, the lack of federal guidance at least suggests the notion that de facto devolution might be a greater consideration than we originally anticipated.

The second factor we consider is the degree of upward intentionality associated with local climate change policy. That is, the degree to which local governments are actively trying to influence higher orders of government. We measured this outcome through responses to the question of how influential do you think your hazards management action is on federal, state, and peer level organizations. The local government administrators' answers were measured on a 4-point scale shown in Table 10.2 below.

These results seem to confirm our thinking on intentionality. Of the respondents who answered this question nearly one-quarter (22.1%) believe their work influences the federal government to a moderate or strong degree. Given that local governments are, at least, two steps away from the federal level of government, this level of anticipated influence seems to us to be quite high. Additionally, well over one-third (37.1%) of respondents assess that their work is moderately or very influential on state officials and policies in the domain of natural hazards management. The

Table 10.2 Influence of Work Unit's Work

	How influential do you think your work unit's hazards management actions are on:					
	Federal Officials or Federal Policies		State Officials or State Policies		Peer Agencies in Other Cities	
	Frequency	Percent	Frequency	Percent	Frequency	Percent
Not influential at all	119	48.0%	71	29.0%	31	12.5%
Slightly influential	74	29.8%	83	33.9%	98	39.5%
Moderately influential	41	16.5%	164	26.1%	89	35.9%
Very Influential	19 n = 248	5.6%	27 n = 245	11.0%	30 n = 248	12.1%

idea of intentionality is further buttressed by responses to this question (and the first) on peer agencies. In the first question, where respondents were asked to consider their motivation for adopting a climate action plan, nearly two-thirds answered that it was because their peers were taking similar action. In this second question, over 48.0% of the respondents answered that their work was influencing their peer jurisdictions (moderately or significantly). This is suggestive of a fairly well-integrated form of networked governance that scholars have argued leads to potentially greater impact on higher orders of government (Engel 2006).

The final factor that we need to consider, is the role of innovation in shaping the climate and hazard management efforts of local officials. To assess the potential for innovation in their policy actions, we consider responses to a question on the use of discretion. Discretion of course, is a key component of "initiative" forms of autonomy that facilitates innovation. In particular, respondents were asked to rate the levels of discretion autonomy they had (on a 4-point scale) with respect to developing risk reduction strategies on natural hazards generally and for climate action plans more specifically. Responses are summarized in Table 10.3.

Responses to this question point to high levels of discretion, particularly with hazards planning, but also with the development of climate action plans. More precisely, almost 80 percent of the respondents noted having at least a moderate level of discretion for developing their local risk reduction strategies on natural hazards and almost 55 percent noted having a moderate or high level of discretionary autonomy in developing a local climate action plan. We interpret these answers to suggest that local (city and county) administrators have a good deal of practical latitude in developing and pursuing innovative solutions to their communities' hazard management challenges, including the specific area of climate change mitigation and adaptation.

These data suggest significant levels of local climate action policy efforts. They do not indicate that bottom-up federalism dynamics are present on climate policy *per se* because we have not assessed their direct impact on policy efforts by higher order governments; asking about perceived influence on higher order governments is a limited measure. However, these results are important in a key way: they are at a minimum highly suggestive of the idea that local climate policy efforts are at least approaching a restructured bottom-up federalism form of policy-making. This is summarized in Figure 10.2 below.

Figure 10.2 depicts three mappings of local climate policy. The first point, at the bottom-left corner of quadrant 1 suggests that local policy efforts on climate policy would be near zero.

Table 10.3 Discretion to Develop Strategies and Plans

	Discretion in Developing Risk Strategy on Hazards		Discretion in Developing Climate Action Plan	
	Frequency	*Percent*	*Frequency*	*Percent*
No Discretion	13	5.4%	23	10.6%
Very Limited Discretion	34	14.2%	75	34.7%
Moderate Discretion	104	43.5%	74	34.3%
High Level of Discretion	88	36.8%	44	20.4%
	n = 239		*n* = 216	

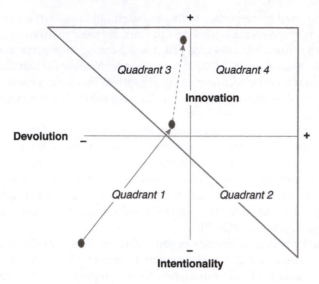

Figure 10.2 Mapping of Local Climate Policy in Practice.

Climate policy would largely be under the purview of higher orders of government (hence zero devolutionary pressures) and subsequently, we would see few efforts by local governments to innovate and influence higher orders of government. Of course, the emerging work in the empirical literature suggests this is not actually the case in the United States. Based on what has been established by prior research, we anticipated that climate change policy would be more aptly characterized by the second point on our figure at the bottom of quadrant 3. However, the descriptive results presented here suggest that local government climate change policy efforts are more intentionally driven than we anticipated. Local policy efforts are more likely to map onto the upper right corner of quadrant 3. This result requires further elaboration and more detailed analysis. Still, the material presented here is strongly suggestive that local policy efforts in the climate change mitigation and adaptation domain, combined with nontrivial political constraints on state and federal action, are pushing climate policy toward a restructured form of bottom-up federalism, as anticipated by the scholarship indicating leadership and innovation by local governments in the United States.

Discussion and Conclusion

On June 1, 2017 President Trump withdrew America from the Paris Climate Accord. He justified this action as being in the best interest of the nation. Thus, while other countries might be off-put with this decision, Trump argued that "[He] was elected to represent the citizens of Pittsburgh not Paris." Immediately following this statement, however, Pittsburgh's Mayor responded in a tweet stating: "Pittsburgh stands with the world and will follow Paris agreement [*sic*]." Further, the U.S. Conference of Mayors issued a statement declaring it: "is a strong proponent of the need to address climate change and we support the Paris agreement." This recent give-and-take between the nation's highest office and its lowest offices, reflects some of the tension that defines, and seems to foster, much of the dialogue and interest around bottom-up federalism.[9]

The core purpose of this chapter is to provide an intellectual basis for assessing local policy efforts, including clarifying more precisely what the nature of bottom-up federalism entails. Further, we attempt to offer at least a very preliminary assessment of what a restructured form of bottom-up federalism would look like in practice by considering the substantively important issue of local efforts on climate change mitigation and adaptation practices. Within that policy domain, it appears that some form of a restructured bottom-up federalism is a plausible way to understand current policy-making activities.

Of course, the descriptive analysis provided here is just that: descriptive. It is necessary to build upon the framework for understanding bottom-up federalism in several ways. First, a more rigorous analysis is required to appropriately characterize American local government efforts on climate change and the degree to which a restructured bottom-up federalism might be taking place at present. Second, a broader assessment of policy-making dynamics across multiple domains is necessary to assess the validity of our asserted framework. Third, and perhaps most important, it is necessary to recognize the conditional nature of the relationships we have outlined here. Concepts such as innovation and intentionality are not truly dichotomous constructs but instead fall on continua with subtle distinctions across variation in actions. As such, identifying the underlying determinants, and how they vary across policy areas and different political and economic conditions is needed to draw robust inferences about how bottom-up federalism functions in practice. Laying out a framework and clarifying the specific demands of the bottom-up concept is a critical first step.

Notes

1   The devolution literature distinguishes between first and second-order devolution. Where second-order devolution refers to the specific transfer of authority "from the state to their cities, counties and other general purpose local governments" (Bowman and Kearney 2011). For more extensive overviews of devolution in general refer to Timothy Conlon (1998), and Alice Rivlin (1992).
2   From Ronald Reagan's inaugural address (1981), taken from Cole, Hissong, and Arvidson (1999).
3   It is worth noting that these authors are, generally speaking, describing the impacts across multiple devolutionary periods and not solely the impacts of the Regan period devolution.
4   Although many scholars working in this area refer to "bottom-up federalism." See for example, Ghamkar and Pickerill (2012).
5   Shipan and Volden refer to the former as benefitting from "snowball" effects and the latter as a result of "pressure valves."
6   Though one might also wish to refer to Pratchett's conceptualization of *freedom from, freedom to and local identity* (Pratchett 2004).
7   The mapping, however, should be viewed only as a general heuristic. As we move forward with a focused empirical research agenda we hope to more precisely measure the dimensions of local policy efforts.
8   The question of course is not nuanced enough to assess the nature of the devolutionary pressure, and indeed the wording of the question suggests a mostly *de facto* form of devolution.
9   In a recent article, Riverstone-Newell (2017) has offered some important insights on the State efforts to advance laws that would preempt local activism.

References

Agranoff, R. and B. A. Radin. 2014. "Deil Wright's overlapping model of intergovernmental relations: The basis for contemporary intergovernmental relationships." *Publius: The Journal of Federalism* 45 (1): 139–159.

Berman, D. R. 2003. *Local government and the states: Autonomy, politics and policy.* New York: M. E. Sharpe.

Bowman A., and R. C. Kearney. 2011. "Second-order devolution: Data and doubt." *Publius: The Journal of Federalism* 41(4): 563–585.

Brenner, N. 2004. *New State Spaces: Urban Governance and the Rescaling of Statehood.* Oxford: Oxford University Press.

Briffault, R. 2004. "Home Rule for the Twenty-first Century." *Urban Lawyer* 36: 258–260.

Butler, H. N., and J. R. Macey. 1996. "Externalities and the matching principle: The case for reallocating environmental regulatory authority." *Faculty Scholarship Series* 1447. Retrieved from http://digitalcommons.law.yale.edu/fss_papers/1447 (accessed October 17, 2017).

Clark, G. L. 1984. "A theory of local autonomy." *Annals of the Association of American Geographers* 74: 195–208.

Cole R., R. V. Hissong., and E. Arvidson. 1999. "Devolution: Where's the Revolution?" *Publius: The Journal of Federalism* 29(4): 99–112.

Conlon, T. 1998. *From New Federalism to Devolution: Twenty-Five Years of Intergovernmental Reform.* Washington, DC: The Brookings Institution.

Eisinger, P. 1998. "City politics in an era of federal devolution." *Urban Affairs Review* 33 (January): 308–325.

Engel, K. 2006. "State and local climate change initiatives: What is motivating state and local government to address a global problem and what does this say about federalism and environmental law?" *Urban Lawyer* 38: 1015–1029.

Gerber, B. J. 2015. "Local governments and climate change in the United States: Assessing administrators' perspectives on hazard management challenges and responses." *State and Local Government Review* 47 (1): 48–56.

Ghamkar, S., and J. M. Pickerill. 2012. "The state of American federalism 2011–2012: A fend for yourself and activist form of bottom-up federalism." *Publius: The Journal of Federalism* 42(3): 357–386.

Godwin, M. L., and J. R. Schroedel. 2000. "Policy diffusion and strategies for promoting policy change: Evidence from California gun control ordinances." *Policy Studies Journal* 28(4): 760–776.

Goggin, M. L., B. J. Gerber, and S. Larson. 2014. "U.S. local governments and climate change: Examining the acquisition and use of research-based knowledge in policy development." *Risk, Hazards and Crisis in Public Policy* 5: 156–177.

Herbers, J. 1987. "The new federalism: Unplanned, innovative and here to stay." Retrieved from www.governing.com/topics/mgmt/new-federalism-unplanned-innovative-here-to-stay.html (accessed October 17, 2017).

Jacob, B., B. Lipton., V. Hagens., and B. Reimer. 2008. "Rethinking local autonomy: perspectives from four rural communities." *Canadian Public Administration* 51 (September): 407–427.

Jacob, B., E. Welch., and T. Simms. 2009. "Emergent management strategies in the public sectors: a case study of alternative fuel vehicles." *Public Organization Review* 9(3): 213–234.

Katz, B., and J. Bradley. 2013. *The Metropolitan Revolution: How Cities are Fixing Our Broken Politics and Fragile Economy.* Washington, DC: The Brookings Institution.

Kincaid, J. 1998. "The devolution tortoise and the centralization hare." *New England Review* (May/June): 36–38.

Krane D., C. Ebdon., and J. Bartle. 2004. "Devolution, fiscal federalism, and changing patterns of municipal revenues: The mismatch between theory and reality." *Journal of Public Research and Theory* 14(4): 513–533.

Krane D., P. N. Rigos, and M. B. Hill Jr. (eds). 2001. *Home Rule in America: A Fifty-State Handbook.* Washington, DC: Congressional Quarterly Press.

Krause, R. M. 2010. "Policy innovation, intergovernmental relations, and the adoption of climate protection initiatives by U.S. cities." *Journal of Urban Affairs* 33: 45–60.

Krause, R. M. 2011. "As assessment of the greenhouse gas reducing activities being implemented in U.S. cities." *Local Environment* 16: 193–211.

Lutsey, N., and D. Sperling. 2008. "America's bottom-up climate change mitigation policy." *Energy Policy* 36: 673–685.

Mintrom, M. 2000. *Policy Entrepreneurs and School Choice.* Washington, DC: Georgetown University Press.

Nathan, R. P. 1996. *The Devolution Revolution: An Overview.* Rockefeller Institute Bulletin. Albany, NY: Nelson A. Rockefeller Institute of Government.

Pratchett, L. 2004. "Local autonomy, local democracy and the new localism." *Political Studies* 52: 358–375.

Rabe, B. G. 2004. *Statehouse and Greenhouse: The Emerging Politics of American Climate Change Policy.* Washington, DC: The Brookings Institution.

Richardson, J. J. Jr. 2011. "Dillon's rule is from Mars, home rule is from Venus: Local government autonomy and the rules of statutory construction." *Publius: The Journal of Federalism* 41(4): 662–685.

Rivlin, A. 1992. *Reviving the American Dream.* Washington, DC: The Brookings Institution.

Riverstone-Newell, L. 2012. "Bottom-up activism: a local political strategy for higher policy change." *Publius: The Journal of Federalism* 42(3): 401–421.

Riverstone-Newell, L. 2014. *Renegade Cities, Public Policy and the Dilemmas of Federalism.* Boulder, CO: First Forum Press.

Riverstone-Newell, L. 2017. "The rise of state preemption laws in response to local policy innovation." *Publius: The Journal of Federalism* 47(3): 403–425.

Sbragia, A. M. 1996. *Debt Wish: Entrepreneurial Cities, U.S. Federalism, and Economic Development.* Pittsburgh, PA: University of Pittsburgh Press.

Selin, H., and S. D. VanDeveer (eds). 2009. *Changing Climates in North American Politics: Institutions, Policymaking and Multilevel Governance.* Cambridge, MA: MIT Press.

Shipan, C., and C. Volden. 2006. "Bottom-up federalism: The diffusion of antismoking policies from U.S. cities to states." *American Journal of Political Science* 50(4): 825–843.

Wright, D. S. 1988. *Understanding Intergovernmental Relations*, 3rd edition. Pacific Grove, CA: Brooks-Cole.

Part IV
Laboratories of Democracy at Work

11 The Legislative Transformation of State–Local Government Relations

Ann O'M. Bowman and Richard C. Kearney

Local jurisdictions in the United States depend on their state governments for sufficient authority and discretion to function effectively. States, however, vary in the degree to which they have empowered their local governments. Certain states have allocated substantial authority to localities, achieving some degree of subsidiarity by allowing lower levels to play a greater role in the operation of government (Vischer 2001). Other states have taken a different, more centralized approach by concentrating power at the state level, thereby circumscribing the range of independent action enjoyed by local jurisdictions. Cross-state variation is important, so too is within-state variation. The distribution of power from a state to its localities is neither immutable, nor is it unidirectional (Stephens 1974). Authority can be conferred on counties or municipalities by the state and in a subsequent legislative session, it can be rescinded. Within a single state, the allocation of power may vary across jurisdictional types and even within types, as in the case of cities with larger populations being granted special powers that smaller cities do not possess. Clearly, the state–local relationship is characterized by numerous power imbalances, varying both across and within states and over time.

The distribution of power is a perennial concern of local governments. A 1973 National League of Cities survey of mayors and city council members reported a widespread perception of a shift in power away from local governments, including the erosion of home rule powers at the hands of state legislatures (Wright 1978). Decades later, the sense that state legislatures continue to chip away at local authority remains potent. For example, in a national survey of city managers, nearly two-thirds of respondents indicated that laws enacted by state legislatures during the preceding decade were often intrusive or preemptive of city government powers or authority (Bowman and Kearney 2012). The media have echoed a similar theme such as an article in *Governing* magazine titled "Devolution and Arrogance: States Can't Resist the Temptation to Boss their Localities Around" (Ehrenhalt 2013).

Clearly, this important and dynamic relationship is worthy of additional research.[1] Indeed, the likely consequences of state restrictions on their local governments is one of the "Big Questions" posed by Hamilton and Stenberg in Chapter 1 of this volume. Our chapter analyzes state legislative actions in the fifty U.S. states during the 2011–2012 biennium, in both regular and special sessions, which directly affected local governments, specifically cities, counties, and towns. The goal is to determine the impact of legislative actions on local jurisdictions, particularly whether these enactments restricted or empowered localities. Also of interest is the substantive focus of these new laws and the degree to which they vary across states. This two-year study is but a snapshot of course but we believe it offers insights about the condition of state–local relations in the U.S.

Finally, we use these findings to consider the implications of the distribution of power and authority in state–local systems of government.

The Issue of Power and Authority in State–Local Relations

States establish the rules of the game for their local governments, giving rise to the often-heard pronouncement that "local governments are creatures of their states" (Frug and Barron 2008). According to the legal doctrine established by Dillon's Rule, local governments may exercise only those powers explicitly granted to them by the state, those clearly implied by these explicit powers, and those absolutely essential to the declared objectives and purposes of the local government.[2] Strict interpretation of Dillon's Rule means that any doubt regarding the legality of a specific local government power is resolved in favor of the state. Dillon's Rule has been adopted in 39 states, and in 31 of them, the rule covers all localities, while in eight states, it applies only to certain types of local jurisdictions (Richardson 2011). Non-Dillon's Rule states operate with variations on the *imperium in imperio* model, an approach that grants local governments exclusive authority in specific functional areas and greater discretion in others (Zimmerman 1983; Wood 2011).

However, the question of local power and authority is not quite so simple as the presence or absence of Dillon's Rule. Most states, including many that have adopted Dillon's Rule, also grant "home rule" to their cities and in some instances, their counties. A grant of home rule empowers local officials to customize their policies to fit their community without excessive interference from the state. For example, Ohio's municipal home rule provision, found in Article 18, section 3 of the state's constitution, declares: "Municipalities shall have authority to exercise all powers of local self-government and to adopt and enforce within their limits such local police, sanitary, and other similar regulations, as are not in conflict with the general laws." Although home rule is considered an important step in the direction of greater local decision-making (Krane, Rigos, and Hill 2001), "no type of home rule equates to total freedom for local governments from state oversight" (Richardson 2011: 14). As the Ohio home rule provision suggests, local authority may give way when it bumps up against the state's general laws. Ultimately, the actual impact of home rule is determined by the state context.

Fuzziness in the concepts of Dillon's Rule and home rule, particularly in how they are practiced, has led to the development of alternative measures of state–local relations. Stephens (1974) analyzes what he terms "the manifestations of power" in state–local relations by considering the distribution of finance and employment across governmental levels. He classifies states according to the extent to which these functions are centralized at the state level or decentralized to the local level.[3] The U.S. Advisory Commission on Intergovernmental Relations (1981) and Zimmerman (1983) gauge "local discretionary authority" by examining the power of localities related to governmental structure, functional responsibility, fiscal authority, and personnel.

In the Wolman et al. (2010: 72) research, "local government autonomy," is defined as a "system of local government in which local government units have an important role to play in the economy and the intergovernmental system, have discretion in determining what they will do without undue constraint from higher levels of government, and have the means or capacity to do so." Comparing the states on these three factors—the importance of localities, their discretion, and their capacity—differentiates the states that grant their local jurisdictions the greatest degree of autonomy (New York, Tennessee, Kansas, and Ohio) from those states providing the least (West Virginia, Connecticut, Rhode Island, and Vermont) (Wolman et al. 2010). They find a mix of

Dillon's Rule and non-Dillon's Rule states in both groups of states—those with high levels of local government autonomy and those with low levels of local government autonomy. This finding underscores the limited explanatory power of Dillon's Rule or home rule as indicators of the actual distribution of power in a state–local system.

Concentration of power by the state or the dispersal of power to local governments affects governmental legitimacy and accountability. Among scholars who study the distribution of governmental authority, many have concluded that, unless compelling reasons exist for centralization, then "local decisions are best made by locals" (Hooghe and Marks 2009: 232). Throughout the world, decentralization has become a mechanism for diffusing decision making and allocating responsibility. According to Krane, Rigos, and Hill (2001: 1), support for a decentralized governmental system is inherent in the U.S. "Local self-government is one of the most cherished and fiercely contested ideas in the pantheon of principles by which Americans organize their system of governance." Opinion research conducted by Schneider, Jacoby, and Lewis (2011) found strong public support for empowered local governments that take responsibility for the problems facing U.S. communities. Decentralization is said to possess numerous advantages including service delivery efficiencies, alignment of program costs with services provided, fostering of policy innovation, enhanced citizen responsiveness, greater government transparency and accountability, and relieving state legislatures of the burden of hearing and deciding on local bills (see Oates 1972; Kincaid 1998; Krane, Rigos, and Hill 2001). Realization of only a few of these purported advantages suggests that the consequences of increased local authority can be substantial. Accordingly, a reduction in local authority makes their fulfillment less likely.

State and Local Governments Encounter the Great Recession

The Great Recession, which began in 2008, hit state and local jurisdictions hard. Passage of the $787 billion American Recovery and Reinvestment Act of 2009 helped postpone the full impact of the decline in own-source revenues and the escalating fiscal stress. The National Governors Association and the National Association of State Budget Officers (2011: vii) reported that "State general fund expenditures were so negatively affected by the recent recession that both fiscal 2009 and fiscal 2010 saw unprecedented actual declines in state spending." In its annual fiscal study, the National Conference of State Legislatures (2011: 1), remarked that "The fiscal impact [of the recession] has been deep and prolonged, with fiscal year 2012 marking the fourth consecutive year that states faced significant mismatches between revenues and spending. To date, state lawmakers have faced—and largely addressed—budget gaps totaling $510.5 billion." Around the country, state rainy day funds dried up to precarious levels as legislators tapped them for short-term relief. Even as the national economy began to improve, most states continued to wrestle with the revenue consequences presented by persistently high rates of unemployment and continued weak consumer spending. Accordingly, many a state cast a covetous eye on revenue sources typically enjoyed by their local governments; similarly, cash-strapped states found it difficult to resist intervening in the operations of their localities.

Throughout 2011 and 2012, the popular media in the United States contained numerous accounts indicating that the state–local relationship was undergoing substantial alteration. For instance, *The New York Times* published an article in March 2011 with the headline, "States Pass Budget Pain to Cities." The magazine *Governing* echoed a similar theme in its April 2011 issue with an article titled, "States Handing Off More Responsibilities to Cities." In California, the media focused on the state's monumental budget shortfall, and the double-edged deal that Governor Jerry Brown proposed to counties: a grant of additional power in exchange for increasing the counties' share of public service provision. State–Local interactions were not solely about fiscal matters. Media outlets devoted much attention to the Michigan governor's announcement in 2012 that he would appoint an emergency financial manager for the City of Detroit, an action that would effectively usurp the mayor and city council's decision making authority.[4] In Ohio, after the city of Cleveland adopted an ordinance prohibiting restaurants from using artificial trans fats in food preparation, local broadcasts covered the state legislature's insertion of an amendment into the state budget bill banning such actions by its local governments.[5] These media examples suggest that the 2011–2012 biennium offers a propitious time for assessing the behavior of state policymakers toward their local governments under conditions of fiscal stress.

To examine the impact of state actions on local power and authority in the aftermath of the Great Recession, as well as to better understand the evolving intergovernmental relationship, we looked at state legislative actions during the 2011 and 2012 legislative biennium.[6] Our inquiry was guided by these research questions:

1   How much legislative activity was directed at local governments during the biennium and how does it vary by state?
2   On average, did state legislative actions empower or restrict local governments, and how much variation exists across states?
3   What are the substantive foci of local government bills passed by state legislatures?

Data and Methodology

Data on local government laws enacted during the 2011 and 2012 legislative sessions in the states were collected in two ways: through searches of "bills enacted" compendia on state legislative websites, and from searching the Lexis-Nexis database StateNet, which reports information on new statutes. To identify laws pertinent to this project, summaries of enacted bills were searched for keywords such as "local," "city" "municipality," "county," "town" and the plural forms of these words.[7] Once these statutes were identified, the subject matter was reviewed. For a law to become part of the dataset, it must have affected the authority, either fiscally or administratively, of general purpose local governments.[8] For example, a law creating a statewide task force to study local government infrastructure expenditures would be identified in the initial search, but would not be included in the dataset because it did not affect localities' authority. Also excluded were state budget bills, laws pertaining to a single jurisdiction which often appear on consent calendars, as well as resolutions related to local governments.

Summaries in StateNet or on a state legislature's website typically provided sufficient information to discern the effect of a new law on general purpose local governments. If not, fiscal notes and bill analyses available on state legislative websites were consulted. If these sources proved insufficient to determine the substance and impact of a new law, then the full text of the statute itself was evaluated.

Laws in the dataset were coded as to their impact on general purpose local government: empowering, restricting, or neutral. After undergoing training, two coders classified the relevant laws.[9] In this formulation, other than the coding for directional impact and substance, no differential weights were assigned to the laws; each counts the same as another.

To be categorized as *empowering* (assigned a value of +1), a law had to intend to reduce an administrative burden borne by cities, counties, or towns, provide funding to them, or grant them additional discretionary authority. To be designated as *restricting* (assigned a value of –1), a law had to intend to remove a power currently held by local governments, preempt local government action, or impose an administrative burden or financial cost on local governments. Laws were classified as *neutral* (assigned a value of 0) if they were neither empowering nor restricting, or if they contained provisions that both empowered and restricted.

The following examples help clarify the coding process. Examples of empowering laws enacted during the biennium include:

- Alabama's law that authorizes municipalities, counties, or any combination thereof to create a public authority for the purpose of promoting and developing tourism;
- Colorado's statute that provides state reimbursement to county governments for charges incurred in pest control operations undertaken by the county;
- Indiana's law related to local government property sales, authorizing a local government disposing agent to hire a broker to sell property instead of using the bid process;
- Michigan's statute that allows local governments to prohibit the sale of alcohol between specified hours on certain days;
- Montana's special allocation of funds to the state Department of Commerce to provide financial assistance to local government infrastructure projects through the Treasure State Endowment Program;
- Oklahoma's statute that decreases the number of months that are required to pass before a municipality may tear down and remove a boarded-up and secured building.

Laws that restrict local governments include:

- Arizona's statute prohibiting a city or town from accepting federal monies for a construction project if as a condition of accepting federal monies the city or town is required to give a preference to union labor;
- California's requirement that county welfare departments inform dependent children in foster care that they may be eligible for preference in state agency internship programs;
- Utah's law prohibiting a city from establishing a local historic district or area in certain circumstances;
- Vermont's statute requiring that the cost of audits of tax increment financing districts conducted by the state auditor of accounts be billed back to the municipalities;
- Virginia's law establishing requirements for local ordinances that address the siting of renewable energy facilities that generate electricity from wind or solar resources;
- Washington's statute requiring counties to have an affordable housing component in the county's impact fees ordinance, and additionally, providing requirements for the affordable housing component.

As noted above, laws that neither empowered nor restricted local governments, or did both, were classified as neutral. Some of these neutral laws simply clarified current law while others contained provisions that authorized local government action but included an extensive set of requirements or restrictions on that action. The substance of the law was determined through a similar process. Enacted bills were categorized as to general subject matter, e.g., government operations, finance, regulation, and so on. Laws with a specified policy component were further classified into policy areas such as public safety, land use, infrastructure, social services, and health, among others.[10]

The keyword search and review produced a total of 1,457 laws directed at local governments enacted in the 2011 sessions; 1,039 laws in the 2012 sessions. It is important to note that state legislatures vary in numerous ways, and at least three of these variations are relevant for this research. First, the continued use of biennial sessions in four states (Montana, Nevada, North Dakota, and Texas) inflates the number of bills passed during a yearly session in those states and reduces the bill passage rate to zero the following year.[11] In a few of the annual session states, such as Arkansas, the second year of a biennium is reserved for fiscal matters thereby limiting the scope of legislation that can be considered. Second, during the 2011–2012 biennium, Ohio and California enacted several omnibus bills to address a range of local government issues, thus those states' total number of bills is lower than it would be had the issues been disaggregated into separate bills. Third, Massachusetts tends to rely more heavily than other states on legislation applicable to a single jurisdiction. Because single jurisdiction bills are not included in our count, the degree to which Massachusetts empowers or restricts local governments is not fully apparent in the data set.

Findings and Discussion

State legislatures had local governments in their sights in the 2011–2012 biennium. Excluding laws applicable to a single jurisdiction or to single-purpose local governments such as school districts, nearly 2,500 new laws affecting general-purpose local governments were enacted, for an average of approximately 50 new laws per state. However, an average masks the substantial—and not surprising—variation that exists across the states. For 2011, the number of new laws affecting general purpose local governments ranges from 2 in Alaska and Massachusetts to 101 in Texas; in 2012, the range extends from a single law in Massachusetts to 84 laws in Virginia. In the first year of the biennium, per state, the average number of new laws affecting local government is 29.1 (standard deviation of 22.8); in the second year, the new laws per state average is 22.6 (standard deviation of 14.6). Table 11.1 reports the enacted laws figures for each state during the two-year period.

Comparing States and their Enactment

Although determining the amount of legislative activity is a useful first step, more important is the direction of those laws: What is the mix of empowering and restricting legislation enacted by lawmakers?[12] Despite the general theme in the media implying that states ran roughshod over their local governments as the Great Recession took its toll, the data suggest a different reality. For the 2011 legislative sessions, the total number of empowering laws (736) exceeds the number of restricting laws (603). (These counts exclude laws classified as "neutral" in their impact.) In other words, of the non-neutral laws passed during the session, 55 percent of them were empowering. Thirty-one states show a positive balance, enacting a higher number of empowering laws than restrictive ones; fourteen states have the opposite pattern. The remaining five states enacted the same number of empowering laws as restricting laws. For the average state, a term we use advisedly, empowering laws (14.7) outnumber restricting laws (12.1). However, across the states, wide

Table 11.1 Number of Local Government Laws Enacted in 2011 and 2012, by State

State	2011 Total	2012 Total	State	2011 Total	2012 Total
Alabama	20	29	Montana	52	—
Alaska	2	6	Nebraska	40	26
Arizona	57	38	Nevada	22	—
Arkansas	75	9	New Hampshire	22	16
California	95	58	New Jersey	28	18
Colorado	28	20	New Mexico	14	8
Connecticut	20	27	New York	35	26
Delaware	5	5	North Carolina	34	20
Florida	29	31	North Dakota	34	—
Georgia	14	15	Ohio	11	30
Hawaii	11	22	Oklahoma	31	28
Idaho	22	14	Oregon	41	12
Illinois	57	36	Pennsylvania	10	17
Indiana	29	29	Rhode Island	33	13
Iowa	11	19	South Carolina	4	8
Kansas	12	12	South Dakota	31	44
Kentucky	8	16	Tennessee	50	27
Louisiana	26	26	Texas	101	—
Maine	26	19	Utah	32	36
Maryland	32	36	Vermont	9	16
Massachusetts	2	1	Virginia	88	84
Michigan	22	30	Washington	35	30
Minnesota	13	11	West Virginia	13	13
Mississippi	32	20	Wisconsin	6	20
Missouri	15	11	Wyoming	18	7
			Total Laws	1457	1039
			Mean	29.1	22.6
			Std. Deviation	22.8	14.6

variation exists, as evidenced by standard deviations of 12.1 and 10.4, respectively. For the 2012 sessions, a similar pattern appears, with empowering laws (530) occurring at a higher rate than restricting laws (411). In terms of the number of laws of each type adopted, 30 states empowered localities more than they restricted them; thirteen states restricted more than they empowered. In the remaining three states convening legislative sessions in 2012, the numbers offset one another. The averages for 2012 are 11.5 empowering laws (standard deviation of 7.8) per state and 8.9 restricting laws (standard deviation of 7.1) per state. To determine the cumulative effect of legislative actions over the biennium, we calculate an impact score for each state by summing the number of empowering laws (values of +1) and restricting laws (values of –1). The annual and cumulative effect of legislative empowerment and restriction of localities is presented in Table 11.2. The two-year period is decidedly positive: 33 states empowered their localities; 12 states restricted them, and in 5 states the empowering and restricting laws offset. The average two-year state impact score is 4.9, however, the standard deviation of 14.4 is further evidence of the wide variation across the states when it comes to empowering and restricting local governments.

States with the greatest empowering impact over the biennium are Virginia, New York, Illinois, Arkansas, and Washington. Of these five states, all but Illinois are considered to be governed by Dillon's Rule.[13] (In Illinois, only non-home rule cities are subject to Dillon's Rule.) As for restricting general-purpose local governments, California leads the other highly restricting states, while Arizona, Utah, Indiana, and Florida, follow by a wide margin. Dillon's Rule applies less comprehensively in this group of states. Arizona is a Dillon's Rule state, Utah is not; in California and Indiana only certain types of jurisdictions are covered by it and in Florida, according to Richardson (2011), the status of Dillon's Rule is unclear.

Also interesting is the trend, admittedly extremely short term, showing how many states reversed course from the first year to the next. Six states (Alabama, Delaware, Georgia, Louisiana, Pennsylvania, and South Dakota) move from the empowering to the restricting category from the first year to the second; however, in only Alabama is the cumulative net effect restrictive. Seven states move in the opposite direction, shifting from restricting to empowering. In three of these states—Colorado, Missouri, and New Mexico) the cumulative net effect is restrictive, although the absolute number was low.

Table 11.2 State Impact Scores, 2011 and 2012

State	2011 Impact	2012 Impact	2-Year Impact	State	2011 Impact	2012 Impact	2-Year Impact
Alabama	2	−7	−5	Montana	8	0	8
Alaska	0	0	0	Nebraska	9	9	18
Arizona	−15	−5	−20	Nevada	0	0	0
Arkansas	15	9	24	New Hampshire	4	4	8
California	−17	−25	−42	New Jersey	7	5	12
Colorado	−3	1	−2	New Mexico	−4	2	−2
Connecticut	0	4	4	New York	11	18	29
Delaware	1	−1	0	North Carolina	−5	−6	−11
Florida	−8	−5	−13	North Dakota	4	0	4
Georgia	6	−2	4	Ohio	4	3	7
Hawaii	2	7	9	Oklahoma	−5	9	4
Idaho	0	−2	−2	Oregon	4	4	8
Illinois	19	6	25	Pennsylvania	5	−2	3
Indiana	−15	0	−15	Rhode Island	17	2	19
Iowa	−1	−5	−6	South Carolina	−2	2	0
Kansas	−1	1	0	South Dakota	6	−1	5
Kentucky	1	4	5	Tennessee	−9	13	4
Louisiana	8	−2	6	Texas	15	0	15
Maine	0	1	1	Utah	−11	−7	−18
Maryland	1	0	1	Vermont	1	4	5
Massachusetts	2	1	3	Virginia	31	25	56
Michigan	1	9	10	Washington	12	12	24
Minnesota	6	8	14	West Virginia	1	5	6
Mississippi	6	11	17	Wisconsin	1	5	6
Missouri	−2	1	−1	Wyoming	13	4	17
				Mean	2.5	2.4	4.9
				Std. Deviation	8.8	7.3	14.4

The Target and Focus of Recent State Enactments

Because of the way the data are coded, we can identify the target of the legislation (general-purpose local governments as a whole or types of local governments—counties, cities, towns—more specifically) and the content of the legislation. As the top section of Table 11.3

Table 11.3 Aggregate Law Content, 2011–2012

Jurisdictional Area	Percent
Local Government	32.1
County Government	28.8
More Than One Type of Local Government	19.3
Municipal/City Government	18.8
Town Government	1.1
Total	100.0
Subject Matter	*Percent*
Government Operations	45.5
Finance	17.7
Substantive Policy Area	14.7
Structure of Government	14.4
Human Resources	5.4
Regulatory	2.0
Structure and Finance	0.3
Total	100.0
Policy Focus	*Percent*
Taxation and Fees	8.2
Land Use	6.9
Public Safety	6.8
Infrastructure	5.4
Environment	5.4
Criminal Justice	4.3
Health	4.0
Transparency	3.5
Education	2.8
Business Licensing	2.5
Vehicle Code	2.3
City Planning	2.3
Economic Development	2.1
Public Utilities	2.1
Social Services	1.8
Emergency Preparedness	1.6
Military/Veterans	1.1
Recreation	0.7
Morality	0.3
Immigration	0.1
Other or none	35.8
Total	100.0

shows, nearly one-third of the new laws are broadly targeted to local governments in general, another 20 percent cover more than one type of local government, typically both counties and cities. As for specific types of local government, 28.8 percent of the new statutes deal with counties, traditionally considered the administrative arms of state government; 18.8 percent focus on cities. Town governments are seldom specified as the target, only 1.1 percent of the bills specifically single out towns.

As for subject matter, fully 83.3 percent of the laws address the operation of local governments. Finance, government structure, and human resources were included as specific government operations coding categories; a more generalized "government operations" classification was used for laws that did not fall into those three categories. Many of these new laws are restrictive in nature, that is, they require local governments to adopt new rules and procedures or they prohibit certain practices in which local governments were engaged. Nearly 15 percent of the new statutes address substantive policy areas; many of the new laws dealing with government operations also contain a policy component. Twenty specific policy areas were included in the coding, with taxation and fees the modal category at 8.2 percent. Land use and public safety are the next most common policy areas at 6.9 percent and 6.8 percent, respectively. The policy areas that produced the most restrictive new statutes are transparency policy (requirements that local governments make information accessible to the public), morality policy (laws prohibiting cities from taking certain actions), and immigration policy (mandates that county government take a particular action on behalf of the state). To a lesser degree, new laws dealing with taxes and fees also have a restrictive impact on local governments by, for instance, redirecting the revenue generated by fees. On average, localities enjoyed the greatest degree of empowerment from new laws related to land use, infrastructure, economic development, and business licensing.

The mechanisms employed by states to restrict localities include outright prohibitions, mandated service standards, preemptions of or constraints on local actions, restrictions on revenue sources, and cost-share shifting. Among the most common tools states utilize to empower their local governments are authorizations to take actions, adoption of programs that contain appropriations for localities, repeal of prior mandates or expenditure requirements, and lifting of restrictions on revenue sources.

Reporting aggregate figures provide a sense of general trends across the nation during the 2011–2012 biennium. However, an examination of three states—one empowering, one restricting, and one in which the impact of the laws offset—captures the variation across them. In Virginia, an empowering state, three-quarters of the new laws address the general category of "local government" rather than specifying a particular type of locality. California, a restricting state, and Kansas, where the impact of the laws offsets, concentrate more of their laws on specific types of local government, particularly counties. Government operations are the most common subjects addressed in the new laws across all three of the states, although some variation exists in the relative emphasis on governmental structure, which is more prevalent in California than in the other two states. The states vary in the policy focus of the legislation they enact. In Virginia, infrastructure and taxation and fees are the two most frequent foci; in California it is criminal justice and health, and in Kansas land use is far and away the most targeted policy topic, with taxation and fees the second-most popular. A common pattern across the three states is the absence of new local government laws dealing with immigration policy or with morality policy.

The Evolving State–Local Relationship

Media reports of state raids on local treasuries and preemptions of authority prompted us to examine the statutory record for a two-year period in the aftermath of the Great Recession. Our methodology for extracting the positive and negative consequences of official state actions regarding local governments is promising as a means of directly measuring state–local outcomes. Our findings are intriguing. If the 2011–2012 biennium is generalizable to other time periods, states are actively engaged in legislating local government affairs, sometimes in a manner that expands local power, other times in ways that diminish local power. Contrary to contemporary media portrayals, the aggregate pattern in the legislation enacted in 2011–2012 is not primarily burdensome or restrictive but rather it is slightly more empowering of local governments. If this trend continues, it may be that some states and their localities are on the cusp of a period that will be characterized by less adversarial behavior. If so, the state–local relationship could yield a series of productive partnerships in which the two levels of government interact more harmoniously.

For a significant subset of states, legislatures did clip the wings of their local jurisdictions in 2011–2012. In those states, how will local governments adapt to the changed circumstances? As fiscal stress accumulates and authority becomes more circumscribed, local governments may be facing what has been termed a "new normal." The implications for public policy could be significant as the locus for decision making shifts from city halls to state capitols and the preferences of local communities become supplanted by the collective will of the legislature. As draconian as this may sound, some research has found that state constraints can function to stimulate innovative problem-solving behavior, at least insofar as municipalities (Krueger and Bernick 2009; Thoreson and Svara 2011) and school districts (Marschall, Rigby, and Jenkins 2011) are concerned. Of course, creativity is not an asset equally possessed by local jurisdictions.

What explains the shifting sands of U.S. state–local government relations? State–local relations in 2011 and 2012 did not unfold on a blank slate; they are built on a state's political traditions, history, and prior state–local relations (Zimmerman 1983). Earlier analysis of the 2011 legislative session suggests that formal legal relationships do not provide much explanation (Bowman and Kearney 2013). Both Dillon's Rule and home rule states address local relations in unpredictable ways. Neither does the nature of state–local relations appear to be driven by political theory, principles of federalism, or the professed value of local self-government or subsidiarity, despite treatises such as the *Federalist Papers,* contributions from public choice theorists on the advantages and disadvantages of scale, and the value of matching jurisdictional political choices and preferences with consequences (Tullock 1969; Olson 1965; Oates 1972). Understanding what is at play requires additional longitudinal research. Although we anticipate that temporal and spatial variance in state–local relations will continue, it is imperative that this supposition be tested. After all, the patterns we found for the 2011–2012 biennium may be aberrational. Research has demonstrated that, historically, cities have struggled to get state legislatures to accede to their preferences (Gamm and Kousser 2013); anecdotal evidence for the 2015 state legislative sessions makes a similar point (Greenblatt 2015).

In the second edition of his book, Deil Wright (1982: 354) quotes from a 1979 American Society for Public Administration paper written by G. Ross Stephens that takes up the issue of the states and their relationships with local governments. In the paper Stephens says, "Given the complexity and diversity in the American federal system, it is almost impossible to generalize about the role of the states vis-à-vis local governments." We certainly acknowledge the difficulties of aggregating and averaging state actions toward their localities in a way that maintains a sufficient level of accuracy and insight about 50 different state–local systems. That said, a fundamental and enduring issue in the study of intergovernmental relations is the distribution of power and authority across governments. Over the two and one-half centuries of the U.S. experiment in federalism, the state–local relationship has changed, but if anything, it is more important and certainly more complex now than ever before. Our research shows that through legislative actions, states continue to dominate the local government landscape; in many cases loosening strictures on localities, in other cases imposing new constraints. Our focus on the legislature does not blind us to the fact that actions taken by a state's executive branch and decisions emanating from the judicial branch also affect state–local relations, often modifying or even reversing actions taken by the legislature.[14] In addition, actions and decisions of the Trump Administration and a Republican-controlled Congress will affect state and local governments in ways that are difficult to predict. Suffice it to say, federal budget cuts, policy shifts, and program changes that affect states negatively will eventually burden local governments. One reality seems indisputable: state–local government relationships will continue to evolve.

Notes

1   Alan Ehrenhalt, an editor at Stateline, commented that although the relationship between the federal government and the states receives the lion's share of attention, "the state–local connection is equally important" (Ehrenhalt 2011).

2   *Merriam v. Moody's Executors*, 25 Iowa 163, 170 (1868). Dillon's Rule was first written in the case of *City of Clinton v. Cedar Rapids and Missouri River Railroad Co.* (1868).

3   In updating the Stephens (1974) index for the period 1978 to 2008, Bowman and Kearney (2011) report modest changes in aggregate levels of state centralization, however within some states, substantial shifts occur over the 30-year period.

4   The governor appointed an emergency financial manager for Detroit in 2013, despite protestations from the city's elected officials. Later that year, the city filed for chapter 9 bankruptcy protection.

5   The city of Cleveland sued the state of Ohio arguing that the state's action was an unconstitutional preemption of its home rule powers. A lower court judge sided with Cleveland in 2012 and struck down the state law.

6   Although the official end date of the U.S. recession is June 2009, many observers contend that its impact continued beyond that date, especially for state governments. For example, as recently as its Fall 2012 Fiscal Survey, the National Association of State Budget Officers declared that "the lingering effects of the recession are still hampering state budgets" (p. vii). See also the Perlman and Scicchitano chapter in this book for additional discussion on the impact of the Great Recession on state and local governments.

7   In Louisiana, the keyword search included "parish" and "parishes" also.

8   In some instances, bills affecting general purpose local governments also addressed single-purpose entities such as school districts. These bills remained in the dataset because of their coverage of general purpose jurisdictions. However, if only special districts, townships, or school districts were covered by the enactment, then it was excluded.

9   The consistency between coders was confirmed through use of an inter-coder reliability test. The Cronbach's alpha coefficient exceeded .8, widely considered to be the threshold for "good" consistency. In cases of disagreement, a third coder resolved the impasse.

10   Many of the laws had a substantive policy component, including some that addressed government operations.

11   Oregon was among the ranks of biennial session states until passage of a constitutional amendment in 2010 that established annual legislative sessions.

12   As noted, our measurement scheme does not capture the scope or salience of state legislation. It is evident from a review of the substance of the laws in the dataset that they vary in the amount of discretion

and authority they grant or rescind. By treating all statutes as equal, we are obviously capturing only a single dimension of legislative actions toward local governments.

13 We rely on Richardson's (2011) designation of states' Dillon's Rule status.

14 For example, in 2012 the Pennsylvania legislature enacted Act 13, a major overhaul of the state's regulation of the oil and gas industry. Among other things, the new law restricted local governments' ability to zone and regulate natural gas drilling. In 2013, the Pennsylvania Supreme Court ruled that these restrictions on local governments violated the state's constitution.

References

Bowman, Ann O'M. and Richard C. Kearney. 2011. "Second order devolution: Data and doubt." *Publius: The Journal of Federalism* 41: 563–585.

Bowman, Ann O'M. and Richard C. Kearney. 2012. "Are U.S. cities losing power and authority? Perceptions of local government actors." *Urban Affairs Review* 48: 528–546.

Bowman, Ann O'M. and Richard C. Kearney. 2013. "How do cities fare when the state legislature is in session?" Paper presented at the 43rd Annual Conference of the Urban Affairs Association, San Francisco, April 3–6.

Ehrenhalt, Alan. 2011. "Alan Ehrenhalt: The relationship between state and local governments," Pew Center on the States. Retrieved from www.pewtrusts.org/en/research-and-analysis/q-and-a/2011/10/14 (accessed April 25, 2012).

Ehrenhalt, Alan. 2013. "Devolution and arrogance: States can't resist the temptation to boss their localities around." *Governing,* September.

Frug, Gerald E. and David J. Barron. 2008. *City Bound: How States Stifle Urban Innovation*. Ithaca, NY: Cornell University Press.

Gamm, Gerald and Thad Kousser. 2013. "No strength in numbers: The failure of big-city bills in American state legislatures, 1880–2000." *American Political Science Review* 107: 663–678.

Greenblatt, Alan. 2015. "In red states, cities can't win." Retrieved from http://governing.com/teplates/gov_print_article?id=293906321 (accessed April 6, 2015).

Hooghe, Liesbet and Gary Marks. 2009. "Does efficiency shape the territorial structure of government?" *Annual Review of Political Science*. 12: 225–241.

Kincaid, John. 1998. "The devolution tortoise and the centralization hare." *New England Economic Review* (May-June): 13–40.

Krane, Dale, Platon N. Rigos, and Melvin B. Hill Jr. 2001. *Home Rule in America: A Fifty State Handbook*. Washington, DC: Congressional Quarterly Press.

Krueger, Skip and Ethan M. Bernick. 2009. "State rules and local governance choices." *Publius: The Journal of Federalism* 40: 697–718.

Marschall, Melissa J., Elizabeth Rigby, and Jasmine Jenkins. 2011. "Do state policies constrain local actors? The impact of English only on language instruction in public schools." *Publius: The Journal of Federalism*. 41: 586–609.

National Conference of State Legislatures. 2011. *State Budget Update: Summer 2011*. Denver, CO: NCSL.

National Governors Association and National Association of State Budget Officers. 2011. *The Fiscal Survey of States*. Washington, DC: NGA/NASBO.

Oates, Wallace. 1972. *Fiscal Federalism*. New York: Harcourt Brace Jovanovich.

Olson, Mancur. 1965. *The Logic of Collective action*. Cambridge, MA: Harvard University Press.

Richardson, Jesse. J, Jr. 2011. "Dillon's rule is from Mars, home rule is from Venus: Local government autonomy and the rules of statutory construction." *Publius: The Journal of Federalism* 41(4): 662–685.

Schneider, Saundra K., William G. Jacoby, and Daniel C. Lewis. 2011. "Public opinion toward intergovernmental policy responsibilities." *Publius: The Journal of Federalism* 41: 1–30.

Stephens, G. Ross. 1974. "State centralization and the erosion of local autonomy." *Journal of Politics* 36: 44–76.

Stephens, G. Ross. 1979. "Fiscal roles of the states in a federal system." Paper presented at the national meeting of the American Society for Public Administration, Baltimore, MD, April 3.

Thoreson, Karen and James H. Svara. 2011 "How local governments are navigating the fiscal crisis: Taking stock and looking forward." In *The Municipal Year Book*, 75–82. Washington, DC: International City/County Management Association.

Tullock, Gordon. 1969. "Federalism: Problems of scale." *Public Choice* 6: 19–29.

U.S. Advisory Commission on Intergovernmental Relations. 1981. *Measuring Local Government Authority*. M-131. Washington, DC: Advisory Commission on Intergovernmental Relations.

Vischer, Robert K. 2001. "Subsidiarity as a principle of governance: Beyond devolution." *Indiana Law Review* 35: 103–142.

Wolman, Harold, Robert McManmon, Michael E. Bell, and David Brunori. 2010. "Comparing Local Government Autonomy Across States." In *The Property Tax and Local Autonomy*, edited by Michael E. Bell, David Brunori, and Joan M. Youngman, 69–114. Cambridge, MA: Lincoln Institute of Land Policy.

Wood, Curtis H. 2011. "Exploring the determinants of the empowered U.S. municipality." *State and Local Government Review* 43: 123–139.

Wright, Deil S. 1978. *Understanding Intergovernmental Relations: Public Policy and Participants' Perspectives on Local, State, and National Governments*. North Scituate, MA: Duxbury.

Wright, Deil S. 1982. *Understanding Intergovernmental Relations*, 2nd edition. Monterey, CA: Brooks Cole.

Zimmerman, Joseph F. 1983. *State–Local Relations: A Partnership Approach*. New York: Praeger.

12 Pulling the Lever

The State's Role in Catalyzing Local Change

Ricardo S. Morse and Carl W. Stenberg

Since the Great Recession, local governments have been confronted with difficult policy and program choices in response to declining economies and growing budget constraints. Decisions to reduce costs, some easy and some not so easy, were made and implemented, such as: salary, travel, and training freezes; across-the-board budget cuts; temporary furloughs and layoffs; vacant position eliminations; fee increases; reserve fund withdrawals; maintenance and vehicle replacement deferrals; and minor service reductions.[1] For some jurisdictions, these cutbacks may not be sufficient to adjust to anticipated intergovernmental trends (Stenberg and Morse 2014).

According to the National League of Cities, local fiscal conditions are improving across the country and revenues are nearing pre-recession levels (McFarland and Pagano 2016). Yet, the effects of the recession on local budgets, coupled with likely state cuts to local aid and downward shifts of services, reductions in federal discretionary grants-in-aid, and increasing unfunded mandates, have led some observers to argue that the next steps include "fundamentally rethink[ing] how . . . the local government functions" (Thoreson and Svara 2011: 82). Policies, programs, and practices, which during better economic times would not have been on the cutback agenda, may now need to be considered as well as more robust collaborative strategies and adaptive realignments (Hilvert and Swindell 2013). Among these are: expanded outsourcing to other local governments, non-profit organizations, and private firms; eliminating, sharing, or merging services; and consolidating local jurisdictions.

For decades, critics of local government structure and advocates for leaner public bureaucracies have called for these and other reforms, yet little progress was evident. Scholars and practitioners recognized that few, if any, purely local problems existed and that most "wicked problems" ignored boundaries and thus required boundary-crossing approaches. Nevertheless, there have been few political rewards or clear financial "drivers" for local professionals and elected officials to take these actions. Jurisdiction has remained a powerful constraint, especially for local officials pre-occupied with reelection (Frederickson 2005). Some public officials, like Chicago Mayor Rahm Emanuel, have observed that "You never want a serious crisis to go to waste," and argued that current and projected economic conditions present an opportune time to launch strategies to reinvent local government structure, functions, and relationships (Greenblatt 2011b: 26). This chapter explores the state's role in leveraging local change.

The State's Role as Catalyst for Local Change

Research on the responses by local governments to fiscal hardship, such as recessions, state aid reductions, and the loss of federal general revenue sharing, has demonstrated the resilience of city and county officials (Miller 2010; Martin, Levey, and Cawley 2012). These studies are also consistent with the chief findings from research on cutback management coping strategies.[2]

By and large, locally-induced change has been evolutionary, conventional, and incremental. Most local governments have not made fundamental changes in their functions, relationships, or structures as a result of the Great Recession (Ammons, Smith, and Stenberg 2012; Stenberg 2011; Hoene and Pagano 2011; Nelson 2012). Yet innovation is certainly occurring, and Thoreson and Svara (2011: 81) find that local governments have "been more proactive and strategic" than in earlier periods of retrenchment but "substantial innovation is only beginning."

As the creators of local governments, states could play a pivotal role in efforts to realign local services and structures to prepare for the fiscal challenges that lie ahead and avoid a protracted period of "fend-for-yourself localism" (Greenblatt 2011a). In this context, state governments could more aggressively push for major changes in local services and structures that cannot be accomplished locally.

State intervention to leverage change has been politically acceptable only under extreme financial exigencies affecting a single jurisdiction. Since the Great Depression of the 1930s, 15 states have established an agency or system for monitoring the fiscal health of municipalities and for assisting jurisdictions experiencing distress (Levine, Justice, and Scorsone 2013). Even where a financial control board or emergency manager has been appointed, only modest changes have been made, which normally have been temporary with the jurisdiction desiring to return to the old ways of doing business (Ammons, Smith, and Stenberg 2012).

Research indicates that many local elected officials and managers believe their state has been more of an adversary than a partner in these efforts, acting intrusively, not cooperatively (Kearney, Swicegood, and Bowman 2011; Bowman and Kearney 2011). As one city manager participating in a 2010 ICMA survey responded: "State agencies rarely provide value to local governments, but always steal resources, increase costs. . .and obstruct local authority" (Kearney, Swicegood, and Bowman 2011: 18). The resulting push-back by city and county officials is attributable to, "a two-word mantra: 'local control.' They see states as meddling in the affairs of local government. And they fear that, under consolidation, communities that always have made decisions for themselves will be forced to abide by the dictates of outsiders" (Goodman 2008: 26).

A *Governing* article on state intervention in fiscally distressed municipalities reached a similar conclusion about the state–local relationship: "Cities don't want to be treated like children. Duly elected officials don't like being told what to do by state overseers; they want a partnership, not a dictatorship" (Farmer 2014: 44). Basically, those holding this view would hypothesize that the states will neither empower local governments to adapt nimbly and entrepreneurially to economic challenges, nor will they provide leadership in facilitating or orchestrating local service and structural responses to fiscal retrenchment. A 2017 National League of Cities survey concluded:

> The rise of preemptive legislation suggests that state governments are concerned about increased local autonomy and the patchwork of regulations that may exist within the state. As a result, a pro-preemption narrative is emerging in an attempt to put cities in their place.
> (DuPuis et al. 2017: 24; see also Riverstone-Newell 2017)

But the narrative does not always result in consistent action. In Florida, for example, the topic of interlocal cooperation has long been an important part of state-level policy conversations, but the state has done very little to incentivize this form of alternative service delivery. In fact, some recent actions may be viewed as an (unintended) disincentive to working together. Governor Rick Scott's review of all independent districts was based on a widespread view that they often have too much authority and too little oversight and accountability. Taxing authority for some independent districts has been rolled back through legislation in recent years based on the same concerns. The governor also abolished the Department of Community Affairs (DCA), the state agency charged with overseeing growth management issues. As a result, significant authority over growth management was essentially handed back to local governments, although bills have been introduced to return that oversight and authority to the state. While studies on service sharing and consolidation have been conducted by the Office of Program Policy and Governmental Accountability (OPPAGA), there does not seem to be a major, strategic focus on assisting or incentivizing local government change. The Florida Legislative Committee on Intergovernmental Relations (LCIR), which historically was an important proponent at the state level for interlocal cooperation and service-sharing, was defunded in 2010.[3]

Other research suggests that state rules can induce local officials to cooperate with other jurisdictions and to take actions that otherwise would be avoided because they would be too politically costly (Krueger and Bernick 2010; Krueger, Walker, and Bernick 2011). For example, a research report on regional consolidation prepared for the Federal Reserve Bank of Boston concluded:

> ... in states with fragmented public service provision, state legislatures could encourage further regionalization by adopting stronger and more targeted regulations and fiscal incentives. Such measures would likely result in accelerated regionalization, compared with the situation in which local governments pursue intermunicipal partnerships and service sharing without these types of intervention.
>
> (Kodrzycki 2013: 28)

The survey of city managers noted above reached the conclusion that devolution has two faces: states are giving localities greater discretionary authority over their finances, especially their ability to raise revenues and issue debt, while at the same time they are "withdrawing state-shared taxes and fees, 'borrowing' from state-funded local government accounts, and imposing new financial requirements on local governments." The authors called this a version of "shift and shaft" federalism (Kearney, Swicegood, and Bowman 2011: 18). Others have called it "devolution by budget cut" (Greenblatt 2011a: 26).

Bottom-Up and Top-Down Approaches

There are three possible approaches states can take to leveraging greater interlocal collaboration and change: a "bottom-up" approach, a "top-down" approach, or a combined approach. The "bottom-up" or "carrot" approach is facilitative, giving localities greater discretionary power to work across jurisdictional and public-private boundaries to forge strategies and build relationships for delivering services more efficiently, effectively, and equitably. This approach is sometimes called "second order devolution" (Bowman and Kearney 2011). Examples include statutory authorization or administrative actions providing for:

- expanded authority for local governments to enter into service sharing, transfer, or consolidation agreements;
- facilitation of local management improvement practices such as collective purchasing and private contracting arrangements;
- expanded authority to use regional councils of governments or state area-wide districts to provide local services;
- liberalization or standardization of procedures for annexation, downsizing governing boards, changing forms of government, and consolidating or dissolving jurisdictions;
- state funding to support local planning studies for charter revisions and other actions to enable shared or consolidated services and merger or dissolution of local units;
- strengthening the power of voters to compel service or jurisdictional mergers;
- designating a state office to provide technical assistance to local government service sharing or merger initiatives and structural reform efforts;
- incentives in state aid formulas for regional collaboration or local unit consolidation; and
- establishing a statewide benchmarking system to provide the public and policy-makers with information about local productivity and progress.

The "top-down" or "stick" approach is directive, where governors or legislators take steps to induce realignment of local services or structures through legislation and other actions, such as:

- imposing limits on local revenues and creation of new local units;
- strengthening the authority and capacity of counties to serve as regional governments, expand their scope of authorized services, and sort-out and mandate transfer of functional responsibilities between counties and municipalities;
- transferring financial and/or administrative responsibility for a service to the state;
- creating metropolitan authorities to provide services on an area-wide or regional basis;
- mandating interlocal cooperation in service delivery and regional consolidation of a local service;
- eliminating or reducing the number of "non-viable" units—like some townships, rural school districts, and small general purpose local units—having very limited size and functional responsibilities or weak financial bases; and
- curtailing or terminating state aid or local revenue authority to units that fail to meet effectiveness criteria (size, cost-savings, etc.).

Svara has observed that states "have generally avoided any systematic examination of the system of local governments used in their states or the need to adapt to changing conditions. No state has undertaken the kind of comprehensive reorganization of local governments observed in a number of other countries" (Svara 2012: 27). Yet there are examples of states attempting to play a catalytic role in local government change. These examples may be viewed as pilot-projects or prototypes that other states may learn from and adapt where appropriate.

Leveraging Examples

Our review of research reports, academic studies, and websites featuring news of relevant state initiatives revealed a range of leveraging examples embracing the above approaches during and since the Great Recession. This review was supplemented by surveys of the executive directors of state municipal leagues and county associations in Fall 2013. The purposes of the surveys were to identify legislation that had been introduced and enacted in any of the above areas between 2010 and 2013, gubernatorial proposals relative to major changes in local services and structures, and related studies by commissions, universities, and others. Officials in 38 states responded to the survey and follow-up telephone interviews.

We found noteworthy initiatives and actions taken in 11 states: Indiana, Michigan, Minnesota, New Jersey, New York, North Carolina, Ohio, Oregon, Pennsylvania, Vermont, and Wisconsin. In only four of these states—Indiana, Michigan, New Jersey, and New York—was state leveraging a component of a broader strategic initiative by the governor and legislature to achieve major state policy goals, such as reducing pressures on property taxes by promoting more efficient and effective local service delivery or making local government operations more transparent and accountable. In these states, initiatives to leverage local change have survived gubernatorial transitions. In two others—Minnesota and Ohio—promising initiatives were taken but they were not part of a broader policy agenda. In the remaining states, the incentives were relatively limited in terms of the funds available and numbers of participating local governments. They were more narrow attempts to stimulate change, most often in particular units, services, or management approaches.

The remainder of this chapter focuses on the four large-scale approaches which we have monitored since 2014. These were selected because they represented a strategic push on the part of state government to spur transformational change at the local level. With respect to the legal relationship between local units and their state government, only Michigan has given localities broad home rule authority and liberally construed devolution of powers while New Jersey and New York have granted them home rule authority over most structural, functional, and financial matters. Indiana granted local governments home rule in 1980, but state regulation of finances, prohibitions on the exercise of powers, and preemptions of authority have limited local autonomy (Krane, Rigos, and Hill 2001: 476–478). Interestingly, governors of all four states have attempted what could be characterized as top-down or "stick" strategies.

Indiana

Indiana was a pioneer in the "top-down" approach to city-county consolidation in the late 1960's with the merger of the City of Indianapolis and Marion County via state legislation to form "Unigov." No other state has taken such a step. The state also has been a partner with local governments in some areas. For example, under the OneIndiana joint purchasing initiative, 160 localities have been able to participate with the state on road salt contract bids, which in 2009 saved $8.5 million, about 40 percent of previous year costs. The Indiana Association of Cities and Towns and the Association of Indiana Counties worked closely with the Departments of Administration and Transportation on the salt partnership.

More than four decades after Unigov, Governor Mitch Daniels proposed a legislative initiative to overhaul local government in 2008. Governor Daniels' call followed release in December 2007 of a report by the bi-partisan Indiana Commission on Local Government Reform, which had been charged by former governor Joe Kernan with examining the structure of local governments in the state and making recommendations for reform to reduce costs and increase efficiency and effectiveness. The commission found: "Our many complex layers of government are often difficult to understand, monitor and hold accountable" (Indiana Commission on Local Government Reform 2007: 3). Indiana has 3,086 units of local government, including 1,008 limited-purpose townships, and 10,700 elected officials, 1,100 of which assess property.

Among the recommendations of the 2007 study were a series of proposals to strengthen and streamline the 92 counties through a single elected county executive and unified legislative body, to eliminate townships, and to transfer all present township responsibilities to the county executive. The proposal would have removed over 5,000 elected officials. All local governments were encouraged to take voluntary action to coordinate and consolidate units and services. A state office would be designated to provide technical assistance to these governments, and a statewide benchmarking system would be established to provide citizens and policy-makers information on local implementation progress and productivity.

Not surprisingly, interest groups opposed Governor Daniels' proposal, and most of the local restructuring legislation failed to pass. However, by 2015 about one-third of the Commission's 27 recommendations had been acted on. Among the accomplishments were shifting property tax assessment duties from townships to the county assessor, which resulted in elimination of 168 elected township assessors, transferring child welfare funding from counties to the state, consolidating emergency public safety dispatch systems, tightening restrictions on school bonds, providing more joint purchasing opportunities for schools, libraries, and local governments, and establishing a statewide benchmarking system.

Among the recommendations on which no action had been taken were those: to establish a single elected chief executive and a unified legislative body for each county; to transfer duties of the auditor, treasurer, recorder, assessor, surveyor, and sheriff to the elected county executive; to transfer duties of poor relief, fire protection, emergency medical services, and cemeteries from townships to the elected county executive; to shift funding for trial courts, probation, and public defenders to the state; and to strengthen powers of voters to compel school and township consolidations.

The Indiana Commission on Local Government Reform represented a serious attempt by a state government to catalyze local government reform. While many of the most substantial recommendations (such as eliminating township governments) were not implemented due to significant political barriers, the Indiana case still represents a substantial "top-down" attempt to drive local government change.

Michigan

Michigan Governor Rick Snyder announced his support for local government consolidation in 2011. With "nearly 1800 separate cities, villages, and townships stretched across 83 counties, consolidation seemed way overdue" (Wattrick 2011). Governor Snyder supported legislation allowing local governments to set up metropolitan authorities, subject to voter approval. Governor Snyder's initiative came in the wake of a 2010 proposal by his predecessor, Jennifer Granholm, to set aside $50 million of the State Aid Fund for a grant competition for school districts to demonstrate savings through consolidation and service sharing. The incentives were intended to help cover the up-front costs of restructuring, such as technology purchases, but the legislature did not include the Fund in its education budget appropriation.

Like locally initiated proposals, Governor Snyder's plan and related legislative proposals to streamline Michigan's 2,314 local governments (1,242 of which are townships), were greeted with opposition and proved politically unacceptable. A consolidation assessment report found no compelling evidence that mergers had slowed the growth rate of governmental costs or bolstered economic development. In response to Governor Snyder, Wayne County Executive Robert Ficano said, "I just think it's unreasonable to think such a large merger would be even feasible at this point" (Wattrick 2011). Another factor was distrust of state government. A 2010 Michigan Public Policy survey of Michigan local government officials found that 49 percent reported that they can "seldom" or "almost never" trust the state government to do what is right; a 2017 poll found that 70 percent of these officials "believe the State government is taking away too much decision-making authority from local governments" (Center for Local, State, and Urban Policy 2010, 2017).

Also in 2011, Governor Snyder proposed and the legislature passed Public Act 63, the Economic Vitality Incentive Grant Program (EVIGP), which accompanied the State's constitutional revenue sharing program and provided financial incentives to cities, villages, and townships for combining operations. These funds were intended to offset costs incurred with mergers, interlocal agreements, and other cooperative undertakings. A year later, Public Act 236 renamed EVIGP the Competitive Grant Assistance Program (CGAP) and appropriated $10 million for the first round of FY 2012 awards, half of which was earmarked for public safety. Counties, authorities, school districts, community colleges, and universities were made eligible. Among the criteria for judging proposals were cost savings, efficiencies, taxpayer benefit, commitment to collaboration and best practices, and completion timeline.

The Michigan Treasury Department awarded $4.3 million to 27 EVIGP projects in the first round of funding. Another $10.5 million was awarded to 32 applicants in the second round of FY 2012. In FY 2013, another $10 million was awarded to 28 communities in two rounds of funding. In FY 2014, more than $19.6 million was awarded to 28 local units, bringing the total incentive funding to over $44 million in the first four years (eight funding cycles) awarded to 115 local government units. Nearly all of the recipients proposed service consolidations—especially fire, police and public safety, 911 emergency dispatch and communications, and information technology—and service collaborations, while only two jurisdictional mergers were proposed—the City of Watervliet with Watervliet Township and Onekama Township with the Village of Onekama. It is worth noting that in FY 2013 program language mentioned a focus on "stimulating . . . new mergers, consolidations, and/or cooperative efforts/collaborations of existing services." FY 2014 announcements stated that "special consideration and preference is given to proposals calling for complete mergers of two or more local units of government."

Turning to Detroit, the governor's "top-down" effort to end the city's long-standing fiscal decline to insolvency through appointment of an emergency manager garnered national attention. Detroit joined seven other Michigan cities having emergency financial managers—Allen Park, Benton Harbor, Ecorse, Flint, Hamtramck, Lincoln Park, and Pontiac. As the largest American city in history to declare bankruptcy, Detroit considered a range of financial and structural options to regain solvency, such as cutting retirement benefits, spinning off the Detroit Water and Sewer Department to form a three-county regional authority or selling it to a private company, transferring street light maintenance from a city department to a special district, and selling city-owned art from the Detroit Institute of the Arts collection. Fiscal exigency spurred discussions between

Detroit and Wayne County officials about merging services such as jails, health, and bus systems, but very few initiatives made it past the conversation stage. However, in the first round of FY 2014 CGAP funding, Detroit was awarded a grant to help facilitate the city joining the statewide records management system. Additionally, Wayne County received a grant toward the consolidation of Detroit's vital records department with the county's department.

In March 2013, the governor signed amendments to the 1990 Emergency Financial Manager Act that require local governments to submit financial projections to the state and give state-appointed emergency managers power to set aside labor contracts, fire local officials, and dissolve a community or school district. In addition to seeking to cut revenue sharing by one-third, Governor Snyder proposed to make such state aid contingent on local adoption of cost-saving measures like securing wage and benefit concessions from public employees and agreeing to consolidate services. By 2015, Detroit was emerging from bankruptcy and Governor Snyder was receiving significant praise for his role in the turnaround, which involved significant collaboration and restructuring.

Despite what seemed like building momentum with the CGAP program, the legislature has not included funding for CGAP since its FY 2014 budget. As recently as April 2017, the Department of Treasury, which managed the program, could give no reason for the lack of funding. It will be interesting to see if there is a push to re-fund the program in future budget cycles.

New Jersey

New Jersey's governor, Chris Christie, and his predecessor both linked the fragmented structure of local government in their state—21 counties, 566 municipalities, 523 school districts, and 234 special districts in 2012—to high property tax burdens. But political support to mandate or induce dramatic changes has been absent or inconsistent. In 2008, former Governor Jon Corzine successfully eliminated a portion of state aid for towns under 5,000 population and imposed a 50 percent aid reduction in one program for towns with 10,000 or fewer residents. In that year the New Jersey Shared Services Association was established as a non-profit, nonpartisan organization promoting greater efficiency in local service delivery and reduced costs of government. The association and its affiliates work with county shared services coordinators to write grants, provide information on best practices, and give advice and administrative support.

Governor Christie, with bipartisan support from legislators, endorsed service sharing as a way of reducing property taxes, although state aid for such purposes was ended. As a result, over half the counties eliminated the shared service coordinator position, which was tasked with leading efforts to explore opportunities such as consolidations of police and schools with neighboring jurisdictions.

Interest in sharing strategies can be traced to a 2006 report by the Joint Legislative Committee on Government Consolidation and Shared Services. The committee recommended creation of a permanent unit to study the structures, functions, and finances of county and municipal governments and underscored the need for consolidation and service-sharing. It called for passage of legislation to achieve greater operational efficiencies by streamlining and facilitating local processes in these areas, including interlocal functional transfers and regional service delivery units. In 2007, the legislature and Governor Corzine approved creation of the Local Unit Alignment, Reorganization, and Consolidation Commission (LUARCC), which operated until 2010. The Commission has not met since that time, and has no staff.

Also in 2007, the legislature passed the Uniform Shared Services and Consolidation Act to help reduce property taxes by promoting local government efficiency. In the introduction to the bill, the legislature noted the obstacles of political resistance, overlapping and antiquated laws, and civil service constraints, and committed to removing these hurdles: "The State largely has employed a 'carrot' approach to incentivizing consolidation and service sharing for over 30 years, and for real progress to occur in reducing the rate of property tax increase, the 'stick' approach is appropriate…". The act re-codified existing laws that authorized local units to enter into agreements to provide or receive services by adopting a resolution and to contract for joint services, and made a number of process improvements. The act sought to make the 1977 Municipal Consolidation Act more attractive by authorizing local governing bodies or registered voters to petition the Local Finance Board of the Division of Local Government Services in the Department of Community Affairs to create a Municipal Consolidation Study Commission to prepare a consolidation plan. Upon approval of the plan by the affected governing boards or voters, the division was directed to create a task force to facilitate consolidation and provide technical assistance. The director of the division was required to establish a Sharing Available Resources Efficiently (SHARE) program to provide grants and loans for local feasibility studies of shared service agreements, joint service operation contracts, or municipal consolidation and for implementation support. Eligible expenditures were consultant fees and one-time start-up costs such as terminal leave benefits. The SHARE program built on initiatives by two previous governors (Christine Todd Whitman and Jim McGreevy) to incentivize "regional efficiency" projects. It was defunded in Governor Christie's 2011 budget.

Senate President Stephen Sweeney, a Democrat, joined Republican Governor Christie in a bipartisan effort to bolster implementation of the joint committee's 2006 recommendations. The legislation introduced in the 2012–2013 session by President Sweeney (S-2) embraced a more punitive "stick" approach. The preamble to the bill stated:

> Experience with the old laws and experience with the "Uniform Shared Services and Consolidation Act" . . . has made it clear that shared services, joint meetings, and consolidation cannot be effective and viable options when the local units are tied to Civil Service rules and tenure provisions limiting their economic feasibility.

Under S-2, New Jersey's Local Unit Alignment, Reorganization and Consolidation Commission, in the Department of Community Affairs, would conduct studies of counties, municipalities, and schools to determine whether functional or structural consolidation would result in efficiencies and tax savings. The commission's proposals would be transmitted to the governor and legislature. At the next general election, voters would be asked to approve the recommended shared or consolidated services; any town that failed to pass these changes would lose state aid equal to the projected cost savings. This legislation would revitalize the moribund LUARCC.

The New Jersey State League of Municipalities opposed the proposal to take away state aid, and unions were opposed because it superseded civil service and tenure provisions (Friedman 2012). Senate President Sweeney explained his position: "My approach quite honestly is the stick approach. If you don't share, we're going to reduce your state aid. Then for the people in the local community, there's no state involvement, there's no state money. They want more expensive government? They got it" (Magyar 2012; Goodman 2008). The Senate passed the bill in November 2012, but the Assembly failed to do so. It was reintroduced in subsequent legislative sessions but did not pass.

In 2013 the governor signed The Common Sense Shared Services Pilot Program Act which implements a pilot program for municipalities in Camden, Morris, Ocean, Sussex, and Warren counties. This legislation permits local governing bodies to remove certain tenured employees who are affected by a shared services agreement.

Another noteworthy New Jersey initiative by the Christie Administration in 2011 was a Local Best Practices Checklist of budgeting, management, and cost-control tools developed by the Division of Local Government Services. Annually, each local government was required to fill out the survey in order to receive the final five percent of its total annual aid allocation. A sliding scale of up to five percent of total aid could be withheld by the division for municipalities failing to reply "yes" or "not applicable" to fewer than 22 of the 30 questions on the current survey. The Best Practices Inventory categories are general management, finance and audit, procurement, budget preparation and presentation, health insurance, and personnel. Responses must be certified as being accurate by the chief administrative officer and chief financial officer, and also certified by the clerk that the results were on the agenda for discussion at a municipal governing board meeting. The first question in the 2016–2017 inventory dealt with shared services: "Has your municipality 1) explored all potential shared services opportunities; and 2) filed a copy of all shared service agreements presently in effect for which it provides the service . . . ?" Municipal officials were directed to comment on whether an agreement had resulted and, if not, to explain the reasons.

An August 2011 survey revealed both progress and challenges that lie ahead for locally initiated service-sharing. With 30 percent of the 566 municipalities responding, 82 percent reported using shared service contracts in the previous year. Several obstacles to shared services were identified, however: "... 40 percent said opposition from citizens was the primary obstacle; 36 percent indicated that concern over the loss of home rule was a driving barrier, and 34 percent indicated issues related to shared service contracts presented challenges" (Sadeghi and Callahan 2011: 5). A Rutgers-Eagleton poll released in April 2014 revealed reduced public support for consolidation compared with a 2010 survey, from 54 to 45 percent Opposition to merger grew from 38 to 46 percent. About one-third of the respondents in both polls indicated consolidation would improve local efficiency and the same proportion believed it would produce little change. One explanation for the decline was skepticism about consolidation producing significant property tax cuts, in the 10 percent range. The 2014 merger of Princeton Township and Borough produced an initial five percent reduction, but its sustainability was questionable (Eagleton Institute of Politics 2014). Sustaining such savings would likely require realigning expensive and politically connected services—police and fire, courts, and schools—which have often resisted consolidation or regionalization.

In summary, shared services has enjoyed a long period of bipartisan gubernatorial and legislative support in New Jersey. Yet this official backing has been wavering and inconsistent. In recent years, as property taxes have risen support for a range of top-down restructuring initiatives has grown from improving management and budget practices, to streamlining operations, to sharing or consolidating services, to merging jurisdictions. A combination of incentives and mandates has been used to leverage local change, although the most drastic steps embodied in S-2 were not enacted in part due to local official opposition. Other initiatives such as LUARCC, the SHARE program, and state aid for shared services coordinators have not been sustained. In some respects, New Jersey's efforts to reduce the size and costs of local government are impressive, but whether they will be sufficient to stabilize or reduce property tax rates remains to be determined.

New York

Five recent New York governors have embraced service sharing and local restructuring. Like Governor Christie, Andrew M. Cuomo has coupled the large number of local governments in the state—including 3,453 counties, cities, towns, villages, school districts, and fire districts—in 2012 with high property taxes. He has led efforts to impose rate caps, reduce individual and business tax burdens, and provide a property tax freeze credit. Incentives to promote local efficiency and reduce the costs of local government through collaboration and consolidation are key components of achieving his agenda.

The Department of State's Division of Local Government Services administers the main incentive program under the Local Government Efficiency portfolio (Local Government Efficiency Grants and Local Government Citizen's Reorganization and Empowerment Grant programs). The department also provides training and technical assistance to help control local costs, promote efficiencies, and coordinate joint service provision.

In an April 2008 report, *21st Century Local Government*, the bipartisan New York State Commission on Local Government Efficiency and Competiveness called for greater state encouragement of local service sharing. Since 2005, a Shared Municipal Services Incentive program had been included in the state budget. In response to the commission's recommendation, the 2008–2009 budget allocated $29.4 million[4] in grants to incentivize shared service initiatives under a new moniker, "Local Government Efficiency" (LGe). The revised program focused its attention on achieving cost-savings through interlocal cooperation. Planning grants were made available to study opportunities to achieve cost-savings through cooperative agreements and shared or consolidated service initiatives, as well as for city or county charter revision studies that covered functional consolidation, service sharing, mergers, or dissolution. In addition to these planning grants, implementation grants were made available to help defray costs such as capital, equipment, and transitional personnel. Cost-sharing between the state and local awardees is 50–50 for planning studies and 90–10 for implementation projects. Planning grants are capped at $12,500 while a jurisdiction's maximum total award is $100,000. For the 2016–2017 program year, $4 million in LGe funds were made available to local governments, with $3.6 million earmarked for implementation projects.

Among the general functional reorganization categories posted on the division's website were education, utilities, public safety, and transportation. Examples of other specific shared services projects for which LGe awards were made included GIS and information technology, office space, zoning and code enforcement, records management, health insurance, courts, and parks and recreation. Between 2006 and 2014, 161 shared services studies and projects and 120 cooperative agreements were undertaken. There were 92 functional consolidation studies and 27 related implementation projects. With respect to dissolution, 52 studies were funded, mostly involving villages, while 12 implementation projects were conducted. There is no available record of the villages that were actually dissolved as a result of an LGe project, although a review of the general government and governmental reorganization award lists reveals at least nine villages that have been dissolved or are in the process of doing so. According to the department, since 2005 New York State has invested over $85 million in 466 LGe projects, which participating local governments expect to result in more than $600 million in savings to taxpayers (New York Department of State 2016: 2).

LGe grants were also offered for "transformative" pilot projects that had cost-savings potential. Examples of possible twenty-first-century demonstration projects eligible for funding included regional smart growth planning and development, multi-county service provision, consolidated school operations, expansion of county services, countywide or multi-municipal policing, and metropolitan municipal corporations. Municipalities that consolidated jurisdictions or services were eligible to receive financial incentives, such as a percentage of the combined property tax revenues, an increase in state discretionary aid, or a flat amount over a five-year period. However, in the end, only one project received funding in this category. The demonstration category has been discontinued.

In 2012, a Local Government Performance and Efficiency Program was included in the LGe portfolio. This program provided awards to local governments that produced recurring financial savings or lowered property tax growth. In 2013 over $12 million in three-year grants was awarded to 13 local governments. The projects varied widely from privatization of services such as home care and nursing homes, to departmental restructuring and re-engineering, to efficiency initiatives. The department's estimated combined annual savings of successful applicants was $38.2 million. Recipients must measure and demonstrate progress each year in order to receive continued funding.

Another LGe restructuring initiative was the New N.Y. Government Reorganization and Citizen Empowerment Act, effective March 21, 2010. Uniform procedures for the consolidation or dissolution of local government units were established, except for school districts and some special purpose districts. Consolidation proceedings can be initiated by joint resolution by governing boards or by elector initiative. In the latter, a majority of the electorate in both jurisdictions must vote in favor of merger in the referenda. If the measures fail, a four-year moratorium takes effect.

In 2012 a Citizen's Re-organization and Empowerment Grant (CREG) program was established to implement the Act's municipal restructuring provisions, including provisions for citizens to petition their town or village to vote on consolidation or dissolution. Grants were authorized for reorganization plan studies or implementation, not to exceed $100,000. A 50 percent local matching cash contribution is required, and projects must be completed within three years. These studies, if implemented and resulting in a governmental reorganization, are also eligible for an increased implementation award in consideration of the local match provided during the study phase. Only local governments covered by the New N.Y. Government Reorganization and Citizen Empowerment Act are eligible for these awards. Service sharing and consolidation studies and initiatives are not eligible for CREG, nor are school district, city, and county applicants. Eight noncompetitive grants totaling $275,000 were awarded in 2013. Among the purposes were an evaluation of the dissolution of a town's water and sewer district and transfer to the county, studies of the fiscal impact of dissolution and ways to achieve greater efficiency, and completion of a dissolution plan for a village. According to the State Department's website, CREG "... is part of Governor Cuomo's continuing efforts to provide taxpayer relief through innovative analysis of governmental functions and services" (New York Department of State 2013). A Citizen Empowerment Tax Credits program provides aid to the survivor of consolidation or dissolution, amounting to 15 percent of the new unit's tax levy, up to $1 million. At least 70 percent of these funds must be dedicated to property tax relief.

Accompanying these "carrots," at Governor Cuomo's request, in 2013 New York's legislature established a Financial Restructuring Board (FSB) for Local Governments. Local governments meeting criteria for "Fiscally Eligible Municipality" can request a 10-person board, chaired by the State Budget Director, to undertake a comprehensive review of finances and operations. The Board makes recommendations to improve financial stability, service delivery, and management. Through the Local Government Performance and Efficiency program up to $5 million in grants and loans could be provided to facilitate implementation of the board's recommendations. Local participation is voluntary, but if a jurisdiction accepts a grant or loan it is required to carry out the board's recommendations.

Governor Cuomo's more recent local restructuring initiatives included both "carrots" and "sticks." The former involved a $20 million Municipal Consolidation and Efficiency Competition, announced in November 2016. Eligible lead applicants for awards to support planned governmental consolidations, shared services, and other efficiency practices are local governments over 50,000 population (57 counties and 34 cities, towns, and villages), although smaller units could join as non-lead consortium partners. Continuing to link the large number of local governments with high property tax rates, the governor's press announcement expressed the purpose of the competition: "Property taxes remain the most burdensome tax in New York and with this competition, we are incentivizing local governments to band together to think outside the box, streamline their bureaucracies, cut costs and deliver real relief to taxpayers." The major goals of this initiative are three-fold:

> ... lower property taxes in the winning consortium of communities, modernize and reduce the number of local governments to achieve a more efficient and adaptable structure for providing local government services, and create an incubator for local government innovation to test and share government consolidation and efficiency best practices.
>
> (New York Department of State 2016)

The governor's "stick" initiative was contained in the 2017 budget, making $715 million in state aid to municipalities contingent on legislative enactment of a bill to amend home rule statutes to require county chief executives or managers to develop shared services plans with their municipalities to save taxpayer costs. After consultation with citizens and approval by the county legislative body, the plan would be placed on the November ballot to make the plan binding. If the efficiency plan is not approved, a new plan would be voted on the next year.

Local government officials and their representatives in Albany opposed Governor Cuomo's budget proposal (Campbell 2017). Further, they disputed the governor's linkage between structure and taxes. County officials, for example, claimed that the costs of state-mandated services consume most property tax revenues. These include schools, Medicaid, public assistance, preschool special education, and legal services for the poor. They also argued that service sharing among local governments has been widespread since the Great Recession, even in the absence of state incentives. Mayors called Governor Cuomo's "stick" proposal another unfunded mandate, which is unnecessary and burdensome. They also pointed out that the $715 million local aid allocation has not been increased since 2008.

In summary, New York State has a long tradition of bipartisan gubernatorial and legislative support for local collaboration. Cooperative agreements and joint service provision have been commonly used tools by municipal and county managers for many years. The Cuomo administration has used the LGe program to bolster collaborative efforts as well as to facilitate service transfers and jurisdictional restructuring. Providing funds to undertake consultant studies, seed start-up costs, and promote citizen understanding of referenda are important ways for the state to leverage change. But the available data indicate that most of the targets have largely been non-controversial, lower cost services and small units like villages and school districts. Whether the amount of state incentive funds is sufficient to attract jurisdictions that otherwise would not pursue such opportunities is unclear, especially to encourage their consideration of costly and controversial reorganizations such as police force consolidation and jurisdictional mergers.

More information is needed on the number of jurisdictions that move from the study to action phase, the response from voters in referenda, the actual cost-savings resulting from streamlining or restructuring, and the impacts on property tax rates. With the exception of the governor's 2017 budget "stick" proposal, it is also unclear whether the Department of State or governor's offices have sufficient "teeth" in the grants to stiffen the resolve of local reformers.

Pulling the Lever

While there has been somewhat greater collaboration among local governments and between cities and counties and non-governmental organizations, and changes have occurred in the mode of delivery of some services, most of the activity involves a limited range of functions and has not permanently altered the size or shape of local units. Coping and adaptive strategies, following a "cutback management" mindset, have been the more typical approach (Ammons, Smith, and Stenberg 2012). But these could still be important tools to leverage change. For instance, the *2013 Municipal Yearbook* reported that over 80 percent of the 1,417 managers who responded to a survey used interlocal collaboration as a management strategy because it "was the right thing to do," leveraged resources, and produced better outcomes (O'Leary and Gerard 2013: 59). Some 86 percent of the respondents indicated they had recently collaborated in such functional areas as fire and emergency response, economic development, infrastructure planning and development, and housing. These results suggest that in many communities there could be a foundation of support for interlocal activity on which state actions to facilitate greater collaboration could be built.

A few states have moved ahead to facilitate or mandate dramatic changes in local service and structural arrangements, but the majority have not done so. There are examples of efforts to incentivize increased interlocal cooperation, service sharing, and outright service or jurisdictional consolidation. Yet, most of these efforts appear to be modest in scope and not part of a larger, strategic agenda to influence fundamental changes in how local governments do business. It is too soon to determine whether these efforts have been successful.

The preceding examples can be thought of as large-scale strategic initiatives to leverage local change around shared services and consolidation. In each state, our coverage is intended to be illustrative, not exhaustive. The jury is still out regarding whether the various initiatives have achieved their intended results. Nevertheless, clearly both "bottom-up" and "top-down" strategies are being pursued, sometimes in tandem. Perhaps these and other initiatives offer insight into how states, in collaboration with municipal leagues and county associations, might fruitfully become catalysts of change in terms of local government service delivery. At least three approaches seem worth exploring based on our preliminary research.

Partnership

Among local officials, there remains considerable suspicion and distrust regarding the motivations of governors and legislators, and with few exceptions they have successfully resisted gubernatorial calls for dramatic changes in the service and structural status quo. As one observer of the "stick" approach to consolidation noted: "Given the opposition, it's not clear that states are pushing consolidation in the right way. Part of the reason they became involved in the first place is that, when municipalities are left to their own devices, they find the political obstacles insurmountable. To date, though, the obstacles have been nearly as great when states are doing the pushing" (Goodman 2008: 27).

In Ohio, for example, the context for service sharing was Governor John Kasich's initiative to cut local financial aid by 50 percent, reduce their share of utility taxes by half, and eliminate an estate tax that earmarked 80 percent of the revenues to localities. H.B. 153 established a Local Government Innovation Fund and a 15-member Local Government Innovation Council to assist local units plan and implement more efficient and effective service delivery through collaborative projects. Over the first three rounds during 2012, 90 grants totaling $6.3 million and 13 loans totaling $4.3 million were awarded through a competitive application process. According to interviewees, less than 20 percent of eligible jurisdictions submitted an innovation proposal. With respect to whether this initiative demonstrated a partnership with the state, one local interviewee was skeptical:

> ... cutting taxes has been the mantra. It hasn't really been about making government more efficient or partnering with local governments. It feels more like "Oh, by the way, we are going to try to throw this bone—the local government fund—and hope you can be more efficient that way."

Employing positive incentives, the bottom-up (or "carrot") approach emphasizes a supportive relationship—as opposed to adversarial—between the state and its constituent units of local government. As one early assessment of states (Indiana, Maine, New Jersey, and New York) "pushing" localities concluded: "The truth, though, is that states don't have to choose between giving local governments a helping hand or a swift kick in the butt . . . The message, it seems, is that if localities are going to come together, state and local government will need to join forces to make it happen" (Goodman 2008: 27).

In 2012, for example, New York's Division of Local Government Services released a PowerPoint presentation to help guide prospective service collaborators entitled "Six Rules for Successful Shared Services Partnerships." These were:

1   Know your own mind (identify goals and outcomes and assess commitment);
2   know your partner's mind (forge a relationship);
3   take the leap (focus on delivery);
4   agree in advance (no surprises, identify costs and benefits, have an exit strategy);
5   take opposition seriously (gauge change resistance, develop "hard" not "soft" options); and
6   invest in the relationship (contract management, culture of improvement and innovation).

States and local governments are best served by approaching local change with a partnership mentality. An encouraging development reported in Chapter 11 of this volume involves several states passing legislation in the aftermath of the recession that empowers rather than restricts local governments. But generalizations about state trends can be risky. In contrast with the Bowman-Kearney findings, the National League of Cities' 2017 survey reported that state actions to restrict local authority in such areas as tax and expenditure limitations, ride sharing, minimum wage, paid leave, and municipal broadband amounted to "an era of preemption" (DuPuis et al. 2017).

Incentives

Most of the state efforts reported from our survey seem to be too modest financially to be significant levers for change. "Carrot"-type incentives likely appeal to jurisdictions already considering service-sharing or other alternative service delivery methods. If state officials are serious about leveraging local change, they have to be willing to provide serious incentives.[5] Minor, incremental benefits are not likely to overcome significant organizational inertia or local interest group or political opposition. Serious resources must be committed in order to influence change where it would not otherwise occur. As indicated in the New York and New Jersey examples, it is also beneficial for incentives to be anchored in a broader gubernatorial and legislative strategic initiative such as property tax relief, performance management, or innovations and best practices. The fact that in these two states leveraging initiatives have survived several transitions in the governorship suggests that they are firmly anchored politically, even though being targets of opposition from local organizations and unions. The programs also should have teeth in terms of state oversight, local reporting, and consequences for poor performance.

As opposed to broadly authorized areas for service-sharing and consolidation, local government representatives could work with state officials to identify specific functions that are "ripe" for collaboration and where an investment of state financial and technical assistance could be a catalyst for change. Likely areas include 911 dispatch, water and sewer utilities, and public safety services (fire and police).

The experience of several consolidated 911 centers in North Carolina is instructive. The director of the state's 911 board made dispatch center merger a top strategic priority and provided significant resources (in the form of over $26 million in grants) to spur action by communities that may not otherwise have acted. Having several million dollars to build a new shared facility can go a long way to allaying concerns over merging agencies across multiple jurisdictions. All of the stakeholders can point to a new facility and know that such a facility would not be possible were it not for the incentive grants.

An area where local service sharing has been facilitated by Minnesota is the Shared Services Grant Program for fire protection administered by the State Fire Marshal and Department of Public Safety. Grants have been available since 2010 for two or more fire services agencies to hire outside consultants to develop voluntary best practices shared services models or feasibility studies and to help cover implementation costs. Among the study coverage requirements are regional fire and rescue shared service district governance, funding for training and equipment, response times, employment issues, and operating procedures (see Minnesota Office of the Legislative Auditor 2012). This strategy is consistent with Ohio's *Beyond Boundaries: A Shared Services Action Plan for Ohio Schools and Governments* report, which recommends: "State associations that have participated in developing this Shared Services Plan should take a leadership role in developing draft agreements; educating their members; facilitating the relationships regionally—both within and across their memberships; training their members in using the tools available to them and communicating about shared services consistently over the next few years" (Ross and Keen 2012: 21).

Timing

Proponents of local change need to be clear-eyed about collaboration taking time to produce desired outcomes. It is important that state incentives leverage real results in terms of local government efficiency and effectiveness. But these results are not often realized immediately. Local representatives could cooperate with state agencies to develop realistic multi-year goals, objectives, and funding streams for shared or consolidated services projects, together with appropriate accountability mechanisms. This is especially the case where dramatic local restructuring such as consolidation and dissolution of units is linked with holding the line on or reducing property taxes.

In Ohio, for example, the Department of Administrative Services has expanded its Lean Ohio network to include local governments. According to its website, the program's mission is to "make government services in Ohio, simpler, faster, better, and less costly" through continuous improvement.[6] Experts are available as internal consultants on the use of tools such as Six Sigma training, strategic planning, data collection and analysis, and meeting facilitation.

Another potentially interesting approach is Minnesota's proposed Accountable Government Innovation and Collaboration (MAGIC) Act. The legislation would give counties waivers and exemptions from statutes and rules to plan, develop, and implement more efficient ways to deliver services through joint or individual pilot projects which, if successful, could become statewide models. Examples of possible projects are lowering water pollution levels and reducing welfare dependency. Affected state agencies must approve county plans, including their outcome goals and performance measures, in advance and success must be demonstrated within three years. The bill was approved by the Senate in 2012, but ultimately stalled in the House and did not pass due to concerns about negative impacts on public employees.

A caveat to the above points is that the research on which they are based is descriptive and any conclusions are preliminary. The recommendations are by necessity not entirely evidence-based but rather suggestive based on what is happening in practice and upon feedback gathered from practitioners in the states examined. More research over time is needed to determine whether service sharing and consolidation have produced greater efficiency and effectiveness, whether and to what extent state incentives can catalyze significant change in the way local governments deliver services, and whether existing state enabling statutes and programs will survive political leadership transitions.

But if predicted economic pressures mount on local governments, it may be prudent for associations representing cities and counties in the state capitol to work with governors and legislators on ways to incentivize interlocal collaboration. Given the power of the functional and structural status quo at the local level, the resiliency of local officials, and the unlikelihood that fiscal crises will disrupt organizational inertia, the state's roles as facilitator of collaborative relationships and catalyst for service realignments could be important. In this respect, governors and legislators could become allies, not adversaries, of city and county managers and elected officials who seek major changes in services or structures but cannot muster the local political support for doing so.

Acknowledgments

The authors express appreciation to Daniel Baird, Jenifer Della Valle, Sarah Hazel, and Ebony Perkins for research assistance on this work. This chapter is a condensed and updated version of a white paper, "Leveraging Local Change: The States' Role: A Policy Issue White Paper," prepared for the Government Affairs and Policy Committee of the International City/County Management Association (ICMA) and published by ICMA in May 2014.

Notes

1   See Kemp (2012) for several articles discussing municipal governments' responses to the "budget crunch."

2   There is a rather robust literature in public administration on "cutback management." A helpful review of the literature can be found in Scorsone and Plerhoples (2010). Charles Levine wrote some now-classic articles on the topic (Levine 1978, 1979). These strategies include the following: (1) to balance budgets local governments tend to rely mainly on spending cuts, while most revenue enhancement areas involve fees with only minimal increases in taxes, if any; (2) to reduce fiscal stress cities and counties tend to focus on productivity and efficiency improvements, instead of adopting new innovative practices, especially those requiring new resource investments; (3) the choice of options usually follows a budget-cutting hierarchy in which the "low hanging fruit" is picked first (such as temporary cutbacks and deferrals and across-the-board budget reductions and spending/hiring freezes) followed by increasingly difficult actions like permanent position eliminations, furloughs and layoffs, and significant reductions in core services; and (4) as budget conditions stabilize and begin to improve, pressures mount to restore the affected services and personnel to previous levels.

3   The LCIR is listed as a "historical committee" on the Florida legislature's website (www.leg.state.fl.us). The site states "this Committee was not funded in the FY 2010–11 General Appropriations Act, and the Committee ceased operations on June 30, 2010."

4   In response to declining state revenues, in 2009, Governor David Patterson reduced the 2008–2009 appropriation from $23 million to $11.5 million. In 2009, the program was further reduced from $11.5 million to $5 million. See New York Department of State (2010).

5   A logical question here is "what are serious incentives?" Unfortunately, there is not a simple answer other than it seems reasonable that a state–local partnership model would include the state authorities asking local government officials about what kinds of incentives would make a difference. The "what kind?" and "how much?" answers are likely context dependent, meaning the unique political and administrative environment in a given state, as well as the unique characteristics of the types of services under consideration.

6   See http://lean.ohio.gov (accessed April 7, 2014).

References

Ammons, David N., Karl W. Smith, and Carl W. Stenberg. 2012. "The future of local government: Will current stresses bring major, permanent changes?" *State and Local Government Review* 44: 64S–75S.

Bowman, Ann O'M. and Richard C. Kearney. 2011. "Second-order devolution: Data and doubt." *Publius: The Journal of Federalism* 41: 563–585.

Campbell, Jon. 2017. "Mayors push back against Cuomo plan." Retrieved from www.democratandchronicle.com/story/news/politics/albany/2017/02/13/mayors-push-back-against (accessed October 17, 2017).

Center for Local, State, and Urban Policy. 2010. "Local government officials give low marks to the performance of state officials and report low trust in Lansing." In *Michigan Public Policy Survey*. Lansing, MI: Gerald R. Ford School of Public Policy, University of Michigan.

Center for Local, State, and Urban Policy. 2017. "Michigan local leaders' views on state preemption and how to share policy authority." In *Michigan Public Policy Survey*. Lansing, MI: Gerald R. Ford School of Public Policy, University of Michigan.

DuPuis, Nicole, Trevor Langan, Christiana McFarland, Angelina Panettieri, Brooks Rainwater. 2017. *City Rights in an Era of Preemption: A State-by-State Analysis*. Washington, DC: National League of Cities.

Eagleton Institute of Politics. 2014. "Despite push by Christie and other officials, New Jersey not yet embracing municipal government consolidation." Rutgers, The State University of New Jersey.

Farmer, Liz. 2014. "Distress signals." *Governing* 27 (March): 42–47.

Frederickson, H. George. 2005. "Transcending the community: Local leadership in a world of shared power." *Public Management* 87: 8–15.

Friedman, Matt. 2012. "S2 is a veiled attempt to remove civil service regulations." *The Star Ledger* (27 February). Retrieved from www.nj.com/news/index.ssf/2012/02/bill_offers_nj_towns_a_choice.html (accessed October 17, 2017).

Goodman, Josh. November 2008. "Attempted merger." *Governing* 21: 22–27.

Greenblatt, Alan. 2011a. "The hand-off." *Governing* 24 (April): 24–28.

Greenblatt, Alan. 2011b. "Rahm's way." *Governing* 24 (June): 24–32.

Hilvert, Cheryl, and David Swindell. 2013. "Collaborative service delivery What every local government manager should know." *State and Local Government Review* 45: 240–254.

Hoene, Christopher W., and Michael A. Pagano. 2011. *Research Brief on America's Cities: City Fiscal Conditions in 2011*. Washington, DC: National League of Cities.

Indiana Commission on Local Government Reform. 2007. *Streamlining Local Government: We've Got to Stop Governing Like This*. Indianapolis, IN: Indiana University Center for Urban Policy and the Environment.

Kearney, Richard C., Jodi E. Swicegood, and Ann O'M. Bowman. 2011. "Second-order devolution? What city managers have to say." *The Municipal Yearbook*. Washington, DC: ICMA: 13–23.

Kemp, Roger L. (ed). 2012. *The Municipal Budget Crunch: A Handbook for Professionals*. Jefferson, NC: McFarland.

Kodrzycki, Yolanda. 2013. *The Quest for Cost-Efficient Local Government in New England: What Role for Regional Consolidation?* Boston, MA: New England Public Policy Center.

Krane, Dale, Platon N. Rigos, and Melvin B. Hill, Jr. (eds). 2001. *Home Rule in America: A Fifty-State Handbook*. Washington, DC: CQ Press.

Krueger, Skip, and Ethan M. Bernick. 2010. "State rules and local governance choices." *Publius: The Journal of Federalism* 40: 697–718.

Krueger, Skip, Robert W. Walker, and Ethan Bernick. 2011. "The intergovernmental context of alternative service delivery choices." *Publius: The Journal of Federalism* 41: 686–708.

Levine, Charles H. 1978. "Organizational decline and cutback management." *Public Administration Review* 38(4): 316–325.

Levine, Charles H. 1979. "More on cutback management: Hard questions for hard times." *Public Administration Review* 39(2): 179–183.

Levine, Helisse, Jonathan B. Justice, and Eric A. Scorsone, eds. 2013. *Handbook of Local Government Fiscal Health*. Burlington, MA: Jones & Bartlett Learning.

Magyar, Mark J. 2012. "New Jersey gets serious about sharing core services." *NJ Spotlight* (February 13): 5.

Martin, Lawrence L., Richard Levey, and Jenna Cawley. 2012. "The 'New Normal' for local government." *State and Local Government Review* 44(1S) 17S–28S.

McFarland, Christiana, and Michael A. Pagano. 2016. *City Fiscal Conditions 2016*. Washington, DC: National League of Cities.

Miller, Gerald J. 2010. "Weathering the local government fiscal crisis: Short-term measures or permanent change?" *The Municipal Yearbook*. Washington, DC: ICMA: 33–36.

Minnesota Office of the Legislative Auditor. 2012. "Consolidation of Local Governments." Retrieved from www.auditor.leg.state.mn.us/ped/2012/consollocgov.htm (accessed February 28, 2014).

Nelson, Kimberly L. 2012. "Municipal choices during a recession: Bounded rationality and innovation." *State and Local Government Review* 44: 44S–63S.

New York Department of State. 2010. *2010–2011 Local Government Efficiency Program: Annual Report*. New York: New York Department of State. Retrieved from www.dos.ny.gov/lg/lge/annrpt2010_final.pdf (accessed October 17, 2017).

New York Department of State. 2013. "New York Department of State Awards Citizen Reorganization Empowerment Grants." Press release, February 21. Retrieved from www.dos.ny.gov/press/2013/creg2-21.html (accessed February 28, 2014).

New York Department of State. 2016. *Municipal Consolidation and Efficiency Competition/Competition Guidelines*. New York: New York Department of State. Retrieved from www.dos.ny.gov/funding/rfa-16-lge-15/MCEC%20Guidance%20112816.pdf (accessed October 17, 2017).

O'Leary, Rosemary, and Catherine M. Gerard. 2013. "Collaborative governance and leadership: A 2012 survey of local government collaboration." *The Municipal Yearbook*. Washington, DC: ICMA: 57–69.

Riverstone-Newell, Lori. 2017. "The rise of state preemption laws in response to local policy innovation." *Publius* 47(3): 1–23.

Ross, Richard A., and Timothy S. Keen (eds). 2012. *Beyond Boundaries: A Shared Services Action Plan for Ohio's Schools and Governments*. Columbus, OH: Office of Management and Budget, State of Ohio.

Sadeghi, Leila, and Kathe Callahan. 2011. *2011 Municipal Management Survey Preliminary Findings*. Rutgers, NJ: Center for Executive Leadership in Government. Retrieved from www.njlmef.org/2011_MunicipalMgmtSurvey.pdf (accessed October 17, 2017).

Scorsone, Eric A. and Christina Plerhoples. 2010. "Fiscal stress and cutback management amongst state and local governments: What have we learned and what remains to be learned?" *State and Local Government Review* 42: 176–187.

Stenberg, Carl W. 2011. *Coping with Crisis: How are Local Governments Reinventing Themselves in the Wake of the Great Recession?* Washington, DC: ICMA.

Stenberg, Carl W. and Ricardo S. Morse. 2014. *Leveraging Local Change: The States' Role*. Washington, DC: International City/County Management Association.

Svara, James H. 2012. "Twenty-first century federalism in the United States (and localities) of America." White Paper prepared for Big Ideas: The Future of Local Government. Alliance for Innovation, November 2–4.

Thoreson, Karen and James H. Svara. 2011. "How local governments are navigating the fiscal crisis: Taking stock and looking forward." *The Municipal Yearbook*. Washington, DC: ICMA: 75–82.

Wattrick, Jeff T. 2011. "Metro Detroit leaders skeptical as Snyder pushes for government consolidation." *M Live* (March 28). Retrieved from www.mlive.com/news/detroit/index.ssf/2011/03/metro_detroit_leaders_skeptica.html (accessed October 17, 2017).

13 Professional Development Applied Projects

Street-Level Laboratories of Democracy

Susan C. Paddock

Deil Wright, arguably the father of the study of and advocacy for intergovernmental relations (IGR) or intergovernmental management (IGM),[1] believed that collaboration was the key to efficient governmental services—that is, providing public services on the most cost-effective basis (Wright 1988). Governmental collaboration involves multiple organizations, with both vertical and horizontal relationships, representing multiple interests (Agranoff and McGuire 2003). It is intended to be a win-win proposition for all parties. Collaboration can help to cut or share costs, improve efficiency, provide the opportunity for front-line employees' involvement, and promote accountability to the public (Benton 2013: 221).

Wright, and others who have followed in his academic footsteps, acknowledged that collaboration relies on trust, and that trust is difficult to build and to maintain. The study of trust in and between organizations recognizes that while organizational structures, policies, and procedures support inter-organizational trust, it is, ultimately, the individuals responsible for organizational actions who either engender or extinguish trust. Gordon (1992: 111), for example, noted that IGR is "highly informal and very dependent on human interactions."

Most models of collaboration involve formal relationships between and among agencies, and depend on the leadership of organizations reaching agreement or consensus on programs and policies. These are top-down models and the collaborative efforts often are organization-wide. The model of collaboration described in this chapter is an alternative approach: bottom-up, employee-directed efforts in the style characteristic of street-level bureaucracy and decision making (Lipsky 1980), that link various state and local government agencies. These efforts rely on trusting relationships developed in a comprehensive training program. This approach serves as an effective means of initiating collaboration in an incubator, laboratory, or pilot-program manner.

The model evolves from experience with collaborative and cooperative projects completed by public administrators as a part of a comprehensive professional development program. This might be termed a "micro" approach to IGM. It leads to a recommendation that organizations may use professional development programs, and especially programs that incorporate applied projects, as a means of exploring or initiating collaborative or cooperative efforts and encouraging innovation in the delivery of public services.

Background

Public administrators participate in at least two different kinds of professional education: credit-bearing masters and doctoral programs, and non-credit professional development or certificate programs. These two approaches differ in several ways beyond the credit characteristic. Degree programs enroll more pre-service students and have a stronger focus on theory. Professional development programs are aimed at in-service students and focus on practical applications and models. In addition, public administration degree programs often incorporate internships in the curricular requirements while non-credit professional development programs have, for the most part, not included such work-life applications.

The Certified Public Manager (CPM ©) program is a comprehensive management development program offered in almost 40 states. The first program was established in Georgia in 1979, and expanded across the nation as a way to improve public agencies' performance and advance best practices. According to the bylaws of the CPM Consortium which govern state-level efforts (www. cpmconsortium.org), CPM programs are offered cooperatively by universities and state governments. They are linked via a section to the American Society for Public Administration. The programs' target audience is middle managers in state, local, federal, and tribal governments, and require 300 contact hours in classes, homework, examinations and applied projects. Although there are variations by state, all programs require comprehensive applied projects as a capstone activity. Applied projects require students to integrate disciplinary expertise in real work situations, using skills in problem solving, decision making and team management (Balanoff and Balanoff 2008; Balanoff 2010; Stern 2014).

Projects are expected to improve organizations' programs, procedures, or policies. They may, for example, examine personnel policies or budgeting practices and recommend changes; research and develop a policy proposal, such as a wellness program; initiate new supervisory practices such as participatory decision making, or implement an employee engagement process; or develop operational manuals, evaluate operational practices, or create internal or external programs. Projects must be approved by both the students' supervisors and the CPM program directors, but are carried out completely by the individual students.

Many of these projects might properly be termed pilot or model programs. As such, their development and implementation reflects that students often are creating "laboratories of democracy." That term was first used by Supreme Court Judge Louis Brandeis in his dissenting opinion in *New State Ice Company v. Liebmann* 285 US 262 (1932). Referring to the Tenth Amendment's language that powers not delegated to the national government were reserved to the states, Brandeis wrote that federalism allows that "a single courageous State may, if its citizens choose, serve as a laboratory; and try novel social and economic experiments without risk to the rest of the country." While first applied almost exclusively to state governments, over time the term "laboratories of democracy" was extended to local governments as well. Governments were able to create new policies based on the experience of other governments, to replicate their successes and avoid their failures. These replications have been both horizontal, to other states and localities, and vertical, from the localities to the states and from the state to the federal level. The Affordable Care Act ("Obamacare"), for example, was developed based on lessons with Massachusetts' health care act, and a proposal for a state government wellness program in Wisconsin was based on the experience of several cities and counties in Wisconsin and in other states.

Applied projects generally are individual projects, completed for and within a student's organization. However, students, all of whom are practicing public administrators, may complete a team-based project. In 2003 the Wisconsin CPM program began to emphasize team-based activities in classes and encourage team-based applied projects. Not only were students encouraged to work with others in the class for their applied projects, but an applied project involving the entire class was added as a requirement. This chapter looks at these projects to determine whether they are effective models of collaboration and cooperation.

The chapter uses both "collaboration" and "cooperation" to describe the projects. A *collaborative* project is defined as one where students, representing two or more agencies, work together with an expectation of benefit to all agencies. This is consistent with the definition by Bryson et al. (2009: 78): "the linking or sharing of information, resources, activities and capabilities by organizations to achieve an outcome that could not be achieved by the organizations separately." For example, representatives of several police departments proposed and developed a combined SWAT team that improved emergency response and saved operating expenses.

By contrast, a *cooperative* project is defined as one where individuals, who may or may not be representing their agencies' interests, work together for a common purpose without expectation of direct benefit to their own agencies. A cooperative project is completed for an agency that may not be the student's. Instead, students provide their talents and abilities to a project that may not be related to their direct work, but which they expect will provide a benefit to another agency or to the greater good. While these projects do not conform to the outcome part of Bryson's definition, they are included here because they demonstrate the "information, resources, activities and capabilities" portion of that definition. In addition, students have experience working in a cross-organizational setting that may be useful in their future management activities. For example, four students worked cooperatively to develop a strategic plan for a port; only one of these students was employed by the port while three were employees of other county departments and subsequently used their planning experience in their own agencies.

Methodology

This study is a qualitative, *ex post facto* analysis of applied projects that were completed as a part of the requirements for the CPM designation. These projects allowed students to study and recommend or take action on an issue or problem, and were expected to contribute to the improvement of an organization. Projects were required to:

- be important to the organization;
- be based on sufficient information or data;
- be able to be completed in the allotted time;
- secure the cooperation of individuals necessary for completion; and
- have the possibility of being implemented.

Projects had to have a relationship to CPM program course content. Students identified, chose, and designed their own projects, with advice and support from CPM program staff and support of supervisors. All students in the program were supervisors or managers, and thus had the ability to carry out projects without explicit agency support for any particular project. Students completed these projects, for the most part, on their own time except where the project required the involvement of co-workers or supervisors. Consequently, no cost for the projects was identified.[2]

All projects were evaluated by CPM program staff at the University of Wisconsin-Madison and were successfully completed. The original goals and objectives for each project were met and there was a tangible result of each project—for example, a specific plan to be implemented, a set of new or revised policies and procedures, or a program or a programmatic evaluation. Projects also met the following evaluation guidelines:

- the paper was well organized;
- the problem or need for the project was clearly identified;
- appropriate analytical tools were used and the analysis was complete;
- appropriate management/leadership principles were exhibited;
- information was accurate and up to date;
- there was a conclusion or solution or recommendation, which flowed logically from the problem identification and analysis;
- effective decision-making approaches were evident; and
- the project was presented clearly and was understandable.

Because of the nature of public agencies, and students' roles within those agencies, successful implementation of projects was not a requirement, but a strong possibility of implementation was required.

The research for this chapter reviewed all projects successfully completed in the Wisconsin CPM program between 1993, when the program graduated its first CPMs, and 2012. The author was the director of the program during this time, and was familiar with all the projects. During that time 469 projects were completed. Almost all of these were individual projects: there was no requirement for collaboration. Only 40 (8.5%) were identified as cooperative or collaborative projects and most of those were completed after 2003, when the program began to emphasize teamwork and collaboration. Of the 40 projects, 29 were identified as collaborative (all students' agencies potentially could benefit from the project) and 11 were designated as cooperative (the lead agency may or may not have benefitted). Seventeen were completed for law enforcement agencies; five for public information or public relations; six for local government general operations; three for health/human services; three for non-law enforcement public safety; and six for other professional areas. Five collaborative projects and four cooperative projects were not implemented. One collaborative class project was included in this study—creating policies and programs for a non-profit community center.

Follow-up with students who completed the projects determined if the projects had been implemented, whether they continued to function, obstacles that either made implementation difficult or impossible, and success factors. The author's conclusions were reviewed by the students to ensure accurate descriptions and conclusions.

While the analysis of these projects is instructive, broader generalizations are limited by the relatively small number of projects, and especially by the number of successful projects. Continued review of completed projects, along with review of training and support provided in the mechanics of supporting collaboration, will be useful in identifying how bottom-up collaboration growing out of professional development programs can be encouraged.

Illustrative Descriptions of Projects

The following brief sketches provide further understanding of the nature and scope of some of the projects described and analyzed in this chapter. All of these projects were implemented.

Collaborative Projects

Regional evacuation plan. The lead on this project was a county representative. The project included the emergency service representatives from all counties in the southeast region of Wisconsin, along with the City of Milwaukee. The result was a template for an evacuation plan that was uniformly implemented across all agencies.

Combined SWAT team. The lead on this project was a local police department representative. Two other police departments collaborated to create a combined SWAT team, saving money on training, equipment, and deployment and thereby increasing SWAT ability to respond.

Affirmative action internship program. The lead on this project was a representative of the state department of justice's crime lab. The state collaborated with the University of Wisconsin-Madison to identify upper-division students from under-represented classes for internships in the crime lab. Because of this project, aimed at creating a more diverse workforce in the lab, students of color accessed internship opportunities and later were hired as permanent employees for the first time.

Plan to maximize health and human services in a time of fiscal stress. The lead on this project was a county representative. As the recession hit, the county was faced with a serious reduction in funding. Rather than cut services, the student led a team that investigated and implemented ways of continuing to provide services by using collaborative approaches such as sharing of personnel and spaces where services were provided and linking similar programmatic activities.

Local government emergency response plan. This project was led by the village clerk, who worked collaboratively with other village departments, local businesses, and citizens to create a plan that could easily be trained to and implemented by identified citizen leaders. Table-top exercises using the plan were used, and the plan later was applied during a storm emergency.

Cooperative Projects

Community information for new refugees. The lead on this project was a representative from a local police department, but the project was not a law enforcement project. Instead, the student identified government resources and information which were needed by the newly-arrived refugees in the community and, working with the local access provider, created a television and video program in the refugees' native languages. This project improved refugees' understanding and use of necessary programs and resources. There was no direct benefit to the student's department.

Policies for a community center. A team of students representing a variety of agencies led this project. They created policies for vehicle maintenance, a manual for the governing board, program plans for youth at the center, a records management system, and other procedures and programs. As a result of these efforts the center director was able to more effectively manage and improve the center's operations.

Truancy program for schools. The lead in this project was a county sheriff, who examined the policies and procedures for identifying and detaining truants. He proposed programs to reduce truancy by providing services for truants that would lessen the likelihood for their becoming habitual truants. The benefit was primarily the school district, rather than law enforcement agencies, although it reduced law enforcement's time spent on truancy concerns.

Strategic plan for the Port of Green Bay. One of the students on this project represented the Port and the other three team members were from other departments in Brown County and did not have an organizational interest in the Port or the plan. All team members brought their decision making and analytical skills to the process of creating the plan and later applied their experience to their own departments.

Project Outcomes and Success

All projects met the requirements of the CPM program; that is to say, they successfully met the established standards. All of them were problem solving projects (Guffey 2003: 43). Some were not implemented, and some were implemented initially but did not endure. The real test of any project's success was its long-term implementation and impact, and that could not be evaluated at the time of the project's submission. Some of the projects were completed as much as 20 years prior to the study. We wondered whether the projects were successful in the long term, and whether the effects originally intended persisted over time. This is the real test of this kind of street-level interagency collaboration.

Students who created the projects were contacted. Brief descriptions were written that captured the essence of their projects. Students were asked whether their projects were implemented, in whole or in part, and whether the projects continue to be operational. When projects were no longer active, or had been implemented and then abandoned, we asked the students what they believed to be the reasons for this outcome.

Twenty-seven of the 40 projects originally identified for this study were reported to have been implemented, and continue to be in operation. This is a significant 67.5 percent implementation rate. The most successful projects involved local government operations; all of those projects identified in this study have had long-term impact. Health and human service projects were somewhat less successful; two of the three projects in this study had long-term impact. Nine of the 17 law enforcement projects had long-term success. None of the public information/relations projects have had long-term, lasting effects.

Creating Successful Collaborative/Cooperative Projects

Nazarro (2003: 23) described the seven steps in creating successful collaborative projects: identifying the project, the partners, the core competencies, the goals, and the needs, creating network relationships, and working together. The CPM projects were evaluated against these seven elements. In the collaborative projects that succeeded, all of these elements were present. The projects were especially good at identifying goals and needs, and in linking individuals' competencies to those. Less-successful projects lacked some or many of the elements, especially in creating long-term networks and relationships.

In follow-up discussions with students, three reasons were identified as critical to project success: project leadership; agency leadership; or project features (see appendix at end of this chapter). Leadership was especially critical. Projects that had long-term effects or continuing application demonstrated a sustained effort of the project leader, not only during the project's creation and its completion and submission to the CPM program, but also after the submission. Students described their initiatives in selling the project to key decision makers in their agencies, in other agencies, or to legislative or decision-making bodies. Sometimes this post-submission activity was made possible since a project leader held a leadership position in an agency. In most cases, however, this continuing attention to the project was a result of the project leader's commitment to the project, his/her willingness to continue to devote time and energy to the project, and his/her agency's leadership support of this continuing effort. Williams (2002) described effective collaborative leaders as "boundary spanners" who are effective at building sustainable relationships, managing influence, managing complexity, and managing roles and accountabilities. Agranoff and McGuire (2003) identified four skills of collaboration: activating the right people and resources; framing and facilitating agreement; mobilizing and inducing commitment; and building trust. While this study did not examine project leadership in depth, discussions with project leaders provided anecdotal evidence that the successful projects had boundary-spanning leaders who exhibited the skills listed by Agranoff and McGuire. For example, all three of the health and human service-related projects were led by assertive leaders who demonstrated, both before and during the projects, their abilities to bring together key players, build relationships across agency lines, and to secure the commitment and trust of others.

None of the studies reviewed as a part of this research focused on the ability of the project leader, and in particular on training provided to the leader, as it affected his/her ability to create and carry through on a project. It may be argued that the kind of professional development provided to the students in the CPM program, who were project leaders, improved their ability to create successful collaborations and, just as important, to follow through. The program challenged participants to assume leadership in class, to work independently, and to function as an effective team member.

Agency leadership support also was important, especially when the student was involved in working with another agency. Managers whose supervisors encouraged their work in the CPM program, including providing time for work on the applied project, demonstrated a commitment to continuing to work with the project after its submission.

Finally, long-term project success was due to the high quality of the project itself, which allowed decision makers to implement it without significant objections. This quality was identifiable at the time of the project's evaluation by program staff; that is, it had a clearly identified problem or need, used appropriate analytical tools and management practices and had a clear and realistic recommendation or solution that reflected the requirements of the existing political and economic conditions. For example, the "Community Resources for New Refugees" reflected an understanding of the difficulty of new, non-English-speaking immigrants in navigating local government policies and laws, as well as the power of the television in communicating with those people. The "Local Government Emergency Response Plan," created for a small village, reflected not only best practices in emergency response but also the need to involve volunteers (citizens and business owners) as well as government officials for an effective response. In no case, however, were the project's elements alone sufficient for its successful long-term implementation; either project leader commitment or agency leadership, or both, were also required.

The projects that were not implemented failed for a number of reasons:

- Although a project included recommendations and conclusions, no plan for implementation, follow-up plan, or next steps were identified, and/or the project leader did not follow up on the recommendations and conclusions. A well-done study of how local governments could improve citizens' understanding of and access to government policies and actions did not include any plan to present those conclusions to local government decision makers.
- Project recommendations were not supported by key policy makers (agency leaders and legislative bodies) or the political environment. A well-researched study on the consolidation of two

police departments, demonstrating improved response time and significant cost savings, was not supported by the governing bodies of those municipalities (one issue was turf: "what logo will we put on the side of the police vehicles?"). Another project that aimed at improving union-management relations through better information was derailed when the Wisconsin legislature significantly changed the status of unions in state and local government.

- Project recommendations required additional effort by affected agencies, with no tangible benefit. A project to improve city-county law enforcement relations was not identified as a priority by any of the affected agencies.
- Although the project was implemented initially, updates necessary for its continuing relevance and usefulness were not made. A legislative outreach program for a state agency was not updated.
- The project leader moved to other priorities or responsibilities not related to the project. The creator of an interagency public relations and communication plan resigned her position to accept another assignment.

Some of these factors are reflected in a 2012 ICMA study which identified challenges that prevent IGM efforts from being successful—in particular, turf wars and political culture (O'Leary and Gerard 2013). However, that study did not identify the critical role of a project leader, and whether that leader held a position of responsibility or authority in an organization. That role may be reflected in Hilvert and Swindell's (2013: 248) conclusion that communities "do not do an adequate job in terms of managing and monitoring" collaborative efforts.

Costs, including bargaining costs, information costs, agency costs, and enforcement costs, generally are a significant concern in IGM efforts (Feiock, Steinacker, and Jun Park 2009). Cost was not considered a factor in success or failure in this study primarily because project participants were not required to track and report those costs. A key cost in any project is staff time. In this study staff time is the project participants' time. Their participation had the explicit support of their supervisors and of agency leadership. The cost of this participation included program tuition but, more significantly, the participants' time attending classes and completing program requirements.

Discussion

Wright (1988: 14–26) identified five features of IGR/IGM efforts. Of these five, three are reflected in this study: the kinds of public officials or administrators involved in IGM efforts; the range of involvement by all public officials, beyond those initiating an IGM effort; and the kinds of program implemented as a result of the collaboration. It is not surprising that projects are more likely to be successful when a project leader has a position of responsibility in an agency. But just as important, at least for the projects studied in this research, was the commitment of the project leader, including his/her ability to promote the project to administrative and political leadership. Also, important, though less so than a leader's commitment, is the quality of the project in terms of its features, details, and presentation.

The importance of project leadership should not be underestimated. Participants in the Wisconsin CPM Program were mid-level administrators; only a few were agency heads, and those were heads of small departments. Yet, by the conclusion of a program that generally took two to three years to complete, those individuals had learned skills and developed relationships that allowed them to take leadership in applied projects. Kellerman (2012) argues that leadership programs have not changed individuals or their organizations. This study suggests that a leadership program can change outcomes. An intensive, applied-project approach, based on a comprehensive curriculum that incorporates discussion of and practice with collaboration can lead to outcomes that support or expand collaboration and IGR efforts.

This study also illuminated the efficacy of a focus on collaboration in a professional development program. More IGM projects were initiated and more of those were successful from 2003 to 2012 than in the previous 10 years due to programmatic changes after 2003 which encouraged students to develop collaborative projects. The CPM program increased its emphasis on collaboration and personal leadership in the curriculum of the program.

In addition, the program increased the requirements in the Capstone class by including a collaborative class project, which was in addition to the individual applied projects. This class project involved all class members, who functioned as a team to define and carry out a project that would be of benefit beyond the students' own organizations. For example, one class worked with a number of communities and private property owners to identify an intercity bike path, secure municipalities' support and property owners' rights of way, and begin the construction process.

Developing trusting relationships between governmental bodies seeking to collaborate is a challenge. Trust is based on a belief in the honesty, fairness, or benevolence of others (Hardin 2002). As Wright (1974: 1) noted, "there are no intergovernmental relations, there are only relations among officials in different governing units." When these interactions are trusting, collaboration is possible. Wright wrote further that, "IGR is the continuous, day-to-day pattern of contacts, knowledge, and evaluations of government officials" and noted especially the growing importance of the "actions, attitudes and roles of appointed administrators." In this study, ongoing relationships developed among participants, during the course of class activities and discussions, inspired trust well before individuals imagined and implemented projects.

Most IGM or collaborative efforts grow out of needs recognized at an organizational level, and initiated by one or more individuals within the organizations. They spend time discussing policies, procedures, and responsibilities. Thus, they may appear to be more formal than the projects that were developed through the CPM Program. These projects were controlled by the agencies only to the extent that the participants sought supervisors' approval. Turf issues, a concern in IGM efforts, emerged only after the projects were well underway—conceptualized, staffed, and initiated. By that time trust trumped turf.

Conclusion

Our study of IGM projects of the Wisconsin CPM program demonstrated a relatively high rate (67.5%) of successful implementation. A review of those successes underlined the importance of the ability of the project leader and of his/her professional development, both during the project and afterwards. This finding reminds us of Lipsky's (1980) discussion of street-level bureaucracy. Lipsky focused on the discretion of street-level public officials in carrying out administrative functions; in the CPM experience, it is the street-level public manager, creating and carrying out a collaborative/cooperative project, who furthers IGM.

This research strongly suggests that as professional development programs become better at identifying student development needs and effective learning strategies, and at creating functioning teamwork and team leadership within a cohort class, it is more likely that students will create IGM projects that can be successfully implemented. In addition, students will be more motivated to continue to monitor projects after implementation. In some way, the model described reverses an IGM process; instead of the IGM educating participants, as suggested by Agranoff (2007), here education led to intergovernmental collaboration.

Professional development programs in public administration should aim at creating programs that encourage and support collaborative efforts. Such efforts are more likely to support successful innovation in the long term, since "a collaborative approach to public innovation seems to have comparative advantages." (Hartley, Sorensen, and Torfing 2013: 821) Successful IGM efforts may well be born in these professional development programs and their street-level public servants.

Notes

1   In more recent decades, intergovernmental relations/management also came to be called collaborative public management or CPM. The projects described here are more properly included in that nomenclature but, to avoid confusion (because the projects were in a Certified Public Manager or CPM Program), IGM will be used throughout this chapter.
2   For a full description of project requirements and process, visit the web site of the Wisconsin CPM Program (http://continuingstudies.wisc.edu/certified-public-manager).

Appendix 1: Key Factors in Successful Projects

Title of Project	Driving Force for Long-Term Effectiveness	Key Factor(s)
Joint Dispatch Center	Key partners involved; plan demonstrated cost savings and improved services, and presented those to legislative bodies	Project leader Project features Agency leadership
Large Scale Regional Evacuation Plan	Experience of working together, and leadership of one individual (project leader)	Project leader
Adolescent School and Community Health Program Procedures Manual	Project leader worked to get manual introduced and used in schools	Project leader
Police Response to Active Shooters in Schools	Key players in police department and school district were briefed on project, and "sold" program to decision making bodies	Project leader Project features
Combined SWAT Teams	Project leader instrumental in working with departments' leaders to implement program	Project leader
Consolidation of Services	Plan presented to agency leadership, and implemented by them	Project leader Agency leadership
Continuing Police Services to the Technical College	Analysis useful in negotiations (not conducted by project leader)	Project features
Affirmative Action Internship Program	Project leaders were/are leaders in state crime lab with authority to implement	Project leaders
Local Government Emergency Response Plan	Plan effective while village clerk still employed; not actively implemented since her retirement	Project leader

Title of Project	Driving Force for Long-Term Effectiveness	Key Factor(s)
Police School Liaison Program for City	Program features presented to leadership of both agencies and adopted by decision making bodies	Project features Agency leadership
Implementing Program Outcome Measures	Project leaders continued to provide leadership and guidance; program outcome measurement adopted widely in state and local governments	Project leaders Public administration environment
Devising a Plan to Maximize Health Services in a Time of Limited Funding	Project leader was/is also the head of an agency charged with most of the health service responsibilities	Project leader
Staffing Study for a New Courthouse	Staffing recommendations presented to county board and adopted	Project elements Agency leadership
Mapping Schools (for crisis responses)	Effectiveness of this project linked to active shooter project; maps not updated to reflect school changes	Project elements
Citizen Police Academy	Project leader is also coordinator of academy	Project leader
Community Resources for New Refugees	Initial success. Major long-term impact was as model for city departments in reaching non-English speakers	Project leader Agency leadership
Manual of Operations for Non-Profit Supporting Fire Service	Project leader was/is also a leader in the non-profit organization, as well as being a municipal firefighter	Project leader
Project Gunlock (Firearm safety program)	Project leader implemented program; this program just one of many responsibilities	Project leader
Truancy in County Schools	Project leader was county sheriff; was instrumental in working with county and school district	Project leader
Strategic Plan for Port of Green Bay	Project leader was/is employee of Port of Green Bay, and worked to have plan implemented	Project leader
Providing Qualified Language Interpreters	Project leader directed implementation, and ensured ongoing support of the program	Project leader
Assessing Security Needs of County Facilities	Project leaders identified specific changes or measures and presented those to critical decision makers and leaders	Project leaders Project elements Agency leadership
Training Modules for Police Sergeants	Project leader held key command position in police department and worked with other departments to demonstrate modules	Project leader Agency leadership
Streamlining the Building Permit System	Project leader shepherded implementation of new system	Project leader
Policies for a Community Center	Center director (a CPM student, but not on the project) implemented policies	Agency leadership
Community Information Program Desktop Manual	Project leader ensured that manual reproduced, and training in its use provided	Project leader
Records Storage	One project leader was head of state records agency and followed up to ensure implementation of recommendations	Project leaders

References

Agranoff, R. 2007. *Managing within Networks: Adding Value to Public Organizations*. Washington, DC: Georgetown University Press.

Agranoff, R., and McGuire, M. 2003. *Collaborative Public Management: New Strategies for Local Government*. Washington, DC: Georgetown University Press.

Balanoff, H. 2010. "The ASPA, CPM connection: Delivering quality professional development programs and educational services to the public sector." *The PA Times* 33(1): 6.

Balanoff, H., and Balanoff, M. 2008. "The National CPM Program." *The Public Manager* 37(3): 76–79.

Benton, J.E. 2013. "Local government collaboration: Considerations, issues and prospects." *State and Local Government Review* 45(4): 221–223.

Bryson, J., Cosby, B., Stone, M., and Saunoi-Sandgren, E. 2009. "Designing and managing cross-sector collaboration: A case study in reducing traffic congestion." *The Business of Government* (Winter/Fall): 78–81.

Feiock, R.C., Steinacker, A., and Jun Park, H. 2009. "Institutional collective action and economic development joint ventures." *Public Administration Review* 69(3): 267–270.

Gordon, G.J. 1992. *Public Administration in America*, 4th edition. New York: St. Martin's Press.

Guffey, M. 2003. "Collaborative networks: The initial design strongly influences the outcome." *The Public Manager* 32(4): 42–44.

Hardin, R. (ed.). 2002. *Trust and Trustworthiness*. New York (Russell Sage Foundation).

Hartley, J., Sorensen, E., and Torfing, J. 2013. "Collaborative innovation: A viable alternative to market competition and organizational entrepreneurship." *Public Administration Review* 73(6): 821–830.

Hilvert, C., and Swindell, D. 2013. "Collaborative service delivery: What every local government manager should know." *State and Local Government Review* 45(4): 240–254.

Kellerman, B. 2012. *The End of Leadership*. New York: HarperCollins.

Lipsky, M. 1980. *Street-Level Bureaucracy: Dilemmas of the Individual in the Public Services*. New York: Russell Sage Foundation.

Nazzaro, M. 2003. "Synergy: An unleashed community power." *The Public Manager* 32(4): 23–25.

O'Leary, R., and Gerard, C. 2013. "Collaborative governance and leadership: A 2012 survey of local government collaboration." In *The Municipal Yearbook 2013*, 34–56. Washington, DC: ICMA.

Stern, M. 2014. "Public sector employee training programs." *The PA Times* 37(2): 13.

Williams, P. 2002. "Competency boundary spanning public administrators." *Public Administration Review* 80(1): 103–124.

Wright, D.S. 1974. "IGR: An analytical overview." *Annals of American Academy of Political and Social Sciences* 416(1): 1–16.

Wright, D.S. 1988. *Understanding Intergovernmental Relations*, 3rd edition. Pacific Grove, CA: Brooks/ Cole.

Part V

Reflections from the Trenches

14 The Unraveling of the Intergovernmental System

A Practitioner's Observations

Donald J. Borut

This chapter is a local government advocate's reflections on the brutal reality of the unraveling of the intergovernmental system and the resulting impact on lobbying by representatives of state and local governments in Washington, DC.

Over the past 20 to 25 years the lobbying strategies and influence of the National League of Cities (NLC) and other state and local public interest groups have profoundly changed. It would be easy to attribute those changes solely to money, the growth of political contributions by special interest lobbyists, and the pressures from the federal deficit. These have been critical. However, they were preceded by changes in the basic relationships, assumptions, and expectations of those in the federal government toward state and local governments.

From 1990 to 2013, I served as the Executive Director of the National League of Cities, a membership organization representing the interests of America's cities, towns, and villages. Through the active involvement of local elected officials and state municipal leagues, NLC lobbies, provides research, training, and other support to local governments and their officials.

A fundamental responsibility of NLC is to represent and advocate on behalf of local governments in Washington, DC. This involves engaging with the Congress and Administration to insure that they understand and appreciate how laws and regulations they enact impact local governments and the services and programs for which they are responsible. More specifically, this includes advocating for resources to implement federal policy priorities and opposing unfunded federal mandates and the preemption of local authority. My personal benchmark for tracking the changes in intergovernmental lobbying begins with the Great Society agenda in the 1960s.

State and Local Governments: From Key Players to Special Interests

There is a large body of literature on the evolution of the relationship of the federal government with state and local governments. The creation of U.S. Advisory Commission on Intergovernmental Relations (ACIR) in 1959 during the Eisenhower administration was the formal recognition of the interdependency of the multiple levels of government and the importance of addressing the complex issues and opportunities resulting from changing federal initiatives. For those in state and local government, ACIR affirmed the importance of the relationship of the federal government to state and local government. The importance and relevance of ACIR was reflected in the appointment and active participation of members of the Intergovernmental Relations Subcommittees of the Senate and House Committees on Government Operations.

In 1967 President Lyndon B. Johnson recognized the interdependence of state and local governments and required that federal agencies seek input from them in the programs of the Great Society. Addressing those administrators responsible for the management of federal programs, he wrote:

> The basis of creative federalism is cooperation . . . To the fullest practical extent, I want you to take steps to afford representatives of the Chief Executives of State and local governments the opportunity to advise and consult in the development and execution of programs which directly affect the conduct of State and local affairs.
>
> (Wellborn and Burkhead 1989: 211)

While I cannot profess to be an expert on the effectiveness of the public interest groups as the critical voices in advancing, promoting, and protecting the interests and needs of state and local government during 1960s and 1970s, there clearly was an appreciation of their role in advancing Presidential agendas. In his 1974 examination of lobbying by governors and mayors, Donald H. Haider credits "government interest groups" with the issuance of the A-85 state/local consultation circular, passage of the Intergovernmental Cooperation Act, the planning/review requirements in the Model Cities legislation, and the passage of General Revenue Sharing (Haider 1974).

The fate of ACIR illustrates how the intergovernmental system has unraveled. Even before the ultimate demise of ACIR in 1996, its resources were reduced and its effectiveness and relevance undermined by those disinterested in intergovernmental relations. At its zenith ACIR supported, enhanced, and enlightened those in the public sector on the challenges and opportunities of co-ordination and cooperation between levels of government. Equally important, it provided a forum to give voice to the fundamental relationships and tensions built into the system of federalism and played out through the real world of intergovernmental relations. While NLC and the other local government public interest groups actively lobbied to continue funding for ACIR, the state groups, most specifically the National Governors Association, were ambivalent and did not actively lobby against defunding.

Senator Daniel Patrick Moynihan (D-NY) observed during the debate on the ACIR's final appropriation, "the ACIR does important, if largely unheralded, work. And we stand on the brink of terminating it. This is a mistake, which we will regret. . .without the ACIR, our knowledge of important matters will never be anything more than meager. The action we are about to take will harm our capacity to govern effectively" (quoted in McDowell 1997: 127; see also Kincaid and Stenberg 2011).

ACIR was a valuable institution, particularly from the perspective of those involved in government at the state and local levels. It is tempting but unrealistic to look back through rose-colored glasses and suggest re-creating an ACIR. It is gone, the political environment has changed, and so have the assumptions and expectations about intergovernmental relations. As John Kincaid has concluded: "Absent significant changes in the national political environment, especially a de-escalation of party polarization, a new ACIR or even a narrowly tailored technical ACIR is unlikely to rise from the dead" (Kincaid 2011: 187; for more information on the history of ACIR see McDowell 2011).

When I arrived in Washington in 1971, the major associations representing state and local officials—the National Governors Association (NGA), the National Conference of State Legislatures (NCSL), the Council of State Governments (CSG), the National League of Cities

(NLC), the United States Conference of Mayors (USCM), the National Association of County Officials (NACO), and the International City/County Management Association (ICMA)—were referred to as the "PIGs" (Public Interest Groups). This horrible acronym that was replaced with a more descriptive (if somewhat pretentious) name, the "Big 7." They worked together through the Academy for State and Local Government, which had a budget and staff. The groups studied issues, developed research and policy papers, and lobbied on issues of shared interest.

The Big 7 also created the State and Local Legal Center to formally represent the collective interests of state and local governments in decisions before the Supreme Court. In many ways decisions by the Court could have as significant and possibly a more significant impact on the powers and authority of state and local governments than congressional legislation and administrative regulations.

Legally, state and local public interest groups and the governments they represent are prohibited from making campaign contributions, unlike groups and organizations representing special interests. In the past, members of Congress recognized and acknowledged the difference. With the increased pressure to generate campaign contributions, the growth in the number of special interest lobbyists, and the declining focus on intergovernmental relations, state and local governments are often treated as just another special interest, rather than an integral part of the system of federalism.

However, when the Big 7 coalesced around a specific issue, they could be remarkably effective in their collective lobbying efforts. While many members of Congress who formerly served at the state and local levels focused their attention on other issues when they came to Washington, others continued to appreciate the interests of state and local governments having been members of and active in the public interest groups. Senators Dirk Kempthorne, George Voinovich, Mark Begich, Mike Enzi, Lamar Alexander, Mark Warner, and Representatives Jim Moran, Mike Turner, and others worked with the Big 7 to encourage their colleagues to understand the needs and concerns of those representing state and local governments through the Big 7. In spite of these efforts, intergovernmental relations have not generated much interest or support from a majority of members of Congress. Senator Carl Levin was brutally candid when he told John Kincaid in 1988: "There is no political capital in intergovernmental relations or serving on ACIR" (Kincaid 2011: 184).

The New Intergovernmental Reality

By the early 1990s local elected officials and those representing the interests of local government were becoming increasingly concerned about the perceived increase in the number and breadth of both unfunded federal mandates and the preemption of local authority. While members of Congress espoused their belief in having decisions made by governments "closest to the people," mandates and preemptions were creating an environment of "shift and shaft federalism," shifting responsibility to local governments without providing the resources. Fewer and fewer Members of Congress and their staffs appeared to appreciate or give priority to both the consequences and un-intended consequences of legislation and regulations on states and localities. There were of course exceptions, primarily those members who had previously served in state and local government.

In discussing unfunded federal mandates it is important to recognize that in many instances state and local officials understand the necessity of a federal mandate. However, they believe the cost of implementing a national mandated policy should be paid by the federal government and not by individual jurisdictions. Furthermore, a "one-size-fits-all" mandate can add significant costs to cities where the mandate is not relevant.

A perfect example is the Safe Drinking Water Act of 1996. Pietro S. Nivola of the Brookings Institution has written that the act was created to

> secure a marked improvement in the health and safety of city-dwellers. But some of the law's subsequent rules have not passed that test. One EPA standard, for instance, requires that trace amounts of arsenic be eliminated from drinking water. This particular requirement will drain hundreds of millions of dollars from local taxpayers at attain a minimal gain in public health.
>
> (Nivola undated)

It also required costly tests for specific toxins found only in specific agricultural areas.

In 1993 the U.S. Conference of Mayors hired Price Waterhouse to conduct a survey quantifying the costs to cities of 10 unfunded federal mandates. These included: Underground Storage Tanks, the Clean Water Act, the Clean Air Act, the Safe Drinking Water Act, the Americans with Disabilities Act, and the Fair Labor Standards Act. Three hundred fourteen cities responded to the survey, representing "approximately one-half of the population among all cities with 30,000 or more residents . . . The total estimated cost for 1993 is $6.5 billion. Estimated costs for the five years 1994 through 1998 total $54.0 billion . . . Cities report unfunded Federal mandate costs consume an average of 11.7% of their locally raised revenues" (Price Waterhouse/U.S. Conference of Mayors 1993: 1–2).

In addition to mandates of specific concern to local governments, state elected officials represented by NGA, NCSL, and CSG have aggressively opposed elements of unfunded federal mandates which placed significant financial burdens on the states. These include Real ID, the Affordable Care Act, and No Child Left Behind.

State and local officials have been equally concerned about federal preemption of state and local authority. Often this is a response to special interests that are unable to prevail locally or at the state level and seek support and redress though federal legislation. Specific examples include the Religious Land Use and Institutionalized Persons Act (RLUIPA), which preempted local zoning regulations, and the Internet Tax Freedom Act, which prevents state and local governments from taxing Internet access.

Accompanying the negative impacts of mandates and preemptions, the level of federal funds budgeted for cities, both directly and as pass-through from states, has been declining as a percent of local budgets. In the 1970s just under 20 percent of local funding came from shared revenues. By 2013, excluding the spike of one-time economic stimulus funds from the 2009 American Recovery and Reinvestment Act, shared revenues had declined to less than five percent with virtually no expectation of a reversal of that trend.

The most visible and significant federal funding source for local government officials has been the Community Development Block Grant (CDBG) program. While it might not represent the largest dollar amount of federal funds provided to local governments, it has been the one program that galvanized the attention, engagement, passion, and direct lobbying by local elected officials. It also provides a lens through which to see the new reality for organizations representing the public sector in Washington.

   The issues of importance to local governments are broad, diverse, and often complex. Sustaining active engagement of local elected officials in advocating on an issue creates a unique set of challenges. CDBG and the general concerns about unfunded federal mandates and preemption of local authority generate visceral and almost universal concern for local elected officials. In brief, local officials are comfortable describing and articulating how these issues can have an impact on their individual communities. Many other issues and programs may in fact have profound negative impacts on cities, but because of their complexities and disparate effects, local officials are less comfortable advocating collectively on their behalf on Capitol Hill.

   During my tenure at NLC, I saw subtle but serious erosion of the comfort, willingness, and capacity of some elected officials to personally lobby members of Congress on behalf of collective priorities important to local governments. While groups and individuals at home continually lobby local officials, these same officials are often not comfortable playing the advocate role in Washington, something I found perplexing. When meeting with a member of Congress, local officials have local issues they want addressed or supported and are unwilling or uncomfortable raising a collective priority or concern of local governments. Instead, a member of Congress often will take control of a meeting, focusing on a program or issue he or she has successfully addressed for the local official. In addition, there is the rarely discussed unstated reality of the human condition, specifically that you can never underestimate anyone's insecurities. Addressing individuals in high or prestigious office, even the most powerful or confident mayors and council members in other situations become intimidated.

   Whatever the reasons, NLC has had the challenge of supporting their members to be clear and explicit in communicating and advocating for shared policy priorities. As a result, a fundamental resource available to a public interest organization like NLC, namely the active engagement of members, has been diminished, resulting in a subtle but important impact on how NLC has been able to lobby.

   Lobbying on behalf of state and local governments has also had to change as a direct result of the unraveling of the intergovernmental system, specifically as members of Congress, administrations, and their staffs gave less consideration to the interdependency of the levels of government. For some this was a philosophical belief in the primacy of the federal government, while for others it was a response to special interest lobbying for national standards. For those concerned about constraints on federal resources, it was a pragmatic option of shifting responsibilities without resources to other levels of government.

   It was gallows humor for local officials to note that local governments were the bottom of the fiscal food chain. There was no level of government to which they could shift responsibilities.

Big 7 Priorities

The following examples illustrate the Big 7 priorities as well as the shifting emphasis from lobbying for grants (except the American Recovery and Reinvestment Act) to defending against unfunded mandates and intrusive regulations.

Federal Unfunded Mandates

No legislation in Washington generated the level of unrestrained opposition by state and local elected officials more than the imposition of unfunded federal mandates.

While local elected officials and their representatives in Washington are equally concerned about unfunded state mandates, they are pragmatic in recognizing the benefit of working with their state colleagues in opposing federal unfunded mandates. Together, the Big 7 provided a lobbying tsunami that helped gain passage of the Unfunded Mandates Reform Act (UMRA) in 1995.

The Majority Leader, Senator Robert Dole, identified UMRA as SB-1 and asked Senator Dirk Kempthorne, a former mayor, to lead and manage UMRA through the Senate. Highly respected by state and local elected officials of both parties, Senator Kempthorne engaged all of the public interest groups in generating support from colleagues across the political spectrum. The legislation passed in the Senate by an overwhelming majority of 86–10 and in the House by 394–28.

UMRA was a high-profile success for state and local governments and those representing them, reflecting the total alignment and concern about unfunded federal mandates, timely political optics, and the then existing comity in the Congress. While the legislation did not eliminate unfunded mandates, it did require that the potential costs of a mandate to state and local governments be identified and considered in the development and adoption of federal legislation.

Presidential Executive Orders

In 1998 President Bill Clinton issued a new Executive Order 13083 on Federalism which changed the way federal agencies were to interpret regulations and rulemaking to favor the federal government over state and local government. This was a major change from Executive Order 12612 established in 1987 by President Ronald Reagan. President Reagan's order was unambiguous: "In the absence of clear constitutional or statutory authority, the presumption of sovereignty should rest with the individual states. Uncertainties regarding the legitimate authority of the national government should be resolved against regulations at the national level" (American Presidency Project 1987). The Executive Order President Clinton signed was ambiguous with caveats that gave agencies discretion to interpret regulations in favor of the federal government (American Presidency Project 1996). Reagan and Clinton grounded their orders based on the fundamental principles of federalism, but significantly diverged in how the principles would be applied.

President Clinton signed his Executive Order while in England without consultation with representatives of state and local government. It immediately galvanized the Big 7 public interest groups in aggressively lobbying the White House and encouraging Republican members of Congress to hold hearings on the order. After many unsuccessful meetings with staff at the Office of Management and Budget, the President's General Counsel quietly intervened and had the order changed.

The American Recovery and Reinvestment Act

When the Congress passed The American Recovery and Reinvestment Act of 2009 (ARRA), the Obama Administration reached out to the Big 7 and sought its input on the development and implementation of the legislation in order to expedite the award process and insure that it would be workable at the state and local levels. This program to create jobs in "shovel ready" projects was intergovernmental relations operating to the advantage of all levels of government and the public.

Internet Taxation

In recent years there have been many other issues on which the Big 7 have been aligned and acted in concert on Capitol Hill. Taxation on Internet sales has been a critical priority for all of the associations, although there have been clear differences over the years on the most effective lobbying strategy. State and local governments depend on sales taxes as a critical revenue source. With the accelerated growth of Internet sales, a federal court decision prevents the collection of the sales tax when the company lacks a physical presence, or nexus, in a state. The tax is owed but the company is not required to collect it. This creates a significant competitive disadvantage for local retail business and deprives state and local governments of the revenues necessary to provide basic services. Although there have been strategic differences within the Big 7 on how to address this priority, the groups agree on the long-term objective of ending preemption of state and local taxing authority.

While the Big 7 continues to work together in lobbying on programs and policies of shared interest, there have been undeniable changes that have impeded the impact of the collective. For the National Governors Association, the increased partisanship of their members has made it more challenging to take a position on critical issues, at times depriving all of the public interest groups of the past high profile leadership and bipartisan support of the governors.

Developing a shared set of advocacy priorities has long been a challenge driven by the organizational and cultural differences of the individual Big 7 members and how each set their agendas. In recent years these organizational differences as well as the personal styles of the executive directors, has added to the challenge of finding common legislative and policy priorities. It has not, however, prevented the groups from continuing to engage and remain committed to advocate on shared priorities.

An interesting if quixotic Big 7 initiative was to organize briefings to expose and inform key congressional staff members on the intergovernmental challenges created in Washington specifically by the explicit and unintended consequences of proposed legislation on state and local governments. Lacking an ACIR, this was an attempt to reestablish an appreciation of the relationship of the federal government to state and local government. It was a good idea but only modestly useful. In the polarized political environment, it is unrealistic to expect members of Congress to invest their energy and focus on state and local government. This trend has called for changes in lobbying strategies.

Changes in NLC Lobbying Strategies

The National League of Cities has a long history of engaging its members in the development of the organization's National Urban Policy and legislative priorities. Through program area committees composed of local elected officials, existing policies are reviewed and modified and new policies are initiated and developed. The product of this work is ultimately reviewed and voted on by the membership as a whole. This process benefits from the engagement of individual councilmembers and mayors with a substantive interest and knowledge in specific program areas.

These officials clearly have the greatest ownership for the NLC agenda and have been totally committed to the process by which policy was made. Perhaps more important, the policy committees provided their "organizational home" within NLC and were extremely protective of preserving the process and the committees on which they served. Efforts to make changes in order to increase the impact and effectiveness of the League's lobbying efforts were actively resisted over the years, given the loyalty, ownership, and historical commitment to the existing structure. The challenge for the NLC leadership and staff has been to find ways to sustain the enthusiasm and engagement of these members, as well as strategically involve other members to create a more robust personal and effective lobbying program.

During my years as Executive Director, we followed a "traditional" set of strategies to advance our lobbying agenda. NLC staff would engage with congressional legislative staff when bills were being crafted, calling on NLC members who had a personal relationship with key members of Congress to encourage their support.

NLC Weekly published the legislative priorities and the status of legislation as it was being developed. Weekly legislative updates were sent out to the state municipal leagues and members of our policy committees identifying specific members of Congress who needed to be lobbied. NLC staff called individual local officials to provide talking points and to request that they make personal calls to their Senators and/or Representatives and to support these officials. The most successful example of this lobbying strategy and process related to preservation of Community Development Block Grant funding.

Prior to NLC's Congressional Cities Conference each March, state leagues were provided with descriptive information on each of our policy priorities with key talking points to share with their state and local elected officials. During the conference, staff provided information, briefing and lobbying training workshops, along with single sheet talking points as well as "leave behind" cards to be given to members of Congress and their staff while visiting Capitol Hill. Conference plenary and workshop speakers were identified and invited to participate based on the policy priorities on our agenda. Some years we provided buttons for members to wear promoting a policy priority and other times we organized rallies on Capitol Hill as well as a briefing session in the Capitol with members of Congress supporting an issue.

The more we could engage individual mayors and council members with members of Congress they personally knew, the greater the prospects of generating support by that member. This was defined as "grass top" rather than "grass roots" lobbying. It was by far the most effective way of engaging NLC members and generating support from members of Congress, but also a costly and staff intensive process.

In the face of the growing impact of campaign contributions from special interest groups and an increase in the number of partisan lobbying organizations, NLC briefly considered retaining a partisan lobbying firm to generate access to key members of Congress, a practice used by many private sector organizations. We were quoted a price of $15,000 per month for "access and personal meetings" with key members of Congress. It was abundantly clear that the cost was too high, the practice was abhorrent, counter to our culture, and ethically questionable, and the outcomes were uncertain. It was a non-starter, but helped prompt a reexamination of how we advocated on behalf of local governments.

In exploring alternative strategies to strengthen NLC's lobbying impact in Washington, DC some members proposed following a strategy developed by the League of California Cities. In 2001 the California League made a strategic and tactical change in how they lobbied at the state level. They increased their dues by 50 percent to hire a field staff of 16 individuals, many of whom had political campaign backgrounds. Perhaps most significant, they adopted an aggressive lobbying strategy that included holding individual state legislators accountable on how they voted on issues important to cities. They publicly identified those who opposed them on issues and gave major positive recognition to supporters.

Some members encouraged NLC to follow this strategy at the national level, arguing that members of Congress needed to be held accountable. While a case could be made at the state level where the interests of cities were high profile, generating prominent attention by citizens, in Washington, DC the range of issues and the lobbying by interest groups are far more diffused. Following the California strategy in Washington was problematic and was more likely to marginalize than enhance NLC's effectiveness. The discussion, however, was important in compelling a continuing examination of how to be effective in changing national political environment.

In an effort to better understand the challenge NLC needed to address on Capitol Hill, we invited a long-time friend and astute political observer to provide his insights on how local governments, NLC, and local officials were perceived. A former city manager, who was serving as the chief of staff to a Republican Senator, pulled no punches in his presentation. What he described was not a pretty picture. His colleagues and the members for whom they worked assumed that NLC and the members we represented were mostly Democrats from larger cities. They had little or no idea or thought about local government needs or interests. While this may have involved a degree of hyperbole to make the point, there was a clear message that could not be ignored. The fact that an NLC survey showed that 43 percent of local elected officials identified themselves as Republicans and 41 percent as Democrats had little impact on the perception of local elected officials.

There was no quick fix to this real problem. Rather it required a systematic effort of increasing personal contacts with staff and members on the Hill and providing greater one-on-one support to local elected officials when they met with members of Congress. It required that the NLC legislative staff allocate even more time to cultivating and building stronger relations with individual congressional staff. Equally important, it involved expanding the way the organization communicated positions on issues both to the public and members of Congress.

NLC and other public interest groups historically depended on press conferences as a major strategy to communicate policy and advocacy priorities to the public, Congress, and administrations. The advent of social media diminished the value, interest, and utility of press conferences, necessitating a major transformation in how NLC communicated its positions. This included using the existing and ever-increasing social media channels, targeting to different audiences, appreciating the importance of redundancy in presenting information, and positioning and expanding NLC's capacity to provide credible data in support of programs and issues.

Lobbying to Defend Local Government Interests

It is instructive to review the nature and range of legislative initiatives, administrative regulations, and Supreme Court decisions that those advocating on behalf of local government confront.

Collective Bargaining

The National League of Cities has not taken a position in favor or against collective bargaining. However, it does oppose federal preemption of the right of state and local governments to make that decision. In the years after 9/11 public safety unions lobbied members of Congress to mandate collective bargaining for police and fire employees. On a regular basis, the public safety unions brought the bill up for a vote. While it was expected that Democratic Members of the House would support this legislation, it was a surprise when an overwhelming number of Republican Representatives signed on to the bill. Given the significance of this legislation for both Democratic and Republican local officials, NLC and other local government organizations have persistently and successfully prevented action in the Senate. For both Democratic and Republican local elected officials, this legislation would be a dramatic preemption of local authority. It is an excellent example of particular interest groups seeking support in Washington when they cannot achieve their objectives at the state and local levels. Depending on the influence of these interests, members of Congress are willing to turn a blind eye to principles of federalism and the intergovernmental system

Religious Land Use Regulations

In 2000 Congress passed the Religious Land Use and Institutionalized Persons Act (RLUPA), an extreme example of the preemption of local authority. Under the act religious institutions, as well as religious-related organizations, can claim discrimination when they want to avoid local zoning regulations. Instead of following the local regulatory appeals procedures, the legislation permits these institutions to bypass them and go directly into federal court. RLUPA personified the ultimate and successful preemption of local authority

Eminent Domain

When the Supreme Court reaffirmed the right of local governments to exercise the power of eminent domain in the 2005 case of *Kelo v. City of New London*, local government took a beating in the court of public opinion, Congress, and state legislatures. Brilliantly framed by opponents as a threat to individual property rights, federal and state legislators rushed to introduce and pass legislation to constrain the use of eminent domain. This issue was so toxic that local elected officials who supported eminent domain were unwilling to publicly defend its use and looked to NLC, which was "politically inoculated," to be the face and voice defending the appropriate exercise of this power. Again, Congress chose to intercede in what is clearly a local government prerogative.

Reductions of Program Support for Local Law Enforcement

An additional challenge directly impacting local governments has been changes in federal priorities that dramatically reduced support for local governments. Following 9/11 the Federal Bureau of Investigation (FBI) was appropriately tasked with reallocating resources to address the threat of terrorism. An unintended but real consequence was a reduction in the FBI's support to local police forces. This was not a reduction in funding, but a cut in program support, adding costs to local budgets and depriving local law enforcement of the professional expertise of the FBI.

Threats to Tax Exemption for Municipal Bonds

Finding ways of reducing the federal deficit is an objective overwhelmingly supported by local elected officials. However, proposals to eliminate the tax exemption for municipal bonds as a means of increasing federal revenues is a major threat to the fiscal viability of municipal governments. Municipal bonds are essential to funding capital infrastructure. The exemption is critical to controlling the cost of financing, and eliminating it could potentially increase costs to local government well beyond the monies cities receive from federal grants. Yet, the two bipartisan commissions that developed deficit reduction proposals included provisions to cut the exemption on municipal bonds. Congress has not acted on these proposals, which might help in controlling the federal deficit but at a significant cost to local governments.

Conclusion

More than anything else, these examples reflect the defensive position local governments as well as state governments confront as they lobby in Washington, DC to give voice to the fundamental concept of federalism and the importance of constructive intergovernmental relations.

Deil S. Wright, the highly respected observer of the intergovernmental system, recognized the shift and impact of the Big 7 on decisions related to the intergovernmental system:

> We have already noted the defensive and reactive posture of the Big Seven and many lesser public interest groups in the 1980s. *Fragile* and *variable* perhaps best describe the nature of the coalition as an effective policy-influencing force on the national scene. *Strong* and *solid* describe most accurately the information, publication, and service base of the several Big Seven organizations. The title of an article on the PIGs captures the singular and collective roles of these associations of officials. "The PIGs: Out of the Sty, Into Lobbying with Style." The state–local lobbies go in different directions with different constituencies; but they still come back together in the face of their common adversary: The Feds. As an institutional force, they have a visible presence. As a coalition with positive clout, however, they are politically peripheral.
>
> (Wright 1988: 283)

As an active participant advocating for the interests of local governments, I believe this critique is understandable, but overstated. I acknowledge that the influence of the public interest groups for reasons already identified has been diminished, but they are not peripheral as reflected in their ability at times to successfully oppose legislation that is anathema to the interests of state and local governments and impact regulatory language.

The challenge for those representing state and local governments is the apparent disinterest, lack of understanding, and diminished priority members of Congress have for intergovernmental relations and the direct and unintended consequences of their decisions on states and localities. Federalism does not appear to be a lens through which legislation is considered.

I would argue that the exponential increase in the number of special lobbyists, the importance of political contributions, and the polarization along partisan/ideological lines diminishes the ability of the public interest groups to be heard. This is not an excuse, but a reality. In the current fiscal and political environment, it is unrealistic to assume that additional federal revenues will be shared with local governments. However, local officials working with their state counterparts have been able to restrain Congresses, Presidents, and federal agencies from adding mandates and preempting state and local authority.

Former ACIR Executive Director John Shannon's 1980s characterization of the state of the intergovernmental system as "fend-for-yourself federalism" is accurate today. Rather than acting as victims or letting the actions and decisions in Washington, DC constrain state and local governments by the unraveling of the intergovernmental system they must and are acting with reduced federal support and, at times, in spite of federal constraints.

To be blunt, local governments are on their own and not necessarily suffering from that new reality. They are proving to be the most creative level of government in the deteriorating intergovernmental system. More often than not creativity in the public sector is a result of local initiatives and regional and public–private collaboration. The public interest groups, the Brookings Institution's Center for Metropolitan Studies, Bloomberg Philanthropies, publications and online organizations like *Governing* and *Citiscope*, and others are promoting and recognizing the innovative and creative leadership of cities, regions, and states. Bruce Katz, Director of the Brookings Institution's Metropolitan Policy Program, is outspoken on this issue: "Washington doesn't really see cities and states as partners anymore, and dysfunction in the capital underscores the fact that state and localities—as opposed to the feds—will be the government innovators going forward" (Holeywell 2013).

With the inauguration of Donald Trump as President local elected officials were prudent in withholding judgment on how the new administration would engage and support local government. However, in the first few months of his Presidency, President Trump had shown little interest or made any significant effort to reach out and/or constructively engage with representatives of local governments. His 2018 proposed budget abolished the 40-year-old Community Development Block Grant program. Executive orders and statements relating to the environment, education and healthcare generated strong questions and concerns from local government organizations and local elected officials.

The one significant exception has been the President's priority commitment to make a major investment in infrastructure. While the method of funding appeared to be heavily dependent on public–private investments, the specifics as of this writing remain unclear. However, this is a critical issue to cities and states and an opportunity to create a constructive set of intergovernmental relations.

Perhaps the most intriguing initiative following the 2016 election was the May 18, 2017 bipartisan announcement by Speaker Paul Ryan and Minority Leader Nancy Pelosi creating the Speaker's Task Force on Intergovernmental Affairs, chaired by Utah's Rep. Rob Bishop, a Republican. At the opening meeting the chair said that the goal of the task force was to examine ways to improve structures so that decisions can be made closest to the people. Representatives from the seven public interest groups were invited to present and engage with task force members.

Speaker Ryan's statement in creating the Task Force was a refreshing appreciation of the deterioration of intergovernmental relations over the past decades. In his May 18 press release announcing the establishment of the Task Force, Speaker Ryan noted:

> Federalism is not a Republican or Democrat principle, but an American principle—and one that is integral to a thriving culture and economy. But in recent years, the principle of federalism has been slowly chipped away at by an overzealous federal government. Under Chairman Bishop's leadership, the Task Force on Intergovernmental Affairs will study ways to restore the proper balance of power between the federal government and states, tribal, and local governments, and eliminate unnecessary regulatory burdens facing communities across the nation."

The mission of the Task Force as defined by the Speaker included:

1   Partner with states, tribes, and local governments to balance the interests of governments
2   Provide a forum for states, cities, and counties to showcase their innovation and creativity in solving public policy problems
3   Examine the effects of federal rules and regulations on state and local partners
4   Develop proposals to partner with and empower states, tribes, local governments, private institutions, families and individuals
5   Examine the extent to which the burdens shared among states, tribes and local governments may be re-allocated to improve the quality of life in all communities.

(Ryan 2017)

While not the reestablishment of ACIR, the Task Force is an important acknowledgement of the impact of federal laws and regulations on state and local government. At a time when partisanship is extreme, defining both the country and Washington, it is refreshing to see an island of bipartisanship, one that speaks to the critical issue of federalism and intergovernmental relations. While the 13 task force members may have a variety of motives and objectives, the fact that the forum was created is in itself significant. Big 7 representatives serve on the Task Force's Advisory Council.

In conclusion, ignoring the changes in intergovernmental relations of course is not possible or responsible. Rather, NLC, the state municipal leagues, and the other national public interest groups must continue to limit the damage of federal action as well as inaction. A key and successful strategy for fulfilling this responsibility has been to give visibility to creative, innovative, and transformational initiatives of local governments and local governance.

References

American Presidency Project. 1987. "President Ronald Reagan's Executive Order 12612—Federalism." October 26. Retrieved from www.presidency.ucsb.edu (accessed August 11, 2015).

American Presidency Project. 1996. "President William J. Clinton's Executive Order 13083—Federalism." May 14. Retrieved from www.presidency.ucsb.edu (accessed August 11, 2015).

Haider, Donald H. 1974. *When Governments Come to Washington: Governors, Mayors and Intergovernmental Lobbying*. New York: The Free Press.

Holeywell, Ryan. 2013. "Forgotten federalism?" *Governing* (May): 36–40.

Kincaid, John. 2011. "The U.S. Advisory Commission on Intergovernmental Relations: Unique artifact of a bygone era." *Public Administration Review* 71(2): 181–189.

Kincaid, John, and Carl W. Stenberg. 2011. "'Big questions' about intergovernmental relations and management." *Public Administration Review* 71(2): 196–202.

McDowell, Bruce D. 1997. "Advisory Commission on Intergovernmental Relations in 1996: The end of an era." *Publius: The Journal of Federalism* 27(2): 111–127.

McDowell, Bruce D. 2011. "Reflections on the spirit and work of the U.S. Advisory Commission on Intergovernmental Relations." *Public Administration Review* 71(2): 161–168.

Nivola, Pietro S. Undated. *Fiscal Millstones on the Cities: Revisiting the Problem of Federal Mandates*. Brookings Policy Brief Series no. 122. Washington, DC: Brookings Institution.

Price Waterhouse/U.S. Conference of Mayors. 1993. *Impact of Unfunded Federal Mandates on U.S Cities: A 314—City Survey, 1993*. Washington, DC: Price Waterhouse/U.S. Conference of Mayors.

Ryan, Paul. 2017. "Speaker and democratic leader announce task force on intergovernmental affairs." May 18. Retrieved from www.speaker.gov/press-release/speaker-and-democratic-leader-announce-task-force-intergovernmental-affairs (accessed June 25, 2017).

Wellborn, David M., and Jesse Burkhead. 1989. *Intergovernmental Relations in the American Administrative State: The Johnson Presidency*. Austin, TX: University of Texas Press.

Wright, Diel S. 1988. *Understanding Intergovernmental Relations*, 3rd edition. Pacific Grove, CA: Brooks/ Cole Publishing Company.

15 American Federalism without a System of Intergovernmental Relations

Parris N. Glendening

The American federal system is one of the great contributions to the philosophy and practice of human governance. The debates, struggles, and even battles over the federal arrangement have been many. This discourse has continued unabated for more than 225 years, and the temper has surged or lagged depending on the crisis of the moment.

It was only during the 1930s with the emergence of the many New Deal programs designed to overcome the Great Depression that discussion moved from a predominately philosophical, constitutional, legalistic study of American federalism toward an understanding of policy and process. Questions about how our brand of federalism actually worked, how it could work better, how policy was formulated and implemented, and how we could solve the great challenges of not just our federal arrangement but also and more urgently, the problems facing our nation started to dominate the conversations.

Born of these discussions was a brand new field of study: American intergovernmental relations. What emerged was not just a new area of academic study. It was an opportunity to understand both how the system worked and how it could be improved. How could our nation implement policies to address the great issues facing America and still maintain the strength and innovation that came from our constitutional structure?

So extensive did the studies on the process of the intergovernmental system become that recent writings are less likely to start as I did for this essay by noting the contributions of the "American federal system." Instead it is far more common and appropriate to note: "The American intergovernmental system was one of the great inventions of the country's Founding Fathers," as colleagues and I observed in 2013 (Rosenbaum, Glendening, Posner, and Conlan 2013).

This massive body of research and literature on American intergovernmental relations is well referenced by others in this book and elsewhere and need not be repeated here. As important as this great collection of academic research and insights was, the real change was the growth of new institutions, organizations, and centers all set up to make the intergovernmental system better.

By the 1980s there was a broad array or organizations working to study and to facilitate the operations of the intergovernmental system. This included, among others, the White House Office of Intergovernmental Affairs (name differed over the years), the Office of Management and Budget Division of Federal Assistance, the General Accounting Office intergovernmental relations unit, the House and Senate Subcommittees on Intergovernmental Relations, and offices of intergovernmental relations in almost every major government agency. First among these intergovernmental centers was the U.S. Advisory Commission on Intergovernmental Relations (U.S. ACIR). The rise and fall of the ACIR (1959 to 1996) reflected the level to which intergovernmental relations was thought of as a *system*. The real emphasis on intergovernmental discussions and analysis, coordination, and implementation was mirrored in the vitality and then decline of the ACIR and the many sister organizations in the national government (Kincaid and Stenberg 2011; McDowell 2011).

During this time, more than half of the states organized state commissions on intergovernmental relations, "little ACIRs," as they became known. These commissions not only worked on intergovernmental relations within their state and relations with the federal government but also often met with sister commissions from other states. The U.S. ACIR urged the establishment of a network of state commissions, the first meeting of which was held in Charleston in 1983. The network subsequently met once or twice a year often concurrently with a U.S. ACIR meeting.

Both the network and the state intergovernmental relations commissions shared the fate of the national intergovernmental relations organizations and slowly faded away, often the result of increasingly hostile and very partisan struggles. A 2010 study by the Council of State Governments—a strong supporter of the state commissions and of creating the network—concluded that the "dynamics of intergovernmental relations today, especially at the state and local level, have shifted from what might be described as coordination and cooperation to competition and adversity . . . In such a climate, the value of the perspectives that commissions contribute to the intergovernmental area is greatly diminished" (Wall 2010). Today there are only 10 such commissions still in operation.

This chapter focuses on American federalism without a system of intergovernmental relations. The implications are important and far-reaching. They are important not only from an academic and research perspective. They are far more important from a policy perspective as we try to address the urgent and significant issues confronting us today.

It is hard to imagine resolution of the major challenges, conflicts, and crises facing this country without having a flexible, innovative, and effective intergovernmental system. Think about the following: Growing income inequality and inequity with unacceptable numbers of citizens in real poverty at a time wealth continues to be concentrated at an unprecedented rate; racism and the explosive conflicts between authority and community; and a continuing deterioration of the environment with the certainty of increasingly violent and frequent climate change-produced disasters necessitating unprecedented mitigation and resiliency efforts. To this list could easily be added: the concerns about an immigration system that neither protects fully the security of the country nor insures the future of our newest arrivals; a revenue system that is so dysfunctional it cannot produce the funds to meet the most basic services and instead finds solutions in passing on costs to other levels of government and/or future generations; and the alarming lack of investment in infrastructure to the point that the nation's roads and transit, water and waste water treatment, etc. are rapidly falling behind much of the developed world.

The solutions to many of these "mega challenges" call out for the resources of the national government and nationwide regulation, enforcement, and compliance. In other areas the decentralized work of a smoothly functioning federal system can bring about needed innovation, experimentation, and diversity of policies. In most instances, it will be a combination of both approaches that works best.

Personal Observations on the Disappearance of the Intergovernmental System

The following are personal observations from my roles as an academician, elected official, and non-profit environmentalist about the rise and fall of the focus on an intergovernmental *system* and some thoughts about a future without that focus. The observations are based not on traditional rigorous academic research but instead on personal real world experiences. The importance lies not in specific events or individual experiences, but rests in understanding what has happened to the study and operation of the intergovernmental system. What are the implications for our federal arrangement and for policy-making and problem-solving in the United States today?

For a young political scientist entering the profession in the late 1960s and early1970s academia was an exciting place, particularly if you had a deep interest in American federalism and inter-governmental relations, as I did. It was a time of insightful new analysis and models, of serious scholarship that stood on the shoulders of encyclopedic works like W. Brooke Graves' *American Intergovernmental Relations* (Graves 1964) and the emergence of centers and journals devoted to intergovernmental studies. In a burst of enthusiasm, my new-found University of Maryland col-league and co-author, Mavis Mann Reeves, and I proceeded to write a leading textbook on federalism and intergovernmental relations, *Pragmatic Federalism* (Glendening and Reeves 1977) and to author dozens of articles and conference papers on the subject.

The academic research and writing were quickly enhanced and understandings deepened by my appointment and subsequent re-election to the Hyattsville, MD City Council in 1973. Hyattsville is a small (18,000) Washington, DC community nested among dozens of similar municipalities in the suburbs of the nation's capital. I learned quickly that being only 18,000 people in a metro-politan area of 5 million meant that the City's success is very much dependent on intergovernmental alliances.

The following year I was elected to the first of two four-year terms to the Prince George's, MD County Council and then to 12 years as elected County Executive. This extraordinarily diverse county of about 700,000 was in a constant series of intergovernmental conflicts, initiatives, and innovative experiments during these 20 years. Major examples included ending federal court ordered forced "bussing" designed to desegregate the public schools, insuring the completion of the "Metro" subway lines in the County at a time when the federal government and the region appeared to be moving away from finishing construction, and the ongoing violence resulting from the crack cocaine drug wars of the 1980s and the resulting conflict with both federal agencies and the District of Columbia. In many ways, it was a challenge of surviving and prospering when Prince George's, the region's poorest and most racially diverse suburb, was bounded by two of the wealthiest, most prosperous counties in the Nation—Montgomery County, MD and Fairfax County, VA.

It was during those years that I actively participated in and led many of the intergovernmental organizations that helped make government successful and effective. At the national level I served on the National Association of Counties (NACo) Board of Directors and on a number of key task forces and committees. As County Executive I served as Chair of the NACo Large County Coalition and then as President of the National Council of Elected County Executives (now called County Executives of America).

Intergovernmental relations had an overwhelming presence in my daily activities during this period. I not only served as the President of the Maryland Association of Counties (MACo), but also participated actively on many key state commissions, task forces, and study groups, including those on education funding, election law revision, and block grants among others. As an active regional leader, I headed a number of regional organizations such as the Metropolitan Washington Council of Governments, the Chesapeake Bay Commission (3 Bay states, DC and the U.S. Environmental Protection Agency), and the Critical Areas Commission (MD Chesapeake Bay front local governments and the State). Significant regional environmental collaboration was achieved through careful intergovernmental negotiations among these groups.

In 1994 I was elected for the first of two terms as Governor of Maryland. The intergovernmental part of my life heated up even more. There was, however, a noticeable change. Intergovernmental interactions moved more from collaboration, conciliation, and defensive struggles to being much more conflictual with often-intensive bitter battles, frequently very partisan. During this period the U.S. ACIR and many like organizations were either phased out or abruptly ceased existence.

It was in this very challenging time for intergovernmental relations that I assumed leadership in a number of national organizations. Among these were the most visible players for state-focused intergovernmental relations, such as National Governors' Association (Chair, 2000–2001), Democratic Governors' Association (Chair, 2001–2002), and the Council of State Governments (President, 2001–2003). I was also an active participant in many other more specialized intergovernmental organizations during this time of extraordinary change in the processes of our federal system. Examples include the Southern Governors' Association, the Education Commission of the States, Southern States Energy Board, Southern Regional Education Board and, shifting focus considerably, completed my elected office tenure serving on the President's Homeland Security Advisory Council (2002–2003). The Council was chaired by former Pennsylvania Governor Tom Ridge, my Republican ally in protecting the Chesapeake Bay.

I outline this intergovernmental perspective of my more than 30 years in elected office not as a "stroll down memory lane" but as a framework for understanding why the increasing lack of focus on an intergovernmental system is dangerous and produces very poor policy outcomes. Most importantly, that lack of focus increasingly makes it difficult to implement fundamental changes that are needed to address the biggest problems facing us, most pointedly for this discussion:

- growing economic inequality and inequity;
- crumbling infrastructure; and
- continuing decline of the environment.

Here I offer a link between observations as a young academic student of federalism and intergovernmental relations and a veteran of many intergovernmental struggles. In 1977 Mavis Mann Reeves and I wrote a very optimistic assessment of how our system worked:

> We write from a point of view—the view that American federalism is pragmatic. We believe that the intergovernmental relations within the system are constantly evolving, problem-solving attempts to work out solutions to major problems on an issue-by-issue basis, efforts that produce modifications of the federal and intergovernmental system . . . As each shift of level or modification of program occurs adjustments are made to accommodate to it, thereby creating more change. The elasticity of the arrangements helps to maintain the viability of the American system. In other words, it is pragmatic.
>
> (Glendening and Reeves 1977: viii)

Today 40 years later that level of optimism no longer exists. Instead of being pragmatic, the federal arrangement has become rigid and inflexible. The intergovernmental system part of it is increasingly weak and unable to address many key issues. Economic disparities continue to increase to dangerous levels as the federal system fails to offer relief on a collective basis and state and local governments are often unable to do so individually. The revenue system has become so flawed that even the simplest task of road and transit maintenance becomes undoable.

Much of this is the outcome of dramatic changes in the American political process. A portion of this collapse of the system is the increasing lack of a focus on the intergovernmental *system* itself. With no ongoing forum for debate and resolution of issues that call out for intergovernmental resolution and lacking a serious analysis of the intergovernmental implications of decisions it is not surprising that the pragmatic federalism of just a few years ago is rapidly disappearing.

Where Are We and How Did We Get Here?

From the beginning of the Republic there has been constant debate about the proper roles for the central government and the states. At times, philosophical and constitutional, at other times descriptive and analytical, and almost always highly political and partisan, Americans have argued and fought over the limits of national power and the role of the states. Our governance arrangement moved from the state dominance of the federal system in the early years of the Republic and again during the 1920s to the great centralization of the New Deal in the 1930s. So abrupt were the changes in the 1930s that many observers expressed sentiments similar to scholar and policy leader Luther H. Gulick's assessment:

> Is the State the appropriate instrumentality for the discharge of these sovereign functions? The answer is not a matter of conjecture or delicate appraisal. It is a matter of brutal record. The American State is finished. I do not predict that the States will go, but affirm that they have gone.
>
> (Gulick 1933: 420)

Although the focal point of power swung back and forth like a giant centralization/decentralization pendulum, inexorably it moved toward greater central power during the next 50 years. Driven by the pressures of new programs to end the Depression, protect Civil Rights, provide senior health care (Medicare), the demands of a federal urban policy and the War on Poverty, the beginning of national environmental programs, the constant international crises of World War II, the Korean and Vietnam Wars, the emergence of the Cold War and the Nuclear Age, and the ongoing struggle against terrorism, it seemed to many that perhaps Luther Gulick's assertions would be realized.

It was in the 1980s, and continuing into the 1990s, that the constant growth of federal presence and power began to lessen. Limits on national government growth in recent years have moved to the point that historical arguments of "States Rights" are increasingly used to justify opposition to programs as far-ranging as clean air regulations, the Affordable Care Act (Obama Care) or high speed rail construction. Some rhetoric became so heated that in the 2008 presidential campaign candidate Governor Rick Perry gave a near endorsement of Texas leaving the Union.

Discussion of the proper role of different levels of government and which government should have primary concern for a particular function are legitimate and, indeed, expected and healthy for the system. A key concern here, however, is the erosion, in some ways the disappearance, of a focus on the intergovernmental *system*.

Starting with the Reagan Administration, national programs were reduced, eliminated, devolved to states and local governments, or transferred to the private sector. This pace has continued, even accelerated. As these changes were made most of the mechanisms of the intergovernmental relations *system* were also set aside.

As programs were reduced, ended, or transferred and the research, data centers, and discussion forums were closed, the academic study of intergovernmental relations declined dramatically. This, however, is not the real loss. Far more important is the absence of an ongoing forum or process to discuss intergovernmental issues. As John Kincaid and Carl Stenberg (2011: 158) noted, "Intergovernmental deinstitutionalization occurred across the board during the 1980s and 1990s." In many ways, the intergovernmental part of major crises facing the country today and the programs advanced to resolve them are as great and even more complex than ever.

Three major issues discussed below—the growing economic inequality in the nation, the challenge of meeting our infrastructure needs, and the urgent need to solve or at least mitigate our many environmental crises—are all at their heart intergovernmental issues. Most the current discussions about the resolution of these challengers are totally devoid of any real intergovernmental analysis. Solutions are advanced at one level of government without any serious consideration of the impact on other levels of the federal partnership. Programs and costs are routinely off-loaded to other governments or left to future generations to solve and finance. In many areas no solution is advanced while fingers point to others to blame.

It is almost as if in the heat of policy debates it is temporarily forgotten that America is a federal system and that major policy decisions by one level of government often impact other levels. An increase or decrease in taxes at one level of government is often felt by other parts of the federal system. Cut expenditures to balance budgets and the fiscal offload is quickly felt elsewhere. In some instances like during the Great Recession, private sector job growth was offset by public sector job loss. This offloading is almost always done without deliberate intent or malice. In fact, even worse, it is generally done without analysis or foresight. It is as if other federalism partners were invisible.

In this debate there is no real forum for intergovernmental discussions. There are increasingly few institutions that undertake objective analysis of intergovernmental implications. There is no public voice for the advancement of needed federal and intergovernmental changes.

My over 30 years of elected office give me a reference point to note just how weakened the intergovernmental focus has become. It was not always this way. I recall clearly during my terms as County Executive and Governor there were some really bright spots in intergovernmental leadership at all levels of government, most notably from the White House.

One of the best examples of serious intergovernmental working relationships among officials at all levels was during the Clinton Administration. Clinton sought to prioritize intergovernmental cooperation by revitalizing ACIR, seeking increased funding from Congress, and placing a White House staffer, Marcia Hale, on the Commission (Warshaw 2009). Just three years later Congress eliminated the ACIR, with the President even withholding his prior strong support after disagreements with the Commission over the issue of unfunded mandates (McDowell 1997).

As governor, I worked on the Personal Responsibility and Work Opportunity Reconciliation Act of 1996 (welfare reform). Governors, mayors, and county executives were all involved in a vigorous debate over significant changes in the six-decades-old welfare program. Many of the meetings were in the White House with high-level members of the Administration. In the end many people were still unhappy with the legislation. Most, however, would agree that opportunities were offered for meaningful input and that we saw modifications in the final program reflecting many of our concerns. Such a level of intergovernmental involvement has not been part of the discussion of many of the most important policy issues before us today.

Another example involved the adoption of Executive Order 13132, which prohibited federal agencies from promulgating new regulations unless they provided funds for direct compliance and unless they consulted prior to adoption directly with state and local elected officials or their representatives or their national organizations. On first blush this Executive Order appeared to help state and local governments in the on-going battle against mandates, preemptions, and other excessive actions by the central government. In fact, it was a substantial weakening of a much stronger Executive Order (12612) signed by President Reagan in 1987. After a bitter political battle outlined in Donald Borut's chapter, major modifications were made that, while lessening Reagan's strong state-oriented federalism, still provided some of the protections and processes sought by state and local governments' organizations. I am not certain there was a dramatic change in agency behavior from either executive order nor did they appear to carry through very well to future administrations. At the time, however, they were important statements about state-centered federalism and about intergovernmental cooperation with other federal partners. This vigorous debate and "big picture" view of how the system should operate is largely missing in recent decades.

It was not only programs like welfare reform or processes like Executive Orders 12612 and 13132 that showed an intergovernmental *system* working well and fundamental principles of federalism being debated. The same intergovernmental system was key for number of huge "mega" public work projects in the Washington, DC area—projects that reshaped the future of the nation's capital. Most notable among those were the construction of the Washington Beltway (1961–1964), the "Metro" subway (1969–ongoing), and the reconstruction of the Woodrow Wilson Bridge (1999–2008). These were complicated, multi-billion dollar projects that involved decades of coordination among dozens of local governments, two states, the District of Columbia, and the national government.

As noted earlier, I was involved in struggles at the end of construction of the first stage of the subway to make sure that Prince George's County received its promised lines. My most extensive participation in the intergovernmental side of this type of project, however, was with the Woodrow Wilson Bridge reconstruction. This bridge carries about 250,000 vehicles per day across the Potomac River as part of Interstate 95 linking Maryland and Virginia. It originates on the Maryland side in Prince George's County.

Serious planning, design, and negotiations started in the early 1980s during my first term as County Executive and continued through my first term as Governor until 1999 when construction started. The intergovernmental actors included 29 federal agencies working through an Interagency Coordination Group. In addition to the numerous U.S. Department of Transportation entities, agencies as diverse as Fish and Wildlife, the Coast Guard, and EPA were involved. Also participating were the most impacted local governments (e.g., Prince George's and Alexandria, VA), the two states via their many state agencies, and the District of Columbia.

Meetings were often complicated, tough, and personal. At stake was much more than the normal questions of who was paying what share or route locations. Many other issues that at their heart involved differing visions about the future of the region. Maryland, for example, insisted that the bridge be constructed "Metro ready" (i.e., constructed with extra lanes and to standards that would bear the weight and vibrations for future expansion of the subway system across the bridge to further connect the capital region by rail transit). Maryland further insisted on wide pedestrian and bike lanes with "bump outs" for walkers and bikers to enjoy the views of the nation's capital and extensive landscaping on the bridge's approaches.

Virginia's two governors during the critical 1994 to 2002 period were strongly opposed to all of those proposals, looking instead to a much more traditional concrete and steel interstate construction that would save several hundred million dollars. Much of the paralysis of the intergovernmental system today is a result of excessive partisanship and ideology. The Woodrow Wilson Bridge project, however, was an example of the system working well on a bipartisan basis. Three presidential administrations (George H. W. Bush, Bill Clinton, and George W. Bush) kept the project moving to completion.

Some of the most interesting conflicts about the bridge overcame expected partisan outcomes. As mentioned above, two Virginia governors tried to block the additional federal funds for what they considered unnecessary "add-on costs." Former Ohio Republican Governor George Voinovich, having been elected to the Senate, was serving as the ranking member of the Appropriations Committee's Subcommittee on Transportation and Housing and Urban Development. I worked with him when he was Chair of the National Governors' Association (NGA), and he was very helpful in securing the additional federal funding even over the objections of his fellow Republican governors. George Voinovich is the only person to date to have served as the Chair of the NGA and President of the National League of Cities, giving him a broad perspective of the importance of having a working intergovernmental system. Today the Woodrow Wilson Bridge stands as a model urban bridge with pedestrian and biker lanes, viewing "bump outs," and ready for a transit line in the future. It is also a model of the intergovernmental relations system functioning.

The same successes were visible on a more horizontal level often without regard to partisan differences. Pennsylvania Republican Governor Tom Ridge, for example, on several occasions supported proposals advanced by Democratic colleagues from Maryland, DC, and the Administrator of the U.S. EPA to protect the Chesapeake Bay over the objections of more conservative Republican governors from Virginia. This reflected added leadership by Governor Ridge considering that Pennsylvania is the only state member of the Chesapeake Bay Commission that is not Bay front.

These two examples of intergovernmental leadership by Senator Voinovich and Governor Ridge demonstrate a working system overcoming partisan differences. Today, the opposite is more often true. An ideological divide and excessive partisan and personal politics have made functioning intergovernmental relations very difficult. Add to this the dismantling of those organizations designed to facilitate a smooth flowing intergovernmental *system*, like ACIR, and we should not be surprised that a "go-it-alone" or "fend-for-yourself" federalism dominates our governance today.

Solving Major Policy Challenges with a Broken Intergovernmental System

There are several very critical and complex issues facing America today. Almost all of these demand intergovernmental discussions and negotiations, intergovernmental solutions, and an effective intergovernmental system for implementation. The challenges of inequality, infrastructure renewal, and environmental protection are very real examples of extreme partisanship, ideology, and major policy differences limiting the effective functioning of an intergovernmental system. Meeting these challenges will mean, of course, a major restructuring of the intergovernmental revenue structure.

Income Inequality

The growing and serious income inequalities in this country matter. This matters because of the growing concentration of wealth and power in a small minority that becomes increasing isolated geographically and culturally from the rest of society. It has potentially serious repercussions to our political system, our policy-making process and our intergovernmental system.

Any approach to lessen these growing inequalities would have repercussions on our federal system of government. One approach would be to increase taxes on higher incomes. Tax hikes could focus on just the wealthiest or could adjust the graduated structure so that those earning more pay more. Changing the income tax structure would have major impacts on the intergovernmental revenue structure. Many state income tax structures are piggy-backed on the federal income tax structure. State adjustments would need to be made. Also, it would undoubtedly provide more money that could be used for intergovernmental transfers or programs that would affect state and local priorities and service expansions.

Another approach would be to support and expand the many services and safety nets for struggling individuals and families. They include a range of services—public education, housing assistance, low fare transit availability, medical support, childcare, and so on. Some of these "income add-ons" are relatively minor, sporadic, and often not even thought of as a means of lowering income inequalities. Free neighborhood parks and libraries, senior center breakfasts and school lunches, and community mental health or dental centers all are examples of small scale but essential "other sources" of income. From a larger, more systemic, perspective the great importance of "big picture" revenue sources such as social security, Medicare and Medicaid, extended unemployment benefits, or food stamps as major sources of "income" cannot be overlooked and could be adjusted to address the income inequality. Again, most of the services indicated are state and local but would require federal dollars in order to add or expand them.

Adding to the concerns about growing income inequalities is the reduction of revenue resources for what is often called "safety net services." Most of the changes in other relatively minor safety net services are the result of a localized decision by a governmental or quasi-governmental entity. When the transit agency increases fares 10 cents per trip, or the community college increases tuition by 4 percent, or the local water utility adds a new $10 a month "distribution fee" to each residential water bill, those most pressed by the growing income inequalities suffer.

These decisions are almost always justified as necessary because "the feds have cut back support for transit," or "the state reduced support for community colleges," or "with the sequester pressure on the budget, we can no longer subsidize individual users for luxuries like fishing licenses." Almost never is the discussion about the increasing inequality impact of these decisions or about the intergovernmental ripple effect that one decision creates. The problem is just "handed off" to another participant in a very complex governmental arrangement. The worker who decides transit is too expensive to get to work or the student who can no longer afford the community college tuition for job required skills are examples of people who drop out of the job market and switch to the unemployment set of supports. The challenge of low-income and of inequality has not been resolved. It has just been transferred to another agency and another level of government.

The third broad resolution of income inequality is to focus on the minimum wage. With the safety net supports and revenues frozen or being reduced and adjustments in the tax structure that would help reduce inequality increasingly unlikely to be approved, it is not surprising that major efforts would focus on changing the wage scale, most particularly the minimum wage.

The federal minimum wage started in 1938 at 25 cents per hour. The whole issue of having a minimum wage has truly been an intergovernmental debate and experiment from the beginning. Massachusetts adopted the first American minimum wage law in 1912, quickly followed by 13 other states and the District of Columbia. The U.S. Supreme Court consistently struck down these and other state and local initiatives as well as a number of federal minimum wage efforts.

The last time the federal wage was increased was in 2009 to $7.25. This has led to an on-going and very bitter political battle. President Obama made an appeal to the nation in his 2014 *State of the Union* message for an increase in the minimum wage. He noted that in the year since he requested congressional approval of an increase, five states (CA, NY, CT, RI, and NJ) had increased their state minimum wage level. The president's plea to his state and local counterparts was: "to every mayor, governor, state legislator in America, I say, you don't have to wait for Congress to Act; Americans will support you if you take this on" (Wogan 2014). Similar appeals were made almost immediately thereafter directly to the governors at the 2014 National Governors Association dinner at the White House. It was as if the president was advancing a unique version of "go it alone" federalism.

These entreaties produced vigorous debate and interesting actions in the federal system. There are currently 29 states that have minimum wages higher than the federal level. Much of the change is occurring locally, in most cases with minimum wages far greater than the national standard *or* the state level. Santa Fe and San Francisco in 2003 became the first cities to have their own minimum wage distinct from their states. A steady stream of local governments adopted their own wage standards in following years.

In June 2014 Seattle adopted a phased-in (by 2017) $15 minimum wage. Los Angeles quickly followed at the same level and other cities (e.g., Chicago and Washington, DC) are rapidly moving in that direction.

In the face of inaction at the national level and in many states, an even more complicated inter-governmental picture has been painted by strategies designed to create a large, multi-jurisdictional area with a higher minimum wage. Led by San Francisco and Oakland, a small group of cities in the South Bay area are coordinating efforts to make the regional local minimum wage $15 per hour. This effort has popular support and is being approved by city and county councils and by popular referenda. Oakland voters, for example, gave an 81 percent approval endorsement. Other coordinated efforts have even crossed state boundaries. Prince George's and Montgomery Counties, MD joined with the District of Columbia in 2014 to adopt an identical new minimum wage for the three jurisdictions ($11.50 by 2016 and then indexed for inflation) that, as the *Washington Post* (2013) noted, created "a contiguous region with 2.5 million residents and a minimum wage higher than any of the 50 states."

Even as these local intergovernmental agreements are adopted, a number of states have pushed back against the higher local government minimum wages and related employee benefits. Fifteen states have enacted preemption laws that prohibit local governments from having wage setting powers. Eleven states have preempted local governments from mandating sick days for private employees. These state-local intergovernmental battles have become increasingly bitter.

Infrastructural Renewal

Since the start of the Republic the central government has been involved in and often the leader of efforts to build a truly national infrastructure. While the Founding Fathers viewed a limited role for the national government in the post-Revolutionary arrangement, they quickly realized the demand for unifying, nation-building infrastructure, or "internal improvements" as it was called then.

The principal of federal support for national infrastructure projects quickly became accepted for an expanding number of investments including lighthouse and harbor improvements, canals, bridges and roads, especially "post roads" to promote the delivery of mail. After the 1830s railroads became a major focal point of federal support, often with major land grants.

Major and historic expansion of federal infrastructure investment occurred under Presidents Franklin Roosevelt, Dwight Eisenhower, and Barack Obama. Roosevelt's New Deal approach was in significant part a massive public works construction undertaking designed to lessen the impact of the Great Depression. The Works Progress Administration (WPA) alone employed more than 8 million Americans, and other alphabet organizations of the 1930s employed millions more. The sheer scope of the WPA projects still staggers the imagination: The Triborough Bridge, LaGuardia Airport, and Lincoln Tunnel in the Northeast; the TVA dams and power distribution system, the Blue Ridge Parkway (NC to VA), and the Overseas Highway in the FL Keys dominated the Southern projects; to the West there was the Hoover Dam, the first freeway in LA, and the Golden Gate Bridge, to name just a few. These were matched with hundreds of schools, courthouses, hospitals, and libraries in communities across the nation.

President Eisenhower, stressing the need for a defense highway system that could rapidly move military personnel and equipment as well as evacuate cities if a nuclear attack threatened, started the Interstate Highway system in 1956. This massive road construction program, almost 50,000 miles, had a dramatic impact on America's post World War II land use development, opening the suburbs and creating a car-dependent society and contributing to the "flight" from many of our largest cities. It is important to note that the Interstate and Defense Highway Act was the beginning of large-scale federal/state/local cost-sharing programs for infrastructure. It became the model for hundreds of infrastructure programs during the following decades.

The Interstate Highway Program, as it evolved over decades, stands as the strongest and most consistent use of a strong intergovernmental *system* for infrastructure investment. While specific projects were often very political, bitterly contested, and the cause of many community and environmental battles, the program used the intergovernmental process for over 50 years investing for billions of dollars in interstate highways, bridges, tunnels, and related projects. There were other major intergovernmental initiatives during this period, e.g., Lyndon Johnson Administration's many urban redevelopment and anti-poverty programs, but none had the consistent intergovernmental administration, magnitude, and impact as the Interstate Highway Program.

The third big burst of federal infrastructure investment was the American Recovery and Reinvestment Act (ARRA) popularly referred to as the Stimulus Program or the Recovery Act proposed by President Obama. This $787 billion (later revised to $831 billion) was a Keynesian economic theory response to the Great Recession of 2008. Designed to save jobs, put the unemployed to work, and help state and local governments deal with major fiscal crises, it offered a broad array of relief and stimulus programs. Included were significant tax incentives ($288 billion), support for Medicaid and other healthcare ($155 billion), education ($100 billion), and aid to low income workers and the unemployed ($82 billion).

Continuing the long history of national government support for infrastructure investment, the Act included $105 billion for infrastructure. About one-half of that amount went to transportation projects through the very popular Transportation Investment Generating Economic Recovery

(TIGER) grants. Twenty-eight billion dollars was allocated for traditional highway and bridge construction projects. Reflecting changing infrastructure needs, $18 billion was allocated to support transit, including intercity passenger rail, especially high-speed rail, new transit projects and Amtrak.

The other half of the Act's infrastructure funding went to a broad range of needs: water, sewage, and environment (e.g., rural drinking water and waste disposal projects and hazardous waste cleanup at Superfund sites); government buildings (e.g., child development centers and housing for service members); and energy (e.g., modernize the electrical grid and smart grid and for power transmission system upgrades). Reflecting modern infrastructure needs, there were significant investments for renewable energy, weatherizing low-income homes, biofuel, and solar and wind projects.

With the exception of the 2009 Stimulus program, there has been a major decline in the dollar value of intergovernmental infrastructure investment. Even the 2009 stimulus was advanced as a one-time expenditure to deal with the economic crisis.

With the stimulus program, there was no real intergovernmental discussion as leaders at all levels of government rushed to avoid a "free fall" of the economy. The surprising thing was how little the states and the governors had been involved in structuring the program. It was understood that this was an emergency and there was a great need to act quickly, and yet most of the states received the first hint of how the stimulus would work only at the time of grant application requests.

There are many reasons for the significant decline in national infrastructure investments. Among them was the 2005 "Bridge to Nowhere" controversy concerning the proposed "earmarked" funding for a $400 million bridge from Ketchikan to Gravina Island, Alaska. The Island's population was about 50 people. This led to a number of anti-earmark efforts in Congress resulting in a general ban on the process by 2010. Not surprisingly the enthusiasm for other capital projects declined sharply after members became unable to direct such funding to their own state or district.

The second big change was the adoption of the Sequester Process (Budget Control Act of 2011). First implemented in 2013 the Act calls for automatic cuts of $1.2 trillion between 2013 and 2021 to be evenly divided between domestic and defense spending. Exempting large entitlements like Social Security and Medicaid insured a major annual reduction in discretionary spending. Budget cuts ranged between 7.6 percent and 9.6 percent for most agencies. Since capital projects are the easiest to cut without causing long-term agency disruption, many reductions impact infrastructure investment.

Last is the major change in the partisan make up and the political philosophy of Congress. Democrats controlled both Houses in 2009. Republicans held majorities in both chambers by 2015. It was not just a change of party. The new majority is fiscally very conservative, vehemently anti-tax, and strongly committed to reducing the size and cost of the national government. The "low hanging fruit" for budget decisions based on this philosophy are often discretionary intergovernmental infrastructure expenditures. Witness the consistent effort to reduce federal aid for local transit construction and operation.

There are currently calls by the White House for "huge" infrastructure investments but the details are still unclear. It is almost certain that the approach will not be utilizing the intergovernmental system, as the Trump Administration's first budget called for dramatic reductions in infrastructure spending.

Environmental Protection

The focus on protecting our environment is a relatively new governmental function at any level of our federal system. For most of our history it was simply not a public issue. If there was a problem, expectations were that the community acting collectively but not through government, or the private sector including individual landowners would deal with it.

Land conservation and site preservation were the main focus of national environmental protection up until the mid-1960s when national legislation still centered on conservation but gave a much broader interpretation of what "conservation" meant and created more aggressive tools to achieve those ends. Major examples included the Wilderness Preservation Act (1964), the National Wild and Scenic Rivers Act (1968) and the Endangered Species Preservation Act (1966). These laws previewed the much broader and more aggressive environmental legislation of the 1970s.

Environmental protection at the state level largely reflected the federal emphasis on conservation and preservation. For example, in 1885 New York business, sportsmen and conservationists came together to create the first state major forest preserve. Designed to both protect forest and the source of clean water for downstate, 715,000 acres of forestland were permanently preserved. This later became the Adirondacks State Park, serving as a model for similar efforts at the state level, especially in New England and the West. These programs set the scene for much broader state environment programs in the twentieth century.

At the local level the early work for the environment centered on clean drinking water, raw sewage removal, and public health especially disease prevention in overcrowded urban slums. New York City created the first local health department in 1866. The other notable and important local environmental forerunner was the emergence of a major system of urban parks.

This, then, was the state of environmental protection efforts in America for the first 175 years. Noteworthy not just because of the singular focus on conservation, preservation, and parks, but also because most initiatives were done by one level of government with very little help from or interaction with other levels. There was occasional cooperation and some financial support, but for the most part there was no meaningful intergovernmental actions or programs for environmental protection.

The situation changed dramatically in the 1960s and especially the 1970s as a large number of urgent and comprehensive laws gave birth to a very complicated intergovernmental system of environmental regulations and programs. The new environmentalism did not occur in a vacuum. In 1892 naturalist John Muir formed the Sierra Club. That organization experienced phenomenal growth in the 1960s and 1970s, as did the National Wildlife Federation, which was started in 1935. The Sierra Club grew from 230,000 members in 1960 to 819,000 by 1970 (Dictionary of American History 2017). These organizations were joined by dozens of new comers the 1960s and 1970s, e.g. League of Conservation Voters, Friends of the Earth, Environmental Defense Fund, Natural Resources Defense Council, and Greenpeace, among many others. Hundreds of similar advocacy groups sprung up at the state and local level all across the country.

Very quickly the environmental movement shifted from land conservation programs to an urgent focus on pollution, especially chemical pollution of our air, water, and habitat, solid waste disposal, and pesticide poisoning. The latter became a major national concern as a result of the intense and widespread reaction to Rachel Carson's *Silent Spring*. Even pop music focused on these issues. Recall Joni Mitchell's "Big Yellow Taxi": "They paved Paradise, put up a parking lot" is the most famous line from that song, but her reference to DDT in the song alludes to Carson's book.

With this backdrop the first Earth Day was held April 22, 1970. More than 20 million Americans, marched, protested, held sit-ins and teach-ins, and demanded change in environmental policy and laws. The tumultuous decade ended with widespread coverage of the Love Canal disaster in which a community in Niagara Falls, NY was discovered to have been built on top of a 70 acre landfill of toxic wastes from the 1940s and 1950s causing a range of major health problems for the residents.

The unprecedented focus by the press, especially television, on major environmental disasters helped generate many significant environmental laws and programs in the 1970s that built on those passed in the 1960s. Among the most important were:

- President Richard Nixon created the Environmental Protection Agency (EPA) to enforce environmental laws and regulations (1970).
- The Clean Air Act regulated air emissions and gave the EPA power to set air quality standards (1970).
- The Noise Control Act authorized EPA to regulate noise pollution (1972).
- The Clean Water Act placed a limit on the flow of raw sewage and other pollutants into lakes, rivers and streams and gave the EPA power to set standards and to enforce them (1972).
- The Endangered Species Act empowerd the U.S. Fish and Wildlife and the National Marine Fisheries Service to list and protect all endangered species (1973).
- The Safe Drinking Water Act protected drinking water against pollutants (1974).
- The Toxic Substances Control Act (1976) required EPA to track and ban chemicals that pose a threat to the environment or to human health (Hartman undated).

In addition, in 1975 Congress authorized EPA to set standards for tail-pipe emissions to reduce automobile produced air pollution. At the end of this extraordinary 10 years of environmental initiatives Congress created and funded the Superfund program to help clean up hazardous waste sites. As one study of this time of great change noted: "During the decade of the 1970s alone, more than twenty major federal environmental laws were enacted or substantially amended, giving EPA and other federal agencies enormous regulatory responsibilities" (Percival 1995).

In two short decades, environmental protection moved from being largely a single focus issue of land conservation implemented by independent levels of government to being the center of a very controversial, bitterly fought, and constantly changing part of the intergovernmental system. Because environmental protection is so complex EPA has used many different approaches during its almost 50 years of existence.

Many programs were primarily voluntary and incentive driven such as the Coastal Zone Management Act. Education, financial incentives, and cost sharing are all tools used for many EPA programs. The other approach is very much a command-and-control use of regulations often resulting in fines or other penalties. The Clean Air Act and Clean Water Act and those programs designed to protect the public such as the Toxic Substances Control Act rely heavily on regulatory enforcement with penalty potential. Many environmental protection policies rely on concurrent enforcement, such as the Endangered Species Program.

Adding to the challenges of environmental protection in an intergovernmental system is the reality that some issues may be purely local, impacting one state or locality, while others are nation-wide. Many are regional, requiring the creation of intergovernmental bodies such as the Great Lakes Commission (8 states and 2 associate member Canadian Provinces) or the Chesapeake Bay Commission, (MD, VA, PA, DC, and EPA).

Environmental policies often pit one state or local government against neighboring jurisdictions with the intergovernmental system responding slowly and ineffectively or not at all. West Virginia's mountain top removal for coal mining has both water and air impacts on surrounding states. I recall a conversation with the then Governor of West Virginia and a personal friend about the problem. His response was "Sorry, but in this State coal mining is King." A decade later the efforts for an intergovernmental solution to that problem continue.

The supply of water is an increasing source of inter-jurisdictional disputes. Georgia as an example has been in a long-running legal and political battle with Florida and Alabama about the amount of water Atlanta takes from the Chattahoochee and Flint rivers "posing a threat to the ecological system" of its two neighbors (Atlanta Journal-Constitution 2017). While Georgia recently scored a major legal victory the problem, made increasingly worse by continuing droughts and water consumption by greater Atlanta's sprawling, growing population, is far from over. Other legal and congressional challenges are certain.

The intergovernmental system has been particularly stressed because of the constantly changing politics of environmental protection. State or local governments often side with significant polluters against the EPA or other regulatory agencies. Siding with major local businesses like a large power company or local paper mill, or trying to protect a major polluting industry, such as coal mining or big chicken farming corporations, often pits the combined resources of states and private industry against enforcement. These struggles frequently end up as multi-year court cases that even challenge the constitutional or legal basis of enforcement (Percival 1995).

Changing political philosophies and ideologies have regularly caused great uncertainty for environmental protection efforts. Ronald Reagan as a candidate for President claimed that President Carter's clean air regulations were responsible for closing many plants and coal mines. Referring to the Clean Air Act of 1970, candidate Reagan speaking in Youngstown, Ohio said: "these 1970 rules have helped force factories to shut down and cost workers their jobs . . . and they will certainly slow the use of coal" (Washington Post 1980).

His appointee as EPA Administrator, Anne Gorsuch, consistently tried to weaken the Clean Air Act and the Clean Water Act as well as end the Superfund cleanups (Little 2004). Her cabinet colleague Interior Secretary James Watt went to extraordinary efforts to increase drilling, mining, forest cutting, and commercial use of federal lands and water. Watt and Gorsuch put a significant brake on the flood of new environmental initiatives and the enthusiasm for environmental protection that had dominated the 1960s and especially the 1970s. Greg Wetstone, then Director of Advocacy for the Natural Resources Defense Council, noted that "Never has America seen two more intensely controversial and blatantly anti-environmental political appointees than Watt and Gorsuch (ibid.).

President Reagan, in the name of reducing the cost and presence of the federal government, made significant reductions in EPA personnel, budget, and enforcement efforts. Gorsuch, claiming to be a follower of the "New Federalism" who would return responsibilities to the states, reduced the EPA budget by 22 percent before resigning under pressure after being cited for contempt of Congress.

The U.S. EPA had several very good administrators from both parties since that controversial period of cutback and weakened mission. However, they could not recapture the innovation, enthusiasm, and level of broad bipartisan support that dominated the environmental protection efforts of the 1960s and 1970s. It was during this time that the idea of a strong intergovernmental *system* largely faded from existence.

Three Concluding Thoughts

America has always been a nation of innovation, experimentation, and change. Over the years, we change as we debate the role of the private sector versus government, or of individual rights versus collective norms, or of the role of the national government versus the states. In this time of extraordinary social, economic, demographic, and political change both in the United States and around the world it should not be a surprise that our federal arrangement and our intergovernmental system will adapt and be modified. It must do so.

As Mavis Mann Reeves and I noted 40 years ago in *Pragmatic Federalism*:

> The most dominant pattern emerging from intergovernmental change is that of pragmatic intergovernmental relations within the federal system—a constantly evolving, problem-solving attempt to work out solutions to major problems on an issue-by-issue basis, resulting in modifications of the federal and intergovernmental systems . . . The very elasticity of the arrangement helps to maintain the viability of the American system.
>
> (Glendening and Reeves 1977: 21).

Individually we may not like the direction of current changes in our system of governance. Or, indeed, we may applaud them. Many individuals and groups will welcome less government, hoping that means less taxes, and/or more functions transferred to the state level. Others will call for a stronger collective intervention by the national government, with its greater revenues and powers. This on-going debate is a reflection of the political system dealing with the great challenges of the day.

The magnitude of the 2016 election results notwithstanding, those changes are still being sorted out. One thing is certain. Our federal system will change dramatically during the course of the next decade or two.

Within this context, I advance three concluding thoughts about a state-centric federalism, the impact of the Trump Administration, and the need for an intergovernmental relations "think tank." Brief references are made to some of the thoughtful "Big Questions" advanced earlier in this book.

State-Centric Federalism

There was a great expansion of the national government's size and powers as the nation responded to the Great Depression and international wars during the more than two decades of the Roosevelt-Truman Administrations. The centralization pattern continued for more than 25 years through four presidencies: Eisenhower (interstate highway program), Kennedy/Johnson (Civil rights, Medicare/Medicaid, and the War on Poverty), and Nixon (EPA and major environmental laws). The centralization of these years was amplified by continuing international wars and crises (World War II, Korean and Vietnam wars, and the Cold War). The Ford/Carter years were relatively quiet transition years on the question of the role of the federal government.

The seismic shift in modern federalism started with President Ronald Reagan's New Federalism. His goals were straightforward: cut taxes; reduce federal spending; and return power to the states. As he stated clearly in his first inaugural address (1981):

> It is my intention . . . to demand recognition of the distinction between the powers granted to the federal government and those reserved to the states or to the people . . . All of us need to be reminded that the federal government did not create the states; the states created the federal government.
>
> *(CQ Researcher* 1981).

The four presidents following Reagan either did not want to expand the federal role or were constrained from doing so for fiscal reasons or by political opposition. Even a liberal chief executive like President Obama was limited in further expansion of the national government's role. His anti-Great Recession stimulus program (AARA) was tightly limited and rapidly phased out by a conservative Congress, and his health insurance initiative (Affordable Care Act) is still a matter of great debate. Neither had the centralizing impact of Roosevelt's New Deal.

These presidents were constrained in many ways by the "four d's" of debts, deficits, demographics, and defense. Barring a very unlikely major increase in federal revenues, this decentralization trend will continue.

Although he was probably elected for several other reasons, Donald Trump's presidency is a strong continuation of the same Reagan principles: reduce taxes and federal revenues; limit the size of government; and return powers and programs to the states. President Trump has shown no explicit awareness of the Constitutional arrangement or of the complexities of our intergovernmental system. His initial proposals, however, would continue significantly the movement to a state-centric federalism.

Both Presidents Reagan and Trump denied strongly that their efforts to return programs to the states was really an effort to reduce the role of government at all levels. Without additional major revenues, that is almost certain to be the outcome given the fiscal challenges that most states already face.

There will be other major changes in the intergovernmental system if some of the current Administration's proposals advance. Many environmental challenges, notably air and water pollution, do not recognize state boundaries. There will be increased state and local multi-jurisdictional efforts to solve these problems. Most immediately there has been a growth in collective resistance to many of these programs by state and local leaders. For example, eight Mid-Atlantic and Northeastern states have joined together to fight air pollution from nine Mid-Western states. Without successful EPA intervention, this will become a protracted legal and political battle for years to come. State and local governments are also organizing in a variety of coalitions to implement the Paris Agreement climate change provisions even if the national government does not do so.

Because of the intense debate on a number of major social issues, state-centric federalism will generate a range of new conflicts between the states and the federal government and between the states and their local governments. Note the battles over Sanctuary Cities, or the coalition of big cities trying to enforce the higher Paris Agreement environmental standards, or the efforts by many states to restrict local adoption of minimum wages that are higher than the state's.

State-centric federalism will have challenges with political, legal and fiscal battles to be sure. We should remember, however, as Mavis Reeves and I said 40 years ago: "In the long run it will be the states' resilience and viability that will maintain the federal bargain and protect against excessive centralization" (Glendening and Reeves 1977: 323).

The Impact of the Trump Administration

The new Administration is a continuation of the decades long political movement for a state-oriented federal system and specifically to a smaller, less intrusive central government. At this early date, it is hard to tell the full, long term-impact of the Trump Administration. A series of political controversies, scandals, and apparent lack of knowledge about how the government process and especially the intergovernmental system work has hindered implementation of any of the President's campaign proposals. The changes in the tax system, the health program replacement, and the extraordinary infrastructure investments for which President Trump advocates would have a significant, even historic, impact on the federal and intergovernmental systems.

Certain impacts, however, are clear from the President's early actions. The new Administration has moved to repeal many of the environmental regulations and to end or reduce many EPA programs. His opposition is based on the same view that Ronald Reagan had about a relationship between these regulations and jobs. As President Trump has stated repeatedly: "I will cancel job-killing restrictions on the production of American energy, including shale energy and clean coal, creating millions of high-paying jobs" (Washington Post 2016).

Further echoing President Reagan's appointments of Anne Gorsuch as EPA Administrator and James Watt to head the Department of the Interior, President Trump appointed Ryan Zinke to be Interior Secretary and Scott Pruitt to be EPA Director. Both are climate change deniers, although each of them modified their positions during Senate confirmation hearings. When asked on CNBC about the relationship of carbon dioxide increasing global warming, Mr. Pruitt responded: "I think that measuring with precision human activity of the climate is something very challenging to do and there's tremendous disagreement of impact, so, no, I would not agree that it's a primary contributor to the global warming that we see" (New York Times 2017). Secretary Zinke has advocated for energy development and mining on public lands and waters as well as further commercial development of federal lands.

Both appointments and the changes they are implementing, especially at the EPA, are already having impacts. States and even whole regions are increasingly pitted against others based on coal burning plants' impact on their states water and air quality. They have generated considerable partisan battles over the wisdom of moving away from environmental protection enforcement. The level of community and political activism around the issue of protecting the environment has not been this strong and widespread since the 1960s and 1970s.

Some states and local governments have vowed to move on their own to continue those protections. Just days after the U.S. withdrew from the Paris Agreement, an alliance of states and local governments announced that they would continue to meet the goals of the Agreement. Former New York Mayor Michael Bloomberg, speaking in Paris after meeting with French President Macron, said: "The American government may have pulled out of the agreement, but the American people remain committed to it—and we will meet our targets" (Los Angeles Times 2017).

Another impact is occurring in the area of infrastructure funding, particularly for mass transit. The President has not yet advanced his often-touted huge new program for infrastructure investment. Preliminary discussions suggest it will not be good policy for state and local governments. Their representatives do not appear to be having any input to the program's early deliberations.

The politics of "no new taxes under any circumstances" appears to have paralyzed national efforts to invest in any meaningful way in new transportation infrastructure. The federal gasoline tax was last raised in 1993. Inflation from 1993 to 2015 was a little over a compounded 64.6 percent, greatly reducing the buying power for the Transportation Fund. States are increasingly moving on their own in this area. Twenty-nine states have legislatively increased the gas tax or otherwise raised new fees to support their transportation needs. In addition, there has been a surge in support for local referenda to raise new taxes for mass transit. For the last decade, the approval rate for these referenda has been just under 80 percent. In the 2016 election, when the President was running on a reduced taxes approach, voters approved $200 billion in local tax increases for transit; $150 billion of that amount was for Seattle and Los Angeles. The latter voted 70 percent in favor of an additional half a cent sales tax on top of the half a cent already used for transit. These approvals are taking place in Republican dominated states as well. Atlanta, Raleigh (Wake County), and Indianapolis voted to increase local taxes to support transit. Ironically, the Indianapolis vote for a local income tax increase was authorized by legislation signed by now Vice President Pence (Davis 2016).

The bottom line is that many state and local governments are moving forward in transportation and especially transit funding as the national government remains paralyzed by a rigid anti-tax philosophy, a strong anti-transit bias, and an excess of partisan rhetoric. An informal "divide the job" systematically as proposed by President Reagan in 1981 may be incrementally taking place now. Unfortunately, there is no real on-going discussion about the intergovernmental impact of this change.

Lastly, it is important to note that while we do not know the details of President Trump's proposed tax cuts, every indication is that it will further the income inequity in America, especially if combined with some of the proposed health care changes. States will not be able to respond in an effective way with changes to their tax codes. Therefore, the most likely solution will be a surge in efforts to increase minimum wages, family leave, etc. This will produce another round of preemption battles as conservative state governments try to block more progressive urban areas from making these changes.

Need for an Intergovernmental Relations Think Tank

As I think through the events of this chapter, I find it necessary to reaffirm a call I made several years ago for the creation of an intergovernmental relations Think Tank (Glendening 2013). While America faces some very serious challenges, we are a strong country. The solutions to many of these challenges are for all of us—citizens, policy and academic leaders, and elected officials—to pull together in a cooperative, intergovernmental, and less partisan approach.

The second part of the solution is to remember that we are a federal system dependent on a smoothly functioning intergovernmental system. Proposed policies, debates, and deliberations and implementation must all recognize the intergovernmental nature of our governance system. As the National Academy of Public Administration memorandum cited above concluded:

> In order to strengthen the federal system emerging needs for public services and public deficits must be addressed; intergovernmental tax reform should be undertaken in a collaborative manner; a means to an institutional framework for the improvement of intergovernmental policy must be initiated; and much work must be done to rationalize that system.
>
> (Rosenbaum, Glendening, Posner and Conlan, 2013)

To the last couple of points, it has been recommended in several recent reports that we backfill with advisory panels and organizations that are intergovernmental in nature, maybe even create a new Advisory Commission on Intergovernmental Relations. I strongly recommend, however, that it be outside of government—not even a quasi-governmental agency. It should be an independent, freestanding "think tank" similar to the Cato Institute or the Brookings Institution, or based at a major university or a consortium of universities.

As an eternal optimist, I affirm that we are a strong nation. We will solve our problems. We have collectively faced bigger challenges in the past than those before us now. We faced those challenges and emerged an even stronger country.

We will best do so, however, if we remember that we are a federal system and depend on a smooth functioning intergovernmental system.

References

Atlanta Journal-Constitution. 2017. *Atlanta Journal-Constitution* (February 14). Retrieved from www.ajc. com/news/state--regional-govt--politics/georgia-scores-major-victory-water-wars-feud-with-florida/kOdvkyyRf6yBFYLsx3bCML.

Carson, Rachel. 1962. *Silent Spring*. New York: Houghton Mifflin.

CQ Researcher. 1981. "Reagan's 'New Federalism'." Retrieved from http://library.cqpress.com/cqresearcher/document.php?id=cqresrre1981040300.

Davis, Stephen Lee. 2016. "Billions in transit measures approved Tuesday." November 10. Retrieved from http://t4america.org/2016/11/10/billions-in-transit-measures-approved-tuesday-unpacking-the-2016-election-results (accessed October 17, 2017).

Dictionary of American History. 2017. "Environmental Movement." July 11. Retrieved from www.encyclopedia.com/earth-and-environment/ecology-and-environmentalism/environmental-studies/environmental-movement.

Glendening, Parris N. 2013. "Forum on Federalism Hearing." Council of State Government Conference, Kansas City, MO, September 21.

Glendening, Parris N. and Mavis Mann Reeves. 1977. *Pragmatic Federalism: An Intergovernmental View of American Government*. Pacific Palisades, CA: Palisades Publishers.

Graves, W. Brooke. 1964. *American Intergovernmental Relations*. New York: Charles Scribner's Sons.

Gulick, Luther H. 1933. "Reorganization of the state." *Civil Engineering* (August).

Hartman, Molly. Undated. "Milestones in Environmental Protection." Retrieved from www.infoplease.com/spot/milestones-environmental-protection (accessed June 2017).

Kincaid, John and Carl W. Stenberg. 2011. "Introduction to the Symposium on Intergovernmental Management and ACIR Beyond 50: implications for institutional development and research." *Public Administration Review* 71: 158–160.

Little, Amanda. 2004. "A look back at Reagan's environmental record." *Grist* (June 11). Retrieved from http://grist.org/article/griscom-reagan (accessed June 2017).

Los Angeles Times. 2017. *Los Angeles Times* (July 14). Retrieved from www.latimes.com/politics/la-na-pol-paris-states-20170602-story.html.

McDowell, Bruce D. 1997. "Advisory Commission on Intergovernmental Relations in 1996: the end of an era." *Publius: The Journal of Federalism* 27: 111–127.

McDowell, Bruce D. 2011. "Reflections on the spirit and work of the U.S. Advisory Commission on Intergovernmental Relations." *Public Administration Review* 71: 161–168.

New York Times. 2017. *New York Times* (March 9). Retrieved from www.nytimes.com/2017/03/09/us/politics/epa-scott-pruitt-global-warming.html.

Percival, R.V. 1995. "Environmental federalism: historical roots and contemporary models." *Maryland Law Review* 54(3). Retrieved from http://digitalcommons.law.umaryland.edu/mlr/vol54/iss4/3 (accessed June 2017).

Rosenbaum, Allan, Parris Glendening, Paul Posner and Tim Conlan. 2013. "Rationalizing the Intergovernmental System." Memos to National Leaders, American Society for Public Administration and National Academy of Public Administration. Retrieved from www.memostoleaders.org/sites/default/files/FINALinMemoStyle_0.pdf.

Wall, Audrey. 2010. "The state of state advisory commissions on intergovernmental relations: do they continue to have a role in the U.S. federal system?" Retrieved from http://knowledgecenter.csg.org/kc/content/state-state-advisory-commissions-intergovernmental-relations-do-they-continue-have-role-us-f (accessed October 17, 2017).

Warshaw, Shirley Anne. 2009. *The Clinton Years.* New York: Infobase Publishing.

Washington Post. 1980. *Washington Post* (October 9). Retrieved from www.washingtonpost.com/archive/politics/1980/10/09/reagan-criticizes-clean-air-laws-and-epa-as-obstacles-to-growth/abed4cf4-b16e-47e9-8e35-5f7e67c49fb6/?utm_term=.7e7ddfcd074b.

Washington Post. 2013. *Washington Post* (December 3). Retrieved from www.washingtonpost.com/local/dc-politics/dc-council-to-vote-on-1150-minimum-wage/2013/12/03/317d68b8-5b72-11e3-a66d-156b463c78aa_story.html?utm_term=.635472c0c3ab.

Washington Post. 2016. *Washington Post* (December 21). Retrieved from www.washingtonpost.com/news/energy-environment/wp/2016/12/21/trump-says-energy-regulations-are-hurting-economic-growth-the-evidence-says-otherwise/?utm_term=.e60230da1dda.

Wogan, J.B. 2014. "Obama to mayors, governors and state legislators: raise the minimum wage." *Governing* (January 29). Retrieved from www.governing.com/news/headlines/gov-obama-to-mayors-governors-and-state-legislators-raise-the-minimum-wage.html (accessed October 17, 2017).

16 Back to the Future?

The Road Ahead

Carl W. Stenberg and David K. Hamilton

While covering different topics from different perspectives, the contributors to this volume have arrived at a number of common conclusions about the current and future condition and directions of intergovernmental relations (IGR) and management (IGM). Even though much has changed since publication of Deil Wright's book *Understanding Intergovernmental Relations* in 1978, much of what Wright wrote holds up to scrutiny and critical analysis. Our authors look backward as well as forward, to capture the spirit and dynamics of intergovernmental institutions, policies, programs, and personalities. This chapter summarizes a few of the major themes that arise from their work, provides some answers to the "Big Questions" about the future directions of IGR and IGM, and identifies areas for further research.

Major Themes

At least five major themes are associated with the evolution of federalism, intergovernmental relations and management over the past five decades. These are:

- continuity and change;
- the transition from government to governance;
- the shifting intergovernmental power balance;
- entrenched partisanship and polarization; and
- institutional voices and values.

Continuity and Change

In general, IGR has undergone significant change even as there has been continuity in programs, responsibilities, and relationships. Governments at all levels have proven resilient to economic crisis and withstood major alterations of the functional and jurisdictional status quo. The Great Recession illustrates the ability of the federal system to respond to crisis and the continuity of the aftermath. During the Recession, the federal government pumped billions of dollars into states and local governments. Essential state and local government services, for the most part, were continued, even as substantial personnel cutbacks were made. After the economic crisis subsided, federal funding returned to almost prerecession levels. The profile of government structures and services, especially at the local level, in the aftermath of the Great Recession closely resembles prerecession arrangements.

As shown in other chapters of this book (see Chapters 3 and 5), federal transfers to states and local governments have not abated and, in fact, are in an upward trajectory. Moreover, the domestic role of governmental agencies has steadily expanded in response to citizen demands and expectations, despite criticisms of "Big Government" and public official promises of "more for less" from government. Cooperative federalism and the marble cake are alive and well. At the same time, federal–state, federal–local, interstate, state–local, and interlocal relationships have become more fragmented, confusing, and coercive.

The problems confronting governments have grown more complex and challenging. They require intergovernmental, intersectoral, and interdisciplinary relationships in order to be successfully addressed. Yet, outmoded governmental structures and public official parochialism often make it difficult for public administrators to readily transcend their jurisdiction and work across boundaries horizontally and vertically. While Deil Wright's Overlapping Authority Model accurately describes the interdependencies and interactions of governments, debate continues over four fundamental federalism questions: Who does what? Who pays the bill? Who is accountable? Who is in charge?

From Government to Governance

Among the significant changes to IGR and IGM have been the steady addition of intersectoral relationships to intergovernmental relationships. The shift from government to governance arrangements, featuring networking and collaboration among public and private partners, has diminished attention devoted to the institutional and bureaucratic features of IGR and IGM. Federal, state, and local agencies are still the predominant players in delivering services, but their work involves interacting with for- and non-profit organizations, faith-based groups, regional and neighborhood bodies, civic organizations, volunteers, and others. In short, the number of intergovernmental players has grown considerably and IGR might well be entering what Benton calls a "Kalideoscopic" phase. As such, the contemporary relevance of picket-fence federalism, together with the overlapping authority model, may be too limited in their purview.

The Shifting Power Balance

The role and influence of the federal government has expanded steadily since World War II under Democratic and Republican Presidents and Congresses. The growth in the number of federal grant-in-aid programs, discretionary spending, regulatory federalism, and unfunded mandates have underscored that the intergovernmental power "tilt" has been in the direction of Washington, DC for many years. This has been the case especially since the 1980s, causing some of our contributors to question the accuracy of Deil Wright's "contractive" phase of intergovernmental relations at that time. Ironically, this post-war growth has occurred despite presidential desires to reduce federal domestic spending and regulations and restrain federal program creation, as well as calls by state and local officials for devolution, states' rights, and recognition of states and local governments as laboratories of democracy. While there have been occasional devolutionary initiatives like the Temporary Assistance for Needy Families welfare reform during the Clinton Administration, as well as administrative efforts to give states greater programmatic discretion and authority such as through regulatory waivers, the power balance remains in place.

The intergovernmental pendulum might swing more in the direction of the states if the federal government's fiscal position becomes unsustainable or if the Trump administration and Congress succeed in "deconstructing the administrative state." For many years the "four d's" characterized federal budgeting—deficits, debt, defense, and demographics—yet domestic spending still grew unabated. Concerns have been expressed in recent years that the federal fiscal positon is unsustainable and that well-entrenched entitlements like Medicaid, Medicare, and Social Security need to be capped or cut. Whether there is sufficient political will to tackle these sacred cows remains to be seen.

Likewise, our authors have noted that the American Recovery and Reinvestment Act stimulus was the last significant step taken by the federal government to bolster state and local economies. In light of current and projected budget conditions and the Trump Administration's agenda, it is unlikely that the federal fiscal "cavalry" will be willing and able to come to rescue states and localities in the future if economic growth falters as spending obligations for education, health care, pensions, and other public purposes continue to rise.

Recent "push-back" actions by governors, legislators, and attorneys general against national policies and regulations—such as Medicaid expansion, health exchange creation, climate change initiatives, and immigrant protection—indicate that states will resist top-down directives from Washington, DC that clash with their political cultures, philosophies, and priorities. In addition, calls to balance the federal budget through constitutional amendment and to reduce the size and scope of federal programs cause uncertainty among state and local officials who fear a loss of discretionary funds, off-loading of functional responsibilities, and continued unfunded mandates. To them, John Shannon's "fend-for-yourself federalism" prediction from the 1980s might become a reality.

Another source of tension and friction over the years has involved the debate over whether, for particular policies or programs, a single, stable national standard is in order or whether 50 different approaches are appropriate. State leaders often remind federal officials of their historic role as "laboratories of democracy," where new and creative approaches to designing and implementing solutions to public problems can be tested, modified, and best practices diffused across the country and shared with federal policy-makers. Massachusetts' and Wisconsin's experiments with universal health care and welfare reform, respectively, influenced the design of federal initiatives in these areas. Currently states are experimenting with a wide variety of social, economic, environmental, and lifestyle policies including minimum wages, gay marriage, gender identity, safe havens for undocumented immigrants, gun control, fracking, marijuana legalization, healthful food requirements, worker protection, broadband access, and plastic bags.

Nevertheless, a compelling case can be made for national action and, ironically, sometimes this is done by political conservatives and business organizations that historically have been wary of federal intervention and supportive of state-by-state actions. Consider the following comments by corporate leaders on regulating automated vehicles. In testimony before Congress, Volvo vice-president Anders Karrberg stated: "The patchwork of state regulations is a concern . . . Congress should encourage [the National Highway Traffic Safety Administration] to update the Federal Automated Vehicles Policy with an explicit request that states refrain from legislating and regulating self-driving cars." With more than 60 bills filed in 20 states to regulate the testing and deployment of automated vehicles, Karrberg asserted that state laws will "... slow the evolution of automated vehicle technology, putting the United States at a competitive disadvantage." Some committee members, however, pointed out that it would take several years to develop national standards and that in the meantime "states should be the testbed for innovation to a great degree here" (Herckis 2017: 23–24).

Partisanship and Polarization

Deil Wright and others have observed that while much of the research and discussion about IGR and IGM involves structures, procedures, programs, finances, and laws, intergovernmental relationships are first and foremost people relations, a concept argued by Perlman, Scicchitano, and Zhang in Chapter 6. This could also be a spirit captured in the picket fence metaphor focusing on the interactions among program administrators at the three levels that transcend governmental structure and levels and that emphasize professional over institutional loyalties. John Kincaid points out that public administrators are responsible for maintaining the largely cooperative nature of relationships in intergovernmental program management, even though overall the system is characterized by coercion. The latter condition is a byproduct of the deterioration of relationships between and among federal, state, and local elected officials. However, partisan politics, philosophical and ideological polarization, and the corrosive influence of money on politics have negatively impacted these relationships and produced dysfunctional IGM coping strategies like across-the-board budget cuts, personnel reductions, unfunded mandates, functional responsibility shifts, and blame-pointing. In this environment, there is little room for compromise, negotiations, and bargaining among the political players. This filters down to the administrators involved in policy formulation and implementation, which often produces policy stalemate.

As polarization spreads from the national to state levels, some argue that these conditions present opportunities for states and especially local governments to lead in policy development. Former International City/County Management Association executive director Robert O'Neill has argued that the current time is "the decade of local government" and the Brookings Institution's Bruce Katz has coined the term "The New Localism" to reflect the growing role of municipalities and counties as policy and program innovators in metropolitan areas. In this polarized environment, it may be the state and local governments that are under the control of the Democrats will lead in the formulation of progressive policies that benefit their communities and citizens—such as in opioid abuse, homelessness, climate change, marijuana use, and Sanctuary Cities—and counteract some of the effects of federal and state aid cutbacks and program withdrawals. In Chapter 10, Jacob, Gerber, and Gallaher discuss some of the local government "bottom-up" policy development efforts.

Institutional Voices and Values

Several contributors have noted that the deinstitutionalization of intergovernmental organizations has created a void in the understanding of IGR and in appreciation of the views of the partners in the federal system on policies and programs that transcend governmental and sectoral boundaries. They recognize that there is a need for such capacity although they are skeptical that an organization similar to the former U.S. Advisory Commission on Intergovernmental Relations (ACIR) could be established in the current political environment. Of course, the work of organizations like the Government Accountability Office and Congressional Budget Office partly fill this void, but their audience is federal, not intergovernmental. The absence of a neutral forum for identifying emerging federalism issues, convening representatives from different levels and sectors to consider common problems, conducting research and analytics, and identifying impacts of policy options on subnational units, among other functions, has been a setback to IGR and IGM (see Chapters 14 and 15). While the creation of a Task Force on Intergovernmental Affairs by Speaker Paul Ryan and Democratic Leader Nancy Pelosi in May 2017 and appointment of "Big 7" representations to an Advisory Council, was encouraging news, whether this body will be successful in filling the intergovernmental consultation void remains to be seen.

At the same time, as Kincaid observes, there are few champions of intergovernmental relations in the Congress and little or no political credit is given for bringing representatives of states and local governments together to advise federal policy-makers and regulators. Intergovernmental consultation and collaboration are no longer valued by most members of Congress, as well as senior federal political executives. As a result, the fiscal and human consequences of federal initiatives on the national policy agenda on the state and local levels are largely unknown—or ignored. There is currently no federal-level government agency tasked with providing credible research on the impacts on the federal system from current Trump initiatives on tax, health-care, and immigration reform, program devolution, and other proposals that would change the current intergovernmental financial and functional balance. The "view from the trenches" contributions to this volume underscore that Big 7 representatives are considered to be just another special interest group pleading their parochial case before federal authorities. The voices of state and local governments and their representatives are not heard or listened to by policy-makers in Washington, DC. These officials are viewed as special interests, yet they have had difficulty getting the attention of members of Congress and other federal officials. Unlike special interest groups, the BIG 7 has no financial or political clout to influence national elections. Their concerns were captured by New Orleans Mayor Mitch Landrieu, President of the U.S. Conference of Mayors, who after meeting with Senators to discuss the post-health care reform agenda said: "We don't feel comfortable or reassured about anything that we see happening in Washington right now" (Lucia 2017a).

"Big Questions" Reconsidered

There are other themes that could be noted, as well as current examples, but the above cover many of the major areas identified by contributors to the chapters of this book. Moving to some more specific questions associated with the transitions that are underway in IGR and IGM, we want to briefly return to some of the eight "Big Questions" identified in Chapter 1. These have already been ably addressed by John Kincaid (Chapter 3) and Parris Glendening (Chapter 15), but we would like to add some of our thoughts. Four of these—deinstitutionalization, coercive federalism, networks and partnerships, and partisanship—have been addressed above. We consider others that are also important below, as they warrant further scholarly attention.

Sorting Out

While there have been calls for a systematic sorting out of intergovernmental roles and responsibilities dating from the Joint Federal–State Action Committee during the Eisenhower Administration, there has been little interest in what some dismiss as a return to the layer cake or dual federalism model. They argue that government has grown too large, complex, and costly to unwind, and that the "web of governance" further complicates significant reordering of roles and responsibilities. Change in the American federal system has been incremental, not systematic. Dividing the intergovernmental job involves navigating an intricate set of political, legal, financial, regulatory, and administrative aspects that have grown over time and become well-ingrained and resistant to change. Elected and appointed public officials tend to be reluctant to give up service responsibilities and allow others to get political credit. Disrupting the programmatic status quo also creates discomfort and uncertainty about impacts on clients and administrative relationships.

The only President since Eisenhower who invested political credit in advancing sorting out was Reagan's "grand exchange" in the early 1980s. Yet, the New Federalism received very little support from the Big 7 and no legislation was introduced in Congress. After two years of discussions, the Administration dropped the initiative. Likewise, the bold proposals by ACIR, Alice Rivlin, and Senator Lamar Alexander to sort out responsibilities to achieve greater systemic efficiency, effectiveness, and equity have attracted few supporters. The experience with the design, implementation, and possible replacement of the Affordable Care Act demonstrates the difficulty of answering the "Who Does What?" question in health care, and it applies to other functional areas.

Block Grants

Block grants have been dwarfed numerically and financially by categorical programs. They also have been unstable as most of the 21 programs have been recategorized over the years and their appropriations have not kept pace with inflation (Stenberg 2008). Initially, this devolutionary instrument was intended to give state and local recipients greater discretion and flexibility in moving federal funds appropriated in a broadly defined area or purpose to their specific priority needs. Block grants were also a tool for federal aid reform, chiefly streamlining the grant system through consolidation of functionally related narrow categorical grants into a broader purpose grant, such as the Community Development Block Grant of 1974, which merged nine categorical grants.

Since the 1980s, however, block grants have been proposed as a means of capping or cutting federal financial contributions, in exchange for giving recipients greater flexibility. This trade-off is evident in the Medicaid reform proposal by the Trump administration, under which a state would receive a set amount of federal money, rather than open-ended match, which it could direct to its greatest needs. The impact was summarized by Connecticut Governor Daniel Malloy (D) as follows: "Block grants, in Republican-speak, means less money today and less money tomorrow and every year thereafter." Alternatively, Arizona Governor Doug Ducey (R), argued that governors could make the tough choices over their health systems, not federal bureaucrats, and that reduced federal funding would be offset. "I think when you lessen the size of the bureaucracy, you're going to find efficiencies and savings" (Lucia 2017b). Given the size of the Medicaid population (74 million people) and the amounts of funds involved (one-third of state budgets), the probability that a block grant would be embraced by governors and legislators regardless of party affiliation is problematic. The unpopular alternatives would be to either cutback eligibility and services or raise taxes to increase the state's financial contribution— and risk the political consequences. It is also noteworthy that two block grants—CDBG and the HOME Investment Partnerships Program, which is the largest source of flexible funding to create affordable housing for low-income households—are targeted for elimination by the Trump Administration.

State–Local Relations

The two chapters in this book covering state–local relations arrive at different conclusions regarding whether overall counties and municipalities have been empowered or restricted by legislatures in recent years. The answers are "both" and "it depends on the area." States also are inconsistent in their treatment of localities. "Dillon's Rule" states have given local governments greater discretion in assuming functional responsibilities, regulating commerce (e.g. minimum wage hikes and plastic bag prohibitions) and the authority to enter into interlocal contracts and joint service agreements. On the other hand, "Home Rule" states have restricted local authority and prohibited counties and municipalities from taking action on their own in a number of areas. It appears that both "Dillon's Rule" and "Home Rule" states address local relations in unpredictable ways. State moves to preempt or devolve authority do not appear to be based on political theory, efficiency, or the value of local self-government.

State–local relations are legally complex and politically contentious. In states where Republications control the governorship and legislature, elected officials are eager to put Progressive city Democratic mayors on a short leash regardless of whether they are Dillon's Rule or Home Rule status (Riverstone-Newell 2017). What is clear from the discussion of emerging intergovernmental developments is that as the federal domestic footprint shrinks, states and localities will likely be expected by affected constituencies to shoulder greater responsibilities. On a state-by-state basis, they will need to answer the four questions posed earlier: Who does what? Who pays the bill? Who is accountable? Who is in charge? In addressing these questions, if the policy paralysis in Washington, DC persists they will need to determine whether they are partners or adversaries in collaborative ventures.

Regional Cooperation and Networked Governance

Two of the "big" questions posed in Chapter 1 were the future of regional cooperation and whether the networked and collaborative nature of IGR and IGM will continue. Regional cooperation is not easy in our intergovernmental system. Cigler (2007) calls it "an unnatural act." However, authors in this volume have referred to it in the context of the "new normal" resulting from the Great Recession. Even though cooperation is an "unnatural act" and much has reverted back to pre-recession days, there is more pressure on local governments to cooperate across governmental boundaries. This not only involves local governments cooperating among themselves but also collaborating with the nonprofit and private sectors in addressing policy and implementation of programs and services. However, there have been few structures, processes, or incentives developed to formalize and encourage cross-boundary efforts (see Chapter 12). Most of the cooperation and collaboration continues to be ad hoc and opportunistic.

Federal policies and funding have supported regional cooperation for many years. The federal government played a key catalytic leadership role starting in the 1960s with comprehensive area-wide planning requirements for transportation and housing program grants. Creation of councils of governments (COGs) and other regional organizations in urban areas across the country was spurred by providing federal operating funds. Federal policy required grant applications for specific programs in metropolitan areas to be reviewed by COGs acting as regional clearinghouses to assure consistency between proposed projects and area-wide plans. Other regional agencies, such as metropolitan planning organizations (MPOs), were established to provide a regional focus for developing transportation plans to spend federal transportation grants.

As demonstrated by authors in this book, the federal government continually relies on states and nonprofit or private agencies to assist in the implementation of its policies. This requires negotiation, compromise, and monitoring. With many actors involved, implementation of programs is not necessarily the same across states. Also, as shown by Johnston and Yurman in Chapter 8, implementation of federal programs by nonfederal agencies may not always meet federal standards. However, given the nature of our federal system and sharp partisan differences, negotiation, compromise, and heavy reliance on nonfederal employees will undoubtedly continue to be the way federal programs are implemented.

Conclusion

The course of intergovernmental relations in recent years has been at times uncertain, controversial, and adversarial. The emerging federal intergovernmental agenda—driven by fiscal constraint, entrenched entitlements, "more for less" citizen expectations, and partisan polarization—indicates that turbulent times lie ahead. The roads to improved IGM and IGR will be filled with many potholes that practitioners will have to skillfully navigate. Federal, state, and local administrators have important work to do as public service leaders, managers, and stewards to keep the wheels of government turning, rebuild intergovernmental institutions, and strengthen collaboration and partnerships.

Federalism and intergovernmental relations scholars also have important work to do. In one of his last published articles, Deil Wright and colleagues conducted a content review of more than 700 articles that were published in the *Public Administration Review* between 1940 and 2007, to determine the extent to which six key terms were noted: FED, IGR, IGM, governance, collaboration, and networking. Among the findings, the authors noted several "gaps in coverage" of the first three terms over the years. Some of these topics appear in our "Major Themes" and "Big Questions Reconsidered" review. Among the paucity of article subjects were the resurgence and transformation of state government, interstate and interlocal relationships such as compacts and contracts, administration of core services like K-12 public education, law enforcement, transportation and infrastructure, and economic development, and state and local implementation and program accountability (Wright, Stenberg, and Cho 2011: 306–307). These and other neglected topics have been analyzed in greater depth by Beverly Cigler (Cigler 2011: 316–334).

We conclude this volume for a call for additional research to fill these gaps, and an encouragement to both scholars and practitioners to follow in Deil Wright's pioneering footsteps to broaden and deepen our *understanding* of intergovernmental relations.

References

Cigler, Beverly A. 2007. "Post-Katrina emergency management: Forum overview." *The Public Manager* 36(3) (Fall): 3.

Cigler, Beverly A. 2011. "Neglected aspects of intergovernmental relations and federalism." In Donald C. Menzel and Harvey L. White, eds. *The State of Public Administration: Issues, Challenges, and Opportunities.* Armonk, NY: M.E. Sharpe, 316–334.

Herckis, Mitch. 2017. "Auto industry is wary of state and local government automated vehicle laws." In *Navigating America's Tough Intergovernmental Challenges.* Washington, DC: Government Executive Media Group, 23–24.

Lucia, Bill. 2017a. "Mayors meet with U.S. senators as legislative agenda shifts away from health care." Retrieved from www.routefifty.com/management/2017/08/us-conference-mayors-senators-congress (accessed August 3, 2017).

Lucia, Bill. 2017b. "For governors, the future of Medicaid." In *Navigating America's Tough Intergovernmental Challenges*. Washington, DC: Government Executive Media Group, 25–27.

Riverstone-Newell, Lori. 2017. "The rise of state preemption laws in response to local policy innovation." *Publius* 47(3): 403–425.

Stenberg, Carl W. 2008. "Block grants and devolution: A future tool?" In Timothy J. Conlan and Paul L. Posner, eds. *Intergovernmental Management for the Twenty-First Century*. Washington, DC: Brookings Institution Press, 263–285.

Wright, Deil S. 1978. *Understanding Intergovernmental Relations*. Boston, MA: Duxbury Press.

Wright, Deil S., Carl W. Stenberg, and Chung-Lae Cho. 2011. "Historic relevance confronting contemporary obsolescence? Federalism, intergovernmental relations, and intergovernmental management." In Donald C. Menzel and Harvey L. White, eds. *The State of Public Administration: Issues, Challenges, and Opportunities*, Armonk, NY: M.E. Sharpe, 297–315.

Index

Note: Page numbers in *italics* refer to figures and in **bold** refer to tables.